OKLAHOMA

American Historical Press
Sun Valley, California

OKLAHOMA

A RICH HERITAGE

Odie B. Faulk & William D. Welge

To my mother, Iva L. Greenawalt Welge,
whose library opened the history of the
world to me. I shall always be grateful.

Photos credited Oklahoma Turnpike Authority, courtesy Oklahoma Transportation Authority.

© 2004 American Historical Press
All Rights Reserved
Published 2004
Printed in the United States

Library of Congress Catalogue Card Number: 2004113065
ISBN: 1-892724-46-4

Bibliography: page 368
Includes Index

CONTENTS

Acknowledgments

As with any project, there are a number of individuals who deserve recognition for their kind assistance. I am grateful to Merlyn Johnson of Guymon; Gary Brown of Enid; General Jay Edwards of the Oklahoma Space Port Authority; Congressman Brad Carson; Jane Thomas and Heidi Vaughan of the Oklahoma City National Memorial; Leslie A. Spears, the Oklahoma City Museum of Art; John Lovett, Curator of Photographs, University of Oklahoma Western History Collections; Phyllis Randolph, Cimarron Heritage Center, Boise City; Gary Reckrodt, Seaboard Farms, Guymon; Michael Dean who provided the necessary contact at the University of Oklahoma Athletic Department; and Debra Copp, Director of Publications, Oklahoma University Athletic Media Relations Office.

I would also like to thank the following persons for giving of their time in helping me understand important aspects of state history: John Marshall of Oklahoma City regarding banking issues; Rick Moore of Oklahoma City pertaining to a variety of matters including Phillips Petroleum Company/ T. Boone Pickens affair; Mayor Norick's office for the perspective regarding the Oklahoma City bombing; and the Honorable Susan Savage, former Mayor of Tulsa now currently the Secretary of State of Oklahoma.

I especially wish to thank the following members of the staff of the Oklahoma Historical Society for their help and encouragement: Judith Michener; Chester Cowen; Rodger Harris; Laura Martin; Bill Moore; Francie Helm; Sandy Smith, for her patience and input; and Chad Williams. There is one person whose talent as a photographer I truly admire and appreciate, Terry Zinn. His eye for capturing all things beautiful is amazing. I particularly want to thank Lillie Kerr for all her work on compiling and scanning many photographs for this project.

And lastly, to my family: Beki, Dan, and Shelby Perkins and Mary Beth, Sali, and Jacob Welge, who have always been there for me.

William D. Welge

Preface

Oklahoma and Oklahoman's have a rich history, culture, and diversity of people. Prior to 1995 most individuals' impressions about Oklahoma were generally negative. Oklahomans were stereotyped into the cowboy or Indian genre or were lumped into the Joad family as itinerate, low self-esteem persons with little or no expectations other than to escape the chronic dust storms of middle-America as depicted by John Steinbeck's novel *The Grapes of Wrath*. This image of Oklahoma and her citizens has persisted for most of the twentieth century. All that changed one gloomy April morning.

On April 19, 1995 the largest domestic terrorist attack to date occurred in Oklahoma City. Within a few hours of the bombing of the A.P. Murrah Federal Building that killed 168 people, the world was made aware of the incident. With continual media coverage of this heinous act against humanity, people who really never had an impression about Oklahoma, or had a stereotypical view of Oklahoma changed. What the world saw that day and the days following, was a deeply compassionate outpouring of individuals coming to aid the injured and assist rescue workers. Later, the Federal Emergency Management Administration (FEMA) dispatched teams from all over the country to assist with the rescue. After the second day, it soon became apparent that rescue operations had become a recovery for remains.

Today, the people of Oklahoma possess a vision for the future. The rebirth of Oklahoma City was made possible by the voters who invested in their community and funded the metropolitan area projects (MAPS), which has created new economic opportunities and a more diverse infrastructure attracting visitors from out-of-state as well as in state.

Tulsa followed the example Oklahoma City set by passing an important bond issue in 2003 to improve the quality of life in that cosmopolitan city. Other towns across the state have taken advantage of community block grants to replace sidewalks, put in new street lighting, and make other improvements.

Oklahoma has become a leader in medical research in recent years. Tulsa and Oklahoma City have attracted some of the finest scientists in biomedical research who are developing new drugs, which may lead to cures for diseases afflicting humankind.

As countries vie for increasing their share of global markets in agriculture, business, aviation, energy resources, and other industries, Oklahoma is competing in every arena by promoting its products and services. However, it's the people, Oklahoma's greatest resource, that make it all happen. The investment needed to reach many foreign markets is there if there are individuals willing to take the risk. One such venture is completion of a successful launch and return of a sub-orbital spacecraft built by private funds. The space port project at Burns Flat is testament to the private sector's commitment toward this goal. This will revolutionize the travel industry as well as provide rapid transportation of goods to new markets across the world.

Oklahoma is a vibrant, progressive and visionary state that looks forward to a second century of new opportunities. The first 100 years, coupled with our infancy period prior to statehood in 1907, were years of growth much like an adolescent youth in need of guidance in order to achieve maturity. Now in the twenty-first century, Oklahoma is in the prime of her collective existence. The state and her people have endured many trials, tribulations, and triumphs. Her future looks bright as she nears the beginning of a second century of endeavors.

William D. Welge

CHAPTER I

Land of Contrast

Southeastern Oklahoma, with its mountains, woodlands, and many rivers, boasts some of the most beautiful scenery in the state. Courtesy, Works Progress Administration, Federal Writers' Project

*F*rancisco Vásquez de Coronado in 1535 came to New Spain, as Mexico was then known, where he had become governor of a large province. Born in Salamanca, Spain, into a family of the minor nobility, he was fair of countenance and light of hair, a handsome young man who had been named a courtier to the king and had been presented at court and enjoyed the viceroy's favor and knew the advantages of wealth and cosmopolitan life.

His comfortable existence changed dramatically in 1540 when he accepted command of a large expedition which was to search for the Seven Cities of Cíbola, a land rumored to contain great wealth somewhere to the north in the *tierra incognita* (the unexplored area north of settlements in Mexico). With 336 Spanish troops and hundreds of Indian allies, he marched into present-day Arizona and New Mexico, there to fight battles with Pueblo Indians and suffer great hardships—to discover only rumors of yet another wealthy kingdom, the Gran Quivira, which supposedly lay somewhere to the east and north of the pueblos of New Mexico. There, according to the Indians, even the humblest peasant ate from golden dishes, the streets were paved with silver, and the chief each afternoon took a nap under a tree adorned with golden bells that tinkled musically when the breeze blew.

From central New Mexico, Coronado and his followers marched for more than thirty days to the east during the spring of 1541, arriving at last at Palo Duro Canyon (near the present Amarillo, Texas). There he sent most of his army back to New Mexico while he marched on to Quivira, taking with him thirty horsemen, six footmen, and several Indian guides. On June 1 they set out riding north, as he wrote, "by the needle" (using a magnetic compass, he would have taken a route slightly east of north). On this course they made about eight miles a day, bringing them by mid-June to the Panhandle of pres-

Opposite page
This redbud tree blooms
during the spring on
Talimina Scenic Drive in
eastern Oklahoma. The
redbud is the official state
tree of Oklahoma. Photo by
Jim Argo

Above
Broken Bow Reservoir in
McCurtain County is one
of Oklahoma's newest
lakes, created in 1969 by
the United States Corps of
Engineers. The lake was
formed by the damming of
Mountain Fork River and
is a favorite of state hun-
ters and fishermen. Photo
by Jim Argo

This artist's interpretation of Francisco Vásquez de Coronado depicts the "Knight of Pueblo and Plains" as he might have looked at the time of his explorations. Courtesy, Bill Ahrendt

falo], for, as I told your Majesty, these animals are very wild and ferocious." On these plains there were no trees, and the men cooked their food as would the pioneers of a later age, over a fire using buffalo chips as fuel. In addition, because there were no major rivers in the area, they were "without water for many days."

As these Spaniards suffered across the High Plains, they little realized that this land one day would be part of the great state of Oklahoma, nor could they know the diversity of the geography of that future state. All they saw was a level sameness, for they were crossing the area that later would be known as the Great Plains. This is a land formed by silt carried out of the Rocky Mountains by a multitude of rivulets, creeks, and rivers. The first feature these Spaniards noticed was the absence of trees. Next they commented about the grass. The vegetation most associated with the southern Great Plains usually was called "shortgrass," for the subsoil did not hold sufficient moisture to allow the growth of the extensive root systems needed by taller grasses. The more level the ground, the more the grass dominated. However, where this land was broken, other types of plants grew: gnarled mesquite trees, some thorny shrubs, and cactus, while along the few creeks of the area tall cottonwoods reached for the sky. These towered above the blue (or buffalo) grass, which was the home of wild hogs, white-tailed deer, pronghorns (antelope), wild turkeys, prairie dogs, ground squirrels, and millions of field mice and jackrabbits. Also, there were dozens of varieties of birds to add a dash of color, a warble of song, and a sudden thrashing of wings.

The best-known native animal to feed on this shortgrass was the American bison, or buffalo. Across the vast plains there was no predatory animal that by itself was capable of killing these great shaggy beasts. A buffalo bull made a formidable enemy, for he often weighed a ton, and with horns and hooves he could fight off most any attacker. Moreover, buffalo were difficult to surprise, for when the herd grazed an old cow usually stood guard, quick to hear anything approaching (these animals had keen hearing). Buffalo were also good runners; only a fast horse could keep up with a stampeding herd. In addition, they were equally commendable swimmers, capable of crossing

ent-day Oklahoma.

This area—in the vicinity of the present towns of Hardesty, Adams, and Tyrone—was extremely flat, an ocean of short grass when Coronado saw it, and everywhere buffalo grazed. "The country where these animals roamed was so level and bare," wrote one of Coronado's men in his journal, "that whenever one looked at them one could see the sky between their legs, so that at a distance they looked like trimmed pine tree trunks with the foliage joining at the top." Coronado's supplies were so depleted by this time that he and his men were reduced to living almost exclusively on buffalo meat secured, Coronado declared in a letter to Charles V, King of Spain, "at the cost of some of the horses slain by the cattle [buf-

Left
*This Wichita Indian vil-
lage, located in central
Oklahoma during the
1850s, resembled the vil-
lages visited by Coronado
during his expedition of
1541. Courtesy, The Okla-
homa Historical Society
(OHS)*

Below
*The Oklahoma High Plains
was a region of vast grasslands, few trees, and little
water. At times it was a
garden producing wild
flowers and abundant
grasses; at other times it
was a drought-stricken
semi-desert, a formidable
land that was the last frontier conquered by non-
Indian settlers. Photo by
Jim Argo*

Right
This mural of an Osage warrior by Monroe Tsa-Toke can be found in the Wiley Post Historical Building in Oklahoma City. OHS

Opposite page, top
Winds in the Oklahoma Panhandle have carved the Dakota sandstone of the area into many unusual shapes, including this one called "The Wedding" or "The Three Sisters." The formation is near Black Mesa State Park in Cimarron County. Photo by Jim Argo

Opposite page, bottom
American bison, or buffalo, once inhabited the Great Plains in herds of more than two million animals. Today, due to massive extermination of the species following the Civil War, only small herds exist on carefully protected wildlife refuges. Photo by Jim Argo

any river to escape an enemy or reach a new feeding ground. On the plains of western Oklahoma, as well as in Kansas and Texas, these buffalo spent their lives grazing contentedly, wallowing in sand to clean themselves, drinking from creeks and streams, and increasing in numbers.

The plains country is a windy region, with winds that freeze in winter, parch in summer, and bring seasonal rains in spring and fall that turn it into a vast marsh on occasion. The area has a "continental weather pattern" (according to modern meteorologists); it gets the extremes of weather conditions known on the North American continent. The storms of spring bring tornadoes, hail, and rain, while the "northers" of winter bring sleet and blinding snowstorms. In the summer winds blow from the south into the nearby Rocky Mountains to melt the snow cover and bring silt-laden water rushing down to form yet another layer on the plains.

The Panhandle of Oklahoma is situated almost exactly between the Arkansas and the Red rivers, the two major rivers that drain the state. Because the Panhandle is the highest part of the state, sloping downward to the southeast from almost 5,000 feet to approximately 300 feet above sea level, these two rivers run in that direction. Since the western two-thirds of the state's land is soft and sandy, the rivers do not cut deep and jagged banks, but rather meander in snake-like fashion as they flow toward the Mississippi. On their way across the state they are fed by other rivers: the Arkansas receives the flow of the Verdigris, the Grand (also known as the Neosho), the

Illinois, the Cimarron, the Canadian, and, at the border of Arkansas, the Poteau. The Red is joined and increased in size from the north by the Washita, the Blue, and the Kiamichi and from the northwest and northeast by the Elm Fork and North Fork, the Prairie Dog Town Fork, and the Salt Fork.

As these rivers approach the eastern portion of Oklahoma, their channels become narrower and better defined, for the land is more resistant to erosion. This portion of Oklahoma consists of rolling hills and minor outcroppings of sandstone. Once the treeless plains give way to prairie and hills, the rivers flow through the Cross Timbers (running north and south almost through the middle of the state). This is an area of

One of Oklahoma's more lovable inhabitants is the prairie dog. A large village is preserved at the Wichita Mountains Wildlife Refuge near Lawton. Photo by Jim Argo

Oklahoma's weather is often unpredictable and frequently severe. The heart of "Tornado Alley," central Oklahoma usually ranks high in the nation in instances of tornadoes each year. Courtesy, National Severe Storms Laboratory, National Oceanic and Atmospheric Administration

blackjack and post oak intermingled with mesquite and smaller shrubbery, while along the rivers' banks cottonwoods give way to long-leaf pine, giant live and white oaks, and finally to stately cypress and pecan groves. In extreme eastern Oklahoma, where the rainfall is heavy, Spanish moss occasionally hangs from the branches of these tall trees. Open patches of ground are covered with Indian paintbrushes, sunflowers, and honeysuckle. Wood bison, a smaller cousin of the great beasts of the high plains, graze these areas along with white-tailed deer, while squirrels chatter and fuss at them from the branches of the trees. Frogs, field mice, and lizards keep a wary watch for hawks and owls.

Contrasting with the plains to the west are the mountains of southern and eastern Oklahoma. The mightiest chain, known to geographers as the Interior Highlands, is a western extension of the Ozarks and consists of the Boston Mountains, the Cookson Hills, and the Ouachita Mountains; the Ouachitas contain several curving ridges known as the Kiamichi, Winding Stair, Poteau, and San Bois Mountains. In the south-central part of the state are the Arbuckles, while to their west are the Wichitas. The Wichita Mountains rise 3,000 feet from the plains and are rich in minerals; for centuries water eroded the earth of these hills, carrying mineral deposits to the Red River and coloring its waters a rusty tint (from which the river received its name). The highest point in Oklahoma, however, is located not far from where Coronado and his treasure-seeking soldiers crossed the Panhandle. Known as Black Mesa, it is not a mountain, but rather was formed by a lava flow some 10,000 years ago and juts 4,978 feet above sea level.

The exact date when humans first entered into what is now Oklahoma is unknown, shrouded in the obscurity of unrecorded history. Archaeologists believe that Paleo-Indians came to the region about 15,000 B.C., bringing with them bone tools and spear points. They were gatherers of fruits, nuts, and berries and hunters of the wooly mammoth. Somewhere between 1500 B.C. and A.D. 500 came the introduction of the bow and arrow, pottery, and basket weaving, and the Native Americans of this time lived in semi-permanent villages near which they cultivated corn. Archaeological digs at village sites have uncovered ornamental pen-

dants, hairpins, shell and bone necklaces, pottery, arrow points, and cooking pits. They had a fully developed religion, and they buried their dead wth artifacts which they thought would be needed in the afterlife.

Between A.D. 500 and A.D. 1350 (known as the Gibson Period) Oklahoma's Indian inhabitants lived in fixed settlements, relied heavily on agriculture, and had developed techniques to fire pottery. They developed trade routes to obtain items they could not produce: to the Gulf Coast for shells, to the Great Lakes for copper and pipestone, and to Nevada and New Mexico for certain types of pottery. A class of artisans produced goods for trade, while a priestly class ruled all aspects of life. The priests were given lavish funerals with burial offerings placed in great mounds (some books refer to these Native Americans as the "Mound Builders").

About 1350, however, came a severe period of drought, causing the breakup of large villages and an end to the practice of mound building as the priestly class declined in importance. Between 1350 and the appearance of Europeans, several advances in pottery-making techniques introduced the use of finely ground mussel shells, mica, and sand as additives to the clay base to improve the tempering of pottery. Stone knives were manufactured, and tools made from bison and deer bone became more common-

Several important archaeological sites are located near present-day Ponca City. Ferdinandina, purportedly the first white settlement in Oklahoma (although in reality a Wichita Indian Village), Bryson Paddock, and Uncas have all produced important finds for archaeologists. This pot was uncovered at the Uncas site. Photo by Jim Argo

place. In the remains of villages built in eastern Oklahoma during this period bison bones are prevalent, indicating that the inhabitants either hunted farther west or the buffalo ranged farther east. This also was the period when Indians began to decorate their clothing, which was made from animal hides, and to weave textiles.

The principal tribes in Oklahoma at the time Coronado made his trek across the Panhandle were adapted to the area and the climate in which they lived. In the southeastern part of the state lived a Caddoan confederation, woodland Indians who supported themselves by hunting and farming. They tended muskmelons, plums, cherries, white grapes, and mulberries, all of which grew bountifully with little or no care. They killed the game that inhabited the forest, and they processed salt for trade. The Caddos were especially noted for their friendliness. They usually welcomed guests by washing their visitors' hands and feet, feeding them well, and giving them the best accommodations in the village. Included among the Caddos were several different groups of Indians related by a common language and tradition: the Natchitoches (in

Left
The artisans of Spiro produced elaborate ceramics and engraved animal bones for trade and for the ornamentation of their leaders. This replica of an effigy pipe is similar to many found at the Spiro Mounds Archaeological State Park by archaeologists excavating the site. Photo by Jim Argo

Above
In eastern Oklahoma, a culture of town builders flourished from A.D. 800 to 1400. Centered near the present-day town of Spiro, these prehistoric people conducted trade with tribes throughout North America, built mounds for ceremonies and houses, and carried out extensive agriculture in the fertile valley of the Arkansas River. Courtesy, Donald R. Johnson

Top, right
These women cultivate corn in a field near the Spiro Mounds. Controlling farmlands, trade routes, and the manufacture of finished goods, the Spiro leaders ruled a large area west of the Mississippi River for some 600 years. Courtesy, Donald R. Johnson

Above
Southeastern Indian traders meet with Spiro leaders to negotiate trade agreements. Courtesy, Donald R. Johnson

Opposite page, bottom
Black Mesa, the highest point in Oklahoma, is located in the northwestern corner of the Oklahoma Panhandle. Photo by Jim Argo

The Caddo Indians were living in the area that became the state of Oklahoma at the time of the first contact with white explorers. Artist George Catlin depicted them gathering wild grapes during his travels in the west in the early 1800s. Courtesy, The Thomas Gilcrease Institute of American History and Art, Tulsa, Oklahoma

present Louisiana), the Cadohadacho, and the Hasinai.

Upriver from the Caddos along the Kiamichi River were the Wichita Indians, a second Caddoan confederation that included the Taovaya, Tawakoni, Yscani, Waco, and Kichai. Originally these Indians lived in northern Oklahoma along the Arkansas River, but they migrated southward when the Osage began moving into northern Oklahoma from present-day Missouri. The Wichitas lived in permanent villages and, like the Caddos, had an economy based on farming and hunting. Generally these two confederations lived in peace, neither relying on raiding and warfare for economic gain. Likewise they lived in peace with the Pawnee, who lived to their north and who also were a farming-hunting tribe.

A second major group of Indians, related by the Siouan language they spoke, were the Osage and Quapaw tribes. They carved

a homeland for themselves in northeastern Oklahoma, living in permanent villages. They cultivated corn and squash, and supplemented their diet by hunting buffalo to the west during the summer. This annual trek was a time of great pleasure, for they returned laden with dried meat to be eaten during the winter, and with hides for clothing, and bones to be carved into implements. Generally these Indians, a tall, well-formed people, were feared by the plains tribes because of their courage and their zest for combat.

In the broken country and plains of western Oklahoma lived the Lipan Apaches, eastern cousins of the warlike tribes of the desert Southwest. These were Uto-Aztecan people, speaking an Athapascan language who apparently had migrated to the region sometime between A.D. 900 and A.D. 1200 from northwestern Canada. Nomadic and fierce, the Lipan Apaches quickly carved a stronghold for themselves on the plains from the Arkansas River south to central Texas, following the buffalo and living in temporary shelters known as wickiups. In physical appearance they were taller than average Indians height, and they were noted orators. Like their neighbors to the east they wove baskets and made pottery, but principally lived by raiding other tribes. Traveling in small bands, because the land would not support large numbers, they followed whatever war leader inspired their confidence. They attacked suddenly, swooping down on unsuspecting Indian villages, seizing all corn, beans, and other food and capturing women and children. They were noted for their cruel and warlike nature, their strength and endurance, and their ability to spread terror among other tribes—except the Osage, whom the Apaches learned to respect as hard fighters.

Change came slowly for these tribes. Decades would slip past with no noticeable change in their economy, their technology, or their society. With no calendar to tell them another year had passed, they dated the events of their lives by the season, a successful hunt, a drought, a raid. Time passed with quiet monotony as they contended with each other and with nature for subsistence, their daily lives almost exactly the same as those of their ancestors. Theirs was not a bleak, brutish existence, for they knew the pleasures of the hunt and the harvest, the generous providence of natural bounty, and the satisfaction of geographic beauty. Yet life for them was uncertain when game grew scarce, the rains were sparse, crops failed, or battles went against them. They suffered from disease, from periodic famine, from man's inhumanity to man. Such an existence was all they had ever known, however, and within it they found reason for hope, for laughter, for dreams.

The years of sole Indian ownership of Oklahoma ended in 1541 with the hoofbeats of an animal never before seen in the area— the horse. Riding these strange beasts were Spaniards, the men of Francisco Vásquez de Coronado, who came looking for streets paved with silver and listening for the sounds of golden bells tinkling in trees. They came searching for the Gran Quivira and the Seven Cities of Cíbola, little noticing—or caring—about the agricultural potential of the land beneath their horses'

hooves, the diversity of geography, or the rights of the native races of the land through which they rode.

Some tantalizing evidence exists that Coronado and his men were not the first Europeans to visit Oklahoma. At Heavener and elsewhere in the state there are carvings on stone which may be pictographs (a form of writing used in the era before the invention of the alphabet). These may have been made by Vikings in the thirteenth or fourteenth centuries or even by visitors from lands bordering the Mediterranean who came as early as 500 B.C. Archaeologists, however, disagree among themselves about the meaning of these pictographs. About Coronado's trek there is no doubt, for his report is detailed and exact.

This painting by C. Wimar shows the impact the horse had on the Osage Indians. Given the greater mobility and speed of horsepower, these Indians could range out on the Great Plains, hunting and warring to expand their influence. OHS

21

CHAPTER II

European Entanglements

Hernándo de Soto led the Spanish group that explored from Florida to Oklahoma and Texas. Reproduced from De Soto and the Conquistadores by Maynard. Longmans, Green & Company, New York (1930)

Coronado and his hand-picked band of thirty mounted Spaniards, along with his footmen and Indian guides, quickly crossed the Oklahoma Panhandle at their slow pace of eight to ten miles each day. Entering Kansas, they continued moving about ten degrees east of north, a route that brought them eventually to the Arkansas River near the present town of Ford. At that point a guide declared he recognized the river and said that the golden city he had described was only a short distance to the northeast.

No doubt with quickening heartbeats, the Spanish explorers crossed the Arkansas and began moving along the north bank of the river at an increased pace of twelve to fifteen miles a day. Three days later, on July 2, 1541, they met natives from Quivira hunting buffalo. Coronado's guide, Sopote, was able to converse with the friendly Quivirans. Riding with these people, Coronado and his band went to the main settlement. What they found there was greatly disappointing. True, the countryside was green and rolling; true, there were trees along the banks of the stream; and true, a few cultivated fields showed great agricultural potential. Yet there were no golden plates, no streets paved with silver, no king holding stately court. Rather, there was a Wichita Indian village of dome-shaped grass huts, filled with tattooed Indians wearing few clothes, little different in appearance from the natives Coronado had seen elsewhere. His seventy-seven-day ride from New Mexico had been for naught.

Eventually Coronado had an interview with the chief of the Wichita tribe, "a man already aged" who wore a metal amulet around his neck (probably of meteoric origin). The chief said there were similar villages in the surrounding countryside, none possessing anything that the Spaniards would consider of value. All the Indians lived in huts of wood and grass construction, all hunted buffalo, and all tended small fields.

Nowhere was there gold or silver or turquoise.

In great disappointment Coronado secured guides from among the Wichitas to lead his group back to New Mexico. This trip was made in almost a direct line from Kansas to the Pueblo country around Albuquerque, which once again brought the party across western Oklahoma. On this part of his trip, Coronado wrote a description of the plains Apaches. He noted that these nomads lived almost exclusively on buffalo meat, that from the hides of these shaggy beasts came the Indians' clothing and tepees, and that they bartered buffalo hides with the eastern tribes for agricultural products. Reunited with the rest of his party in New Mexico, Coronado returned empty-handed to Mexico to report to the viceroy in the spring of 1542.

While Coronado was yet in New Mexico that spring, Fray Juan de Padilla, a Franciscan priest, expressed a desire to return to Kansas to Christianize the Wichita Indians and bring them under the domination of the Spanish king. With Coronado's approval, he selected one soldier to accompany him— Andres do Campo, whose name would indicate a Portuguese background. Also accompanying Padilla were two Mexican Indians who had taken the vows of lay brothers, Lucas and Sebastián.

The Wichita Indian guides, the priest, Campo, and the two lay brothers returned to Quivira and spent the summer of 1542 seeking converts. Their success was so small that the priest, hearing of the Kaw (or Kansa) Indians to the east, determined to take his gospel message there. On the journey however, the small party was ambushed. During the struggle, Fray Juan de Padilla was killed and the other three—Campo, Lucas, and Sebastián—were captured and held as slaves for almost a year. Their masters probably were Kaw Indians who worked them but did not treat them badly. Nor did they watch their captives too closely, for in the summer of 1543 the three managed to slip away, walking south toward Mexico.

As they crossed Oklahoma the brothers took turns carrying a large wooden cross as a sign of penitence. Along this route they were joined by a dog that apparently preferred Spanish to Indian allegiance. This animal proved invaluable, by catching rabbits and other small game when the small party could not beg something to eat from the Indian tribes they encountered. Five long years of walking took them across Oklahoma, Texas, and northern Mexico, and finally in 1548 they reached safety at the Spanish town of Panuco (present Tampico, Mexico). During their heroic trek, they pioneered a road to the north far shorter than the one followed by Coronado, but it was not to be used by other Spaniards.

At the same time Coronado was crossing Oklahoma in search of the Gran Quivira, another Spanish expedition led by Hernándo de Soto was heading westward from Tampa Bay, Florida, after landing there on May 25, 1539. After discovering the Mississippi River, De Soto and his army crossed into Arkansas—and perhaps the extreme eastern border areas of Oklahoma. De Soto's private secretary, Rodrigo Ranjel, noted in his journal that the area abounded with corn, pumpkins, beans, wild game, and fish, and frequently members of the expedition killed woodland buffalo for meat. Ranjel's narrative also noted that many Indian villages were protected by stockades. At one point De Soto's expedition apparently was within 200 miles of Coronado and his men, but neither knew of the other's presence.

Eventually De Soto despaired of finding wealth, for he had reached the edge of the plains country where he found food harder to secure. Therefore he and his men turned back in 1541 to winter on the banks of the Mississippi. There De Soto died of a fever on May 21, 1542. Luís de Moscoso assumed command, and after many adventures brought 320 survivors safely to Panuco (Tampico) in 1543. The official report of the De Soto-Moscoso expedition was similar to that made by Coronado: to the north there was no gold, no silver, nothing of wealth, just natives willing to fight for their supplies of food. Spaniards therefore had no reason to return to the region that would become Oklahoma.

Gradually during the remainder of the sixteenth century, Spanish settlement crept northward from the central valley of Mexico until, in 1598, a finger of settlement was thrust northward into New Mexico. This colony was founded by Juan de Oñate, who hoped to discover the wealth that Coronado might have overlooked. Thus in 1601, with New Mexico firmly established as a colony, Oñate led a full-scale expedition to the northeast, paralleling Coronado's trek to

René Robert Cavelier, Sieur de la Salle, made the first complete exploration of the Mississippi River, discovering its mouth in 1682. He thenceforth claimed all lands drained by the river for King Louis of France. Reproduced from A History of the Mississippi Valley *by Spears and Clark. A.S. Clark & Company, Cleveland (1903)*

Kansas and reaching the same Wichita Indian village. His report of this expedition was similar to Coronado's: "What I am sure of," he wrote, "is that there is not any gold nor any other metal in all that country." The Oñate foray across Oklahoma to Kansas brought to an end the early period of Spanish exploration. Everyone was convinced that no riches were to be found in the area, and there was an excess of good farm land elsewhere. A quiet century would follow leaving the Indians undisturbed in directing their own affairs.

In the late seventeenth century, René Robert Cavelier, Sieur de la Salle, was responsible for the return of Europeans to Oklahoma. Born in France in 1643, La Salle immigrated to Canada where he gained a reputation as a woodsman and leader of men. Hearing of a great river to the south, he gradually became obsessed with a desire to be the discoverer of its mouth. This dream he realized on April 9, 1682, when he stood near the Gulf of Mexico at the mouth of the Mississippi River—"The Father of Waters"—and intoned the ritual formula for taking possession of new lands:

In the name of the most high, mighty, invincible, and victorious Prince, Louis the Great, by the grace of God, King of France, and of Navarre, Fourteenth of that name, I . . . have taken, and do now take . . . posses-

sion of this country of Louisiana.
Oklahoma, which was drained by the Mississippi, thus was aclaimed by the French.

Even as he fulfilled one dream, La Salle conceived another: he wanted to plant a settlement at the mouth of the Mississippi to ensure that the vast territory he called Louisiana would forever remain French. In 1685, however, his ships carrying colonists missed the mouth of the Mississippi (which was hidden in a mass of delta islands), and he planted his settlement on the coast of Texas at Matagorda Bay. This settlement, which he named Fort Saint Louis, proved ill-fated. In the spring of 1687 La Salle was killed by unhappy colonists, and within a short time the local Indians overran the little settlement.

The French were determined to settle on the Gulf Coast, however, and in 1699 Iberville le Moyne established a settlement at Biloxi. Three years later came another colony at Mobile. Le Moyne's intent was to make profits by trading European goods to the Indians for furs and by sending out his own trappers to gather more pelts. Then in 1712, Louis XIV decided to give Louisiana to a private businessman for development. This enterprising Frenchman, Antoine Crozat, was in charge of settling the area between Biloxi and the Mississippi to the west. In return for the investment, Crozat expected to reap profits from the fur trade, and to introduce French goods into the Spanish colo-

Above
This painting by O.C. Seltzer illustrates the fur traders and trappers of Oklahoma and the West. Courtesy, The Thomas Gilcrease Institute of American History and Art, Tulsa, Oklahoma

Left
French coureurs du bois, or runners of the woods, were often illegal Indian traders who conducted extensive trade with the Wichita and Comanche Indians of Oklahoma. Reproduced from The Story of Oklahoma *by Wright. Webb Publishing Company (1929)*

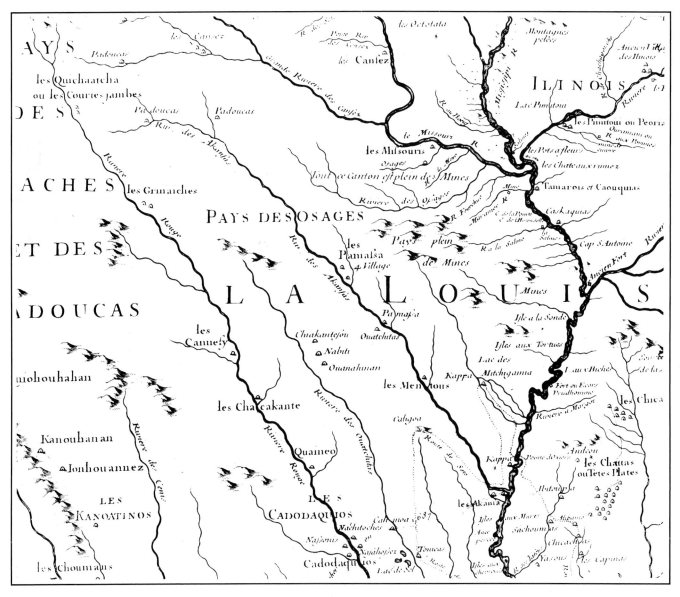

Map labels: les Octotata, Montagnes pelées, Ancien Ville des Ilinois, Pointe Rau, les Canlez, R. de la Charche..., A Y S, les Canlez, Padoucas, ILINOIS, R. ou Rivig, Lake Pimitoui, les Quichaatcha ou les Courtes jambes, Grande Riviere des Canlez, le Missouri, R., les Pimitoui ou Peoria, Ouamiami ou K. aux Pommes, D E S, Padoucas, Padoucas, Ru. des Akansas, les Misouris, les Pots a fleurs, les Chateaux rumez, Osages, Tout ce Canton est plein des Mines, A C H E S, les Grimaiches, Riviere des Osages, Tamarois et Caouquias, R. Fourche, Cascaquias, PAYS DES OSAGES, Pays plein de Mines, R. a la Salne, Cap S. Antone, Riviere, E T D E S, Rouge, les Pamalsa, Village, Mines, Ancien Fort, A DOUCAS, Ru. des Akansas, L A, L O U I S, Pamafra, Mines, les Cannely, Chuakantefou, Ouatchitas, Isle a la Sonde, niohouhahan, Nabiti, Isles aux Tortues, Ouanahuman, Lac des, les Chatcakante, Riviere des Ouatchitas, les Menilous, Kappa, Mitchigamia, Fort ou Ecors Prudhomme, les Chica, Caligoa, Riviere a Margot, Kanouhanan, Riviere des Cenis, Rivere Rouge, Quaineo, Antlou, Kappa, Pointe d'Ozier, les Chattas ou Tetes Plates, Jonhouannez, Hutoupa, LES KANOATINOS, L E S, Cali moa 637, Isles aux Mares, Aligon, Chuachta, CADODAQUIOS, Nachitoches, Sachoumas, les Choumans, Nafsonis, Natahofsez, Tomcas, Cadodaquios, Lac de Sel, Isles aux, Yasous, les Capinas

This French map of 1718 shows the locations of the Mississippi Valley and Plains tribes when contacted by French traders and trappers operating out of New Orleans. Courtesy, Library of Congress, Geography and Map Division

nies in Mexico (although this was strictly forbidden by Spanish laws that held that all goods sold in New Spain had to come only from the mother country). Nevertheless, Le Mothe Cadillac, Crozat's governor in Louisiana, received orders to make this effort.

As leader of the crucial first expedition, Governor Cadillac selected the daring and enterprising Louis Juchereau de St. Denis, a native of Canada fluent not only in Spanish but also in several Indian dialects. In 1713 St. Denis led a small party of French traders up the Red River. That autumn he traded with the Natchitoches Indians, reconnoitered the area, and established a trading post named for the local natives. Possibly he explored into the present Oklahoma before traveling in 1714 across Texas to the Rio Grande to attempt trade with Spaniards. He was arrested, however, as a foreign intruder,

his goods were confiscated, and he was taken to Mexico City for questioning by the viceroy.

The sudden appearance of Frenchmen in Texas caused Spanish officials to order the colonization of East Texas, a task undertaken in 1716. Two years later, San Antonio was settled as a halfway station between Spanish outposts on the Rio Grande and those in East Texas. Eventually San Antonio would become the center of Spanish activity in Texas. That same year Bienville le Moyne founded New Orleans, which would become the capital of French Louisiana.

In the three decades that followed, Spanish and French officials in Louisiana and Texas contended for supremacy in trade with the Indians of the Great Plains, especially those in North Texas and Oklahoma. This was done partly for the profits involved,

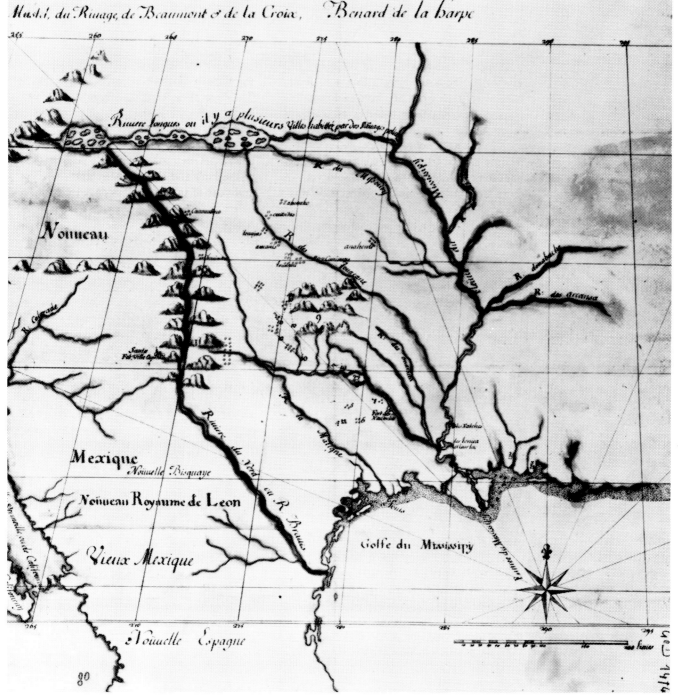

Carte des Nouvelles découvertes faites en 1719, dans la partie de l'ouest de la .. Province de la Louiziane, Par le S. Benard de la Harpe Commandant des troupes aux Nassonittes, et les Sieu Hust. du Riuage, de Beaumont & de la Croix, Benard de la harpe

but more for the loyalty and military support of these tribes. European colonists, Spanish and French, were so few in number that the nation which won the loyalty of the Indians would dominate the area. In short, the Indians of Oklahoma had become pawns in a game of imperial rivalry for mastery of the interior of North America.

In this contest the French proved superior.

French traders, called *coureurs du bois* (literally "runners of the woods"), used the Mississippi and its lower tributaries, the Red and the Arkansas, as highways into Oklahoma. Soon canoes, pirogues, and flatboats were plying these streams carrying French guns, ammunition, knives, axes, beads, cloth, ribbon, and assorted trade goods upriver to be traded for bales of muskrat, beaver, and other furs, even tanned buffalo robes, which made their way to New Orleans and eventually to France to be used to make fashionable clothes. Each French trader was an agent of empire for his distant king, for the government of the region had changed.

In 1717 Louis XV revoked the charter given Antoine Crozat, awarding it to John Law, a refugee from Scotland, who used it as the basis for one of the greatest swindles in history. Forming the "Louisiana Company," Law began selling stock and from the income gained from sales, he began paying handsome dividends—and then sold yet more stock at even higher prices. Law was hailed as a financial genius—until 1721 when the "Mississippi Bubble" burst and Law fled France. Thereafter Louisiana was a royal colony administered by a governor appointed by the crown.

During and after the frenzied period of Law's company, sons of France were quietly roaming the Mississippi Valley—and Oklahoma—trading and expending French influence among the Indians. In 1719 Charles Claude du Tisne went up the Mississippi to the Missouri River to open trade with the Osage and Missouri Indians. Then, moving southwest into northern Oklahoma, Du Tisne visited Wichita villages along the Arkansas (near the present Newkirk). His goal was to reach New Mexico for he had hopes of opening trade with Spanish settlers there.

Another trader, Bénard de la Harpe, came from New Orleans in the spring of 1719 to Indian villages along the Red River in eastern Oklahoma. La Harpe there dispatched one of his aides, the Sieur du Rivage, westward to explore the possibility of opening trade with Spaniards at Santa Fe. In June 1719 Du Rivage reported that he had visited Wichita villages on the Red River, given presents to the Apaches he encountered, and had met a tribe of newcomers to western Oklahoma, the Comanches.

La Harpe, meanwhile, had moved north from the Red to the Canadian to the Arkansas River (at the future site of Haskell in Muskogee County), where he found Indian villages with some 7,000 natives living in "dome-shaped houses of straw and reeds covered with earth." In their fields they raised corn, beans, pumpkins, and "prodigious quantities" of tobacco. In the vicinity they hunted bear and deer, and there was good fishing in the river. Each October the

tribe hunted buffalo in the plains to secure a winter's supply of meat and a year's supply of hides. Already the horse had become a part of their culture. La Harpe noted that the Wichitas were "unable to do without them either in war or hunting." He wrote that the Wichitas were "people of good sense, cleverer than the nations of the Mississippi, but the fertility of the country makes them lazy. They are always sitting around their chief and usually they think only of eating, smoking and playing." After two pleasant days of being feasted, La Harpe left, instructing one of his men to "carve on a post the arms of the king and the company and the day and year of taking possession." In his report he recommended that the Louisiana Company should establish a permanent trading post with these friendly Indians, using this as a base from which to open trade with the plains natives.

La Harpe was so impressed with Du Rivage's report about the Comanches that he determined to make a personal visit westward "to make an alliance with [them] . . . in order to shorten the way into New Mexico . . ." Going up the Arkansas, he paused at every Indian village along the way to give presents of guns, powder, shot, knives, and hatchets to the chiefs, and he spoke of the advantages of friendship with France.

La Harpe was not alone in visiting the Comanches and Apaches, for other French *coureurs du bois* had learned the route from Louisiana to western Oklahoma. Such visits alarmed Spanish officials in Texas and New Mexico, for they feared that if the French gained total influence among these tribes the natives might drive all Spaniards out of the region. Moreover, the French were trading firearms and alcoholic beverages to the Indians, which was prohibited by Spanish law. When these officials complained to the viceroy, the Marquis de Casafuerte, however, he decided (from the security of his office in Mexico City) that French trade with the plains Indians was harmless, and chose to ignore the threat.

French officials in Louisiana regarded the opening of trade with the plains Indians as extremely significant. Du Tisne was called for a personal report to Governor Bienville, who in the early 1720s decided to attempt an alliance with the Comanches. He named Etienne Venieard, Sieur du Bourgmont, to head another expedition to western Oklahoma. Bourgmont was a dashing adventurer married to an Indian and fluent in several dialects. After months of preparation, Bourgmont set out in February 1723, arriving in the Comanche country in the spring of 1724 and making contact with several bands of the tribe. These lords of the plains proved friendly to the Frenchman, and some of the chiefs returned to New Orleans with Bourgmont where they were given guns, ammunition, and steel knives.

These new weapons of war, along with the ones they acquired in trade with the French, so strengthened the Comanches that they grew more powerful than the neighboring Apaches, and the balance of power on the plains was upset. The Comanches, cousins of the Arapaho, originally had lived in the Rocky Mountains, but about the turn of the eighteenth century they had emerged onto the plains to capture mustang horses. Mounted on these and equipped with French weapons, they started moving south in search of a better homeland. In 1706 they made their first recorded appearance at Santa Fe, and by 1743 they had moved as far south as San Antonio, driving their Apache enemies before them. Spaniards in Texas bore the brunt of French trade with the Comanches, for Spaniards steadfastly had refused to supply any tribe with firearms. Almost without realizing it, the Spaniards thereby were forced into a disastrous alliance with the Apaches, who were desperately seeking some way to combat the advancing Comanches.

French influence with the plains tribes continued to grow, thanks to the efforts of remarkable frontiersmen such as Bénard de la Harpe, who reached Santa Fe in 1724. Other French explorers crossed Oklahoma to arrive at the foothills of the Rocky Mountains by mid-eighteenth century, placing themselves in the good graces of the natives along the way because of their non-restrictive trade policies. They would sell anything—firearms, firewater, ammunition, gunpowder, and knives, along with mirrors, beads, ribbons, and vermilion. They liberally gave gifts and cultivated friendships, and thus through their economic policies they were an instrument of imperial destiny for France. In 1741 Fabry de la Bruyere set out in company with soldiers and trappers in an attempt to map the route from Louisiana to Santa Fe. He ascended the Arkansas to the Canadian River and pushed up it to the

point near the present boundary between McIntosh and Hughes counties, but there he was halted by shallow water and sandbars.

By the mid-eighteenth century French influence in Oklahoma had become so significant that many Indian tribes had forsaken their old ways to become commercial fur hunters. Bales of fur came out of Oklahoma each year by pirogue and flatboat on the Arkansas and Red rivers. The French left behind children who were part European, as well as place names including Poteau, San Bois, Fourche Maline, Cavanal, Sallisaw, Bayou Menard, Verdigris, Salina, and Vian Creek (originally known as Bayou Viande). The French flag also flew over Wichita villages on the Canadian and Arkansas rivers. Like the Spaniards in Texas who allied with the Apaches, however, the Frenchmen who traded in Oklahoma had identified themselves too closely with one tribe, the Wichita, who were bitter enemies of the powerful Osage nation. As Osage attacks increased from the north, Wichita bands gradually moved south to form two new villages on the Red River: San Bernardo, in present Jefferson County, Oklahoma, and San Teodoro, in what is now Montague County, Texas. By 1749 only one Wichita village was still on the Arkansas: Fernandina (near the present Newkirk). Fernandina fell before an Osage onslaught in 1757, and the residents moved south to San Bernardo and San Teodoro. There they built palisaded walls around their towns, and they sought an alliance with the masters of the plains, the Comanches.

The Osages, Wichitas, and Comanches were pushing Spaniards in Texas hard. A year after Fernandina fell to the Osages, the Comanches destroyed a Spanish mission built for Apaches at San Saba, Texas. That raid in 1758 triggered a Spanish reprisal the following year when the viceroy in Mexico City determined to avenge what he saw as an insult to Spanish honor. In August of 1759 Colonel Diego Ortíz de Parilla led a force of 380 soldiers and more than 100 Apache allies north to strike the Comanches. Arriving at the Red River in October, Parilla found the Comanches and their Wichita allies inside a palisaded fort surrounded by a moat, over which flew a French flag. A Spanish charge proved fruitless, and general fighting ensued. That evening Colonel Parilla counted his casualties

The Plains Apache Indians were fierce rivals of the Comanches and Wichitas during the period of French control of Oklahoma. OHS

and learned that his Apache allies had stolen many of his horses and had escaped into the night. Parilla wisely chose to retreat, leaving behind the eleven cannons so laboriously brought from San Antonio and which proved unable to batter down the walls of the Indian fort.

Parilla's report of French influence among the plains Indians caused considerable consternation among officials in Mexico City. Yet the Indians so outnumbered Spanish soldiers on the northern frontier that it was hopeless to think of total war as a solution. Swallowing his pride, the governor of Texas hired Athanase de Mézières, a French trader from Louisiana, who persuaded the Comanches to return the cannons abandoned by Parilla.

Spanish fears of French influence on the plains tribes ended in 1762. The close of the Seven Years' War (known in America as the French and Indian War) saw England victorious in Canada, India, and the Continent. Spaniards, who had been dragged into this conflict on the side of France, suffered the loss of Florida to England, while France lost so decisively it feared the hated British would get all former French colonies in North America. To compensate Spain for the loss of Florida—and to prevent England from taking it—France gave Spain all the Louisiana Territory west of the Mississippi River, thereby making Oklahoma Spanish once again.

During the next four decades the region was under Spanish rule, although the traders coming up the Red and Arkansas rivers were Louisianans of French descent—the sons and grandsons of the *coureurs du bois* who had opened the region to trade. The governor at New Orleans tried to halt the traffic in guns for which the Wichitas had been famous, and their prosperity began to wither away, as did their power and influence as traders and allies of the Comanches.

During this last phase of European ownership, Oklahoma was still a source of furs, but on a declining scale.

It was during this period that Bénard de la Harpe's dream of using Oklahoma as a highway of commerce to New Mexico finally was realized. In September 1786 Governor Domingo Cabello y Robles of Texas called Pedro Vial to his office and hired him to open a road from San Antonio to Santa Fe. Vial, a Frenchman from Louisiana, went north from San Antonio to San Bernardo and then up the Red River to its source, reaching Santa Fe on May 26, 1787, after traveling more than 1,100 miles. The following year Vial made a similar journey from Santa Fe to the village on the Red River, from there to Nacogdoches in East Texas, and then to San Antonio.

The route Vial pioneered from Santa Fe to the Wichita village on the Red River was used by some traders who went from New Mexico to San Bernardo and then on to New Orleans. Thereafter a regular traffic soon developed between Louisiana and New Mexico. Huge two-wheeled carts, little changed from those used in biblical days, came squealing down from Santa Fe loaded with woolen blankets, piñon nuts, even furs, and returned carrying imported items needed in the west. Spanish coins were used to pay for food and lodging along the way, and today treasure hunters still find gold and silver coins *(pedazos de ocho)* buried near the banks of the Red River.

Such was the nature of European Oklahoma: a place where golden villages were sought, where Spaniards and Frenchmen battled for Indian loyalties, and where roads crossed the region. This era came to an end not because Spaniards or Frenchmen desired it, but because of events in Europe. The kaleidoscope of history was turning in Paris, Madrid, London, and Washington, and this would determine Oklahoma's future.

CHAPTER III

Oklahoma Becomes American

*T*he revolution which began in France in 1789 was a fire that burned fiercely. Within three years it brought Louis XVI and Marie Antoinette to the guillotine, and France moved from monarchy to republic and then to anarchy. Out of the ashes of this social fire in 1799 came Napoleon Bonaparte, an emperor with visions of restoring his nation to greatness as a colonial power. Casting his eyes to the south, he saw a weak Charles IV on the throne of Spain, a king who had abdicated the day-to-day affairs of government to Prince Manuel Godoy. Napoleon summoned Charles IV and Prince Godoy north to inform them that he wished Louisiana returned to France. On October 1, 1800, they drafted and signed the secret Treaty of San Ildefonso, which retroceded Louisiana to France.

With Louisiana again French—on paper—Napoleon quickly moved to take actual possession. In November 1801 he sent his brother-in-law, Marshal V.E. LeClerc, with an army of 10,000 men to suppress a slave rebellion against French ownership of Haiti and then to occupy Louisiana. When LeClerc arrived on the island of Santo Domingo, he found the former slaves united and ready for war under the leadership of Toussaint L'Overture. At first the battles were won by Frenchmen, and L'Overture was captured by intrigue (later to die in a French prison in the Alps).

However, LeClerc's soldiers had no experience with tropical diseases, particularly yellow fever. Unaccustomed to the ravages of this scourge, they died in incredible numbers. More and yet more troops arrived from France only to become infected and die, as did LeClerc. After 27,000 men had been sent to the New World and Haiti still had not been reconquered, Napoleon at last realized he would have to grant the island-nation its independence. Nor could he spare additional men to occupy Louisiana, for by

1802 war with England again loomed. The French emperor clearly understood that when this war began, England, with its control of the seas, could easily take Louisiana from him. Determined that the hated "nation of shopkeepers" would not own this territory, he decided to sell it to the United States, commenting early in 1803:

I know all the value of Louisiana . . . . A few lines of a treaty have given it back to me, and hardly have I recovered it when I must expect to lose it. But if I lose it, it will be dearer one day to those who compel me to abandon it [England] than to those to whom I wish to deliver it [the United States].

In the United States, almost since it was recognized as an independent nation, Americans had been casting covetous eyes on Spanish Louisiana, and particularly the port of New Orleans. Frontiersmen in the backcountry of Tennessee and Kentucky were floating their produce down the Mississippi to that city for shipment to the East Coast. Spanish officials periodically halted this flow of goods, causing the frontiersmen to complain loudly to their national government. By 1801 the newly installed president, Thomas Jefferson, was listening—and hoping for an opportunity to make a change.

Jefferson heard of the secret Treaty of San Ildefonso and, at first, watched to see what move the French might make. When nothing happened—because of yellow fever in Haiti— he decided at last to act. In January of 1803 he asked the Senate to name James Monroe as minister extraordinary with authority to work with Robert Livingston, the American minister in France, to seek the purchase of New Orleans from Napoleon. The Senate concurred, and Congress voted a secret appropriation of two million dollars for such a purchase.

In France, war with England was rapidly approaching. Early in March, Napoleon told the British ambassador that France must have ownership of the island of Malta or war with England would result. War obviously was what he would get, and both nations began feverish preparations. Thus on April 10 Napoleon told his finance minister, the Marquis Francois de Barbe-Marbois, "I renounce Louisiana. It is not only New Orleans that I cede; it is the whole colony without reserve." The next day Robert Livingston was told that

the United States was to be the unwitting beneficiary of European intrigues.

James Monroe arrived the following day, April 12, armed with orders from Jefferson to attempt to buy New Orleans. It was Livingston, however, who conducted most of the negotiations with Barbe-Marbois. Napoleon had told Barbe-Marbois that he would accept fifty million francs; the marquis, hoping to impress his emperor, doubled that amount when he made his first offer to Livingston. The American minister countered with an offer of twenty million francs. Back and forth the haggling went until at last a figure of sixty million francs was set—with the United States requesting twenty million francs to indemnify Americans who had claims against France. This final sum, in total, amounted to fifteen million dollars. When the agreement was signed on April 20, 1803, Livingston commented, "We have lived long, but this is the noblest work of our lives."

That noble work proved a headache for President Jefferson when the treaty reached his desk. He had long maintained that the national government had only those powers specifically granted it in the Constitution— and nowhere in that document did it state that the government could acquire territory. Yet he strongly wanted Louisiana. All his life he had idealized agriculture as a way of life, for he thought farming developed moral and political virtue in people. He therefore wanted the United States to be a land of yeoman farmers, and the Louisiana Territory, he believed, would provide sufficient land for the farms needed by Americans for the next 500 years. Caught in this dilemma, Jefferson first considered a constitutional amendment to authorize the purchase; the amendment would also have provided for creating an Indian state in part of the Louisiana Territory. Yet Jefferson knew that amending the Constitution took time, perhaps years, and he had no time. He was continually receiving letters from Livingston urging quick ratification of the treaty before Napoleon's fertile mind found another use for Louisiana.

Jefferson therefore sent the treaty to the Senate. That body concurred that, although the Constitution did not specifically state that the nation had the right to acquire territory, this right was inherent in national sovereignty, and the treaty was ratified. On December 15, 1803, American commissioners were in New Orleans to take possession from Frenchmen, who only a short time before had themselves taken ownership from Spaniards. The ceremony of raising the American flag was then repeated at other places, such as St. Louis, in the months that followed. The land later to be known as Oklahoma (except for its Panhandle) had become part of the United States.

The Louisiana Purchase immediately brought new problems, however. The actual boundaries of the area were unclear, for neither Spain nor France had ever drawn specific lines separating Louisiana from Texas and New Mexico. The French negotiators who sold the territory to the United States recognized the vagueness of this boundary, Napoleon himself commenting, "If an obscurity did not already exist, it would, perhaps, be good policy to put one there." By this he meant that the United States thereby was free to claim as much Spanish territory as it could defend. After the transfer to American ownership, the Spanish commissioners at New Orleans, Manuel Salcedo y Salcedo and the Marques de Casa Calvo, withdrew west of the Sabine River (the present boundary between Louisiana and Texas) to await developments.

Jefferson wanted to quickly determine the limits of the land he had bought. Even before the purchase, his curiosity had led him to propose an exploratory party into the American West, resulting in the expedition of Meriwether Lewis and William Clark, who trekked to the mouth of the Columbia River in Oregon and back to St. Louis between 1804 and 1806. Simultaneously Jefferson sent explorers into the Southwest to learn the sources and courses of the Red and Arkansas rivers, important in setting a boundary between American and Spanish territory. No exact maps existed, and knowledge was a weapon that negotiators could use to advantage.

In April 1804 Congress appropriated $3,000 for Sir William Dunbar and Dr. George Hunter to lead the expedition in search of the rivers' headwaters, but the effort failed. The two scientists were blocked by Spaniards in Texas, who did not want Americans to gain a favorable boundary settlement. Therefore Dunbar and Hunter spent the money exploring for four months in the Quachita River Valley of Arkansas, an area already settled by American frontiersmen. Although Dunbar and Hunter made no geographic discoveries, they did gather valuable scientific information.

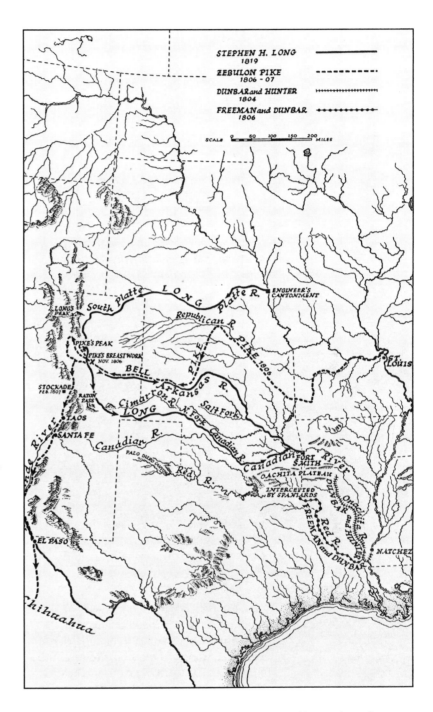

Before Jefferson could send yet another expedition westward, General James Wilkinson, commander of American forces in Louisiana, ordered young Lieutenant Zebulon Montgomery Pike into the region to search for the headwaters of the Arkansas and to open commerce with the plains Indians. Wilkinson's reasons for sending Pike are unclear, but the general was heavily involved with former Vice-President Aaron Burr, who perhaps had thoughts of taking some Spanish territory by force.

Lieutenant Pike set out from St. Louis on July 15, 1806, going west by way of the

This map shows the routes of the American explorers in the Great Plains from 1804 to 1819. OHS

Lieutenant Zebulon M. Pike, the "lost pathfinder," led the first American expedition across the Great Plains in 1806. His assistant, Lieutenant James B. Wilkinson, was the first American to record his travels through Oklahoma. OHS

Missouri and Osage rivers. He was accompanied by James B. Wilkinson, son of the general, twenty-three whites, and fifty-one Osage and Pawnee Indians. Turning south at the mouth of the Osage River, the group arrived at Osage villages near the Lake of the Ozarks. From there they made their way northwestward to Pawnee villages on the Republican River (near the present Kansas-Nebraska border). Pike found the Pawnees unfriendly, having recently been visited by a 600-man Spanish force from New Mexico commanded by Lieutenant Colonel Facundo Melgares. A Spanish flag flew over the village, and around the chiefs' necks were Spanish medals, but Pike persuaded the Pawnees to replace the Spanish flag with the flag of the United States. He and his party then rode to the Arkansas River, reaching it near the present town of Great Bend, Kansas. At that point, because

young Wilkinson was seriously ill, he and six men were allowed to begin a return trip to the Mississippi by way of the Arkansas River.

Pike subsequently pushed into Colorado, discovered the peak that today bears his name, and turned south into New Mexico. There he was captured by Spanish soldiers, taken to Santa Fe and then to Chihuahua City for questioning, and finally marched across Texas to Louisiana, arriving there on July 1, 1807.

Meanwhile, Lieutenant Wilkinson and his six companions were struggling down the Arkansas River and crossing the northeastern part of Oklahoma. They started downriver on October 28, 1806, hoping to reach friendly Indians or traders before the winter became too harsh, but their boats immediately ran aground on sandbars and ice. Soon they abandoned their boats, each man carrying a gun, a buffalo robe, and a few cups of corn. Two weeks later they reached the site of the present Wichita, Kansas. There they decided to try the river once more, and ten days were consumed in felling trees and fashioning canoes. Again, however, the boats snagged on sandbars and ice. Moreover, the canoe holding the major part of their food and ammunition overturned, and these essential supplies were lost.

As the men crossed into Oklahoma they seemed doomed, but there they were befriended by Osage Indians who offered to kill fresh meat for them while they rested in an Osage camp. While there, Wilkinson was told that Tuttasuggy, an Osage chief, was ill and needed medical attention. Wilkinson agreed to help, traveling on November 30 by mule to an Osage village located near the present Ponca City. This marked the first entrance of an official American exploration in what soon would be the Indian Territory.

On December 1, Wilkinson and his six companions resumed their journey, fighting ice on the river day after weary day. They rested for three days at the mouth of the Salt Fork River, Wilkinson using the time to write in detail on the hunting habits of the Osages and the location of their villages. On December 10, they were at the site of Sand Springs, pausing there to make a small side journey up the Cimarron River, which Wilkinson labeled the Saline because the Osages gathered salt along its marshes. By December 23, the party rested at an

Osage village at the confluence of the Verdigris and Grand rivers. There Wilkinson took another side trip, this time sixty miles up the Verdigris to the Osage village of Chief Clermont (near present Claremore). Clermont was the hereditary chief of the Great Osage, but when he was a child his place had been assumed by Pawhuska (White Hair) with the aid of Pierre Chouteau, a trader working out of Missouri. Pierre's halfbrother Auguste Chouteau, a merchant living in St. Louis, had been given a monopoly on trade with the Osages in 1794, but in 1802 his license was revoked by the governor-general of Louisiana. Unwilling to lose this profitable trade, he sent his halfbrother Pierre to persuade the

Osages to leave their traditional homeland in Missouri to live along the banks of the Arkansas in Oklahoma, and some 3,000 Osages agreed to move, driving out both Caddos and Wichitas.

Leaving the Three Forks area where Muskogee eventually would grow, Wilkinson and his party on December 29 arrived at "a fall of near seven feet perpendicular" (Webbers Falls). At last, on January 7, 1807, the weary travelers arrived at Arkansas Post (where the Arkansas joins the Mississippi). There their journey ended.

The reports of Pike and Wilkinson left President Jefferson still without exact knowledge about the Arkansas and Red rivers, and he was so anxious to learn the

Osage Chief Pawhuska settled his band in north-central Oklahoma on the fringe of the Great Plains. OHS

geography of the area that he had already sent another expedition into the region. In April 1806, Thomas Freeman and a party that included Captain Richard Sparks and Peter Custis moved up the Red River to Natchitoches, Louisiana. Late in May, Freeman set out upriver with thirty-seven men in two flatboats and a pirogue.

They immediately encountered great hardship, for just above Natchitoches was the Great Raft, a logjam extending more than seventy miles along the river. Sweating and cursing, they cut their way through this maze of wood following the serpentine course of the river. Adding to their misery was the fear of what lay ahead, for on June 8 Freeman received word that a large Spanish army was moving up from San Antonio to intercept the Americans and prevent their exploring and mapping the Red River. When at last Freeman's party reached the Great Bend of the Red, they were warned by Caddo Indians that Spaniards were in the area.

The two parties met on July 28. Captain Francisco Viana and 150 Spanish soldiers were waiting near the site of Wichita Falls, Texas. Freeman, faced with a superior force, agreed to turn back, and after a harsh return journey reached the Mississippi River in August 1806. Although the expedition had failed to find the source of the Red, it had mapped 635 miles of the river

and had gathered a considerable amount of scientific information about the region.

Less interested in knowledge than profits were the civilian traders who, like the Chouteau brothers, began working in Oklahoma at this time. When Lieutenant James Wilkinson was making his way down the Arkansas in January 1807, he met James Bogy and a party of traders coming upriver. Bogy had secured a license to trade with the Osages, and had loaded a boat with goods. At the Three Forks area Bogy ascended the Verdigris a short distance, erected log cabins, and began trading for pelts. Despite the conflict between the tribes contending for supremacy in the region, he would stay.

In 1811 another official American expedition would venture into Oklahoma, this one led by George Champlin Sibley, son of John Sibley, who was in charge of the Red River and Sulphur Fork Indian Factory, a licensed trading post in Louisiana. Sibley, who was to solicit the plains Indians' friendship for the United States, first visited the Osages, then went to the Great Salt Plains and explored the Salt Fork River (in present Alfalfa County). In the process he made copious notes about the geography of the region.

Despite the many explorations, Oklahoma largely remained a mystery to map makers. Moreover, the headwaters of the Red and Arkansas rivers still had not been discovered. Despite this scarcity of hard knowledge, the United States and Spain, once the Napoleonic wars ended in 1815, negotiated their way toward an agreement about the boundary separating the Louisiana Territory and Texas. When finally signed, the Treaty of 1819 (also known as the Adams-Onís Treaty) provided for the boundary to begin three marine leagues out in the Gulf of Mexico, proceed up the south or west bank of the Sabine River to its intersection with the 32nd parallel, go due north to the Red River, move west along its south or west bank to its intersection with the 100th meridian, run due north to the Arkansas, proceed along its south or west bank to its source, then run due north to the 42nd parallel, and follow that parallel to the Pacific Ocean. The American desire to have total ownership of the Sabine, Red, and Arkansas rivers (rather than run up the middle of each river, as usually was the case in drawing boundaries) stemmed from earlier difficulties with Spain over the right of transit on the Mississipi. No such quarrel could

develop if the United States totally owned these rivers. From this eventually would come Oklahoma's complete ownership of the Red, which it shares as a boundary with Texas (a point that became extremely important when oil was discovered in the bed of the river).

Following this treaty the United States naturally needed to learn the source of the Arkansas and Red rivers and to have these streams mapped accurately. Sent to accomplish these tasks was Major Stephen Harriman Long. During the summer of 1820, Long, accompanied by nineteen soldiers and Dr. Edwin James, a scientist, journeyed first to the source of the Arkansas, and then into Oklahoma, leaving half his command to float down the Arkansas under the leadership of Captain John R. Bell. In Oklahoma, Long mistook the Canadian for the Red River and set out down it, eventually reaching the Arkansas and joining with Captain Bell to continue into Arkansas Territory, which had been created the previous year. Once again Oklahoma had been penetrated by Americans.

In his report Long asserted, as had Pike, that the Great Plains constituted a "Great American Desert" on which only a nomadic population could live. He argued that the region was forever unfit for habitation by people depending on agriculture for a living, saying that, although some of the soil was

fertile and that some timber and water were present in isolated spots, the area could never be of any value—except as a buffer to prevent too wide a dispersement of the American population. In short, Long saw the Great American Desert as a barrier to westward expansion. Because of his pessimistic report, few frontier Americans wanted to move there.

Nevertheless, the United States was the owner of this vast expanse of land, and it occurred to some national leaders that, if farmers could not exist there, it might be an ideal place to remove all Indians living east of the Mississippi. As early as 1803 Thomas Jefferson had written of the possibility of

Right
This map was part of Stephen Long's report. It clearly shows the area labeled the "Great American Desert" crossing western Oklahoma. Courtesy, The Thomas Gilcrease Institute of American History and Art, Tulsa, Oklahoma

Opposite page, top
During Stephen Long's expedition across the central Great Plains, the explorer contacted several Indian tribes. An important tribe located strategically in eastern Kansas was the Kansas or Kaw Indians. Here warriors of the tribe attempt to impress Long and his men with a war dance. Courtesy, The Thomas Gilcrease Institute of American History and Art, Tulsa, Oklahoma

Opposite page, bottom
The report of Stephen Long's expedition in the Great Plains was illustrated with views of the lands that they crossed and of the explorers themselves. Here the caravan marches through the foothills of the Rocky Mountains in eastern Colorado, heading south to Oklahoma. Courtesy, The Thomas Gilcrease Institute of American History and Art, Tulsa, Oklahoma

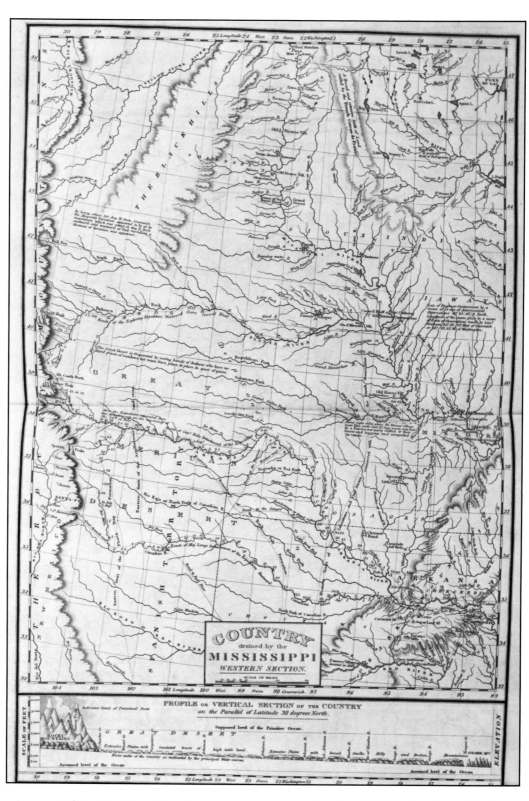

using part of the Louisiana Purchase as a home for eastern Indians. Little came of this suggestion until 1823 when Secretary of War John Calhoun began worrying with the problem of what to do with these Native Americans.

Calhoun drafted a plan for removing all eastern Indians to the Great American Des-

ert, noting that 53,625 Cherokees, Creeks, Choctaws, and Chickasaws still owned 33,573,176 acres in Georgia, Alabama, Mississippi, North Carolina, and Tennessee, while 5,000 Seminoles owned a sizable portion of Florida. These Indians, Calhoun suggested, should be removed to an "Indian Territory." President James Monroe, in pre-

senting this plan to Congress in his annual message on January 27, 1825, stated that it would "promote the interests and happiness of these tribes," to which "the attention of the Government has long been drawn with great solicitude." In 1830 Congress agreed with this proposal, setting aside the Indian Territory and requiring all non-Indians within that area to leave unless specifically licensed to trade with the Indians. However, some Indians from the eastern states already had been forced to move to the territory long before Congress legislated the policy as a national goal.

CHAPTER IV

The Indian Territory

Pushmataha was principal chief of the Choctaw Nation prior to and during removal. He allied his tribe to the United States during the War of 1812 and the Creek Wars, winning the admiration of General Andrew Jackson. OHS

At the time of the adoption of the Articles of Confederation during the midst of the American Revolution, one of the most hotly debated issues involved the western land claims of the various states. Some, such as Maryland and Pennsylvania, had definite western limits, while others, such as Virginia and Georgia, laid claim to almost unlimited acres in the West. By July 1778, eight states had signed the Articles, but New Jersey, Delaware, and Maryland refused until all states had ceded their claims to the western lands. Representatives from Maryland argued that the Revolution was a common effort, and therefore the western lands should be a common heritage. The Continental Congress responded in 1780 by asking those states with land claims in the West to surrender them. New York shortly thereafter led the way, followed by Virginia and most other states with claims. Thereupon the Articles of Confederation were ratified. Not until 1802, however, did Georgia finally cede its western land claims, and then only with the provision that the national government extinguish all Indian land titles within that state.

In the northern part of the United States, the policy of removal (or extermination) moved forward rapidly. By the end of the War of 1812, most of the Northeast and some of the Northwest Territory had been cleared of native inhabitants. In the Southeast, however, most of the so-called Five Civilized Tribes—the Cherokees, Creeks, Choctaws, Chickasaw, and Seminoles—were stoutly resisting white encroachment. A few of their number had surrendered and had moved westward, especially among the Cherokees. One small group from this tribe had moved to Texas perhaps as early as 1813 onto land allotted them by the Spanish government in that province (but to which no land title was given). Another slightly larger body of Cherokee had settled in Arkansas.

Yet the majority of the members of the

This chickie, or Seminole Indian dwelling, was similar to most used by that tribe and others of the Five Civilized Tribes prior to their adoption of white ways. OHS

Five Civilized Tribes desired to stay on their traditional lands, and devised several strategies to remain there. They cooperated with the national government, hoping for protection from citizens of the various states. They signed treaties whereby they surrendered part of their lands in order to be guaranteed ownership of their remaining traditional lands. The Cherokees, for example, signed away parts of North Carolina, South Carolina, Tennessee, Kentucky, and Alabama in order to retain acres in eastern Tennessee and northern Alabama.

Another strategy of the Five Civilized Tribes was to adopt white ways in the hope of winning acceptance by their non-Indian neighbors. They adopted white dress and white patterns of farming, owned slaves, sent their children to school, welcomed missionaries and became Christians, and fought on the American side in the War of 1812. Despite these policies, they found no white acceptance—and little federal protection. Land-hungry frontiersmen, land speculators, and gold hunters looked with greed and envy on the fertile acres owned by the Indians, and gradually a series of laws were enacted in Georgia, Alabama, and Mississippi designed to force the Indians westward. Everywhere there was the argument that the federal government had not lived up to its commitment, made during the ratification of the Articles of Confederation, to remove the Indians. Thus the Indians, despite their resistance, gradually lost skirmish after skirmish to retain their homelands. They lost in state legislatures, in Congress, and finally in the courts.

The first major removal resulted from a meeting of leaders of one group of Cherokees, American officials, and the headmen of the Osages. At this meeting in St. Louis in 1808, the Osage agreed to cede all their land east of a line running directly south from Fort Clark (on the Missouri River) to the Arkansas River. Included in this cession was almost all of the land within the present state of Arkansas north of the Arkansas River, as well as a significant portion of the present state of Missouri. The following January, President Jefferson gave permission for the Cherokees to send exploring parties westward to examine and reconnoiter "the country on the waters of the Arkansas and White rivers, and the higher up [farther upriver] the better, as they will be longer unapproached by our [white] settlement." According to this treaty of removal, heads of Cherokee families were to receive 640 acres, while those not heads of families, called "poor warriors" in the treaty, were to receive "one rifle and ammunition, one

44

blanket and one brass kettle, or in lieu of the brass kettle, a beaver trap." In addition, the government said it would provide flat-bottomed boats to aid any Cherokee moving west.

By the terms of this treaty, such emigration was voluntary, but by 1817 there were some 2,000 Cherokees who moved westward from Tennessee and Georgia into present Arkansas. In their new homeland, east and north of present Fort Smith (between the Arkansas and White rivers), they began erecting homes, clearing land, and planting crops, and in 1813 Major William L. Lovely was sent by Colonel R.J. Meigs, Cherokee Indian agent in Tennessee, to serve as sub-agent to the Western (or Arkansas) Cherokees.

The major problem with this scheme of removal was that the Osages still were contesting for ownership of the land onto which the Cherokees settled. As early as 1814 Subagent Lovely was recommending that a military post be opened on the Arkansas River to keep peace in the region. By the summer of 1816, with no troops yet posted and intertribal warfare more intense than ever, Lovely called for a meeting at the Three Forks area (the present Muskogee) between the Arkansas Cherokees and the Southern Osage. At this council Lovely asked Chief Clermont and the Osages to cede yet another vast tract of land, more than seven million acres, to the United States. On July 9 the Osage chiefs signed the accord agreeing to what became known as Lovely's Purchase. This involved the land bounded on the east by the old Osage line, on the south by the Arkansas River, on the west by the Verdigris River up to the falls, then in a straight line northeast to the saline springs on the Grand River, and from there due east to the Osage line. The Cherokees would become owners of this new land, said Lovely, and thereby peace would return to the region. Lovely did not live to see his hope realized, for he died shortly after securing the purchase that would bear his name.

In the summer of 1817, with warfare still raging between the two tribes, American commissioners met with Eastern Cherokee chiefs to persuade them to remove to Arkansas, thereby throwing their old homeland open to white settlement. The Cherokees agreed, and in return were promised payment for their costs of removal and military

protection in their new homeland. As a result of this treaty, another 4,000 Cherokees would remove westward in the next two years, bringing the total number of Cherokees in Arkansas to some 6,000, and in 1817 Fort Smith would be erected at the junction of the Arkansas and Poteau rivers at a place known as Belle Point.

Yet the strife between the Cherokees and Osages continued to rage, so much so that on September 25, 1818, the United States signed a treaty with the Osages at St. Louis in which the Osages reconfirmed their agreement to Lovely's Purchase made in 1816. This tract then was given to the Arkansas Cherokees as a hunting ground and as a path to the plains for killing buffalo. The hope was that this would bring peace, but soon the Osage and Cherokee nations were at war once again. Because of this, in 1822 Colonel Matthew Arbuckle, commanding officer at Fort Smith, recommended that a garrison be placed at the mouth of the Verdigris River to keep peace in the region.

Orders to this effect were issued early in 1824, and on April 9 Colonel Arbuckle marched his 7th Infantry troops upriver, and on April 22 selected the location of what became known as Fort Gibson, named in honor of Colonel George Gibson, then commissary general of subsistence. Colonel Arbuckle also sent troops to the Red River near its junction with the Kiamichi River to found Fort Towson, named for Nathan Towson, a hero of the War of 1812. Fort Gibson eventually proved to be the most useful post, for it was located near where several major confrontations would occur and because it was situated on three navigable streams (the Arkansas, the Grand, and the Verdigris). Fort Towson proved difficult to supply because the Red River often was unnavigable. In 1825 a road was surveyed to connect Forts Smith and Gibson, paralleling the present route of U.S. 64. Later a road was opened between Forts Smith and Towson, while other roads, really little more than cart paths, were opened across other parts of southeastern Oklahoma.

At the same time the government was persuading the Osages to cede land for Cherokee settlement, it was also pressuring the Quapaws to sign away a huge strip of their homeland. This cession, signed in 1818, defined a tract of land bounded on the south by the Red River and on the

Right
This sketch of Fort Towson, located near the Red River in southeastern Oklahoma, shows the parade ground and barracks of the troops. This post was abandoned in the 1830s as the frontier of the Five Civilized Tribes moved westward. OHS

Below
Reconstruction of the Fort Gibson Stockade was completed during the 1930s. This post is the oldest military fort in Oklahoma. OHS

Malmaison, *the plantation home of Greenwood LeFlore in Mississippi, showed the degree of civilization of the mixed-blood members of the Five Civilized Tribes. When the Choctaw Nation was removed to Indian Territory, LeFlore chose to remain in Mississippi rather than move with his people. OHS*

north by the Canadian and Arkansas rivers. In claiming that this huge area (almost one-third of the present Oklahoma) had become open to settlement by eastern tribes, however, the government ignored the legitimate claims of many other tribes to parts of this land, including the various Caddoan people and, in the west, the roving bands of plains tribes. However, with this treaty signed by the Quapaws, the federal government increased its pressure on the Five Civilized Tribes to remove westward.

Moreover, Congress in 1820 further defined the boundaries of what was increasingly becoming an "Indian Territory." When it passed the Enabling Act for Missouri to enter the Union as a state, Congress set 36°30' north latitude as the dividing point between Missouri and Arkansas. The Indian Territory thus was the area between the Red River and 36°30' north latitude and between the western edge of Arkansas and the 100th meridian.

After some Cherokees recognized the inevitable and began moving westward, part of the Choctaw Nation followed suit. For two decades the white settlers of Mississippi had been pressing the federal government to open Choctaw lands to settlement, and in 1820 Chief Pushmataha represented the tribe in negotiating with General Andrew Jackson, spokesman for the United States. By terms of the Treaty of Doak's Stand, signed in 1820, the Choctaws, in return for part of their traditional homeland, were given the recently ceded Quapaw Strip (from the Red River north to the Canadian and Arkansas and east into present Arkansas). Any Choctaw warrior who would move west was to be given a rifle, a bullet mold, one year's supply of ammunition, a blanket, a kettle, and money to cover the value of the improvements he had made on the land he left behind. About one-fourth of the tribe eventually left under the terms of the Treaty of Doak's Stand.

Immediately after this treaty was signed, whites in Arkansas protested that it gave away large amounts of land already settled by them. Congress in 1824 responded by defining the western boundary of Arkansas as beginning forty miles west of the southwestern boundary of Missouri and then running due south to the Red River. This pleased whites in Arkansas but greatly disturbed the Choctaws who had removed westward. In 1825 a delegation of Choctaws went to Washington to protest, resulting in yet another agreement, this one setting the western boundary of Arkansas at 100 paces west of Fort Smith and then running due south to the Red River. Thereby the Choctaws re-

gained a forty-mile strip of territory. They were also promised $6,000 a year "forever," a removal of all whites from Choctaw lands, and prevention of any future white settlement on land belonging to the Choctaws.

Also in 1825 the Osage were induced to cede their remaining land in Oklahoma. In 1808, 1816, and 1818 they had made agreements to surrender land, and each time they vowed to live in peace with their neighbors. Yet these promises had always been broken and incessant warfare had raged. The opening of Forts Smith and Gibson failed to bring peace to the region. In 1825, however, faced with rising debts to other tribes and with declining numbers, the Osage, represented by Chiefs Clermont and Pawhuska, agreed to cede all their remaining land except for a reserve fifty miles wide along the southern border of Kansas from the 95th to 100th meridian.

Next to feel the pressure to move were the Creeks. Already in 1814, by the Treaty of Fort Jackson, they had lost domain along the Coosa and Tallapoosa rivers because some of the tribe had fought against the United States during the War of 1812 (the so-called "Red Sticks"). In 1818 they had been forced to cede another fifteen million acres, largely in Georgia. These two losses caused a majority of the tribe to oppose any further cessions—even to oppose talks that might possibly lead to cessions. In 1824 the will of the majority was demonstrated by a tribal order decreeing the death penalty for any Creek who proposed selling land to the whites. Yet within the tribe there were members who foresaw the inevitability of a move westward. This faction was led by William McIntosh, a half-breed related to the governor of Georgia. McIntosh believed the Creeks would prosper only when removed from white influences and pressures. Twice in the early 1820s he tried to sell tribal lands in exchange for a new domain in the West, but both times he was thwarted by conservative Creeks.

In 1824 the United States government, under pressure from Georgians to remove the Creeks, approached the tribe about selling some of its land. McIntosh and his followers indicated a willingness to negotiate, and the Treaty of Indian Springs was signed on February 12, 1825. This provided for the purchase of all Creek lands in Georgia and eastern Alabama in return for land between the Arkansas and Canadian rivers in the

Indian Territory, along with a cash bonus of $400,000.

Although the Treaty of Indian Springs was signed only by McIntosh and fifty other Creeks, the government was so desperate to remove the Creeks from Georgia that it chose to recognize this as binding and sent it to the Senate for ratification. Within a month the Senate voted its approval, causing consternation in the Creek tribal council. The council immediately sent a delegation to Washington to protest that the treaty was illegal, while simultaneously ruling that McIntosh was guilty of treason and subject to the death penalty (as stipulated by Creek law in 1824). On April 30, 1825, a large group of warriors surrounded McIntosh's home. Everyone inside, except McIntosh and one other signer of the treaty, was allowed to leave, after which the house was set afire. When the two men emerged, they were shot. The Creeks always maintained that this was a legal execution, not murder.

President John Quincy Adams, who took

Chilly McIntosh was the son of William McIntosh and the leader of the pro-removal faction of the Creek Nation. OHS

Sequoyah developed a syllabary for his tribesmen, making them among the most literate people in the world at that time. OHS

office on March 4, 1825, also thought the Treaty of Indian Springs was fraudulent, and he nullified it. Public opinion in Georgia, however, was against the Creeks, and finally the tribal leadership realized that bloodshed was inevitable unless some new accord was reached. Therefore a delegation was sent to Washington in the spring of 1826, and a new treaty was signed on April 26, voiding the Indian Springs treaty, but stipulating that most of the Creek lands in Georgia were to be exchanged for a new home for the tribe along the Canadian River plus an immediate cash settlement of $217,600 and an annual allotment of $20,000. In addition, the government was to furnish transportation for this move westward. The McIntosh Creeks, as that faction was called, were to be moved westward at government expense, to settle on unoccupied land somewhere west of the Mississippi River, and to receive $100,000.

The McIntosh Creeks were the only members of that tribe to move immediately. Led by Roley McIntosh, son of the slain chief, this group began settling along the west bank of the Verdigris River early in 1828. The government purchased the improvements made by Auguste and Pierre Chouteau, and after the McIntosh tribe moved there, the old Chouteau trading post became the Indian Agency headquarters. The McIntosh group was fortunate, because the site was near Fort Gibson, giving them protection from the still-belligerent Osages. By 1830 more than 2,000 Creeks were living at this site between the Verdigris and Grand rivers. The majority of the Creek Nation resisted removal, however, and moved from Georgia to settle on remaining tribal lands in Alabama.

During this same period, the government was having problems with white encroachment onto Cherokee lands in present Arkansas. At the time of Lovely's Purchase, the Cherokees were granted the land for hunting and as a path to the plains for pursuing buffalo. By the early 1820s, however, continued white settlement in that area caused the Cherokees to fear that the arrangement might be threatened. In 1822 they sought a congressional guarantee of their right to this land, but nothing was done. Again in 1826 they made the same request of Congress. This caused whites, some of whom were living illegally on the land encompassed by Lovely's Purchase, to petition Congress, through

the Arkansas territorial legislature, for the area to be opened to white settlement. When Congress agreed, settlers rushed in, and almost overnight Lovely's Purchase was transformed into Crawford County by the Arkansas territorial legislature.

The Western Cherokees were shocked and dismayed by this action, as it left them surrounded by white settlers and with no outlet to the plains. They again sent a delegation to Washington to protest that by terms of the Treaty of 1818 they had been promised an outlet to the west. One member of this delegation was Sequoyah, who already had gained fame for the Cherokee syllabary he had invented. The result was a new treaty signed on May 6, 1828, which provided for an exchange of Cherokee land in Arkansas for a new home bounded on the north by the southern border of Kansas, on the south by the fork formed by the Arkansas and Canadian rivers, and on the east by the western boundary of Arkansas. The treaty also promised the Cherokees a permanent outlet to the west, and provided for the removal of all whites from the Indian Territory. The Cherokees were to be paid for all the improvements they had to leave behind in Arkansas and they were given fourteen months to make the move.

When the provisions of this treaty were announced to the Western Cherokees, many of them threatened to inflict on the negotiators the same punishment meted out to

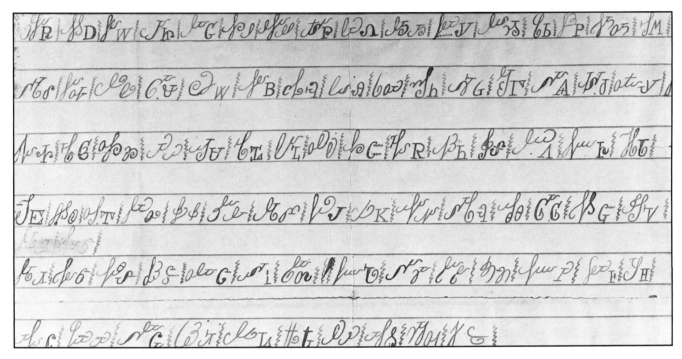

William McIntosh by the Creeks—death. In the face of a binding treaty, however, they had no recourse and began preparations to leave. Simultaneously, the whites in what had been Crawford County did not want to move eastward. Their anger was appeased somewhat by the grants of land made them to the east in Arkansas, and they likewise packed to move, spurred in part by the government's threat that any white not out of the Indian Territory by December 27, 1828, would forfeit any claim to land in Arkansas.

The treaty of 1828 had one additional feature: it sought to reward the genius of one Cherokee: Sequoyah. Born about 1770 in the village of Taskigi, Tennessee, Sequoyah was the son of the trader named Nathaniel Gist. His mother, who was part Cherokee, was abandoned by her husband shortly before the birth of her child. Sequoyah used his Indian name until he approached manhood, at which time he assumed the name George Guess (as he understood his father's last name to be spelled). Crippled for life in a hunting accident, he became an excellent silversmith. As an adult his curiosity was piqued by "talking leaves," as he called books. In 1809 he determined to master this secret and apply it to his own people. After a dozen years of ridicule and insults, he invented a Cherokee alphabet of eighty-five or eighty-six characters, each representing a sound in the tribal language. In 1821 he demonstrated his invention before the Cherokee council, which approved his work. Within two years thousands of Cherokees had mastered the syllabary, stimulating the printing of books and some newspapers in the Cherokee language, allowing Cherokees in the West to communicate fully with their kinsmen still in the East. In the treaty of 1828 the United States government recognized the importance of Sequoyah's work by awarding him $500 and adding another $1,000 for the Cherokees to buy a printing press.

As a result of the treaty of 1828, the Arkansas Cherokees rapidly moved into the Indian Territory, and they soon erected homes on their new land. Conflicts with the Osage continued, for some members of that tribe were still living on the land promised by the government to the Cherokees. Despite these clashes, the Cherokees cleared land and planted crops.

In their new homeland the Western Cherokees were joined in 1829 by Sam Houston. Born in 1793, Houston had grown to manhood in Tennessee, lived among the Cherokees there from 1809 to 1812, and was given the name "The Raven." Houston in 1819 became attorney general of Tennessee, then a congressman for four years, and finally governor of the state in 1827. In January of 1829 he married Eliza Allen, but in April that year he divorced her, resigned as governor, and fled to the Indian Territory to live among the Cherokees once again. Just a few miles northwest of Fort Gibson he erected Wigwam Neosho, a trading post,

Sequoyah's Cherokee alphabet is depicted in the scholar's own handwriting. Courtesy, The Thomas Gilcrease Institute of American History and Art, Tulsa, Oklahoma

and took a Cherokee wife, Talihina (or Tiana). Twice he represented the Cherokees in dealings with the federal government, traveling to Washington on their behalf. However, in 1831 he was defeated for membership on the tribal council, and the following year he moved to Texas (there to become a hero of the Texas Revolution and twice president of the Republic of Texas).

While the Western Cherokees were successfully settling the Indian Territory, their eastern kinsmen, along with members of the other Five Civilized Tribes, were having difficulties. In Georgia there was mounting white pressure on the Cherokees despite the 1827 tribal constitution patterned on that of the United States; this abolished "tribal government" and established a constitutional republic. The following year the Eastern Cherokees elected John Ross as principal chief. Ross, who was only one-eighth Cherokee, nevertheless adopted the viewpoint of the full bloods and worked diligently to prevent further land cessions or removal westward.

The governor and legislature were determined in 1828 to force a removal, however, and that year passed legislation which made tribal members subject to state laws and declared it illegal for Indians to testify against whites in court. Thus whites who took Indian lands were immune from prosecution because the Indian owners could not testify against them. When gold was discovered on Cherokee land in 1829, the legislature of Georgia declared it unlawful for the Cherokees to prospect for or to mine gold on their own land. That same year the legislature abolished the Cherokee government and announced that all Cherokee lands were the property of the state. The tribal council was forbidden to meet except to discuss removal westward. Another law, aimed at the missionaries working among the Cherokees, required any white living among the Indians to have a permit from state officials.

The Cherokees knew their rights were guaranteed them by treaty with the United States government, but the future was made clear to them when Congress on May 28, 1830, passed the Indian Removal Act, a response to the belief that the West was a "Great American Desert." The Indian Removal Act decreed that Indian lands in the East should be exchanged for land in the West. Although this law did not call for enforced removal, it did recommend it strongly

and empowered the president to work for it. Two years later Congress passed a second Indian Removal Act further strengthening its recommendation of the forcible westward removal of all Indians east of the Mississippi River.

Among the Cherokees, thanks to their own inclination and to the work of dedicated missionaries, the tribe had an educated group of leaders who understood the workings of the American government and thus believed that one other route lay open to them: an appeal to the federal courts. When the state of Georgia in 1831 arrested eleven missionaries for preaching and teaching among the Cherokees without permits from the state, and subsequently sent two of these men, Samuel A. Worcester and Elizar But-

ler, to prison, the Cherokees made their appeal to the federal judiciary. Eventually this dispute reached the United States Supreme Court in the case *Worcester* v. *Georgia*, and in 1832 the Court ruled in favor of the Cherokees by declaring that their status as a "domestic dependent nation" meant that state laws could not be enforced in treaty-guaranteed Cherokee territory. Rulings of the Supreme Court were enforced by the executive branch of government, however, and President Andrew Jackson, a frontiersman from Tennessee, refused to carry out the ruling. Worcester and Butler stayed in the Georgia prison. Thereafter, the fate of the Indians was sealed. They would be moved, willingly or unwillingly, to the Indian Territory.

CHAPTER V

The Trail of Tears

Moshulatubbee, a full-blood Choctaw chief, led his people westward over the Trail of Tears to settle southeastern Indian Territory. Courtesy, Smithsonian Institution

*B*y 1830 only a small part of the Five Civilized Tribes was living in the Indian Territory: some 6,000 Cherokees, 2,000 Creeks, and one-fourth of the Choctaws. The others were tenaciously clinging to their reduced homeland in the Southeast, many hoping that justice somehow would yet prevail. On the other side, however, were whites equally determined that these Native Americans would be moved westward—peacefully if possible, at bayonet point if necessary.

When faced with pressure to move, most Cherokees responded by asking that the provisions of their treaties with the United States be honored. They were instead met with a firm federal demand for removal. In October 1832 President Jackson's representative, E.W. Chesser, conferred with tribal leaders to state this demand clearly. Principal Chief John Ross personally headed a delegation to Washington to respond that the tribe would never consent to removal.

On this trip Ross learned that, although his voice carried weight in Cherokee councils, it had no impact in Washington. Born near Lookout Mountain, Tennessee, in 1790, Ross was the son of a Scottish father and a mother one-quarter Cherokee and three-quarters Scottish. His Indian name was Cooweescoowee, and he was educated by private tutors and then at Kingston Academy in Tennessee. His rise to prominence in the tribe began in 1819, when he was elected a member of the Cherokee National Council. Two years later he became president of the council, a position he held for five years. In 1822 he helped write the Cherokee constitution and was elected assistant chief. Then in 1827 he became principal chief, a position he held until 1839 (although he spoke Cherokee so poorly that he refused to make public speeches in that language. He spoke in English with an interpreter standing by his side to render his words into Cherokee).

Left
John Ridge had at one time opposed cession of tribal lands, but, seeing the inevitable, he signed the Treaty of New Echota, exchanging tribal holdings in Georgia for land in the Indian Territory. He was later assassinated by anti-Treaty supporters of John Ross. OHS

Far left
Major Ridge was leader of the Cherokee Treaty Party supporting removal to Indian Territory. Cherokees opposing removal assassinated him, his son, and nephew after they arrived in the Indian Territory in 1839. OHS

Despite his strong statements in Washington, Ross found several headmen willing to accept removal when the tribe met in council in May 1833. Major Ridge, his son John Ridge, and Elias Boudinot, who spoke for a significant minority of the tribe, suggested that Ross was fighting a losing battle and that the tribe should accept the inevitable. Called the Treaty Party, the Ridge-Boudinot group generally consisted of mixed-blood Cherokees, while the anti-removal group, Ross Party, as that faction was known, largely consisted of full-bloods. Major Ridge had earlier helped execute a headman who in 1808 had signed a treaty selling Cherokee lands, and his son John had been extremely outspoken for many years against removal. Boudinot, a nephew of Major Ridge and editor of the *Cherokee Phoenix,* had written rousing editorials denouncing federal bureaucrats, Georgia functionaries, and members of the tribe who were trying to remove the Cherokees to the Indian Territory. The three men gradually had come to believe, however, that removal was inevitable and that the tribe would prosper in the West (later there would be charges that these three men were bribed by the federal government to speak in favor of removal, but no evidence supports this).

In 1834 the state of Georgia showed its determination to be rid of the Cherokees by passing legislation calling for a survey of Cherokee land and opening it to white settlement by lottery. John Ross lost his property in this way. That same year the Georgia militia marched to New Echota, the Cherokee capital, and smashed the *Cherokee Phoenix* printing press. Such actions caused the Treaty Party to gain yet more followers.

This split in the Cherokee Nation emboldened the federal government. Late in 1835 officials of the Indian Office announced that a general council would be held in December that year at New Echota. To insure that a treaty resulted, federal officials had Ross arrested and held while negotiations were underway. The Treaty of New Echota, concluded on December 29, 1835, provided for a total cession of all Cherokee lands in the Southeast in return for five million dollars and land in the Indian Territory. Leaders of the Treaty Party agreed, although they were warned by the Ross Party that their signatures would constitute their death warrants.

Ross, when freed, protested the treaty and even went to Washington to lobby against its ratification. Nevertheless, the Senate accepted it, and President Jackson signed it into law, although Ross concluded that a majority of the Cherokee Nation would refuse to move. The followers of the Ridges and Boudinot, some 2,000 Cherokees, did emigrate voluntarily. They were paid for their cost of removal and given subsistence for their first year in their new home. The Treaty of New Echota promised them joint ownership of the Cherokee lands

ᏣᎳᎩ ᏧᎴᎯᏌᏅᎯ.

CHEROKEE PHŒNIX.

NEW ECHOTA, WEDNESDAY JUNE 18, 1828.

...S BOUDINOTT ...KLY BY ...HARRIS, ...EE NATION. ...dvance, $3 in six ... at the end of the ... an read only the price will be $2,00 be paid within the ... ll be considered as ...bers give notice to ...mmencement of a ... six subscribers, ... for the payment, gratis. ...e inserted at seven-

Male negroes	7	Total	24
Female negroes	17		
Whole population			1,383

There are in this District, eight white men married to Cherokee women, and one Cherokee man married to a white woman.

There are in this District, 211 spinning wheels, one grist mill, one blacksmith shop, 308 ploughs, fifty-three looms, 323 sheep, 2,419 swine, 1,506 black cattle, 554 horses.

CHICKAMAUGA DISTRICT.

Males under 18 years of age	484	
Males from 18 to 59 years of age	396	
Males over 59 years of age	43	
To...		92...

...of both sexes, seven blacksmith shops, one turnpike, five ferries, six public roads, one threshing machine, one store, ninety-three goats, 243 sheep, 6,080 swine, 1,730 cattle, 815 horses, 372 ploughs, seventy looms, 327 spinning wheels, twenty-nine wagons, three saw-mills, six grist mills, two cotton gins.

CHATTOOGA DISTRICT.

Males under 18 years of age	420	
Males from 18 to 59 years of age	400	
Males over 59 years of age	30	
Total number of males	—	850
Females under 15 years of age	339	
Females from 15 to 40 years	365	
Females over 40 years of age	95	
Total number of females	—	790
Total of males and females		1,649

The following ... day made to ...okee nation: Newto... Friends an... happy that a... sumed in the ... you and the St. This has all... of becoming ... several membe... For the whole ... respect, and w... of you, we hav... friendships. I... violence to our ... do we lower t... of the United

Above
Pictured is a detail from the front page of the June 18, 1828, Cherokee Phoenix, *which was published at New Echota, Georgia, by Elias Boudinot. This unique newspaper, printed in both English and Cherokee, typified the level of culture attained by members of the Five Civilized Tribes. OHS*

Far right
Elias Boudinot, editor of the Cherokee Phoenix, *was an outspoken critic of efforts to sell tribal lands to the Americans, however, he joined with his uncle Major Ridge and his cousin John Ridge and signed the Treaty of New Echota. OHS*

already assigned in the Indian Territory, and they were allowed to buy an additional 800,000 acres (a strip of land twenty-five miles wide and fifty miles long—in present Kansas adjoining the state of Missouri—for $500,000). In addition, Article 2 of the treaty gave the tribe the Cherokee Outlet, a broad strip of territory stretching from the Cherokee land in northeastern Indian Territory west to the 100th meridian, providing them access to the buffalo plains.

Members of the Ross Party learned to their sorrow that the federal government indeed intended to enforce the Treaty of New Echota. General John E. Wool, a fatuous soldier of little competence more at home behind a desk than in the field, was sent in 1836 to begin the task of removing the Cherokee holdouts. At first Wool harangued the Cherokees to accept the inevitable, but when talking proved futile he erected fenced camps in which Cherokees arrested by his soldiers were held until a sizable party could be gathered and shipped westward. For two years Wool and his troops sent approximately 2,000 of the more than 16,000 Cherokees in Georgia to the Indian Territory. Wool and many of his soldiers hated this job; only Georgia militiamen proved enthusiastic for the task. Ross repeatedly requested delays and worked unceasingly to prevent

removal, but at last President Martin Van Buren grew impatient and sent General Winfield Sott to take command of 7,000 soldiers and speed up the process.

Scott, a competent soldier and humane man who tried to do an unpleasant job without causing undue hardship and suffering, coordinated his troops and began making wholesale arrests, but some of his troops

Major General John E. Wool was initially responsible for the removal of the Cherokee Indians from Georgia to Oklahoma. His inept handling of his task caused great hardships for the Indians, and he was subsequently replaced by General Winfield Scott, who capably handled the removal. Courtesy, The Thomas Gilcrease Institute of American History and Art, Tulsa, Oklahoma

and many of the Georgia militia committed rape, robbery, and even murder. The Cherokees suffered from hunger and disease, and the death rate rose rapidly among the sick, the aged, and the young. In July 1838 Ross returned from another unsuccessful trip to Washington and found the suffering so intense that he dropped resistance as a weapon. He asked Scott to let the Cherokees themselves oversee their own removal. Scott agreed at once, and by August the *nuna dat suhn'yi*—Trail of Tears—was a reality. Waiting until the heat of summer had passed, Ross sent his people west by overland trail and by boat. Cholera and measles took a heavy toll. Among the dead was Ross' wife, who expired near Little Rock, Arkansas. By December 1838 the last party of Cherokees put Georgia behind to march toward the sunset of the Indian Territory. The Cherokees had been removed.

The following year, 1839, Mirabeau B. Lamar, president of the Republic of Texas (and former secretary to the governor of Georgia) determined to rid that nation of all its native inhabitants. Under his direction the Cherokees who had removed to Texas while it was owned by Spain were driven north into the Indian Territory. For the first time in some four decades the entire Cherokee Nation was together—but at a terrible price in human life.

As the Cherokees were fighting unsuc-

cessfully to stay in Georgia, the remainder of the Five Civilized Tribes were undergoing a similar experience. The first to remove entirely were the Choctaws. When Alabama and Mississippi enacted laws discriminating against Indians, the Choctaws began serious negotiations with the United States, and in September of 1830 the three district chiefs of the nation—Greenwood LeFlore, Moshulatubbee, and Nitakechi—signed the Treaty of Dancing Rabbit Creek. In return for all their lands in the southeastern United States, they were given land between the Red River on the south and the Canadian and Arkansas rivers on the north, and between the Arkansas border and the 100th meridian. The federal government agreed to transport the tribe and to furnish members with food for the first year after their removal. As many tribal members as possible would move "during the falls of 1831 and 1832," and the remainder would move during the autumn of 1833. Any tribal members not wishing to move were to receive individual allotments of land and become citizens of their state of residence. Finally, the federal government, represented in negotiations by Secretary of War John

Steamboats carried members of the Five Civilized Tribes to new homes in the Indian Territory during the Trail of Tears. Later the Arkansas River was an important supply route for the Indians and whites in the territory. OHS

The misery and grief of the Indians on the Trail of Tears is depicted in this painting by Echohawk. Family members lay a lost one to rest in the cold prairie, while even the trooper charged with their forced removal looks on with compassion. Courtesy, The Thomas Gilcrease Institute of American History and Art, Tulsa, Oklahoma

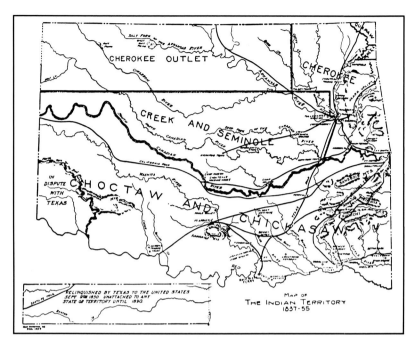

This map shows the original lands of the Five Civilized Tribes following removal to Indian Territory from circa 1830 to 1855. OHS

Eaton and General John Coffee, promised the tribe that its new homeland would never, for any reason, be made part of a state or territory and that it would forever be governed by its own laws. This feature was to allay tribal fears that their experience in the Southeast would not be repeated if whites someday coveted their new home.

To aid in this removal, the government in 1831 opened an agency headquarters fifteen miles up the Arkansas River from Fort Smith. Agents of the Indian Office of the Department of War would help settle the Choctaws once they had completed their exodus. Less than thirty-six months were required to remove the sovereign Choctaw Nation to the Indian Territory, but there was intense suffering because of poor planning on the part of government functionaries and intensely cold weather. Almost half the 12,000 members of the tribe chose to remain in Mississippi and Alabama—only to meet discrimination and the eventual loss of their lands to whites who overran their acres with impunity. They would later move to the Indian Territory during the late 1830s and 1840s.

The same state laws that forced the Choctaws to move westward also affected the Creek Nation. Already that tribe had been forced out of Georgia into Alabama, and there was no enthusiasm for yet another move to join the McIntosh faction already in the Indian Territory. By 1832, however, the tribal leaders recognized that their days in the East were numbered, and a Creek

delegation, headed by Opothleyahola, negotiated the Treaty of Washington signed on March 24. In return for ceding their lands in Alabama, the Creeks could either move to the Indian Territory to live on the land given to the McIntosh Creeks, or they could accept an allotment of land in Alabama (640 acres for a chief, 320 acres for every other head of a family), receiving the deed after five years. In return, the government agreed to pay the tribe $12,000 a year for five years and then $10,000 annually for fifteen years. Implied in this treaty was federal protection for those Creeks who chose to remain in Alabama, and only 630 members of the tribe agreed to removal. The others elected to stay in Alabama under the mistaken impression they were safe at last.

In the Indian Territory, inaccuracies in the maps setting boundaries of Creek and Cherokee lands caused conflicting claims among the tribes. Under the treaty of 1826, the Creeks were granted land along the Arkansas River near the mouth of the Verdigris; that same land also had been given to the Cherokees by a 1828 treaty. This dispute was settled in 1833 when the Cherokees agreed to allow Creek ownership of the disputed area. It was in this area around the Three Forks that the McIntosh Creeks had settled, and it was to this same area that the 630 Creeks who migrated in 1832 came.

Those who remained behind found their lot hard indeed. Their livestock was stolen, and whites took their homesteads by means both violent and fraudulent. The federal government did nothing even when peaceful Creeks were murdered while working their fields. Finally in 1836 the Lower Creeks unified under Chief Eneah Emothla to fight back. Alarmed Alabamans proclaimed a "Creek Rebellion" and appealed for federal troops, who were sent under command of General Winfield Scott. Scott was assisted by almost 2,000 Upper Creeks commanded by Opothleyahola; the Lower Creeks were defeated, and their suffering began in earnest. The 2,495 captives—men, women, and children, the sick and the aged—were bound in chains and sent westward, many of them dying during a winter march in 1836 to 1837. Another party of 300 captives was moved aboard a riverboat previously declared unsafe, and when it sank all of the Indians died.

At the same time the government demanded that the Upper Creeks remove westward despite their assistance in putting down the "Creek Rebellion." Opothleyahola led his people to the Indian Territory, with an estimated 3,500 Creeks perishing during the move. In the Indian Territory they chose to separate themselves from the earlier migrants of the McIntosh faction and settled farther south along the Canadian and Deep Fork creeks.

The Chickasaws, like the other Five Civilized Tribes, were also under great pressure to remove. During the early 1830s leaders of this tribe, recognizing that such a move was inevitable, sent a delegation west, but it failed to find a suitable home. Then in January 1837 a Chickasaw delegation met with leaders of the Choctaws at Doaksville (adjoining Fort Towson) to forge the Treaty of Doaksville, which provided for a Chickasaw home along the western edge of what had been Choctaw lands. This treaty also stipulated a unified Choctaw-Chickasaw tribal government (one clause stated that in cases of disagreement there would be an appeal to the President of the United States for settlement).

The removal of the Chickasaws was better managed and more orderly than other Indian relocations among the Five Civilized Tribes. Most Chickasaws had time to prepare, gathering their livestock and slaves and storing provisions for the trek. Moreover, the distance to be traveled was not as great for them as for the other four tribes. By 1840 the Chickasaws were living in their new home along the Washita River. Yet a majority of the tribe did not favor a unified government with the more numerous Choctaws, and this feature of the Treaty of Doaksville would cause trouble for several years.

The last of the Five Civilized Tribes to face removal were the Seminoles, a subgroup of the Creek Nation noted for their warlike ways. Traditionally they had lived in Florida, southern Georgia, and southern Alabama, welcoming to their ranks runaway slaves and those Creek warriors who had fought against the United States during the War of 1812 (the Red Sticks).

When the United States bought Florida from Spain in 1819, whites entering the area began demanding that the government remove the tribe. In 1832 James Gadsden, representing the United States, negotiated the Treaty of Payne's Landing, calling for

the Seminoles to remove to the Indian Territory as soon as a suitable home could be found. The tribe was given three years to make the move, and the government agreed to pay the cost of removal plus a one-time payment of $15,400 and an annual payment of $3,000 for fifteen years.

Osceola, a Seminole leader, spoke against this agreement. Born about 1800 on the Tallapoosa River in Georgia, Osceola was the son of William Powell, a Scottish trader, and a Creek wife. In 1808 his mother moved to Florida, there to associate with the Seminoles. Osceola, although still a youngster, fought at the Battle of Horseshoe Bend with the Red Stick Creeks, and in 1818 he was in the thick of fighting against American troops led by Andrew Jackson. In 1832 he lived near Fort King, Florida, and rose to prominence and tribal leadership among the Seminoles.

Late in 1832, under the terms of the Treaty of Payne's Landing, seven Seminole chiefs and Agent John Phagan journeyed to the Indian Territory to look for a home for the tribe. During this visit the delegation,

Osceola led the hostile Seminole Indians in the First Seminole War until his capture by General Thomas Jesup. He was succeeded by Billy Bowlegs in leading the futile attempt to repel Army troops and resist removal to Indian Territory. Courtesy, Western History Collections, University of Oklahoma Library

while at Fort Gibson, met with Creek leaders who offered to allow the Seminoles to settle on Creek lands. In February 1833 the two groups signed the Treaty of Fort Gibson, and the Seminole delegation returned home to prepare to move. During a discussion between American commissioners and Seminole leaders, some Seminole chiefs indicated their disagreement with the Treaty of Fort Gibson by refusing to touch a pen; Osceola did so by plunging his knife into the paper.

On December 28, 1835, Osceola and his followers killed Chief Emathla, one of the signers of the Treaty of Fort Gibson, along with Indian Agent Wiley Thompson. That same day Osceola's men surrounded 110 American soldiers near Fort King and killed 107 of them, triggering the six-year Seminole War. During this conflict Osceola achieved national prominence because of his victories in several major battles against American soldiers. On August 16, 1836, for example, he almost overwhelmed Fort Drane, Florida, leading to widespread criticism of the Army and especially of General Thomas Jesup. Jesup ordered Osceola captured under a flag of truce, which was accomplished on October 21, 1837. First imprisoned at Fort Marion, Florida, Osceola later was moved to Fort Moultrie, South Carolina, where he died on January 30, 1838, of mysterious causes. A majority of the tribe surrendered in the spring of 1839

and were moved westward, leaving only a few small bands to continue guerrilla warfare against the United States (until the government allowed them to remain in Florida; this war cost twenty million dollars and the lives of 1,500 soldiers).

While the Seminole War was in progress, the government moved peaceful Seminoles and captive warriors to the Indian Territory and by 1842 there were some 3,000 Seminoles living on Creek lands between the southern and northern forks of the Canadian River.

During the movement of the Five Civilized Tribes to the Indian Territory, the federal government also moved two additional tribes there: the Quapaw (who once had claimed ownership of the land that eventually belonged to the Choctaws and Creeks) and the Senecas (who at one time had lived in New York). Both tribes had suffered a drastic reduction in numbers since their first contact with whites. In the 1600s the Senecas had been a major part of the six-nation Iroquois Confederacy. Yet they were crushed during the wars of the eighteenth century, and had been overrun during the white settlement of the Ohio Valley. By the 1830s the tribe numbered only a few hundred and was living on a reservation in Ohio. In 1831 the government decided to move them to the Indian Territory because whites wanted their 90,000-acre reservation, and by treaty that year the Senecas agreed to give up that land

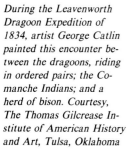

During the Leavenworth Dragoon Expedition of 1834, artist George Catlin painted this encounter between the dragoons, riding in ordered pairs; the Comanche Indians; and a herd of bison. Courtesy, The Thomas Gilcrease Institute of American History and Art, Tulsa, Oklahoma

in return for 130,000 acres between the Grand River and the southwest boundary of Missouri (north of the Cherokee preserve). Another small party, the Seneca-Shawnee (Mixed Band), was brought to the area after an 1832 agreement.

The Quapaws likewise had once been a numerous people, but the population had been reduced by wars with whites and with other Indians. In 1818 they had ceded the land they owned in Oklahoma for a reservation in Arkansas, then had been removed south of the Red River where they lived with the Caddos. This proved an unhappy time for the Quapaws, for the Caddos gave them marginal land that was flooded annually by the Red River. Moreover, the humid, balmy climate produced fevers that killed hundreds of Quapaws. In desperation the 300 survivors illegally returned to Arkansas to find homes on abandoned land and to petition the federal government for relief. In May 1833 they signed a treaty granting them a reserve of 96,000 acres between the Missouri and Grand rivers (north of the Seneca land). With their own home assured them, the Quapaw gradually ended their wandering about the Indian country and settled on their lands.

When the tribes newly moved to the Indian Territory came into conflict with the Indians already on the land, they turned to the federal government for assistance, and federal agents tried to negotiate a compromise. A major conflict, for example, occurred between the Osages and Cherokees, and it continued until all the Osages moved north into Kansas (about 1840). More serious than this, however, were the frequent raids on newcomers by the Comanches, Wichitas, Kiowas, and Kiowa-Apaches.

The Wichitas, a Caddoan tribe, considered the prairies of central Oklahoma to be their hunting grounds, while the Comanches coveted the buffalo and antelope roaming the plains. The Comanches lived along the upper reaches of the Canadian, Red, and Cimarron rivers, and were closely allied with the Wichitas, who inhabited the middle section of the Red River. Frequently the two tribes joined to form hunting and war parties that raided south into Texas and even deep into Mexico. The Kiowas and Kiowa-Apaches, equally possessive and fierce, roamed western Oklahoma and the Texas Panhandle, also joining the Comanches on occasion to form raiding parties. All four tribes considered hunting

parties of the Five Civilized Tribes to be intruders and attacked them, and they journeyed to the eastern part of the Indian Territory to attack villages established by the newcomers. In addition, all four of the plains tribes were enemies of the Osages, which compounded the difficulty of keeping the peace. As long as such raids were small and infrequent, the government tried to ignore them. But when raids grew large and numerous, the government was compelled to take action.

Such an occasion arrived in 1832, and a federal commission led by Governor Montfort Stokes of North Carolina and accompanied by United States Indian Commissioner Henry L. Ellsworth met with the Cherokees and Osages to settle old disputes and to avoid future bloodshed. Noted writer Washington Irving accompanied this commission and wrote about its adventures in his delightful *A Tour on the Prairies.* Yet despite the visit of the Stokes Commission, war soon erupted between the Osages and the plains tribes. In the summer of 1833 the Osages, led by Chief Clermont, located an unprotected Kiowa village near the Wichita Mountains and attacked. When the war party returned eastward with some fifty scalps, it left the village strewn with dead

United States dragoons, in field dress (on horseback) and parade dress (on foot), made the difficult journey across southern and western Oklahoma during the summer of 1834. Commanded by General Henry Leavenworth, this expedition suffered intensely from disease and heat. OHS

OKLAHOMA: A RICH HERITAGE

bodies and burning tepees. The federal government felt compelled to take action, as a general war might result—and thereby delay the removal of the Five Civilized Tribes.

To demonstrate the might of the United States government, General Henry Leavenworth, who recently had taken command of the region from the ailing General Matthew Arbuckle, ordered the erection of three camps on the frontier. These were Cantonment Leavenworth, near the mouth of the Washita River, and Camps Arbuckle and Holmes on the Canadian River. General Leavenworth in 1834 personally inspected the frontier with a large body of troops drawn from Forts Gibson and Towson. One member of this party was artist George Catlin, who preserved the history of the region through the medium of his canvas. This party first marched west to the Washita River, intending to move further west to confer with the Comanches and Kiowas. At the Red River, however, General Leavenworth and more than half his men became ill, and Colonel Henry Dodge assumed command.

Dodge marched west to hold a meeting with the Kiowas, Comanches, and Wichitas, exchanging prisoners ransomed from the Osages for Osages and white captives held by the plains tribes. One individual released was the son of Judge Arthur Martin, who had been captured by the Kiowas after his father was killed near the site of the present Madill, Oklahoma. At this time Dodge had fewer than 200 healthy soldiers with him, so when negotiations were completed he hastily retreated to Fort Gibson, returning late that summer to learn that General Leavenworth had died from his illness.

At Fort Gibson a conference was held between representatives of the plains tribes who had accompanied Dodge back to the post and leaders of the Cherokees, Creeks, Choctaws, Delawares, Osages, and Senecas. Little was accomplished, but all agreed to meet again the following year.

The meeting in 1835, a large affair, was held in August at Camp Mason, a new post established by General Matthew Arbuckle on the western edge of the Cross Timbers beside the Canadian River (in present Cleveland County). Arbuckle (returned to command in place of the deceased Leavenworth) and Montfort Stokes represented the United States. Indian leaders at the conference represented the Cherokees, Creeks,

Choctaws, Delawares, Osages, Senecas, and Quapaws, and there were delegations present from the Comanches, Kiowas, and Wichitas. A general treaty resulted in which the tribes in the eastern part of the Indian Territory were granted the right to travel and hunt on the western prairies and plains. Only the Kiowas refused to sign this agreement (in 1837 they would be forced to agree to it, as would the plains Apaches with whom the Kiowas had become allies). Yet despite the assurances contained in this treaty, warfare continued between the plains Indians and the woodland tribes recently removed to the Indian Territory.

The other newcomers to the Indian Territory during the 1820s and 1830s, other than a few licensed traders, were the soldiers who came to man Army posts such as Gibson, Towson, Leavenworth, Washita, Arbuckle, and Cobb. Many of these posts proved short-lived, like Fort Coffee, which was erected on the banks of the Arkansas between Forts Smith and Gibson in 1834 to control illegal liquor traffic. Despite the presence of the cannon at this post, whiskey continued to move upriver, and Fort Coffee was abandoned in 1838. Fort Gibson remained the major military installation in the Indian Territory until the eve of the Civil War.

Duty at these posts was hard and dangerous for the soldiers. The men erected their quarters themselves, cutting logs or quarrying stone, moving these to the desired location, and erecting them according to plans drawn by their officers. They fought malaria and bilious fevers, ate government hardtack and bacon, escorted supply wagons, scouted new territory, and sometimes fought Indians or white renegades—all for eight dollars a month. Little wonder that so many of them deserted at the first opportunity.

By 1840 almost all Indians who once lived east of the Mississippi River had been removed westward, and the people of the United States hailed this as a great national achievement. In the process all of present-day Oklahoma (except the Panhandle) had been allotted by treaty to one tribe or another. Yet in this land there was no celebrating, for the nations were struggling to reestablish themselves economically in their new homeland and to heal the tribal divisions between those who had fought removal and those who had accepted it as inevitable.

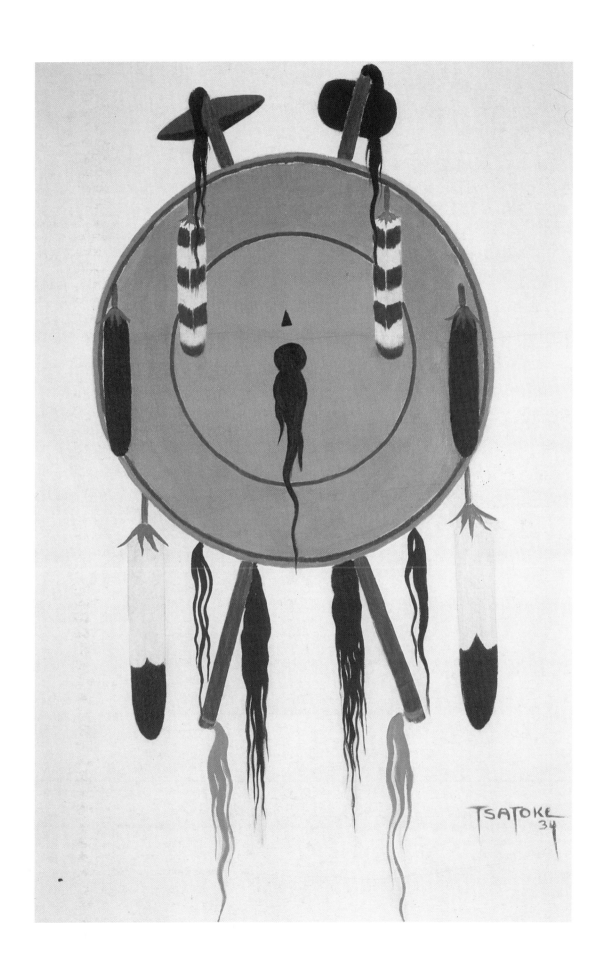

Top
The third mural, Indian
Immigration, *covers Okla-
homa's history from 1820
to 1885. Courtesy, Charles
Banks Wilson*

Above
The fourth mural, Settle-
ment, *covers Oklahoma's
history from 1870 to 1906.
Courtesy, Charles Banks
Wilson*

These colorful Indian murals by artist Monroe TsaToke can all be found in the Wiley Post Historical Building in Oklahoma City. The upper left illustration depicts a Kiowa chief, the upper right illustration is a Kiowa woman with her child, in the lower left, is a Kiowa fancy dancer, and in the lower right is a Comanche chief. OHS

Right
This untitled work by
*Monroe Tsa-Toke, of an
Indian with a pipe, is also a
mural in the Wiley Post
Historical Building in
Oklahoma City. OHS*

Below
Indian Friendship, *by
James Auchiah, is another
mural in the Wiley Post
Historical Building in
Oklahoma City. OHS*

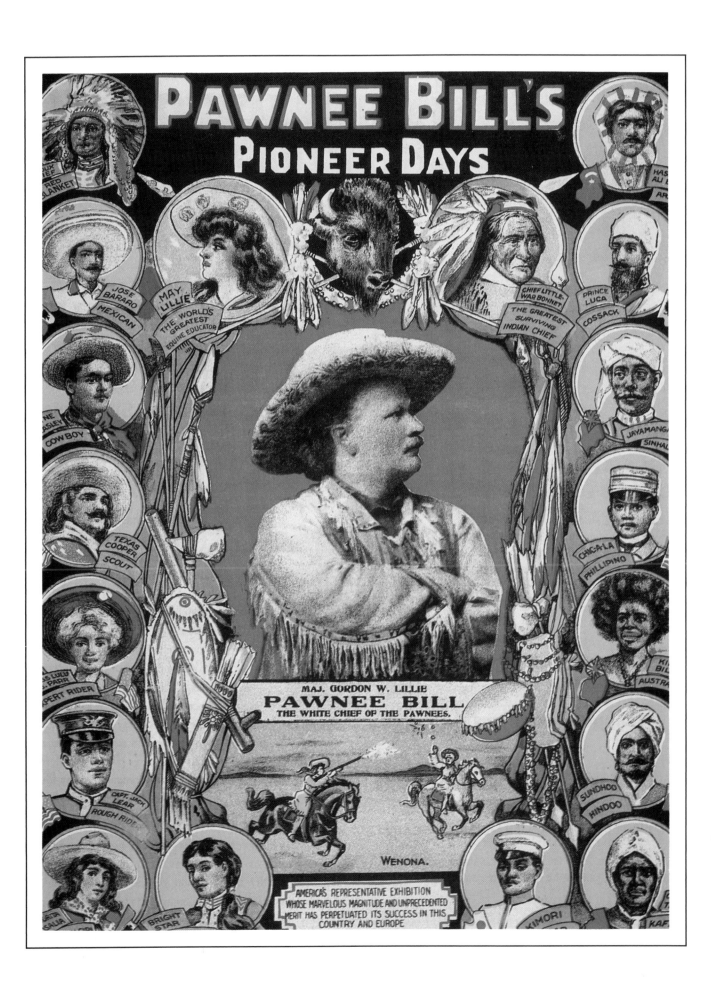

Indian Republics in a New Land

*T*he Native Americans removed to the Indian Territory in the second, third, and fourth decades of the nineteenth century arrived in their new homeland eager for a time of tranquility in which to reestablish their tribal identities. They were refugees from years of persecution and struggle with whites, and they came in search of peace. Tranquility was elusive, however, for within most of the tribes there were conflicting factions vying for positions of leadership.

The most seriously divided of the Nations were the Cherokees, who were split into three factions: the Old Settlers, consisting of those tribesmen who had moved to Arkansas and then to the Indian Territory prior to 1830; the Treaty Party, made up of the Ridges, Boudinot, and their followers who had removed westward voluntarily; and the Ross Party, who had taken part in the Trail of Tears. The federal government apparently hoped that, once in the Indian Territory, the entire Nation would be dominated by the Treaty Party, but Ross and his adherents were too numerous and too bitter to accept this leadership. In fact, on June 22, 1839, Major Ridge, John Ridge, and Elias Boudinot were killed for signing the Treaty of New Echota (members of the Ross Party always insisted that these were legal executions, while adherents of the Treaty Party saw the deaths as brutal murders). Stan Watie, brother of the slain Boudinot, assumed leadership of the Treaty Party. It was Watie, who, after viewing his dead brother's face, said, "I will give ten thousand dollars for the names of the men who did this."

Born on December 12, 1806, south of New Echota, Georgia, Watie at birth was named Degadoga ("He Stands"), and was the son of a full-blood Cherokee named David Watie and Susanna Reese, a half blood. When his parents converted to Christianity he took the name Isaac S. Watie, later preferring to be known as Stand Watie. His father fought on the side of the

United States during the War of 1812 against the Red Stick Creeks at the Battle of Horseshoe Bend. Watie was educated at a Moravian mission school and then returned to a quiet existence on the family farm. In 1828 he entered Cherokee politics when he was chosen clerk of the Nation's Supreme Court under the constitution of 1827. In the confrontation between whites and Cherokees in Georgia, Watie played a small but active role, but gradually he came to believe in the inevitability of removal. In the Indian Territory, after his older brother Elias Boudinot and the Ridges were killed, Watie became the leading opponent of John Ross for almost three decades.

Following the death of the three leaders of the Treaty Party, Ross and his party seized power, but the principal chief found it necessary to have a bodyguard of 500 to 600 men almost all the time for fear of reprisal. In this bloody struggle for power, a constitution was drafted in 1839 at Double Springs, some ten miles north of Fort Gibson. The three sharply divided Cherokee factions were all present, but the constitution adopted at this meeting did not restore peace, and violence continued despite the efforts of would-be peacemakers within the tribe and the Army.

Several federal officials voiced the opinion that no accord could be reached among the various factions, and that separate reservations might be required. Legislation, introduced in Congress in 1846, resulted which would have separated the tribe. Fortunately, John Ross and a Cherokee delegation arrived in Washington before the bill could be passed. These men convinced President James K. Polk that a commission should be appointed to study the matter. Polk responded by naming William Armstrong, superintendent of Indian Affairs of the Western Territories, as chairman and Albion K. Parris and Edmund Burke as commission members.

For almost six months this presidential commission visited leaders of each faction and negotiated the Treaty of 1846. This recognized a United Cherokee Nation, reaffirmed the tribe's claim to its lands in the Indian Territory, pardoned past crimes by Cherokees, and granted funds (as compensation) to the families of the Ridges and Boudinot.

With peace restored, the tribal constitution of 1839 at last could be implemented.

The constitution provided for a two-house legislative body consisting of a National Committee of Sixteen (two members from each of the eight districts into which the Nation had been divided) and a council consisting of three members from each of the eight districts. Sitting together, the two houses were known as the National Council, with the principal chief, as executive, who had veto powers and who was aided by an assistant principal chief. The judiciary consisted of a supreme court and a circuit court system, while a treasurer was selected by the National Council. To maintain law and order justices of the peace would be appointed by the principal chief of each district, and each district elected its own sheriff. Under the new civil government, schools were opened, books and newspapers were printed, and churches were organized. In addition, the tribe established a Male Seminary in Tahlequah, capital of the Nation, and a Female Seminary at nearby Park

Stand Watie, leader of the Pro-Treaty party of the Cherokee Indians following the assassination of his brother, uncle, and cousin, led the Confederate Cherokees during the Civil War, rising to the rank of brigadier general of the Confederate Army. OHS

Hill.

Unfortunately a few members of the Cherokee Nation were unable to return to peaceful ways after the Treaty of 1846 was implemented. A report in the *Cherokee Advocate* in 1845 observed: "The great mass of the Cherokees remained uncorrupted and incorruptible. But some . . . became drunkards, some idlers, and others were seduced from the path of virtue and innocence. From among those last enumerated, may be found some of those depraved but unfortunate beings who, while indulging the habits and vices imbibed from the whites, commit the crimes that are occurring in our country." Several gangs of outlaw Cherokees had begun operating in the vicinity of the present Stilwell, spreading terror and destruction. The most famous of these groups was the "Starr Gang," captained by Thomas Starr and his brothers. For almost a decade this gang enjoyed success in thefts, robberies, and murders, but in 1858 gang members were gunned down by a Cherokee posse. Other outlaw bands met a similar fate, and peace gradually returned to the Cherokee Nation.

Yet horrible economic suffering during these same early years in the Indian Territory hampered a return to prosperity among the Cherokees and the Creeks. Fields had to be cleared and planted, a process that took time. Many of the newcomers, not understanding that the region was subject to flooding, settled alongside streams, and in their first years frequently saw their homes washed away, their livestock drowned, and their crops ruined. The promised government rations either were not forthcoming or else were provided by some contractors so intent on cheating that much of what did arrive was rotten. Moreover, the climate proved unhealthy for the newcomers, and hundreds died of "bilious and intermittent fever" (malaria and typhoid). Proud people accustomed to refinements of living were forced to endure in rude shelters, subsist on whatever food could be gathered, and work long hours rebuilding farms and homes.

The Creeks arriving in the Indian Territory in the late 1830s benefitted from the pioneering work of the McIntosh branch of their Nation. This group, led by Roley McIntosh, son of the slain William McIntosh, arrived in the valley of the Verdigris years before the majority of the tribe and had laid out farms (utilizing slave labor). By the time the other Creeks arrived, the McIntosh faction had determined what crops would grow well in the area, and had food supplies on hand to aid the newcomers.

Once reunited in Oklahoma, the Creeks

After removal from Georgia to the Indian Territory, the Cherokee Indians set about the task of rebuilding their nation. Rose Cottage, near Park Hill, was the home of Principal Chief John Ross, who ably led his people through the dark post-removal days. Courtesy, Western History Collections, University of Oklahoma Library

reinstituted their traditional political system comprised of semi-independent towns, each with a village chief, and "Upper" and "Lower" nations with a hereditary chief ruling over each. Although the two divisions of the tribe had been enemies during the Alabama "Creek Rebellion," there was peace between them until the outbreak of the Civil War. The legislature for the Nation consisted of two houses, the upper house composed of "kings" representing the towns, and the lower house composed of one "warrior" from each town plus an additional "warrior" for every 200 people in each town. A principal chief was elected in the Upper and Lower nations by males over the age of eighteen, and a judicial system meted out justice. The Creek General Council met in present McIntosh County and were presided over by the two hereditary chiefs representing the Upper and Lower nations. Within this system the Creeks made rapid progress, with southern plantation homes rising where only a few years before had been trees and prairie grass. A few of the more prosperous Creeks, such as the McIntosh and Perryman families, farmed large acreages and sold surplus corn and other produce to the Army at Fort Gibson.

Because the Choctaws were the first of the Five Civilized Tribes to remove most of its members to the Indian Territory (by the early 1830s), this nation likewise was the first to produce a new written constitution. Adopted in 1834, it was a revision of a document first drafted in 1826. It divided the Choctaw Nation into three districts: Pushmataha, Moshulatubbee, and Okla Falaya (or Red River), each with its own chief elected for a four-year term (each limited to two terms). The tribal General Assembly consisted of nine members from each district and met annually, while a judicial body also was elected. Each district had a police force consisting of six "lighthorsemen." A bill of rights attached to this constitution assured every Choctaw citizen of the right to trial for any crime, and it guaranteed all males twenty-one years of age or older the right to vote. For a time the Choctaw capital was at Nanih Wayah (near present Tuskahoma), but in 1850 it was moved to Doaksville.

The three chiefs, sitting together, had the power to veto legislation (two of them constituted a majority); however, the assembly could override a veto by a two-thirds vote.

In the first election held in 1834, Nitakeechi was elected chief of the Pushmataha District, Joseph Kincaid chief for the Moshulatubbee District, and George Harkins (nephew of Greenwood LeFlore, who had remained in Mississippi) was chief of the Okla Falaya District. Progress under this system was rapid and the tribe became prosperous.

The Chickasaws, when forcibly moved to the Indian Territory in the late 1830s, were ordered, much against their will, to integrate with the Choctaw Nation. However, the Treaty of Doaksville, under which they received land in the western part of the Choctaw preserve, was specific on this point. The Choctaws simply added a fourth district, named Apuckshumnubbee, to their government for the Chickasaws, and they were given thirteen representatives in the General Assembly. The newcomers were un-

Colonel Zachary Taylor ordered the establishment of Fort Washita to protect the Five Civilized Tribes from marauding Plains Indians. OHS

76

John Jumper, Seminole principal chief, negotiated a treaty with the federal government and the Creek Nation for a separate homeland for his tribe in 1856. OHS

dians, Colonel Zachary Taylor, commanding the Department of the Southwest, ordered the establishment of Fort Washita at the mouth of that river in 1842. This lessened the threat of Comanche raids, and thereafter the Chickasaws began to prosper.

The Seminoles, unlike the other four members of the Five Civilized Tribes, had not been farmers in their original homeland, and they suffered greatly from what they considered to be harsh winters in the Indian Territory. They were a hunting people, and they resisted efforts to make them farmers in the Indian Territory. The greatest problem facing the Seminoles, however, was their Creek landlords. The Creeks were more numerous, given to agriculture, and owned slaves. The Seminoles traditionally had protected runaway slaves and had brought a number of blacks west with them. When the Creeks began claiming these blacks as slaves, difficulties erupted between the two tribes. To avoid clashes, the Seminoles tended to remain near Fort Gibson for a time, but by the mid-1840s they had begun to settle along the banks of the Canadian River near Little River. They never developed extensive farms or a written constitution, but lived in twenty-five scattered villages, each with its own chief and council of warriors. A general tribal council, headed by Chief Micanopy, met each year to make laws for the tribe although the Creek General Council had veto power over these laws. In 1856 the Seminoles, led by Chief John Jumper, negotiated a treaty in Washington with the chiefs of the Creek Nation and secured tribal autonomy. Afterward they built a new capital at Wanette (in present Pottawatomie County).

happy with being forced to submit to the Choctaw laws, methods of policing, and judicial system, but were unable to change it until 1855. Then they were separated by formal agreement with the United States, and allowed to establish their own system of government, which proved similar to that of the Choctaws.

The Chickasaws also had to contend with the constant raiding of their lands by the fierce plains nomads. Because the Chickasaws were principally located in the Washita Valley on the western part of the Choctaw Nation, they lived so close to the plains that they were a tempting target for plains raiders. The Comanches and their allies, the Kiowas and Kiowa-Apaches, had major war trails leading south into Texas, and on these forays there were always a few warriors who would decide to turn east and raid the Chickasaws. To defend these peaceful In-

In moving west and reestablishing themselves in the Indian Territory, the Five Civilized Tribes, along with the Seneca, Ottawa, and other tribes, were aided by missionaries representing several Christian sects. In their enthusiasm to "civilize" the Indians, various church leaders lobbied the federal government for financial help, and on March 13, 1819, Congress established an annual fund of $10,000 to be used to employ "persons of good moral character" to instruct the Indians in agriculture and to teach their children reading, writing, and arithmetic. Naturally these funds were doled out to missionary organizations, such as the United Foreign Missionary Society, one of the principal lobbyists for this legislation.

Bloomfield Academy was established prior to the Civil War to educate Chickasaw Indian women. OHS

Union Mission was the first missionary station established in Oklahoma. The first printing press and the first book printed in Oklahoma were located there. Photo by Jim Argo

The United Foreign Missionary Society was created on July 25, 1817, in New York City by representatives of the General Assembly of the Presbyterian Church, the General Synod of the Reformed Dutch Church, and the General Synod of the Associated Reform Church. Its purpose was "to spread the gospel among the Indians of North America . . . ." Once Congress began appropriating funds, the society sent Epaphras Chapman and Job P. Vinal, two Presbyterian missionaries, to explore the possibility of establishing a mission among the Cherokees then in Arkansas. The two men found, however, that a competitor had already staked a claim there—the American Board of Commissioners of Foreign Missions, founded in 1808 by four students at Andover Theological Seminary. Therefore Chapman and Vinal traveled on to the Osage country to select a site on the Grand River some twenty-five miles above the Arkansas.

On the return trip to New York City, Vinal died, leaving Chapman the task of beginning the work. Chapman realized that more was required than simply evangelizing the Indians, for by an act of Congress the federal funds were to be used to "civilize" the natives. So in recruiting for his mission, Chapman selected a farmer, a carpenter, a blacksmith, a physician, and women to teach domestic skills. When Reverend Chapman began his return trip, he and his fellow missionary, Reverend William F. Vaill, had seventeen adults and four children in their party. After some ten months of travel and hardship, they arrived in the Indian Territory on February 18, 1821. Their station was named Union Mission, and on August 27 they opened the first school in the Indian Territory with four Osage children. Soon thereafter Hopewell Mission, located farther north on the Grand River, was established.

Other missionaries soon came to the Indian Territory, some traveling with the Indians from the Southeast. The Western Cherokees, for example, had asked for missionaries in 1820, and the American Board responded by founding Dwight Mission in Arkansas, named in honor of Timothy Dwight, one of the board's members. When the Cherokees traded their land in Arkansas for new homes in the Indian Territory, Dwight Mission moved westward with them, as did Mulberry Mission, another American Board establishment founded in Arkansas. In the Indian Territory, Dwight Mission was located on Sallisaw Creek (in present Sequoyah County near the town of New Dwight), while Mulberry Mission was located near the present Stilwell. In 1829 Mulberry moved and was renamed Fairfield Mission. In 1830 the board established a third mission for the Cherokees called Forks of the Illinois because of its location on the Illinois River.

For a time there was wasteful duplication of effort between the missionaries of the American Board and the United Foreign Missionary Society. In 1826, however, the two societies were united into the American Board of Commissioners for Foreign Missions. As the Five Civilized Tribes began arriving in the Indian Territory in large numbers, missionaries were assigned to work with them. Each mission station tried to accomplish the same result: conversion of everyone to Christianity, schooling for the children, and vocational education for adults, along with medical assistance for the sick. For example, when the Creeks settled in the Three Forks area, the American Board assigned Abraham Redfield of Union Mission to serve the newcomers. In anticipation of his arrival in their midst, the Creeks built a two-room schoolhouse measuring 16-by-30 feet. This was the first Creek school in the territory.

Congregational missionary Samuel Austin Worcester traveled with the Cherokees over the Trail of Tears. Released from imprisonment in Georgia, Worcester established himself in the Indian Territory at Park Hill in 1835. Two years later he moved his printing press from Union Mission (where it had operated temporarily) to Park Hill to establish the leading center of both secular and religious training in the Cherokee Nation. Worcester annually published the *Cherokee Phoenix,* a newspaper partially in

the syllabary of Sequoyah, and the *Cherokee Almanac,* along with portions of the Bible in the Cherokee language. Worcester was a stern and devout leader who remained an influence among the Cherokees until his death in 1859.

The Moravians, who were not partners in the American Board, came to the Indian Territory and founded New Spring Place Mission in present Delaware County, while the Baptists also opened a mission in Delaware County and published religious material, including the *Cherokee Messenger.* Methodist circuit riders continually rode among the newly settled Indians to preach the gospel, as well.

Often these missionaries faced hostility from the traders licensed to work among the Indians, for the ministers constantly fought

Cyrus Byington was a missionary to the Choctaw Indians. He developed a written language for the tribe, translating the Bible and other written texts to help educate his adopted people. OHS

against the sale of whiskey in the territory. Occasionally there were feuds between contending denominations—and even fights within certain denominations. Nevertheless, the Indians realized their children needed schooling, and many of them converted to Christianity. Therefore the missionary work continued, and their schools increased in size and quality. By the mid-nineteenth century the Cherokees, Choctaws, and Creeks had made notable advances in agriculture, education, and comfortable living, while the Chickasaws were trying to overcome the disadvantage of living too near the plains raiders. Even the Seminoles were gradually making progress. The forced uprooting of these various tribes from their traditional homelands, according to one observer, had done "more at a single stroke to obliterate Indian ideas than could have been accomplished by fifty years of slow development." By 1850 these changes had been made, and the future looked bright for the newcomers to the Indian Territory.

Right
The oldest remaining church building in Oklahoma, Wheelock Mission was established in 1832 by the Reverend Alfred Wright to minister to the Choctaw Indians following their removal from Mississippi. Photo by Jim Argo

Opposite page, top
Following the removal of the Choctaw Indians to Indian Territory from Mississippi, the nation was divided into three districts. The elected chiefs from each district were provided houses by the federal government. This cabin, located near Swink, was one of the original homes built in the Indian Territory and is the oldest remaining home in the state. Photo by Jim Argo

Opposite page, bottom
The Choctaw National Capitol was located at Nanih Waya, near Tuskahoma. This building was first used for the tribe's house of representatives and later became a school for tribal children. OHS

Bottom
The Cherokee Nation was subdivided into several districts after removal to the Indian Territory. One of these districts had its council house and courthouse located near Gore. This replica depicts the style of construction prevalent in the Indian Territory before the Civil War. Photo by Jim Argo

CHAPTER VII

Broken Promises, Broken Dreams

The primary crossing of the Red River on the Texas Road was at Colbert's Ferry. The route of the Texas Road was later used by cattlemen driving herds northward into Kansas and Missouri, and the Missouri, Kansas & Texas Railway followed its path when the rail line was constructed from 1870 to 1872. Photo by Jim Argo

*T*he chance discovery of gold in January 1848 by an employee of John A. Sutter, feudal baron of the Sacramento Valley in California, directly affected events in the Indian Territory within a year. As word of the discovery spread across the United States, all sanity seemed to vanish from the public mind. As the *New York Herald* commented in a special edition:

Husbands are preparing to leave their wives, sons are parting with their mothers, and bachelors are abandoning their comforts; all are rushing head over heels toward the El Dorado on the Pacific.

Wherever and whenever men gathered that winter of 1848 to 1849, the talk was of California and the gold strike. By the spring of 1849 tens of thousands of eastern Americans were ready to depart for the gold fields to pick up the fortune they thought was awaiting them.

Businessmen in Fort Smith, Arkansas, knew that these Forty-Niners would spend large sums outfitting in any city that became known as a jumping-off point for an overland trail, so in late 1848 they called on General Matthew Arbuckle, commanding at Fort Smith, to win his support for the construction of a military road from Fort Smith to Santa Fe, New Mexico (where Forty-Niners could use the existing Gila Trail to reach California). The road would bring Fort Smith the business its merchants desired—and at federal expense. When Arbuckle gave his approval, local residents then went before the state legislature to solicit its support, and that body duly petitioned the Secretary of War to authorize a military expedition to open a wagon road from Fort Smith to Santa Fe by way of the Indian Territory. By spring of 1849 Congress had appropriated $50,000 for surveys from the Mississippi River to the Pacific Coast, and the Fort Smith route was in-

cluded.

Some 2,000 emigrants gathered at Fort Smith that spring to take advantage of the military escort provided by the troops assigned to this survey, spending large sums and driving up the price of horses, mules, oxen, and food supplies. Commanding the infantry and dragoons was thirty-five-year-old Captain Randolph B. Marcy, a native of Massachusetts and a graduate of the United States Military Academy. His orders were to blaze a suitable trail across the plains and to escort the gold-seekers through the domain of the plains tribes.

Leaving Fort Smith on April 4, 1849, soldiers and civilians alike fought their way through a sea of mud caused by heavy rains in February and March. Startled residents of the Indian Territory, waiting for drier weather to plow and plant, could only stare in wonder as this wave of gold-seekers and soldiers struggled across their land. At last the column came to the Canadian River. There Marcy decided this stream would be an unavoidable signpost for future travelers and determined to follow it westward. This journey proved largely uneventful except for the wonder and excitement generated by the geological formation to be known as Rock Mary. Discovered on May 23 (in present Caddo County), it was named for seventeen-year-old Mary Conway, one of the travelers who was a cousin of President James Madison and granddaughter of a governor of Arkansas. Several junior officers of the

party raced to the crest, planted an American flag there, and named it Rock Mary in her honor. (In subsequent years this red fifty-foot-high sandstone formation served as a guidepost to travelers across the flat grasslands of that region.)

Arriving in Santa Fe on June 28, Marcy and the caravan had averaged thirteen miles a day. During the return trip, made without hindrance of civilians, Marcy tried a different route. From Santa Fe he went down the Rio Grande to the town of Dona Ana, then east to the Pecos River and across northwest Texas to enter the Indian Territory at the town of Preston, a ford on the Red River. From Preston his column proceeded to Fort Washita and thence to Fort Smith. Thereafter this route across the southern part of the Indian Territory, named Marcy's Trail in the captain's honor, would be the principal route used by gold-seekers and settlers crossing from the mid-Mississippi Valley to the great West. The trail was also used by many Cherokees who also wanted a share of the riches so widely believed to be waiting in California.

Even the Butterfield Overland Mail, which on September 16, 1858, began operating stagecoaches from St. Louis to San Francisco, followed Marcy's Road. From Fort Smith westward, the Butterfield passed through what one traveler called "two hundred miles of the worst road God ever built." Waterman L. Ormsby, a reporter for the *New York Herald* who was on the first

The California Road blazed by Captain Randolph Marcy crossed western Oklahoma. Wagons journeying along the road left deeply cut wagon ruts in the sandstone of present-day Red Rock Canyon State Park near Hinton. Photo by Jim Argo

stagecoach making this run, expressed fear of the Indians west of Fort Smith, but was surprised to find that Choctaws had been hired as station keepers and were excellent at their jobs. Ormsby wrote:

The night was beautifully clear and bright, and I was tempted to stay up and enjoy it; but I had become too much fatigued with the journey to be able to withstand the demands of somnolence, and wrapping myself up in my shawls, was soon obliviously snoring on the extended seats of the wagon. I

awoke but once during the night, having been jolted into a position where my neck felt as if there was a knot in it. They had stopped at a station to change horses, and for the time not a sound could I hear. I had been dreaming of the Comanche Indians, and in the confusion of drowsiness first thought that the driver and the mail agent had been murdered, and that I, being covered up with blankets, had been missed; then I recollected that I had a pistol and thought of feeling for it; but finally I thought I would not stir, for fear the Indians would see me—when I was brought to my senses by a familiar voice saying "Git up there, old hoss," and found it was the driver hitching up a new team.

Ormsby might have been astonished to learn that his fear of Indians was matched by an Indian fear of whites—and of other Indians. During the decade of the 1850s the new owners of the Indian Territory were not left alone to develop the homes they had carved for themselves and their families. Constantly they were bothered by raids conducted by plains tribes, while the federal government was under pressure to remove even more Indians to the territory. The result was increased federal involvement in tribal affairs.

The Comanches were the principal raid-

Rock Mary, a natural outcropping along the California Road, became a landmark for travelers crossing western Oklahoma. This drawing of the formation is by German artist H. Mollhouser, who accompanied Captain A.W. Whipple on an 1854 surveying expedition. OHS

This map of the Indian Territory shows the important routes and trails that crisscrossed the region prior to the Civil War. OHS

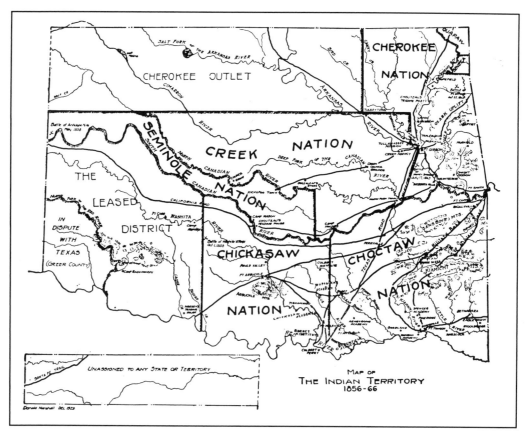

ers in the Indian Territory and in Texas. In theory this tribe had a claim to land in the Lone Star State, but when Texas came into the Union it was granted ownership of all its public lands—and the state government wanted to remove these Indians from the state. In 1855 the federal government leased from the Choctaws and the Chickasaws the area between the Canadian and Red rivers in the southwestern corner of Oklahoma as a reserve onto which the plains raiders could be placed at some future date. In addition, the Army, to make its presence more visible to the plains tribes, established Camp Radziminski on Otter Creek (in present Kiowa County), and the following year opened Fort Cobb (at the site of the present town of Fort Cobb). At the insistence of the federal government, the Comanches were given a reservation in Texas in 1855, but were forced by irate civilians to leave four years later and were assigned to part of the Leased District. In theory they were to confine themselves there. In reality, however, they continued to raid south of the Red River and among the Five Civilized Tribes to the east.

The removal of the Comanches to north of the Red River signaled difficult years ahead for the inhabitants of the Indian Ter-

ritory. During the late 1850s this area increasingly was surrounded by whites who began looking with covetous eyes on lands supposedly given to the Indians in perpetuity. Texans were moving beyond the 98th meridian along the south bank of the Red River, and to the north, Kansas was being settled.

During the 1854 debate in Congress about the creation of Kansas Territory, the future of the Indian Territory was discussed. Senator Robert Johnson of Arkansas proposed that year that the Indian Territory also be considered for statehood. He wanted to divide the Indian Territory into three new territories: Cherokee, Muscogee (to consist of Creek and Seminole lands), and Chata (to be made up of Choctaw and Chickasaw lands). He suggested that the region be surveyed, that tribal members be given an allotment of acres, and that surplus lands be opened to settlement by non-Indians. When all three territories had sufficient settlers to meet the requirements for statehood, they would be reunited and admitted as the state of Neosho.

All tribes in the Indian Territory united in opposition to Senator Johnson's plan, asserting that they had been promised their new homelands would never be violated for any reason. Because of this strong opposition, as well as binding treaty obligations, Johnson's bill was not passed by Congress, but the idea did not die. The desire to break up the Indian republics to allow white settlement became dormant until some way could be found to void the government's treaty obligations to the tribes. Then came the Civil War, giving the government the excuse it was seeking.

As war clouds darkened the horizon of the United States in the late 1850s, the leaders of the Five Civilized Tribes found their position difficult. Slavery was traditional among them and was an established

Above
Stagecoaches like this one jolted and lurched along the crude trail across southeastern Oklahoma during the heyday of the Butterfield Overland Mail route. OHS

Left
During the heyday of the Santa Fe trade, the Santa Fe Trail which ran from Westport, Missouri, to Santa Fe, New Mexico, carried thousands of wagons and tens of thousands of draft animals. The Cimarron Cutoff crossed the northwestern corner of the Oklahoma Panhandle. In this photograph the ruts left by the wagons still remain on the Oklahoma prairies. Photo by Jim Argo

part of their agricultural pattern. Thus their sympathies were Southern. It was Southerners, however, who had driven them from their traditional homelands in Georgia, Alabama, Tennessee, Florida, and Mississippi. On the other hand, the federal government was protecting them in their new homes, but newly elected President Abraham Lincoln held abolitionist views and spoke openly of allowing white settlement in the Indian Territory. Then, with the outbreak of war in April 1861, the federal government withdrew its troops from all posts in the Indian Territory, thereby admitting it could not protect the Indians from Confederate attacks. Lincoln and his advisers did not want the Indian Territory to be swallowed by the South, but defense of Eastern states seemed far more important to them.

The newly organized Confederate States of America wanted the Five Civilized Tribes as allies. The Indian Territory could be a useful buffer against a Union invasion of Texas, as well as a strategic staging area should Southern forces invade Kansas. In Texas the secession convention early in 1861 sent delegates to ask the Five Civilized Tribes to ally with the Confederacy. In February these delegates found the Choctaws, Chickasaws, Creeks, and other tribes willing to side with the Confederacy. The Texas delegates were unable to secure a favorable response, however, from Chief John Ross of the Cherokees.

Ross moved slowly because he did not want to act emotionally. He feared what might befall his tribe should the Union win the war. Moreover, he knew that many

Albert Pike, pictured in Masonic regalia, negotiated treaties of alliance between the Five Civilized Tribes and the Southern Confederacy in 1861. He later commanded the Indian troops involved in the Battle of Pea Ridge in 1862. OHS

Cherokees, particularly the full bloods of the anti-treaty party, were cool toward the South. The old division within the tribe caused by the Treaty of New Echota, which had forced the Cherokees to move westward, had already been reopened. In 1859 the Reverend Evan Jones restructured the Keetoowah Society a pro-Union, abolitionist organization, while Stand Watie and his followers organized chapters of the Knights of the Golden Circle to promote a pro-slavery and pro-Southern attitude in 1860. The Keetoowahs, known as "pins" because of the emblem their members wore, were openly fighting the "Knights" by late 1860, and the Cherokees were a divided people once again, although Ross was able to postpone a decision to align the Cherokees with either side during the summer of 1861.

The withdrawal of federal troops from the territory decided the issue, for shortly afterward a Confederate force from Texas arrived. Many Indians who had wanted to remain neutral—and even many who were pro-Union—thereupon were forced to accept the South and to take up arms. Realizing this advantageous position, Southern officials acted quickly. Albert Pike, a lawyer at Little Rock, Arkansas, who had handled some legal matters for the Choctaws and was trusted by the Civilized Tribes, was sent by the South to make treaties with these nations as well as with the plains tribes, treaties that would ally them with the Confederacy.

Arriving at Tahlequah early in the summer of 1861, Pike began negotiations with the Cherokees. When Ross dragged these talks on with no end in sight, Pike left and in the next several weeks signed treaties with the other four Civilized Tribes. These assured their friendship for the Confederacy in return for perpetual Southern recognition of the Indians' title to their lands. Journeying on, Pike concluded similar agreements with the plains tribes, even with the Comanches, who promised to raid into Union Kansas rather than Confederate Texas. Returning then to Tahlequah, Pike in October concluded a Southern alliance with the Cherokees. Ross reluctantly had decided, following early Confederate victories in the war, that his tribe had to come to terms with the South—although many Cherokees were opposed to his actions.

Pike's treaties called for the Indians to raise troops for the South: one regiment of Cherokees, another of Choctaws and Chickasaws, and a third from the Seminoles and Creeks. The Confederacy, in return, would provide equipment and pay and would protect the Indian Territory from Union invasion, in addition to paying the annuities which the United States previously had paid the tribes. The Five Civilized Tribes quickly kept their end of the bargain by raising 5,000 soldiers. Prominent among their leaders was Stand Watie, who on July 12, 1861, was commissioned a colonel in the Confederate Army.

The first battle in which Indian troops were engaged was against their fellow tribesmen. This resulted because Opothleyahola, the Creek leader, was unhappy with the treaty signed by his tribe with Pike. He had been absent when the negotiations had taken place, but his signature had been placed on the document. Upon his return he refused to recognize any alliance with the

Douglas H. Cooper was Indian agent to the Choctaw and Chickasaw Indians prior to the Civil War, and later commanded the Department of Indian Territory for the Confederacy during the war. His defeat at the Battle of Honey Springs jeopardized Confederate control of the Indian Territory. OHS

89

Confederacy, and those Upper Creeks faithful to him, along with their families, livestock, and slaves, began gathering at his plantation, where they retreated to a camp on the Deep Fork of the Canadian River. There he and his followers, who also included some Delawares, Seminoles, Shawnees, and Comanches, came to be known as the "Neutral Indians," and they decided to remove to Kansas, setting out November 5. By this time his following numbered some 6,000 men, women, and children.

Unfortunately for them, the pro-Confederate Indians refused to allow neutrality. On November 15, 1861, Colonel Douglas Cooper, a former Choctaw agent, set out with a force of 1,400 Indians and Texans to stop them from reaching Kansas and to recover the Creek treasury that Opothleyahola possessed. Cooper's scouts soon located the Neutrals, and on November 19 the Battle of Round Mountain (the first battle of the Civil War in Indian Territory) was fought. Opothleyahola's warrior's were fighting for the welfare of their families. Led by two Seminoles, Billy Bowlegs and Alligator, they defeated Cooper's Confederates while Opothleyahola led the Neutrals farther north to a new camping place at Caving Banks (Chusto-Talasah) on Bird Creek.

Cooper was determined to force Opothleyahola's people to join the Confederacy, so reinforced by a regiment of Cherokees early in December he again sent out scouts to locate the Neutrals, and on December 9 a second engagement was fought. The Neutrals used the natural fortifications at Caving Banks to good advantage, and the Confederates were driven back a second time. Before Cooper could take further action, his regiment of Cherokees withdrew, and the Confederate leader retreated to Fort Gibson to reorganize.

Cooper remained steadfast in his determination to overwhelm the Neutrals and make them join the Confederacy, and when he was reinforced by 1,500 Confederates from Van Buren, Arkansas, commanded by Colonel James McIntosh, he again took the field during the third week in December. Marching up the Verdigris River from Fort Gibson, McIntosh located the Neutrals northeast of Caving Banks at a place called Chustenahlah (near the present Skiatook). There on December 26 the Neutrals twice turned back Confederate charges, but a third assault destroyed the resistance of the tired and under-supplied Neutrals. That night a fierce blizzard blanketed the area, and the freezing chill numbed Opothleyahola's followers, who were without shelter. McIntosh followed those Neutrals who escaped capture as they fled toward Kansas, harassing them and capturing stragglers. Hundreds died before reaching Union lines, and many of the survivors lost limbs to frostbite. Eventually some members of this Neutral column would return to the Indian Territory in Union uniforms.

With Opothleyahola's followers gone, the Confederacy reigned supreme in the Indian Territory—but only for a short time. The North recovered quickly from its early defeats in the Trans-Mississippi West and organized a large army for a sweep into Arkansas in the spring of 1862. Led by General Samuel Curtis, this force crossed southern Missouri to confront Confederate defenders in Arkansas commanded by General Sterling Price. Faced with this Union threat, Major General Earl Van Dorn, commanding Confederates in the West, ordered Brigadier General Albert Pike to take all forces from the Indian Territory and join Price to confront Curtis' force. Pike, who had been given overall command of the Indian Territory, was headquartered at Fort Davis (named for Confederate President Jefferson Davis) located on the southwest side of the Arkansas River at the Three Forks area (in present Muskogee County).

Pike responded to Van Dorn's orders by taking all his Indian forces into Arkansas, leaving the territory without defense—in violation of the agreements he had negotiated (these had stipulated that no Indian troops would be withdrawn from the territory without permission of the tribal governments, which was never secured). Van Dorn's hope for a quick victory over Union forces in Arkansas was not realized. At the Battle of Pea Ridge, fought on March 6 to 8, 1862, the Confederates sustained heavy losses and had to retreat. The Indian regiments fought bravely and well, Stand Watie and his Cherokees captured a Union artillery battery, but Van Dorn in his report slighted their contribution. This so enraged Pike that he withdrew to the southern part of the Indian Territory to establish Fort McCulloch on the west side of the Blue River (in present Bryan County), leaving Douglas Cooper in command at Fort Davis.

Cooper's position never became secure.

Colonel John Drew's Confederate Indian troops deserted en masse to the enemy twice during the Civil War, once before the battle of Caving Banks, and then prior to the fall of Tahlequah. He did, however, lead his Cherokees valiantly and well throughout the war. OHS

The Confederate defeat at Pea Ridge left him without adequate men and supplies to defend the northern part of the Indian Territory. Union officials realized Cooper's weakness, and in April 1862 the "Indian Expedition" was organized to regain control of the territory. This expedition consisted of troops from Kansas and other Northern states along with volunteers from Opothleyahola's followers. Commanded by Colonel William Weer, a Kansan, this force on June 2 set out down the Grand River from Baxter Springs, Kansas.

Once in the Indian Territory, Weer's command constantly was harassed by Stand Watie's Cherokees until on July 3 the two forces met in open battle at Locust Grove. For a time it seemed Watie and his men

would repel the Union invaders, but a withering Yankee cannon fire broke the Confederate line and insured a Northern victory. Following this victory, Weer sent one column to occupy Fort Gibson and another to take Tahlequah. The fort fell easily, but Tahlequah was well defended. For a time it seemed that siege of the Cherokee capital would be necessary, but the full-blood Cherokee regiment of Colonel John Drew deserted to the Union side, leaving the town open. On July 12 Weer's troops occupied Tahlequah without firing a shot. Chief John Ross and his family, who were in Tahlequah, thereupon moved to Philadelphia, Pennsylvania, where he helped organize Unionists in the Indian Territory through his agents.

The Confederate defeats at Locust Grove, Fort Gibson, and Tahlequah made it appear that nothing could stop Weer from marching all the way to the Red River; however, the column halted of its own accord. Many of Weer's soldiers were unhappy at the thought of advancing further into the Indian Territory because Watie's cavalry was harassing their detachments, and they feared their line of supply from Kansas (and their line of retreat, if that became necessary) would be cut if they advanced toward the Red River. Moreover, a rumor was circulating among the Federals that a Confederate force equal in size to their own was across the Arkansas at Fort Davis. When Weer argued at Tahlequah for an advance, he was charged with insanity and disloyalty by Colonel Frederick Salomon of Wisconsin and a band of Union officers and men; they relieved Weer of command and then retreated to Kansas during the summer of 1862. This gave the Confederates time to reorganize, and Stand Watie, elected Cherokee chief by pro-Southern members of the tribe, was able to spread terror in southern Kansas and southwestern Missouri by raiding undefended towns. Watie also burned Ross' home at Park Hill, Rose Cottage, as well as the Cherokee capitol building in Tahlequah.

By the fall of 1862 the situation in the Indian Territory was degenerating toward chaos. William A. Phillips, aided by agents sent by John Ross, organized the pro-Federal Indian Home Guard, and was spreading fear among Confederate Indians along the Verdigris River. And William C. Quantrill had arrived from Kansas in mid-1862 with his band of cutthroats, called irregulars, to

Far right
Colonel Tandy Walker commanded the Confederacy's Second Indian Brigade, composed of Choctaws, Chickasaws, and Caddos, during 1864 and 1865. OHS

Below
The Battle of Honey Springs was the largest Civil War engagement fought in the Indian Territory. The Union victory insured that Indian Territory would not remain in the hands of the Confederacy. This marker was erected by the United Daughters of the Confederacy to honor the Confederate soldiers who fought in the battle. Photo by Jim Argo

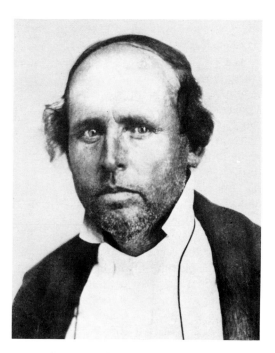

wreak havoc. Despite Watie's efforts to provide order and stability in the Cherokee and Creek country, the area was suffering from its own miniature civil war and from lawlessness.

Union planners then decided to recapture the Indian Territory, and in October 1862 General James G. Blunt led a Federal column into the area from Arkansas. Douglas Cooper, still officially in command of Confederate forces north of the Canadian River, moved his troops to Fort Wayne, a post first established in 1838 (in northeastern Adair County) but moved a few months later to present Delaware County and abandoned in 1842. His hope was to make a thrust into Kansas, diverting Blunt's forces there to protect that area. Blunt learned of Cooper's presence, made a forced march, and engaged the Confederates in battle on October 22. During the one-hour contest near old Fort Wayne,

the Federals tried to engulf Cooper's troops, but failed. Cooper was able to retreat, but his defeat effectively opened the Cherokee country to Union control—and it encouraged the full-blood Cherokees to ally with the North.

The pro-Union Cherokees met in National Council at Cowskin Prairie in February 1863, elected Thomas Pegg acting chief, reasserted that John Ross was the legitimate chief of the Cherokees, repudiated the treaty with the Confederacy, declared Stand Watie's Confederate Cherokee government illegal, confiscated all the property of pro-Confederate Cherokees, and freed all slaves in the tribe. When pro-Confederate Cherokees called for a National Council to meet at Webbers Falls on April 25, Colonel William A. Phillips, commanding the Union Indian Brigade at Fort Gibson, crossed the Arkansas and attacked the pro-Southerners, who fled in disorder. Thereafter until the end of the Civil War, there were two Cherokee governments contending for supremacy, with Union sympathizers in the majority.

Desperate for supplies, on May 28 Watie led his pro-Southern troops to attack a Federal supply train steaming to Fort Gibson. There he met defeat, as he did again in June when he attempted to capture a Union wagon train. Watie then retreated to Honey Springs, a Confederate supply depot on the Texas Road south of Three Forks, where he joined forces with Douglas Cooper to rally their troops for an attack on Fort Gibson,

which was seen as the key to the Union presence in the Indian Territory.

At Fort Gibson, General Blunt and his troops crossed the Arkansas below the mouth of the Grand and engaged Watie and Cooper on July 17. Heavy rains preceded this Battle of Honey Springs, and the Confederates had allowed their gunpowder, already of inferior quality, to become damp—to their great disadvantage during the fighting. Blunt used the large number of cannons he had brought to good advantage, and after bitter fighting the Confederate line broke. At Webbers Falls the local residents listened to the echoes of cannon fire and learned the outcome of the battle when retreating Confederates were followed by Union troops who burned the town.

Late in August 1863, when General William Steele and a Confederate force approached Fort Gibson, Blunt again came out to do battle. The Federals followed part of Steele's troops to Perryville, and there defeated the Confederates and destroyed their supply depot. More Confederate supplies were lost at North Fork Town, and on September 1 a Union force captured Fort Smith, thereby closing the upper Arkansas to any Confederate traffic. The fall of Fort Smith signaled the end of any real hope for a Southern victory in the region—and signaled the onset of great suffering. Roving bands of thieves and killers, especially the men of William Quantrill, cloaked themselves behind the Confederate flag and spread terror in the territory. Medical supplies and food were in desperately short supply.

Early in 1864 the Confederacy made a last attempt to reassert its authority. Two new Indian units were formed: the First Indian Cavalry Brigade, composed of Cherokees, Creeks, Seminoles, and Osages and commanded by Stand Watie, who was promoted to brigadier general; and the Second Indian Cavalry Brigade, composed of Choctaws, Chickasaws, and Caddos and commanded by Colonel Tandy Walker. Watie thereby became the only Indian general on either side during the Civil War. Although he was openly critical of the Confederacy for abandoning its Indian allies, Watie and his men continued to fight. They conducted guerrilla raids that thrust deep into Union territory, and they had some notable successes. At Cabin Creek on September 18 to 19, 1864, they captured 250 Federal supply

wagons and distributed food to needy Indian refugees.

Despite such limited successes, the South was defeated. On April 9, 1865, Robert E. Lee admitted the inevitable and surrendered his army to Ulysses S. Grant at Appomattox Courthouse in Virginia. Some Confederates in the Trans-Mississippi West swore to continue the war indefinitely, but in May General Edmund Kirby Smith, commander of the department, surrendered. In mid-May the Indian Territory leaders of the various tribes called for a united meeting at Council Grove to discuss a course of action, but disbanded when threatened with Union force. Meeting again at Camp Napoleon (on the Washita River), these leaders agreed to unite in negotiations with the United States. On June 23, 1865, General Stand Watie formally surrendered his troops, the last Confederate force to quit the field. At long last the bloody war was over.

Colonel William A. Phillips led the Union Indian Home Guard and was a stalwart friend of Indian refugees devastated by the war. OHS

93

Reconstruction and Pacification

Not all residents of the Indian Territory had allied with the Confederacy during the Civil War, but all would suffer in the decade that followed. The eleven states that had seceded would feel the presence of federal troops and basic changes in their laws, but none of them would endure the hardships imposed on the natives of the Indian Territory. Some Northern leaders not only wanted vengeance for Indian participation in the rebellion, but also to destroy tribal government and to nullify tribal ownership of land.

Residents of Kansas were most interested in breaking up the reservations. They were bitter at the destruction and death caused by raiders operating out of the Indian Territory, and they wanted retribution. In addition, they wanted tribes still in Kansas moved to the Indian Territory, leaving Indian land in Kansas open to white settlement. Some Kansans wanted to end the concept of Indian reservations completely, forcing all heads of families to take an allotment and opening the remaining acres to white homesteading. Such a desire had been voiced during the Civil War by Senators Samuel Pomeroy and James Lane of Kansas, who in 1862 had proposed that treaties with the Five Civilized Tribes be voided and the Indians of Kansas moved to the Indian Territory. Congress passed this measure in 1863, and it became the basic plan for reconstruction of the Indian Territory.

The blow was delivered in the fall of 1865. Leaders of the Five Civilized Tribes, with chiefs from the Osage, Wichita, Caddo, Seneca, Shawnee, Quapaw, and Comanche nations, met with federal officials at Fort Smith in September. Representing the United States were Dennis Cooley, Commissioner of Indian Affairs; Elijah Sells, Superintendent of the Southern Superintendency; General William S. Harney, representing the Army; Colonel Ely Parker, a Seneca mixed-blood; and Thomas Wistar, a mem-

Pro-Southern Cherokee delegates to the Fort Smith conferences included, from the left, John Rollin Ridge, Saladin Watie, Richard Field, E.C. Boudinot, and W.P. Adair. OHS

ber of the Society of Friends. In his opening statement Commissioner Cooley told the Indians that by joining the Confederacy they had "lost all rights to annuities and lands," that their treaties had been voided, and that their tribal laws no longer were valid. Each tribe would have to negotiate a new treaty with the United States, free all slaves, and cede a portion of their lands for use by other tribes.

The Indians were stunned by the severity of this pronouncement. This was especially hard on the Cherokees, for its pro-Union tribal government had already confiscated the property of all Cherokees who had sided with the Confederacy. John Ross and others spoke so vehemently against the proposals that no treaties could be negotiated immediately, and the conference recessed to resume in Washington the following year. At the conclusion of the meeting in Fort Smith, simple treaties were signed wherein the Indians renewed their allegiance to the United States.

The fall and winter of 1865 to 1866 was a time of terrible suffering in the Indian Territory. Few crops had been planted the previous spring, and hunger took a heavy toll. Survivors, suffering from malnutrition, fell prey by the hundreds to cholera, which ravaged the refugee camps. When at last the survivors of the Cherokee, Creek, and Seminole tribes returned home, it was to find waste and destruction; contending armies had stripped the countryside of livestock, knocked down fences, and burned homes, while unplowed fields had returned to grass and weeds. Moreover, those tribes which had split into Northern and Southern factions during the war (Cherokee, Creek, and Seminole) faced internal quarrels that still pitted brother against brother.

In the negotiations in 1866 the United States was represented by Commissioner Cooley, Elijah Sells, Colonel Parker, and Secretary of the Interior James Harlan. The quarrelsome Cherokees sent two delegations, one headed by an ill John Ross, the other by Stand Watie and several pro-Southern Cherokees who were demanding that the Cherokee tribe be divided into two separate nations. The Choctaws and Chickasaws were served by Peter Pitchlynn, the Southern Creeks by D.N. McIntosh, the Northern Creeks by Chief Oktarsars Harjo Sands, and the Seminoles by John Chupco. Because of differences within the tribes, the Indians were negotiating from a position of weakness, while the American negotiators were united in their desire to force the Indians to give up part of their lands.

Four treaties were signed—one with the Creeks, one with the Cherokees, another with the Seminoles, and one with the Choctaws and Chickasaws. Known as the Treaties of 1866, these four agreements sharply reduced tribal prerogatives. Slavery was ended and the freedmen ordered adopted into the tribes. All five nations had to agree to allow railroads to build across the territory, and there was agreement in principle to an intertribal government for the territory. The contending Cherokee delegations agreed to a single treaty when the federal government promised to restore the confiscated property of the pro-Confederates. The most crushing feature of these treaties was the loss of land. The Cherokees had to cede their 800,000 acres in Kansas, while the federal government assumed de facto ownership of the Cherokee Outlet. The Cherokees were forced to agree that the government could settle other tribes in the Outlet and in what had been the principal Cherokee reservation as the need arose. The Seminoles had to sell their land to the government for fifteen cents an acre, but they did receive a new reservation of 200,000 acres in the western section of the Creek Nation—which they had to buy at fifty cents an acre. Creek lands were sharply reduced. The tribe lost more than three million acres in the western half of their reserve for the government's price of thirty cents an acre. The Choctaws and Chickasaws sold what had been known as the Leased District to the government for $300,000.

The signing of the Treaties of 1866 saw life in the Indian Territory drastically changed. No longer were the Indians masters of their own destiny, makers of their own laws, or sole owners of vast stretches of land. No longer were their constitutions the sole foundation on which their governments operated. In addition, they had to overcome chaotic economic and social conditions. Using the same stoicism with which they faced removal and resettlement in the 1830s, they set about rebuilding homes, fencing land, and plowing and planting, and they began healing the wounds of tribal divisions during the Civil War.

In the Cherokee Nation the old hatreds had been intensified by the war, and they had divided along the old lines: those who had opposed the Treaty of New Echota and who had supported the Union on one side,

Daniel N. McIntosh commanded a Confederate Creek regiment during the Civil War. He later represented his tribe during the treaty conferences at Fort Smith in 1866. OHS

and those who had favored the treaty and had supported the South on the other side. When John Ross died unexpectedly on August 1, 1866, while negotiating in Washington, the situation grew worse. Strangely, however, some of his followers joined adherents of Stand Watie to form the Union Party in 1867, and thereafter this group for almost two decades would control the tribe despite opposition from a hard-core band of disciples of John Ross.

The end of serious factionalism among the Cherokees in 1867 marked the beginnings of economic recovery for the tribe. Aided by missionaries sent by Presbyterians, Baptists, and Moravians, the Cherokees rebounded quickly, and by the early 1870s prosperity was returning. Schools were established for Cherokee children, crops were replanted and herds rebuilt, and their courts restored social order.

The Creeks, who also had been divided by removal and by the Civil War, were unable

to restore peace and harmony so quickly. Samuel Checote, a Confederate veteran, was elected primary chief in 1867, but Union sympathizers within the tribe refused to accept him. This led to open warfare within the tribe in the early 1870s, and federal troops were required to restore order. For more than two decades thereafter, only the presence of soldiers at nearby Fort Gibson prevented continued violence. With such quarrels openly evident, it was difficult for the tribe to return to prosperity, although a

new tribal constitution, adopted after Chief Checote's election, did allow tribal leaders to effect some progress. Under this organ of government, the tribal reserve was divided into six judicial districts with a supreme court at Muskogee providing ultimate resolution to disputes, while companies of light-horsemen provided police protection. The Creeks were a hard-working and ambitious people, and by 1880 their fields again were green, thousands of horses and cattle grazed their pastures, and schools educated their children.

The Seminoles suffered most terribly from factionalism. At the end of the Civil War they were moved to a new reserve and began rebuilding—only to learn that they were still on Creek land. They bought another 175,000 acres from the Creeks at one dollar an acre. Yet on this land there was no peace, for the Seminoles were still divided according to Civil War loyalties: John Chupco and the pro-Union forces against John Jumper and the pro-Confederates. Living apart from one another, each band developed its own government until the 1880s, when the division mended and the tribe began cataloging its laws; although the statutes were never published. As a people the Seminoles had never liked farming, and

because of their several moves and political
divisions they were hesitant to begin tilling
the soil on their new reservation. Only the
threat of starvation at last forced them to
begin planting and harvesting, but prosperity
did not visit the Seminole part of the Indian
Territory.

Ironically the tribes that suffered the
least during reconstruction were the two
that had supported the Confederacy most
strongly: the Choctaws and Chickasaws.
Their lands in the southern part of the territory were least touched by war, and the
tribes were not divided by factionalism after
the conflict ended. Therefore life in these
two nations was not disrupted economically
or socially. Moreover, they were able to sell
coal from mines in their land when railroads
built through, and the range cattle industry
came to the Chicksaw Nation.

In the immediate aftermath of the war,
while the various Civilized Tribes were attempting to rebuild, the Army had returned
to occupy posts such as Fort Gibson, but
there were so few troops that they did little
to restore order. Until 1870 Army officers
acted as agents to the tribes, after which
they were returned to civilian agents—often

Northern carpetbaggers seeking personal enrichment rather than interested in helping the Indians. In 1874 control of the Five Civilized Tribes was centralized as the Union Agency, which the following year opened its headquarters at Muskogee.

Another major problem during this era was the status of the freedmen. These former slaves did not receive land, although they were reluctantly granted citizenship by all the Five Civilized Tribes except the Chickasaws. Many of the freedmen squatted on land in the territory. Without money—and largely without hope—some freedmen turned to stealing as a means of livelihood. To control them, vigilante law was exercised by members of the Five Civilized Tribes, a practice that sometimes led to abuses and needless cruelty. Some freedmen, caught with a stolen horse, cow, or hog, were executed on the spot, while many were severely flogged for lesser offenses. Eventually the blacks settled near one another for self-protection, a practice that led to the development of several all-black communities.

Controlling the white outlaw bands operating in the territory proved more difficult. In the immediate post-Civil War years the Indian Territory was being ravaged by roving bands of outlaws, restless veterans trained in the recent conflict in hit-and-run tactics, killing, and robbery. Such notorious figures as the James brothers, the Younger gang, and the Daltons regarded the territory as a good hideout and as a place where theft could be committed without fear of capture,

while homegrown outlaws such as Ned Christie contributed to the lawlessness. Indian courts had jurisdiction only over issues involving Indians, but not over crimes committed by whites—even those involving a white against an Indian. These cases, along with cases involving federal laws, had to be tried in the nearest United States District Court.

Immediately after the Civil War the nearest federal court was at Van Buren, Arkansas; Indians had to ride many miles and miss days of work to appear there. Tribal leaders therefore urged the government to establish a district court at Muskogee where the Union Agency was located. On March 3, 1871, the government transferred the court for the Western District of Arkansas, whose jurisdiction included the Indian Territory, to Fort Smith. Judge William Story presided during the next three years, but his effectiveness was terminated when he was called before a congressional committee to explain how $714,000 had been spent in his district in just three years. Following Story's resignation, President Grant appointed Isaac C. Parker to the bench, and the situation changed dramatically.

For twenty-one years following his appointment in 1875, Judge Parker was known as "the law west of Fort Smith" and as "the hanging judge." More than 13,000 prisoners would be arrested in the Indian Territory and taken to Fort Smith for judgment, and Parker was a stern, puritanical man who did not flinch in handing out the death sentence—151 of them, of whom eighty-three were executed. Parker was described by contemporaries as "white of hair and beard, with pink cheeks and slightly rotund," a man "with a twinkle in his eye and a little contagious chuckle which always made [youngsters] think of Santa Claus."

The United States marshals served as Parker's executives, assigning warrants and writs to be served by deputies in the field. They worked in bad weather and good, in extreme cold and stifling heat. They expected violence, for few criminals in "the Nations" wanted to be brought before Judge Parker. These deputy marshals also performed their work for no salary, only fees. Each received seventy-five cents a day to feed his prisoners, ten cents a mile for travel, and two dollars for each paper served. If in the course of duty he killed a man, he not only lost his fees, but also had to pay

jurisdiction, and conflicts between them and the district court at Fort Smith were common. Once in 1872 a group of deputy marshals entered a Cherokee court to arrest the defendant, Ezekial Proctor, who was on trial for killing an Indian; the marshals wanted him for killing a white man. When the Cherokees refused to give up their prisoner, guns were drawn and fired until seven deputy marshals and four Cherokees were dead. Despite such quarrels, however, Judge Parker and the Federal District Court at Fort Smith did reduce outlawry in the Indian Territory.

The tribes removed to the Indian Territory from Kansas added to the confusion and uncertainty in the area. Kansas was experiencing a growing demand for land, especially that assigned to various tribes of Indians, owing to passage of the Homestead Act in 1862, the tendency of many people

Among the ablest of the deputy marshals who served in the Indian Territory was Bass Reeves (pictured at the far left). He earned a reputation as being fearless, and he always brought in his man. OHS

burial expenses. This work was extremely hazardous—sixty-five deputy marshals lost their lives in the line of duty—yet good men continued to serve, men such as Bill Tilghman, Chris Madsen, and Charlie Colcord. Blacks such as Grant Johnson, Bass Reeves, and Ike Rogers served with equal valor and honesty—but without the fame that came to their white counterparts.

The Indian courts were jealous of their

to move west after the end of the Civil War, and almost unlimited immigration from Europe, along with the introduction of pioneering techniques and inventions, such as barbed wire, the windmill, the sod house, and drought-resistant kinds of wheat. To clear lands for white settlers the government decided to move these natives to the Indian Territory, and after 1865 a steady stream of new exiles flowed there.

Additional Indian reservations were established following the Civil War in the Indian Territory. Indians from as far away as California and Washington were removed to Oklahoma to free lands for non-Indian settlers. OHS

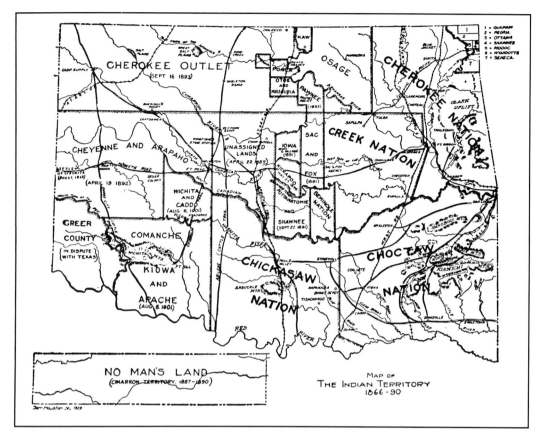

MAP OF
THE INDIAN TERRITORY
1866-90

So many whites had already encroached on the reserves these Indians had in Kansas that it required little inducement by the government to get them to move southward. First to arrive in the territory were the Pottawatomies, who in 1867 were settled between the Canadian and the North Canadian (west of the Seminoles). Just to the north of the Pottawatomies the so-called Absentee Shawnees were given a small reserve, as were the Iowa, while the Sac and Fox also were removed in 1867 to a reserve west of the Creek Nation between the Cimarron and North Canadian rivers.

Another tribe forced from Kansas was the Osage. Residents of the Sunflower State wanted the Osage land, which had been given to the tribe by the federal government in exchange for the reserve given to the Cherokees in the Indian Territory that once had been the home of the Osage Nation. As a result, in 1870 Congress heeded Kansans' demand for removal of the Osages by passing an act creating a new reservation for the tribe in the Indian Territory. The Osages accepted this move peacefully because, five years earlier, they had signed a treaty which, in principle, agreed to their removal southward. They bought title to a reservation in the Indian Territory from the Cher-

okees with the money paid them for their land in Kansas, bounded on the east by the 96th meridian and on the west by the Arkansas River. Individual Osages who wanted to remain in Kansas, accept a homesteader's allotment, and adopt white ways were allowed to remain in that state, but their acres were overrun by whites and they were cheated out of their land. They soon joined the remainder of the tribe in the Indian Territory. Ironically, it was an area their ancestors had left at the insistence of the federal government.

Kansans were still not content, however, and soon they wanted the reserves that belonged to all remaining Indians inside their borders. Yet to yield were the Kansas (or Kansa, or Kaw). Linguistically related to the Osages, the Kansas were given 100,000 acres in 1872 along the Arkansas River in the northwest corner of the Osage Reservation.

In Nebraska the Pawnee tribe found its situation similar to that faced by Indians in Kansas. Their reservation along the Loup River had been created in 1857, but almost immediately settlers and the territorial government began lobbying for their removal elsewhere to allow white settlement. In addition, the Pawnees faced frequent raids by the warlike Sioux. Because of this—and lured by tales of happy natives in the Indian Territory—the Pawnees agreed in 1872 to cede their reservation in Nebraska in return for a new home along Black Bear Creek between the Arkansas and Cimarron rivers. Congress failed to appropriate the promised funds for this move, but it was made anyway between 1873 and 1874.

The Ponca, another tribe in Nebraska, faced the same pressures, and in 1876 its members agreed to removal. Arriving in the Indian Territory in 1877, they lived for a time with the Quapaws, then received a tract of land along the western bank of the Arkansas. A few years later the Oto and Missouri tribes were moved to a home just south of the Ponca. By the 1880s this area along the Arkansas had been designated the Ponca Agency, and to it came yet another displaced people, the Tonkawas. A Caddoan folk, the Tonkawas had been moved in 1859 from Texas to the Leased District, but there they suffered continual abuse from the more warlike Kiowas and Comanches. In 1884 they were allowed to resettle along the Salt Fork of Arkansas (northwest of the Poncas).

The area inhabited by the Senecas and Quapaws was also used to settle several small bands of dispossessed Indians. Between 1865 and 1880 the Wyandottes, Peorias, Miamis, and Ottawas were located peacefully in this region, receiving land taken from the Quapaws and Senecas for their part in the Civil War. In 1873 that part of the Modoc tribe that had followed Captain Jack into rebellion in northern California and southern Oregon was given 4,000 acres taken from the Eastern Shawnees who had been settled there during the 1830s.

As new tribes arrived in the territory, the Bureau of Indian Affairs created individual agencies to watch over them. Gradually some of these were closed, their duties transferred to central agencies or to subagencies. By 1889 there were eight agencies operating: the Kiowa-Comanche Agency at Fort Sill, the Sauk and Fox Agency near present Stroud, the Darlington Agency near Fort Reno (for the Cheyenne-Arapaho), the Wichita-Caddo Agency near Anadarko, the Quapaw (or Neosho) Agency near present Miami, the Union Agency at Muskogee (for the Five Civilized Tribes), the Osage Agency at Pawhuska, and the Ponca Agency near present Ponca City.

While the tribes in the eastern and north-ern parts of the Indian Territory accepted these changes peacefully—if not happily—the warlike and fierce raiders of the plains refused to accept white authority or adopt white ways. Theirs was a nomadic existence, their economies based on raiding in addition to the slaughter of buffalo. The government attempted to settle these tribes on reservations by diplomacy, but military conquest proved the only permanent solution.

At the end of the Civil War, peace-longing congressmen and officials in the Indian Office, along with representatives of various religious denominations, still hoped for an easy solution to the threat posed by the plains Indians. At their insistence a council was called with tribal leaders of the Kiowas, Cheyennes, Arapahos, and Comanches to meet in October 1865 near present Wichita, Kansas. Known as the Little Arkansas Council, because of the stream running nearby, the plains tribes ceded all their lands north of the Arkansas River to the United States, promising to limit their wanderings to the Panhandle of Texas, the western part of present Oklahoma, and southwestern Kansas and to be no threat to white settlers. However, this treaty proved of short duration and the tribes continued their raids into Kansas and Texas.

Two years later, Congress sent yet another commission west to negotiate at Medicine Lodge Creek in southern Kansas. Chiefs of the Kiowas, Comanches, Kiowa-Apaches, Cheyennes, and Arapahos gathered to confer with Commissioner of Indian Affairs Nathaniel Taylor, John Henderson, Samuel F. Tappan, General W.S. Harney, General Alfred Terry, and Colonel C.C. Augur. The American commissioners warned the nomadic Indians that, with the movement of white farmers onto the plains and the eventual slaughter of the buffalo, they soon would be forced to turn to agriculture themselves, supplementing their diet with government-issued beef. In response Kiowa Chief Satanta summed up the feelings of the tribes gathered there: "I love to roam over the wide prairies, and when I do it, I feel free and happy, but when we settle down we grow pale and die." Comanche Chief Ten Bears spoke in a similar vein:

I was born upon the prairies, where the wind blew free, and there was nothing to break the light of the sun. I was born where there were no enclosures, and where every-

Left
Lieutenant Colonel George Armstrong Custer led the Seventh Cavalry in an assault on the Cheyenne camp of Black Kettle in the winter of 1867. OHS

Far left
Major General Philip Sheridan, Civil War hero and commander of the military department of the Missouri, was charged with the subjugation of the Cheyenne and Arapaho Indians in the winter of 1867 to 1868. OHS

Bottom, left
A Cheyenne Indian camp in western Oklahoma is shown following the defeat of the tribe at the hands of the Seventh Cavalry in 1867. OHS

Below
Black Kettle, a Cheyenne peace chief, survived the Sand Creek Massacre in Colorado, but fell during Custer's attack on his village during the Battle of the Washita. Courtesy, Western History Collections, University of Oklahoma Library

thing drew a free breath. I want to die there, and not within walls.

Despite these plaintive calls for freedom, the American commissioners already had decided that the Indians would have to give up yet more land, accept small reservations, allow railroads to be built, and permit whites on what had been Indian land. In return they would receive houses, schools, churches, and instruction in agriculture. The Kiowas and Comanches were to be settled in the Leased District, while the Cheyennes and Arapahos were to have a reserve in the Cherokee Outlet.

Once the Treaty of Medicine Lodge was completed, the Indians returned to their old habits of following the buffalo and raiding. With the onset of winter, they went into winter quarters believing that the Army, as usual, would not undertake a campaign then. Yet Major General Philip Sheridan, commanding the Department of the Missouri, was angered that the tribes paid so little heed to the treaty just concluded, and he determined to punish them, particularly the Cheyennes of Chief Black Kettle. This tribe, driven from Colorado in 1864 follow-

ing the infamous Chivington Massacre at Sand Creek, was not living on their reservation in the Cherokee Outlet between the Cimarron and Arkansas rivers. Instead they had moved south to settle on the North Fork of the Canadian and along the Washita River. Early in 1868 Sheridan ordered his soldiers to establish a post later named Fort Supply on Beaver and Wolf creeks (in western Woodward County) from which they could mount a winter campaign.

Troops massed at Fort Supply when it opened in November 1868. Heavy snows began to fall just as scouts returned to report that Black Kettle and the Cheyennes were encamped on the upper Washita River. Lieutenant Colonel George A. Custer and eleven troops of the 7th Cavalry set out, not waiting for reinforcements, and on the morning of November 27 the impetuous Custer led his men into Black Kettle's village. This engagement, later known as the Battle of the Washita, was a victory for the Army. Black Kettle and more than 100 Cheyenne men, women, and children were killed, hundreds of Indian horses were shot,

Above
General Custer's captives from Black Kettle's camp are pictured being escorted to Camp Supply following the Battle of the Washita. Courtesy, Western History Collections, University of Oklahoma Library

Top
Custer's Demand, a painting by Charles Schreyvogel, depicts the soldier's order for the surrender of the Cheyenne and Arapaho Indians in the spring of 1868. Courtesy, The Thomas Gilcrease Institute of American History and Art, Tulsa, Oklahoma

and the village and its supplies were destroyed, while fifty Indians were captured. Custer, however, as he later would do at the Little Big Horn, had divided his command, and thirty soldiers commanded by Major Joel Elliott were killed. This winter strike so disheartened some Cheyennes that they, along with some Arapahos and Kiowas, moved onto the reservations to which they had been assigned—and stayed there.

Sheridan continued this massive winter campaign, striking the Kiowas and the Comanches, leading to the establishment of a reserve for them near the site of Fort Cobb. In addition, Sheridan established Camp Wichita, which soon was renamed Fort Sill. With its completion, the Army's cordon of

posts stretched from Fort Supply to Fort Sill, a valiant—if vain—attempt to keep the plains tribes from raiding into Texas. That same year the Cheyennes and Arapahos were assigned to a new reservation on the North Fork of the Canadian River (north of the Kiowa-Comanche reservation and west of the 98th meridian) by presidential proclamation. The agency for this reservation was first located at Pond Creek, but in 1870 it moved to become the Darlington Agency. Fort Reno would be built near this agency in 1874.

Despite this winter campaign and the building of new forts, the Comanches still roamed the plains and raided into Texas. Particularly inclined to this life was one band of the tribe, the Kwahadi, led by Chief Quanah Parker. The son of Chief Pete Nokona and Cynthia Ann Parker, a captive white girl who lived among the tribe more than twenty years, Quanah Parker was the bold, resourceful leader of a proud, free, and fierce people. Joining Parker and his Kwahadis were Kiowas and their leaders Satanta, Big Tree, and Satank. They likewise scorned farming and the confined life of the reservation.

When Ulysses S. Grant was inaugurated as president in 1869, he turned over administration of the reservations and agencies to members of various religious denominations, hoping the Native Americans would become Christianized and forego their old habits, customs, and economic system to live in harmony with whites. This became known as Grant's "Quaker Policy" because the Society of Friends (Quakers) played a prominent role in its implementation. As part of this plan, Lawrie Tatum, a Quaker from Indiana ignorant of Indian customs but long on brotherly love, was placed in charge of the Comanches and Kiowas at Fort Sill. Good-hearted and honest, Tatum could not control the reservation or halt the raiding. When he admonished one chief to keep his young men from joining forays south of the Red River, the chief told him that if he wanted these attacks to cease he would have to move Texas far away so his warriors could not find it.

One major cause of Indian raiding during this period was the slaughter of the buffalo, an animal which played a key role in the economic system of these tribes. Prior to the 1870s buffalo had been hunted by Indians, and professional hunters had killed them to feed railroad crews. In addition, sportsmen came from afar to hunt the beasts. There was a small commerical market for hides, which were used (with the hair on) as robes in sleighs and carriages. Despite the killing done to 1870, however, no one thought the animal was in any danger of extinction, for all attempts to tan buffalo hides into commercial-grade leather had produced a spongy product of little value. As late as 1869 one herd crossing the tracks delayed a Kansas Pacific train for nine hours.

With the discovery of a tanning process in Germany in 1871, the price paid for a single hide soon jumped to as much as three dollars, and a boom rapidly developed. Soon the techniques of the trade had also been developed. A hunter—the one doing the shooting—was the leader of a party. He hired as many men as he thought he needed to skin the buffalo he killed. A party might include as many as fifteen skinners, normally greenhorns who wanted to learn the business. Hunters at first used a Springfield .50 caliber Army rifle loaded with seventy grains of powder and a swedge ring ball. Soon, however, almost all of them switched to the .50 caliber Sharps rifle, which seemed made especially for killing buffalo. This was a large, heavy weapon designed not for the saddle but for a man hunting on foot. Its killing range, 600 yards, was so great that one Indian was moved to remark that the weapon "shoots today and kills tomorrow."

When a hunter sighted a herd, he approached it from downwind, for buffalo had a keen sense of smell. Once near the herd, the hunter aimed for a bull and shot it, hoping the others would mill about rather than stampede. When a herd did mill—the hunters called this a "stand"—the hunter often could kill a dozen or more of the beasts before the others began to run. Soon there were conflicting claims as to who had killed the most buffalo. One report claimed that Tom Dixon had killed 120 buffalo in one stand and that in a period of one month and five days he had slaughtered 2,173 of these shaggy beasts. Because of such wholesale slaughter, the northern herd (north of the Arkansas River) began to thin, and hunters went to Fort Dodge to ask the commanding officer about hunting south of the Arkansas in violation of treaties with the Indians.

Quanah Parker, a half-blood Comanche, led the Kwahadi Comanches in their transition from Plains nomads to reservation Indians. OHS

107

"Boys," replied the commanding officer, "if I were a buffalo hunter, I would hunt where the buffalo are." They did, and soon the southern herd also was thinning toward extinction.

The result of this slaughter was increased pressure on the plains tribes to leave their reservations to raid. Texans, in turn, complained loudly to Washington about these incursions, but officials there dismissed the assertions of these former Confederates. Finally in 1871 General William T. Sherman, commanding general of the Army, decided to inspect the region to determine the truth. In north Texas he saw the devastation wrought by the raids, and there near Fort Richardson he narrowly missed being killed by one party of marauders. A wagon train just hours away was attacked, seven people were killed, and their bodies were mutilated.

Sherman went directly to Fort Sill, there to meet Kiowa Chief Satanta and hear him brag about having led this raid. Sherman arrested him, along with Chiefs Satank and Big Tree, and sent them to Texas to stand trial. Satank was shot while trying to escape, while Satanta and Big Tree were convicted and sentenced to death. Their sentences were commuted, however, by the reconstruction governor of Texas, and they were imprisoned at Huntsville—only to be pardoned by that same governor in 1873. Satanta and Big Tree immediately led more raids in revenge for their captivity. Satanta

was captured on one such raid, brought to trial, and again was sentenced to prison. Four years later he committed suicide rather than spend his years in the Texas State Penitentiary.

Nevertheless, the raids continued, and by 1874 Quanah Parker and his Comanches, along with the Kiowas, had the frontier of north Texas aflame with their incursions. In response the government declared that all Indians off the reservation were renegades and subject to punishment, and the Secretary of War ordered the Army to capture them. The result was a five-pronged attack called the Red River Campaign, centering on the Panhandle of Texas (near Palo Duro Canyon). The maneuver involved Colonel Ranald S. MacKenzie, coming north with a large force; from Fort Sill came another body of troops; coming from the northeast was a third body of troops led by Colonel Nelson A. Miles; a fourth contingent of men marched from Fort Union, New Mexico; while a fifth column marched east from central New Mexico. More than 3,000 soldiers were engaged in this effort.

In the course of this campaign, carried out during the winter of 1874 to 1875, fourteen battles were fought. In one of these, an engagement at Tule Canyon, Captain (later General) Adna R. Chaffee made military history by shouting to encourage his soldiers, "If any man is killed, I will make him a corporal." By the spring of 1875 the Co-

manches' spirit had been broken. They were largely without horses and provisions, and most of their women and children had been captured and taken to Fort Sill. In small groups the warriors began trickling into that post to surrender. On June 2, 1875, Quanah Parker and more than 400 Kwahadis admitted defeat and laid down their arms at Fort Sill. Seventy-five Comanche and Kiowa leaders were arrested, tried, and sentenced to imprisonment in Florida, a few years later to be returned to their people at Fort Sill.

With the conquest of the Kiowas and Comanches, the Indian wars in the territory at last came to an end. Reluctantly they began scratching the earth to grow food for themselves and their families, for the paltry rations given them by the government were inadequate. They would be joined at Fort Sill in 1894 by Geronimo and proud Apache survivors of the wars in Arizona, but by that time the day of sole Indian ownership of the territory was past.

CHAPTER IX

Iron Horses and Longhorn Cattle

Frederic Remington sketched this stampede of Texas longhorns. A common occurrence on the trail drives from Texas to Kansas, the stampede was only one of many hazards that made the life of a cowboy exciting and brief. Courtesy, Bob L. Blackburn

*I*n the years immediately following the end of the Civil War, the eastern part of the United States was industrializing and urbanizing rapidly, and the people there needed a reliable system of transportation. The Far West would be connected to the booming East by a transcontinental railroad in 1869 with the completion of the Union Pacific, but the Indian Territory, with its native population, small towns, and lack of manufacturing, was slower to see rails laid.

Transportation had long been a problem in the region. The Arkansas and its major tributaries had provided ready highways for commerce, but these streams were inconsistent, rising and falling rapidly depending on rainfall and snow melt. The Red River similarly was a moody mistress for steamboats and flat-bottomed skiffs. Thus the Indian Territory at the end of the Civil War had no reliable system of transport other than wagons, but these slowed—and often stopped—when rains turned the few roads into quagmires of mud.

Between 1870 and 1880 the Army Corps of Engineers worked to improve navigation on the Arkansas and Red rivers, and goods did move by steamboat up the Red to the mouth of the Washita and up the Arkansas as far as Wichita, Kansas. The boats used on these streams were not the floating pleasure palaces that plied the Mississippi; rather they were sternwheelers of extremely shallow draft, woodburning carriers of freight and frontiersmen. There were always problems. Low water could halt transport or strand boats on sandbars.

By this period the railroad had proved to be the best means of moving people and freight. It represented the future, and the right to lay tracks across the Indian Territory was part of the Treaties of 1866, despite the protests of the various nations. Most Indian leaders did not want railroads crossing their lands for fear they would bring whites to the region, whites who would demand the

right to settle in the area and thereby threaten Indian control. The directors of several railroads were interested in pushing track across the territory because they hoped to get land bonuses in it and because this area lay between Kansas and Texas as well as between Arkansas and Colorado. The Cherokees would resist rail construction through their land, but to no avail; the snorting and puffing and shrill whistle of the iron horse soon would be heard in a country that previously had known only the wagon and buckboard.

The first line to push onto Indian lands was the Missouri, Kansas, and Texas (usually called the Katy), a branch line of the Union Pacific that operated in the states for which it was named. The owners of the line hoped to get three million acres in land subsidies within the Indian Territory, but Congress late in 1866, when it granted permission for the Katy to build across this area, could not give the land bonus because the area was not part of the public domain. Nevertheless, the Katy worked rapidly in order to forestall competition, and by 1870 the roadbed had been surveyed and track was being laid, largely following the old Texas Road from southeast Kansas to the Red River near the mouth of the Washita (at Colbert's Ferry). As the Katy built

southward, the towns of Chouteau, Gibson Station, Muskogee, Eufaula, McAlester, and Atoka became terminal points. By January 1873 locomotives were pulling freight and passenger cars across the Indian Territory in a north-south direction.

At the same time, the St. Louis and San Francisco, usually called the Frisco, was entering the territory on an east-west route. A subsidiary of the Atlantic and Pacific chartered to run between St. Louis and San Francisco, the Frisco began laying track through the Quapaw reservation west of the Missouri boundary in May 1871 and reached the Katy's tracks by September 1. At this strategic junction, where a city was bound to grow, there was a major quarrel. The Cherokee Nation, which opposed the laying of tracks through its lands, passed a law requiring one square mile to be reserved at every railroad station with lots sold only to Cherokee citizens. Elias C. Boudinot, son of the slain Cherokee leader and an influential mixed-blood Cherokee who served as attorney for several railroad interests, tried to gain control of 1,000 acres at the junction of the Frisco and Katy in order to start his own town, which he named Vinita in honor of sculptress Vinnie Ream. The Cherokee National Council disallowed Boudinot's claim, took control of the area, and renamed

These men are bridge building on the Wichita Falls and Northwestern Railroad, a branch line of the Missouri, Kansas, & Texas Railroad in western Oklahoma. Courtesy, Western History Collections, University of Oklahoma Library

the town Downingville in honor of Prinicpal Chief Lewis Downing. During the quarrel between the Nation and Boudinot, the Vinita Hotel, which Boudinot had built, was burned by his opponents. (Later the town's name would be changed back to Vinita.)

For almost a decade the Frisco's tracks ended at Vinita, but in 1882 the road was extended to a Creek village called Tulseytown (later to become the modern city of Tulsa) at the junction of the Arkansas and Cimarron rivers. In the latter part of the nineteenth century the line would build across to Oklahoma City, and in 1896 it would extend on to Quanah, Texas.

Another major railroad to enter the Indian Territory in this period was the Atchison, Topeka, and Santa Fe, better known simply as the Santa Fe. A branch line headed south into the territory in 1886 from Arkansas City, Kansas. Once its tracks entered the Indian Territory, Santa Fe officials immediately began lobbying in Washington to have the region through which it ran, the so-called Unassigned Lands in the center of the Indian Territory, opened to white settlement.

The Rock Island, yet another major carrier, built on a north-south line across the

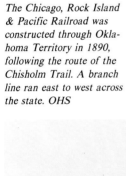

Pictured is a Rock Island locomotive of the 1880s. The Chicago, Rock Island & Pacific Railroad was constructed through Oklahoma Territory in 1890, following the route of the Chisholm Trail. A branch line ran east to west across the state. OHS

territory in 1890, while the Choctaw, Oklahoma, and Gulf (later to become part of the Rock Island) in 1894 laid tracks from El Reno to Oklahoma City and southeast to McAlester by the following year. There it joined company track that ran on east to Wister. The track between McAlester and Wister had been laid in 1888 by a small line named the Choctaw Coal and Railway Company to transport the growing amount of coal being mined in the Choctaw Nation. The firm went bankrupt in 1891 and was acquired by the Rock Island.

The Kansas and Arkansas Valley connected Fort Smith, Arkansas, with Coffeyville, Kansas, while yet another line laid track from Fort Smith to Paris, Texas, in the early 1880s, crossing the Choctaw Nation. Other small lines in the territory included the Split Log; the Kansas City, Fort Scott, and Gulf; the Fort Smith and El Paso; and the Chicago, Kansas, and Nebraska. Most of these were eventually absorbed by one or another of the major lines. By 1903 more than 2,500 miles of track crisscrossed the area that became Oklahoma.

While various railroad companies were hurriedly constructing lines across the Indian

Territory, another major industry was developing: the cattle business. The animal involved in this business was the Texas longhorn, a direct descendant of the unseemly, lanky animals brought by Spanish conquistadors to the New World and then driven north from Mexico into Texas. By the 1820s, when Americans began moving into that area, the longhorn was running wild in south Texas, for it had found conditions there ideal: the climate was mild, the grass grew tall, and predatory animals were few. Domestic cattle brought by Anglo-Texans interbred with the longhorn, producing a different animal with almost unlimited color variations: brindle, blue, mouse-colored, duns, brown, cream, yellow in several shades, black, white, red, and splotchy combinations. Weighing about 800 pounds by age four, with some grizzled veterans of ten tipping the scales at 1,000 pounds, the longhorn was big at the shoulders, flat-ribbed, and thin at the hips. The animal's body was so long that the back frequently swayed as it walked. Packers asserted the animal was "all legs and horns," but there was considerable beef on his large frame—though much of it was stringy and tough. Cowboys declared that the longhorn, despite its independence and mean nature, was the best animal ever devised for trail driving. These long-legged animals had tough hoofs, great endurance, and the ability to walk up to sixty miles without water, farther than cattle of improved blood—the "high grade" stuff of a later period. A natural rustler, the longhorn seemed to thrive on almost any plant it could get into its mouth. His long legs carried him tirelessly over great distances, and he was unaffected by heat, hunger, and the unmelodious singing of cowboys. These virtues compensated in part for the distressing inability of the breed to produce quality beef.

When Texans returned from the Civil War, their Confederate currency was worthless and their economy was wrecked, but they did have beef—millions of longhorns free to anyone who could round them up in the brush country or buy them at four to five dollars a head. This was beef that would bring forty to fifty dollars a head at northern and eastern markets, although Texas had no rail connections. In 1866 a few enterprising Texans attempted to drive cattle through highly populated areas of the Indian nations, destroying crops and infect-

Joseph G. McCoy built cattle pens at the small Kansas town of Abilene for the herds of cattle from Texas he hoped to attract. He later was active in early Oklahoma Territory politics, narrowly being defeated for congressional delegate in 1890. OHS

ing milk cattle with splenic fever. Better known as "Texas fever," this disease spread by ticks carried on the longhorns; the hardy Texas cattle were immune. The tribes in the Indian Territory brought pressure to halt the longhorn drives across their lands, as did farmers in Arkansas, Missouri, and eastern Kansas.

It was twenty-nine-year-old Joseph G. McCoy who provided a solution. He persuaded the Kansas Pacific Railroad to build to the middle of Kansas, beyond the farmers' frontier (and west of the lands of the Five Civilized Tribes through which cattle were trailed northward), and establish loading pens there. This caused the birth of Abilene, Kansas, for merchants, gamblers, and assorted others flocked to the railhead to separate the cowboys from their pay. To publicize this railhead, McCoy hired Jesse Chisholm, a mixed-blood Cherokee, to pioneer a trail south and tell Texas cattlemen of this place to market their cattle. In 1867, the first year this trail was open, 35,009 cattle were marketed at Abilene, but in the next four years more than a million longhorns would be loaded there to be shipped to packing houses in Kansas City or Chicago. Each spring a river of beef would run north from Texas up the Chisholm Trail to Abilene, or up the Western Shawnee Trail, which in the Indian Territory started at Boggy Depot and ran to Sedalia, Missouri,

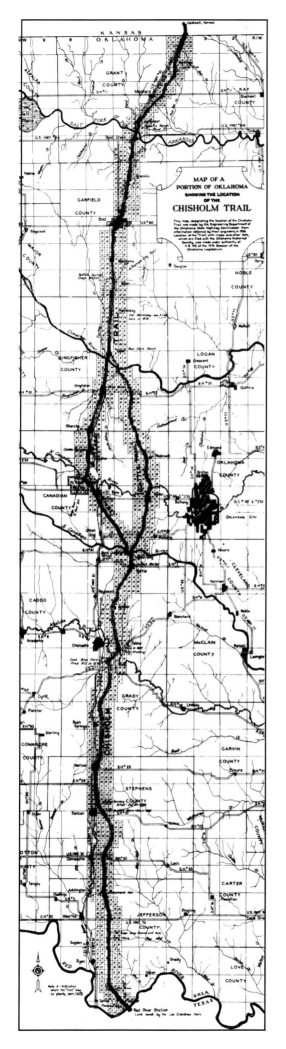

Left
Jesse Chisholm had been a trader in the Indian Territory and, along with Black Beaver, blazed a trail from Texas to Kansas. The Abilene Trail would eventually be renamed the Chisholm Trail. OHS

Far left
A map of the Chisholm Trail in western Oklahoma was drafted by the Oklahoma Department of Highways in the 1930s to locate the route of the trail and to preserve its heritage. OHS

and later to Baxter Springs, Kansas.

As the farmers' frontier advanced beyond Abilene and as the Santa Fe built across southern Kansas, other cities briefly boomed as "cowtowns": Newton, Wichita, Ellsworth, and then Dodge City, the "Queen of the Cow Town" from 1876 until the closing of the frontier about ten years later. The Great Western Trail was opened in 1876, running from south Texas north to the Red River (west of present Childress at Doan's Store) and then proceeding north across the Indian Territory.

Cattle drives across the Indian Territory and the profits realized by Texas cattlemen soon gave rise to a new industry north of the Red River: cattle grazing and ranching on Indian lands. Vast tracts owned by the Five Civilized Tribes were vacant because no tribesmen were farming them, and on this land grew blue stem and gramma grasses rich in the nutrients cattle needed to fatten. Interspersed among the grass-covered hills were creeks usually containing water, even during dry summer months. The climate was colder than in Texas, but cattlemen soon learned that this was an advantage; cattle that wintered in the Indian Territory lost their ticks, which could not

stand the cold weather. Thus the cattle no longer were carriers of splenic fever. Cattlemen who could claim rights in the Nations either by blood or by marriage crowded into the region, while some Indians took up ranching themselves.

The largest pasture of fine grass in the territory was the Cherokee Outlet, a 6.5 million-acre strip of land extending along the southern boundary of Kansas from the Arkansas River to just west of present Laverne. Prior to 1879 Texas drovers often paused in this area to fatten their cattle before taking them on to Abilene or Dodge City. If the market was glutted, the longhorns were held at the Outlet until prices rose. In 1879 the Cherokees decided to seek payment for grazing rights and began charging ten cents a head for pasturing cattle there. The cost per head rose rapidly, for the Cherokees quickly realized the value of this pasturage. For a time grazing rights reached one dollar a head, but soon fell back to about forty cents. In 1883 the cattlemen using this area decided to organize. At Caldwell, Kansas, that year they organized the Cherokee Strip Live Stock Association to prevent illegal grazing in the Outlet, to halt rustling there, and to negotiate with the Cherokees for a favorable contract. This was reached that same year: $100,000 per year rental for a period of five years. The agreement was renewed in 1888 at a fee of $200,000 per year. A lease

signed, the Association fenced the Outlet into pastures, subleasing plots to individual cattlemen who paid two cents per acre rental to the Association, which in turn paid the Cherokees. Within a short time most other tribes in the Indian Territory had made profitable leases with cattlemen—to the benefit of both.

Life within these leased tracts was hard. Ranchers erected only temporary quarters, paying young cowboys twenty-five to thirty dollars a month for long days of hard work. The Indians did not police these areas, and the states of Kansas and Texas had no jurisdiction in the territory. Therefore the Cherokee Strip Live Stock Association or individual ranchers had to perform the functions of government and try to protect life and property.

The typical cowboy of that era wore heavy woolen trousers; a woolen shirt whose sleeves were held up by sleeve garters; a large hat that protected him from rain, snow, and hot sun; a neckerchief knotted around his neck to be pulled up to cover his nose in wintry cold or blowing dust; and boots that fitted well into stirrups. Only in winter did the cowboy don a coat, for it tended to bind his arms and hold in the heat. Instead he wore a vest in which he kept his watch, his tobacco, and any coins he might possess. He took great care in selecting the gloves he wore year-round, which usually were of buckskin. His boots were a

Branding calves in the Indian Territory was a yearly event. Roundups were coordinated by cattlemen's associations, and mavericks were distributed to association members. Courtesy, Western History Collections, University of Oklahoma Library

source of great pride, although he tended to be awkward in them when not on horseback. Finally, he wore chaps made of heavy leather and fitting as a second pair of trousers, to protect his legs from thorns. Somehow chaps became a symbol of the trade to newcomers, who wanted to "look like cowboys."

Because most of the young men coming into the occupation had read lurid tales of what their life was supposed to be like, they also wanted a pistol to strap around their waists. In practice, the weapon most often proved a bother, just extra weight to be carried, for few cowboys had the money to buy the ammunition needed for practice to become expert shootists. Gradually most young range workers discarded the weapon except when they went to town and wanted to look like cowboys.

Another item of great pride to a cowboy was his saddle. This was designed as a place for long hours of work, so it was much like a chair, but with a horn for roping. On the average these saddles weighed thirty pounds. Each cowboy was expected to provide his own saddle; thus selling it meant he was totally broke and without prospects.

Perhaps it was long hours in the saddle that made the cowboy quiet, bottling up his emotion even among his closest friends. When he did talk, it was a salty language born from his occupation. For example, one old cowboy, when asked late in life to what he attributed his longevity, replied, "Try to get your beefsteaks three times a day, fried in taller [tallow]. Taller is mighty healing,

and there's nothing like it to keep your stomach greased-up and in good working order." This life also produced a raw sense of humor that appreciated the ignorance of greenhorns and the ever-present danger. Once in the Cherokee Outlet, when a horse rolled over on its rider and killed him, the foreman and the other five cowboys in the group dug a shallow grave on a hillside. With the body placed, the foreman solemnly asked the group, "Does anybody know the right words to say?" When no one answered, the foreman commented, "Well, throw some dirt on the son of a gun, and let's get back to work."

The cowboy found his life filled with monotony and hard work. Cattle had to be tended, for the brutes had a knack for getting themselves into trouble. They had to be pulled from quicksand, eased out of barbed wire, and dragged out of mud. They had to be doctored and helped during calving time. Barbed wire fences had to be strung and repaired—a particularly nasty job. Post holes had to be dug and wire strung. Harness had to be kept in repair, saddles mended, and other equipment looked after. Horses had to be broken—"gentled" was the word cowboys used, but "broken" was more apt, for about one in five horses had to be almost ruined before it could be ridden, while one in a hundred could never be ridden. Nor did the cowboy have a favorite horse he loved above all other animals—that was a fiction of the pulp writers. Because these horses were grass fed, the cowboy had to change mounts frequently.

Broken bones and death were constant threats. To be thrown from a horse meant bruises at the least; often it meant a broken leg, usually set improperly. One kick from a temperamental horse could kill, while a simple ride across the countryside could mean death if the horse was sufficiently mean to deliberately run under a low tree limb at high speed. A terrified herd stampeding at night could bring injury or death to a cowboy in a hundred ways; "stompede" was the cowboy pronunciation of a word one old-timer defined as "one jump to their feet and another jump to hell." Equally hazardous was an unexpected blizzard in winter which could trap a cowboy on the range where he might freeze to death. Sleeping on hard ground brought arthritis to many a cowpoke, and it exposed them to rabies from

the bite of infected skunks and other wild animals. Even the simple act of roping could result in the loss of a finger or two if these were caught between rope and saddle horn when a thousand-pound steer hit the end of the rope. Little wonder that the average working life of a cowboy was only seven years.

Yet young men continued to seek out the life, 20 percent of them black and 10 percent of them Indian. To them no other life seemed to hold such romance, such glamour, such chance for glory. Their occupation continued unchanged into the twentieth century, for the rich grass in the Indian and Oklahoma territories attracted ranchers even after the dramatic changes that were to unfold in the years between 1887 and 1907.

Frederic Remington made a brief trip to Indian Territory as an artist and writer in the 1880s. While there he sketched the branding of cattle to be issued to the Cheyenne and Arapaho Indians for their subsistence. Part of the fees charged by these and other tribes for the right of crossing their reservation was a number of cattle for meat. OHS

OKLAHOMA

CAPT. PAYNE'S

OKLAHOMA COLONY

Will move to and settle the Public Lands in the Indian Territory before the first day of December, 1880. Arrangements have been made with Railroads for

LOW RATES.

14,000,000 acres of the finest Agricultural and Grazing Lands in the world open for

FREE HOMES

For the people—these are the last desirable public lands remaining for settlement Situated between the 34th and 38th degrees of latitude, at the foot of Washita Mountains, we have the finest climate in the world, an abundance of water, timber and stone. Springs gush from every hill, The grass is green the year round. No flies or mosquitoes.

The Best Stock Country on Earth.

The Government purchased these lands from the Indians in 1866. Hon. J. O Broadhead, Judges Jno. M. Krum and J. W. Phillips were appointed a committee by the citizens of St. Louis, and their legal opinion asked regarding the right of settlement, and they, after a thorough research, report the lands subject under the existing laws to Homestead and Pre-emption settlement.

Some three thousand have already joined the colony and will soon move in a body to Oklahoma, taking with them Saw Mills, Printing Presses, and all things required to build up a prosperous community. Schools and churches will be at once established. The Colony has laid off a city on the North Fork of the Canadian River which will be the Capital of the State. In less than twelve months the railroads that are now built to the Territory line will reach Oklahoma City. Other towns and cities will spring up, and there was never such an opportunity offered to enterprising men

MINERALS!

Copper and Lead are known to exist in large quantities—the same vein that is worked at Joplin Mines runs through the Territory to the Washita Mountains, and it will be found to be the richest lead and copper district in the Union. The Washita Mountains are known to contain Gold and Silver. The Indians have brought in fine specimens to the Forts, but they have never allowed the white men to prospect them. Parties that have attempted it have never returned.

In the early spring a prospecting party will organize to go into these Mountains and it is believed they will be found rich in GOLD AND SILVER, Lead and Copper.

The winters are short and never severe, and will not interfere with the operations of the Colony. Farm work commences here early in February, and it is best that we should get on the ground as early as possible, as the winter can be spent in building, opening lands and preparing for spring.

For full information and circulars and the time of starting rates, &c., address,

T. D. CRADDOCK,
General Manager,

GEO. M. JACKSON,
General Agent,

The Run
for Land

Among the Choctaw delegates to Washington in 1866, when the tribe was negotiating a new treaty following the end of the Civil War, was Allen W. Wright, who first suggested that the Indian Territory be renamed "Oklahoma." Wright derived the name from two Choctaw words: *okla,* meaning people, and *homa* (or *huma*), meaning red. Oklahoma, he suggested, would be an appropriate name for a land that was "home of the red man." In 1869 a bill was introduced in Congress to effect this change, but the word usually was applied only to the empty part of the area. The remainder continued to be known as the Indian Territory, an officially designated but unorganized territory.

The Treaties of 1866 had contained provisions whereby the Indian Territory might become organized—and thus introduced into the state-making process. Delegates from the various tribes were to work out the details in conference, their expenses paid by the federal government. This intertribal council met at Okmulgee in 1867 and again in 1869, but no plan of organization emerged. Then, with the introduction of a bill in Congress to create a "Territory of Oklahoma," the tribal leaders met yet again in 1870. This time they drafted a document known as the "Okmulgee Constitution." This established a framework for a governmental union of all tribes in the territory (even including a bill of rights), but it made no mention of the United States. Subsequently the various tribes refused to ratify this document, nor was it accepted by Congress. Each year thereafter until 1876, when Congress ceased appropriating funds to pay the costs involved, the intertribal council met, but no satisfactory plan for organizing the territory could be reached. Indian leaders feared such organization would be a first step to abolishing tribal governments and allowing whites into the area, thereby ending Indian control of their own destinies.

Allen W. Wright, a Choctaw chief, first proposed the name "Oklahoma" for the Indian Territory in 1866. OHS

This fear was well-founded, for there were thousands of landless whites who wanted fertile acres on which to homestead. By the late 1870s most of the West had been carved into separate territories, and the good farming and ranching lands were settled. Only in the Indian Territory could these people see unoccupied acres suitable for farming. Naturally they coveted this land, and they began clamoring for Congress to open it to settlement. Joining landless whites in this demand were railroad officials anxious to see more settlers on the land—farmers and ranchers who would buy and sell and require rail shipments. Equally anxious to see the Indian Territory opened were merchants in the adjacent states of Kansas and Texas, businessmen who knew such an opening would expand their trade territory. Congressmen favoring business and railroad interests responded to the pressure, and legislation periodically was introduced to throw the land open to settlement.

Indian leaders, particularly among the Five Civilized Tribes, naturally opposed white settlement. They knew that if the unassigned lands were opened to homesteading, white frontiersmen would not be satisfied. Soon they would demand an end to the reservations, the alloting of a homestead to each Indian head of family, and the opening of the remainder to non-Indian settlement.

Thereby tribal governments would end—and with this the way of life the Indians had come to know in their territory. Ranchers joined Indian leaders in protesting the opening of the Unassigned Lands, they were grazing their herds for small fees on these acres. Missionaries and eastern humanitarians also insisted that the opening of the territory would represent further despoliation of the Indians. Others fighting the opening included a horde of government bureaucrats, who feared a loss of influence—and their jobs; licensed traders, beef contractors, and merchants doing business with the Indians; and whiskey peddlers illegally supplying alcoholic beverages to the red owners of the land.

Not content to wait for Congress to act, Elias C. Boudinot, the mixed-blood Cherokee who had attempted to organize the town of Vinita, was convinced that progress for Indians in the territory would come only with breaking up the reservations, alloting homesteads to tribal members, and opening the remaining land to white settlement. Of particular interest to him was the tract of some two million acres taken from the Creeks and Seminoles at the end of the Civil War as a home for Indians from other parts of the United States, but never used for that purpose. This vast block was known as the Unassigned Lands (and, increasingly, as the Oklahoma District).

In 1878 Boudinot failed to lobby through Congress an Oklahoma Territory Bill, which would have opened the Unassigned Lands to white settlement. Therefore he tried another way to accomplish his goal. On February 17, 1879, he published an article in the *Chicago Times* in which he argued that fourteen million acres of land in the Indian Territory were legally a part of the public domain. He wrote that this land had been taken from various tribes to be used for the resettlement of other Indians, but had never been so employed and so had reverted to the public domain. With the article was a map he had prepared that showed what he considered the area open to homesteading: the Unassigned Lands, Greer County (then part of Texas but later added to Oklahoma), and parts of the Comanche, Kiowa, Wichita, and Cheyenne-Arapaho reservations.

Reprinted widely, Boudinot's article triggered the "Boomer" Movement, composed of whites anxious to settle in the Indian Territory. One leader who emerged in 1879

was Charles C. Carpenter, who previously had led prospective settlers onto Sioux lands in the Black Hills of South Dakota. Carpenter began speaking publicly of taking whites into Oklahoma, causing leaders of the Five Civilized Tribes, along with several Indian agents, to protest loudly to Washington.

President Rutherford B. Hayes issued a stern warning to these prospective settlers to stay out of the territory, a warning relayed by General Phil Sheridan, commander of the Department of the Missouri. This show of opposition caused Carpenter to abandon his effort, and his followers dispersed.

David L. Payne proved less easily discouraged in his drive to open the Indian Territory. Born in Indiana in 1836, Payne, after an average education, became a frontier guide in the process visiting the Indian Territory several times. After service in the Civil War, he was elected to the Kansas Legislature and then became a captain in the 19th Kansas Cavalry. Then, settling in Wichita, he again served in the Kansas legislature, after which he became a doorkeeper for the House of Representatives in Washington, D.C. When he lost that position, he returned to Kansas and became leader of the Boomer Movement ("booming" the opening of the Indian Territory). During the next several years he supported himself by charging a fee of two, three, or even five dollars for membership in his "colony."

Payne proved persistent in his efforts. Several times he led colonists into what he called Oklahoma, only to be turned back by the Army. He also took the government to court at Fort Smith, Arkansas, and he hired a newspaperman from Chicago to write his

Elias C. Boudinot, the son of the assassinated leader of the Treaty Party of Cherokees, called for the opening of the Unassigned Lands to non-Indian settlement and the eventual statehood for the Indian Territory. OHS

The Intertribal Council, held in Okmulgee in 1878, attempted to create a territorial government for the Indian Territory. Lack of support from the Five Civilized Tribes led to the failure of the movement. OHS

biography in order to stir interest in his efforts. Because of his work the border towns of Kansas grew as prospective homesteaders moved to them to be near Oklahoma should it be thrown open. In addition, Boomer camps sprang up along the Red River in Texas. Several times the secretaries of the War and Interior departments urged Congress to enact laws making it a criminal offense to trespass on Indian lands, but Congress never complied.

On November 28, 1884, while Payne was organizing yet another attempt at colonization, he died suddenly at Wellington, Kansas. His lieutenant, W.L. Couch, aided by Samuel Crocker, inherited leadership of the movement, and in December of that year Couch led several hundred followers to the future site of Stillwater and began constructing crude houses. Bitter wintry cold prevented a full force of soldiers from arriving until January 25, 1885, when Colonel Edward Hatch and 350 soldiers came from Fort Reno. Hatch chose to starve out Couch

and the Boomers rather than fight, and they were escorted back to Kansas.

While the Boomers were attempting to gain a foothold, legal or otherwise, their story was being spread aross the country in newspapers. Particularly active in this effort was Milton W. Reynolds, who wrote exten-sively about what he labeled "The Land of the Fair God." Often writing under his In-dian name, "Kickingbird," Reynolds did much to spread the word about the fertility and richness of Oklahoma.

At last Congress could ignore the situa-tion no longer. Even Secretary of the Inte-rior Henry M. Teller changed his mind after Couch's abortive effort to settle at Stillwater. On January 30, 1885, Teller rec-ommended that the Oklahoma District be thrown open to settlement. The Indian ap-propriation bill passed on March 3 that same year authorized the president to nego-tiate with the Cherokees, Creeks, and Sem-inoles for land to be homesteaded. Four years later the negotiations were completed: the Creeks ceded their unoccupied lands for $2,280,000, while the Seminoles received $1,912,942. President Benjamin Harrison signed the act and proclaimed that the lands would be opened on April 22, 1889. David Payne's dream had come true.

Yet there still was the question of the method by which the two million acres would be allotted to settlers. By 1889 there were tens of thousands of people wanting land. Governmental officials knew that on the day of the opening there would be chaos as these land-hungry individuals fought each other for a homestead. At last the bu-reaucrats decreed a land run. On March 23 President Harrison issued a proclamation stating that this run would commence at high noon on April 22; that the acreage would be subject to the provisions of the Homestead Act of 1862, which allowed a settler to acquire 160 acres; and that no person inside the Oklahoma District prior to noon on April 22 could legally homestead. Sections 16 and 36 in each township (of thirty-six square miles) were set aside for the benefit of public schools, and thus were not open to settlement, and the Secretary of the Interior was instructed to make provi-sions for appropriate townsites not exceed-ing 320 acres each. Finally, the Army was instructed to supervise the run and keep out those who tried illegally to enter the area prior to the run. Such people were known as "Sooners," and some estimates of their numbers run as high as 30 percent of all would-be settlers.

From all parts of the United States peo-ple came to participate in the run, camping

in Wichita and Arkansas City in southern Kansas, and Dallas, Fort Worth, and Gainesville in north Texas while they waited. A banner on one wagon in Kansas summed up the hard life of the pioneer and the hopes these people had for their new promised land: "Chintz-Bugged in Illinois, Sicloned in Nebraska, White-Capped in Indiana, Bald-nobbed in Missouri, Prohibited in Kansas. Oklahoma or Bust!"

As the day of the opening neared, the ban on whites in the Indian Territory was lifted temporarily so the Boomers could camp along the outer boundary of the Oklahoma District rather than wait in Kansas or Texas. To the appointed places they came, and there they prepared for the run. Some chose to make the dash in wagons loaded with everything they owned; others decided they could make better time on horseback; still others chose to ride the Santa Fe, which had fifteen passenger trains ready to haul them. Because those coming up from the South first would have to cross the Canadian River, a treacherous stream, most Boomers chose to make their entry from the north.

A reporter for the *Arkansas City Traveler* headlined his story of that momentous run "An Empire Opened in a Second," describing how a cavalry sergeant stood beside an American flag and shouted, "Let'er Go Gallagher!" What followed was a mad stampede of 60,000 or more people. They ran for glory—and land. By dusk that evening almost the entire two million acres had been claimed by individuals planting wooden claim stakes, each about two feet long. Some who made the race got nothing for their effort, while occasional disputes flared over who had reached a particular town lot

or quarter section first. There were also some who made the run to a favored spot, only to find someone whose horse was not sweaty, and angry cries of "Sooner" were hurled, a charge that immediately meant a fight. There was violence—and ironically one of those who died in such a quarrel was William Couch.

"Cities" sprang into existence that afternoon. "Born grown" were Oklahoma City, Norman, Guthrie, Edmond, and Kingfisher. By the following morning each sported shops, stores, and banks operating out of tents, and within a few days some enterprising individuals had wooden buildings erected.

In the rush to open this area to settlement the federal government unfortunately had made no provision for any type of government. The settlers survived by invoking vigilante law where necessary and by following a form of rough democracy. They acted as if there was constituted authority and elected city councils, mayors, and chiefs of police. In the effort to keep the peace these officials were aided at times by United States marshals and by the soldiers in the area.

The need for legitimate government was belatedly solved when Congress, on May 2, 1890, passed the Oklahoma Organic Act which joined the Oklahoma District with "No Man's Land" to form the Oklahoma Territory. No Man's Land was that strip of territory that constitutes the present Panhandle of Oklahoma that had not been made part of Texas, Kansas, New Mexico, or Colorado, and thus was without any government. In the post-Civil War period it had been the home of so many outlaws that

for a time it was called Robber's Roost. Beginning in 1886 it had been settled by cattlemen and a few farmers, and they enforced vigilante justice. The following year they petitioned Congress for organization as the "Territory of Cimarron," but Congress ignored the area until 1890 when it was joined to the Oklahoma Territory.

The Organic Act of 1890 provided for the president to appoint a governor and three federal district judges who, sitting together, constituted a territorial supreme court. The legislature was to be composed of a lower house of twenty-six members and an upper house of thirteen members. There were to be seven counties in the territory: Logan, Oklahoma, Cleveland, Payne, Kingfisher, Canadian, and Beaver (all of the Panhandle), and Guthrie was designated the territorial capital. Until the legislature enacted a code of laws, Oklahoma Territory was to be governed by the laws of Nebraska. The Organic Act also provided that as Indian reservations were thrown open to white settlement, that land would be added to the Oklahoma Territory.

In making appointments to the seven territorial offices, President Harrison caused some hard feelings in Oklahoma by naming five people from out-of-state: George W.

Harrison Avenue, Guthrie, on June 22, 1889, two months after the land run, shows the rapid development of that city. Already the wood-frame buildings were being replaced by brick structures, and soon streetlights would be installed. OHS

Steele of Indiana as governor; Warren Lurty of West Virginia as United States marshal; and Edward B. Green of Illinois, Abraham J. Seay of Missouri, and John Clark of Wisconsin as supreme court justices. Robert Martin of El Reno and Horace Speed of Guthrie were appointed as secretary of the territory and as United States District Attorney. Steele, born in 1839, was an old friend of the president, a lawyer, a Civil War veteran, and a former congressman. When he arrived by train in Guthrie for inauguration on May 22, 1890, the disgruntled cries about carpetbag officials temporarily quieted. An hour-long parade, which included a contingent of girls from Miss Williams' horseback riding class, moved from the railroad depot to the temporary capitol and ended with a round of speeches in which Steele said, "I am determined as far as in my power to make my coming here both lucky to myself and lucky and useful to the people of Oklahoma."

Because of his Army service Steele was accustomed to giving orders, and within a month he had county government functioning and the United States marshal had taken a census indicating almost 60,000 people in the territory. Elections for legislative seats were held on August 5, and the Republican Party gained a slight majority: fourteen of the twenty-six House seats and six of the thirteen positions in the Council (as the upper chamber was called). The Democrats elected eight and five respectively, while the People's Alliance Party, better known as the Populists, was represented by four in the House and two in the Council. The close split between the two major parties enabled the Populists to enjoy considerable power: one of its members was chosen Speaker of the House and another President of the Council.

The territorial legislature, which convened on August 27, had much to do during its first session. Most needed was a code of laws, but the legislators instead spent endless hours debating about the permanent location of the capital. The logical choices were Guthrie and Oklahoma City because they were the two largest towns, each with about 5,000 people. When Governor Steele vetoed a bill that would have moved the capital to Oklahoma City, disgruntled legislators voted to move it to Kingfisher, a town of about 1,200 people; Steele likewise vetoed that. The capital would remain in Guthrie, but the debate would continue.

The governor did sign other acts passed by the legislature: one to create a territorial university at Norman, another to begin an agricultural and mechanical college at Stillwater, and yet a third opening a normal (teacher training) college at Edmond. The legislature also made provisions for a system of public schools and appropriated $50,000 for salaries, books, and supplies. In November it elected David A. Harvey as Oklahoma's delegate to Congress; in winning the office, Harvey defeated Joseph G. McCoy, the man who had opened the cattle market at Abilene.

The Territorial University was founded in Norman in 1890. This is the first administration building of the University of Oklahoma, pictured in 1900. OHS

Steele, who was resented as an outsider and hated for filling the appointive positions with non-Oklahomans, did persuade the federal government to allocate $47,000 to purchase food for the needy in the territory, and he convinced officials of the Santa Fe to send $10,000 worth of wheat to farmers to be used as seed (to be repaid when the first crop was harvested). Both these efforts were popular, for a drought in the summer of 1890 had left thousands in dire need.

Governor Steele, however, never wanted to make Oklahoma his home. Rather, he preferred to return to Indiana and be re-elected to Congress. Thus on October 3, 1891, he resigned. Later he would say, "Well sir, when I got there I found matters in pretty bad shape. Civil laws had been laid down . . . but there were no officers to enforce these laws . . . . Peace and order was restored and today the people out there are civilized and prosperous. The only thing they pine for is excitement."

While Steele was yet in office, a second land run occurred, for the day of unoccupied Indian lands was ending. In 1889 President Harrison appointed a commission to negotiate with tribes for unassigned lands. This commission was composed of General Lucious Fairchild, Judge Alfred M. Wilson, and John F. Hartrauft. When Fairchild and

Hartrauft resigned, they were replaced by David H. Jerome and Warren Sayre. This group, known as the Cherokee Commission or Jerome Commission, persuaded the Sauk and Fox, the Shawnee, the Iowa, and the Potawatomie to open 868,414 acres to white settlement. The run for this land on September 22, 1891, was marked by the same excitement as the opening of the Unassigned Lands two-and-a-half years earlier; 20,000 people, three times the number of claims available, rushed in. The addition of this territory allowed the expansion of Payne, Cleveland, and Logan counties and the creation of Lincoln and Pottawatomie counties.

The Jerome Commission then turned its attention to the Cheyenne and Arapaho tribes, and in October 1890 persuaded these tribes to accept allotments. The remainder of what had been reservation land, more than four million acres, was sold to the government for one and a half million dollars, and it was opened by run on April 19, 1892. Only 25,000 people took part in this rush, as the western portion of this land was thought too dry for farming. Much of it was not homesteaded in the run, but eventually would be settled and transformed into farms and ranches. Many of those who chose to locate in that area were Mennonites, and

On September 16, 1893, over 100,000 people participated in the largest land run held in Oklahoma, that for the Cherokee Outlet. OHS

through their industry they showed the rich promise of this land. From the Cheyenne-Arapaho lands came Blaine, Dewey, Roger Mills, Custer, Washita, and Day counties, while Kingfisher and Canadian counties were expanded. (Day County would later be abolished by the constitutional convention.)

Next came the greatest run of all, that into the Cherokee Outlet. The Jerome Commission tried to negotiate with the Cherokees for this land in 1889, but the tribe refused an offer of a dollar twenty-five an acre. At that time the Cherokees were receiving an annual rental of $200,000 for this area from cattlemen, and one group of ranchers was offering them three dollars per acre for the Outlet if the Cherokees could get permission from the government to sell it. This was refused, and in 1891 the president ordered the cattlemen out of the Outlet, thereby denying the Cherokees any revenue from it. Giving in to the pressure, the Cherokees reluctantly sold the 6,220,854-acre Outlet on December 19, 1891, for $8,595,736—about a dollar forty an acre. The Pawness and Tonkawas had also been persuaded to take allotments and open the remaining parts of their reservations to white settlement, so when the great run occurred on September 16, 1893, there were almost six-and-a-half-million acres to be converted into farms and ranches. Congress, however, decreed that the settlers had to pay for this land, a fee that ranged from a dollar twenty-five an acre in the western portion to two dollars and fifty cents an

acre in the east.

Approximately 100,000 people gathered from across the United States to race for the 40,000 homesteads available, and rumors flew thick and fast as the great day neared. Some said that no trains would be allowed to make the run, others that the trains would be allowed to move at only five miles an hour. According to one story, only wagons drawn by a team of white horses and driven by red-headed girls could participate. In camps water sold for five cents a cup, and dry sandwiches hauled out from Wichita or Arkansas City sold at exorbitant prices. This was the last great block of land to be opened, and Kansas merchants tried to make as much money as possible.

The race was to begin at noon on September 16, the start to be signaled by Army troops discharging a firearm at each appointed place. At Hennessey someone fired a gun five minutes early, and the crowd surged into the Outlet. At Arkansas City, Kansas, a pistol shot sent 5,000 horses running eleven minutes before noon. Troops at both places tried to stop the Boomers, but their efforts were futile. Two hours after the race began, all was quiet. The land had been claimed, and Woodward, Woods, Garfield, Grant, Noble, Kay, and Pawnee counties had been created. The opening of the Cherokee Outlet was the last great run, although there was one small dash for land in 1895 when the Kickapoo reservation was opened to settlement.

No opening occurred in 1896, but Okla-

homa did expand that year when the Supreme Court ruled that what had been Greer County, Texas, belonged to Oklahoma. The question involved was which branch of the Red River constituted the main bed of the stream. Texans claimed that the North Fork was the main channel, while Oklahomans naturally asserted that the South Fork was the main channel (and therefore the correct boundary between them). On March 16, 1896, the Supreme Court ruled in favor of Oklahoma. Texans living on the land were allowed to claim their homesteads and file for an additional quarter section at one dollar per acre.

Yet another major tract of Indian land was opened to white settlement in 1901, some two million acres taken from the

Kiowas, Comanches, Caddos, Wichitas, and Apaches. This time the government chose not to have a run because of the lawlessness and disorder that had been associated with previous openings. Instead, this land was opened by lottery. Any adult, male or female, could register for a quarter section at Fort Sill or Fort Reno. Between June 9 and July 28 more than 165,000 hopefuls registered for the drawings, which were held between July 29 and August 5. Cards were drawn from the boxes until the 1,500 homesteads had been taken—and any single woman who won immediately received several proposals of marriage. Next came a drawing for the right to buy lots in the three townships of Lawton, Hobart, and Anadarko. The proceeds from this sale,

Left
*Whenever three pioneers
got together on the American frontier, it was said,
they would immediately
clamor for territorial status. In Oklahoma the population of the Unassigned
Lands soon after the run
exceeded 50,000. This po-
litical rally held at Lexing-
ton was one of many calling
for the establishment of an
Oklahoma Territory. Cour-
tesy, Western History Collections, University of
Oklahoma Library*

Opposite page, top
*The first substantial home
of many Oklahoma settlers
was a dugout. Courtesy,
Museum of the Great
Plains, Lawton, Oklahoma*

Opposite page, bottom
*Civic improvements came
shortly after the opening of
the Unassigned Lands and
the settlement of towns.
Telephone lines had been
strung, and streets were being prepared to be paved
in Oklahoma City soon
after the turn of the century. Courtesy, Bob L.
Blackburn*

some $700,000, were given to the three new counties (Kiowa, Comanche, and Caddo) to be used to erect county buildings and to run the county governments until taxes could be collected.

Finally in 1906 came the opening of the Big Pasture Reserve in southwestern Oklahoma, consisting of land belonging to the Comanches and Kiowas that had not been included in the lottery of 1901. Totaling 505,000 acres, it was sold at public auction in 160-acre tracts for an average of ten dollars per acre. No individual could purchase more than one quarter section. In the years between 1901 and 1906 some additional small parcels of land were opened through the closing of the Ponca, Kansa, and Missouri-Oto reservations; tribal members received allotments, and the remaining acres were opened. The Osages likewise received allotments, but inasmuch as that Nation had a deed to its lands (by purchase from the Cherokees), there was no surplus for white settlement; each Osage received approximately 500 acres as an allotment.

During these runs, lotteries, and auctions, two sections in each township generally were withheld for the support of public education, and other blocks of land were reserved for the Wichita Mountain National Forest and for Fort Sill. The income from leasing these school lands helped finance the 1,000 public schools that were open in Oklahoma by 1900. These openings caused the population of the territory to grow from some 60,000 in 1890 to more than 400,000 by 1900.

For these new citizens of Oklahoma Territory, life at first proved hard. Usually those who settled on the land fell into one of three categories: farmers, some of them destitute and seeking a place to begin anew or else well-to-do farmers, moving to escape the extreme temperatures of the north; speculators making every run in order to get land for quick sale; and people with little purpose, drifters and irresponsible vagrants who never lived long in one place. Most were young men desperately intent on making a success in the new land, for they realized the frontier was closing and that Oklahoma might be their last chance for inexpensive land. Descriptions of these settlers range from "polite but crude" to "secretive and talkative." In their new homeland they suffered from shortages of fuel and building materials, they knew loneliness and isolation, and they toiled long hours to clear and plow fields, erect fences, and put up some type of shelter, generally a sod dugout. Many came without furniture, and thus their new accommodations were rough-hewn and makeshift.

Once in Oklahoma they struggled to get a crop in and then tried to eke out an existence until harvest time. When drought came, as it frequently did, many of the men left the farm to seek employment in town while their women and children remained behind to walk along the creeks gathering plums, berries, wild greens, and black haws. As one pioneer woman recalled, "We ate mulberries that first spring that grew wild on the creek, and we had so many I never

Marshall McCully, a homesteader in the Cherokee Outlet, constructed this sod house on his claim in present-day Major County. The structure is now preserved and operated as a historic site by the Oklahoma Historical Society. OHS

liked them since." Gradually their lot improved as crops were harvested and sold. As that same pioneer woman remembered, "It was hard going at first, but we got a little ahead every year, until we added to our one room, and even had nice furniture. I kept some chickens, we had our own cow, a garden, and lived very well. Our menu never varied much—corn bread, sorghum molasses, and a lot of gravy—but we stayed healthy." One sign that a family was doing more than "getting by" was when it moved out of a dugout into a frame house.

During the first years in the Cherokee Outlet the only crop that seemed to do well was turnips, and people often ate these three times a day. Housewives taxed their cooking abilities trying to find new ways to prepare turnips. One story that was often told concerned a man from Enid who, on a trip to Oklahoma City in the fall of 1894, came down to the hotel restaurant for breakfast and, without looking at the menu, absentmindedly told the waitress, "I believe I'll have my turnips fried this morning."

Those who settled in the towns fared somewhat better, although their lot was not easy. There were quarrels over ownership of lots, and, as in Oklahoma City, rival township companies causing endless arguments over titles. Some who made the run hoped to get choice lots which could be sold quickly at a handsome profit, but most came with the intention of building a home and business. A few merchants arrived with train carloads of lumber and merchandise, and in a few days they had wooden stores open and doing a brisk business. Other less prosperous storekeepers had to make do in tents for weeks and even months. And there were a

few scoundrels intent on fleecing the new settlers—as, for example, the well-dressed man who arrived in Guthrie with a large iron safe; placing a board across two barrels, he erected a large sign stating that his "bank" was open and then, after taking in thousands of dollars in deposits, departed the territory never to be seen again. Most town dwellers, like their counterparts on farms, worked hard, put aside a few dollars each month, and gradually saw their lot improve.

Suffering perhaps more than any other group were the blacks who came to Oklahoma seeking a new home where they might find social equality. Blacks long had been associated with the region, for they had come as slaves to the Five Civilized Tribes, as runaways, and as soldiers. During the late 1870s many blacks fled Mississippi and Alabama to homestead in Kansas (the "Exodusters" they were called), and they had founded all-black communities such as Nicodemus (in central Kansas). A leader in this movement was Edward P. McCabe. Born in 1850 in Troy, New York, McCabe eventually reached Chicago, completed a law degree, and became a staunch Republican. Moving to Kansas, he worked hard for the party and at age thirty-three was named state auditor of Kansas. By the late 1880s, however, the town of Nicodemus was dying and McCabe's political power in Kansas was waning. He chose to migrate to the new Oklahoma Territory, as did many other blacks in Kansas. In this move they were aided by the Oklahoma Immigration Association, founded to help blacks move to the new territory.

Arriving in Guthrie in May of 1890, McCabe found rumors circulating that through his political connections in the Republican Party he was to be named governor, and Oklahoma was to be an all-black state. Such did not prove to be the case, however. McCabe's goal's were to show that black colonization would work and to carve out a new power base for himself. His vehicle for both was the town of Langston, which he helped establish shortly after he arrived. His newspaper, the *Langston City Herald,* promoted black migration, instructed prospective settlers on the preparations they should make, and warned of frauds being perpetrated by fast-talking promoters on unsuspecting blacks. One typical fraud involved a promise that for thirty-five to fifty dollars land claims would be guaranteed, but after getting the money the promoters fled. McCabe did increase black immigration to Oklahoma. In 1890 there were approximately 22,000 blacks in the Oklahoma and Indian territories. By 1900 this figure had risen to 56,000.

Soon after his arrival in the Oklahoma Territory, McCabe became treasurer of Logan County. In 1894 he was named secretary of the Republican Territorial League, and three years later he became assistant territorial auditor. Moreover, he was able to persuade the legislature in 1897 to create a Colored Agricultural and Normal College at Langston so that blacks could secure an education. Despite McCabe's efforts, however, Langston's population gradually declined from a high of around 2,000 people to about 250 in 1907; only the presence of the college saved it from extinction. In 1907, with the coming of statehood and dominance by a white-oriented Democratic Party, McCabe left Oklahoma, his dream of a sanctuary where blacks would receive justice seemingly blocked.

For all Oklahoma's settlers, frontier life was not totally bleak. Long hours of hard labor made them appreciate small luxuries and opportunities for socializing. Revivals, community dances, all-night sings, communal Christmas observances—all made life more enjoyable by ending for a short time the loneliness of the new, hard land.

Outlaw gangs, however, did continue to disturb honest people both in the Oklahoma and Indian territories, finding the isolation and shortage of peace officers on the frontier to their liking. The Daltons, the Doolins, and the Starrs could hide in the Indian Territory after committing their crimes, but gradually the marshals and sheriffs caught up with them. Some outlaws were sent to prison in Kansas (Oklahoma Territory made an agreement with Kansas whereby prisoners were sent to the Kansas State prison at Lansing). Others were killed or driven out of the territory by peace officers such as Heck Thomas, Bill Tilghman, Chris Madsen, Charles Colcord, or Frank Canton. Shortly after the turn of the twentieth century, most of the outlaw gangs had disappeared.

Gradually the speculator and drifter moved from Oklahoma to seek elsewhere that which they would never find. Left behind were the solid, hard-working people who would build a dynamic culture and a vibrant economy. Yet troubling the solid citizens these years was a desire for total self-government free from carpetbag northern politicians appointed in Washington. They wanted statehood—and were willing to work for it.

Prosperity came slowly to Oklahoma settlers, but by the mid-1890s many farmers had progressed from sod house or dugout to a frame home. OHS

CHAPTER XI

Politics, White and Red

Chitto Harjo was the leader of the "Snake Indians" who opposed allotment and abolition of tribal governments in the 1890s. Harjo was arrested by federal marshals and United States cavalry in 1901. His followers were assigned allotments in the western portion of the nation, land that in the 1910s became valuable with the discovery of the Cushing Oil Field. OHS

*L*ate in life George W. Steele, Oklahoma's first territorial governor, commented, "I did not expect to become permanently identified with Oklahoma, so I concluded to step aside and make room for someone who did." He submitted his resignation on October 3, 1891, but served until November 8 when Robert Martin, secretary of the territory, assumed the position of acting governor. Steele, who had intended to serve only five or six months, had completed seventeen months in office. He then returned to Indiana and was reelected to Congress. When he died in Marion, Ohio, in 1922, the flag in Oklahoma was flown at half-mast.

Martin's tenure was brief as acting governor—slightly less than three months. Born in Pennsylvania in 1833, Martin was a graduate of Westminster College in Ohio, a lawyer, a veteran of the Civil War, and a minor politician. He came to Oklahoma in 1889, settling at Harrison on the North Canadian River. Through old friends in Ohio (Senators John Sherman and William McKinley) he was appointed first secretary of the territory and thus became acting governor when Steele resigned. His duties as governor proved extremely light: issuing the Thanksgiving proclamation in 1891, signing the charter of a bank in Stillwater, and performing ceremonial duties on several occasions. When President Benjamin Harrison was considering names for a new territorial governor, Martin's name was taken from the list because the president thought him an extremely effective territorial secretary. Martin relinquished the office on February 2, 1892, and resided in Guthrie until his death in 1897.

When Steele resigned, the people of Oklahoma, tired of "carpetbagging," were loud in their demand that the president appoint a resident to the office and Harrison honored these demands—to some extent. He chose Abraham J. Seay, an associate justice of the territorial supreme court. Born in

The home of territorial governor Abraham J. Seay is preserved by the Oklahoma Department of Tourism and Recreation as an historic site. Located in Kingfisher, the Seay Mansion preserves a piece of Oklahoma's early history. Photo by Jim Argo

Virginia in 1832, Seay moved to Missouri with his family at age three, later finding success as a teacher, lawyer, judge, businessman, banker, and politician. A Republican, he was a Civil War veteran financially secure who wanted some appointive office. This came in 1890 when he moved to Oklahoma as an associate justice.

Inaugurated governor on February 2, 1892, Seay offended some Oklahomans by his appointment of non-residents to territorial jobs, which caused a split in the Republican Party in the territory: those supporting him and those opposing him. During his sixteen months in office, however, there was growth and change: the Cheyenne-Arapaho lands were opened to white settlement, an official territorial exhibit was sent to the Columbian Exposition in Chicago, and a legislative session was held during which Seay urged the upgrading of the territory's public schools. He also worked actively on behalf of higher education, and he pushed hard for statehood. In the election in the fall of 1892, no party emerged with a clear majority, and Seay proved unable to work in harmony with either house. His major accomplishment was to get $10,000 appropriated to buy "seeds for the Seedless." Seay was also noted for his favorable attitude toward

blacks and his unfavorable attitude toward "Jim Crow" laws, although some members of the legislature wanted to restrict the rights of blacks, as in several Southern states at this time. Yet Seay's tenure as governor was short because Grover Cleveland, a Democrat, was elected President in 1892. On May 10, 1893, Seay spoke at the inauguration of his successor, stating that he felt as if he were participating in the "graveyard ceremonies of . . . [my] own funeral." Afterward he devoted himself to his business interests, which included banks, hotels, and land. He died in 1915 and was buried in Kingfisher.

William C. Renfrow, the only Democrat—and Confederate veteran—to serve as territorial governor, was born in North Carolina in 1845. Moving to Arkansas after the Civil War, he lived there until 1889 when he moved to Norman to become majority stockholder in a bank and a local landowner. Taking office on May 10, 1893, Renfrow suffered few outcries of "carpetbagging," but his appointment of Democrats to many positions formerly held by Republicans did outrage many newspaper editors, most of whom were Republican. Especially outspoken was Frank Greer, publisher of the *Oklahoma State Capital* (later the *Daily*

State Capital) at Guthrie.

During Renfrow's four years in office the Cherokee Outlet, the Kickapoo Reservation, and Greer County became part of the territory. Despite working with a legislature sometimes dominated by Republicans, Renfrow secured legislation that in 1897 opened the Colored Agricultural and Normal School at Langston (now Langston University) and Northwest Normal School at Alva, and he pushed for creation of a territorial insane asylum at Norman. Moreover, Renfrow continually urged that the Oklahoma and Indian territories be combined and admitted as a state. The election of a Republican president in 1896 meant the end of Renfrow's administration, and on May 24, 1897, he saw his successor inaugurated. He then established the Renfrow Mining and Royalty Company to mine lead and zinc, and in 1920 went into oil exploration with his Mirindo Oil Company. He died in 1922 and was buried in Russellville, Arkansas.

With Republican William McKinley in the White House early in 1897, Cassius M. Barnes was appointed governor. Born in 1845 in New York, he grew to manhood in Michigan, where he trained as a telegrapher and went to work for Western Union at age twelve. During the Civil War he was a military telegrapher. After the war he moved to Arkansas, where he became involved in business and politics, then came to Oklahoma in 1889 as receiver for the United States Land Office at Guthrie. While the Democrats were in office, he studied law, was admitted to the bar, and was active in fraternal organizations such as the Masonic Lodge, the Knights of Pythias, and the Grand Army of the Republic. During the election of 1896, Oklahoma's Republicans split badly, and Barnes led the minority faction which did support McKinley's presidential bid, and on April 21, 1897, he was appointed governor.

The campus of Southwestern Oklahoma State University in Weatherford was established as a normal school during the administration of Governor Cassius M. Barnes. OHS

Barnes' main contribution as governor was the improvement of educational facilities in the territory. He encouraged the legislature to appropriate funds and erect buildings at the new normal school at Alva and at the Colored Agricultural and Normal College at Langston. He also persuaded the legislature in 1897 to create Southwestern Normal at Weatherford and in 1901 the University Preparatory School at Tonkawa (present-day Northern Oklahoma College), bringing to seven the number of territorial institutions of higher learning. Moreover, Barnes sought more funds for common school education and for better care of the insane, the aged, and the disabled. Working with Dennis T. Flynn, Oklahoma's delegate to Congress, Barnes secured in 1900 congressional passage of a Free Homes Bill. This allowed free settlement on unoccupied lands in the territory and canceled back payments owed to the government for homesteads taken in prior land runs, saving Oklahomans an estimated fifteen million dollars that otherwise would have been spent on land.

Continued feuding within Oklahoma's Republican ranks brought a delegation to Washington in 1901 petitioning that Barnes not be reappointed by President McKinley. To heal the party split, McKinley heeded the petition and appointed William M. Jenkins to succeed Barnes. Barnes retired to practice law in Guthrie—and later served two terms as its mayor. In 1910 he moved to Leavenworth, Kansas, and later to New Mexico, where he died in 1925. His body was returned to Guthrie for burial.

Jenkins, who had been secretary of the territory, was the first non-Civil War veteran to govern Oklahoma. As an adult he had practiced law in Iowa and Kansas until making the run for land in the Cherokee Outlet in 1893 and settling in a dugout in Kay County. A friend of President McKinley, he was appointed secretary of the territory in 1897. In this position he steered a neutral course between the two factions of the Republican Party. For this reason he was named governor on April 15, 1901, fol-

Territorial Normal School, later renamed Central State University, was the first territorial school of higher education to hold classes in the territory. Old North Tower is the symbol of this institution charged with training Oklahoma's teachers. OHS

lowing Barnes' ouster.

During Jenkins' short term in office, Oklahoma expanded with the opening of the Kiowa-Comanche and the Wichita-Caddo lands. Jenkins made needed reforms in the method of leasing school lands, including introducing an equitable system of appraising them for lease. When he attempted to remove certain members of various territorial boards governing the educational institutions, however, he ran afoul of the factional split in the Republican Party. In October 1901, only six months after his inauguration, formal charges were lodged with the Secretary of the Interior that Jenkins secretly owned stock in the Oklahoma Sanitarium Company of Norman and was profiting from its contract with the territory to care for the insane. At this point many of his political friends deserted him, and President McKinley had been assassinated. Theodore Roosevelt met with Jenkins on November 28, 1901, at the White House, and told him that while he did not consider him dishonest, he was indiscreet and could not continue in office. Two days later a presidential order formalized Jenkins' removal, stating that the governor had "an entire lack of appreciation of the duties of his office." Two years later an Oklahoma legislative investigation completely cleared him of any wrongdoing. He lived until 1941, most of that time in Sapulpa.

The territorial secretary, William C. Grimes, served a ten-day stint as acting governor while President Roosevelt searched for a candidate that would close the split in the Republican Party. When long-time Oklahoma resident Thompson B. Ferguson was appointed, Grimes returned to his duties as secretary. Ferguson, educated to be a teacher, had gradually turned his attention to journalism before making the run of 1889. However, he returned to Kansas soon afterward, coming back to Oklahoma in 1892 to establish the *Watonga Republican.*

Ferguson well understood the pitfalls of trying to reunite the Oklahoma Republican Party, for during Jenkins' term he had compared Oklahoma to a bronco, and on another occasion saying that to govern it "requires just as much bravery as it did to sail into Manila Bay, or to face the deadly Spanish Mausers at San Juan Hill."

After a quiet inaugural on December 9, 1901, Ferguson soothed partisan factions in the Republican Party by making all his

Thompson B. Ferguson served the longest term of office as Oklahoma's territorial governor, from 1901 to 1906. OHS

appointments on the basis of merit. Moreover, he moved to acquire the property and buildings at Fort Supply, recently abandoned by the Army, to be used to house the insane. This enabled him to end the contract with the Oklahoma Sanitarium Company in Norman, long a cause of quarrels. Ferguson worked hard to promote wise money management and sound financial planning, and he worked to secure additional funding for education, viewing with special pride the record $1,459,623 appropriated for common schools in 1904. He also wanted to cut the number of institutions of higher learning, however, stating, "One good Normal, one good University, one good Agricultural College is all that is required." The legislature pleased him in 1905 by enacting legislation allowing the consolidation of rural school districts. He also helped organize the territorial board of agriculture authorized in 1902. Ferguson was proud of Oklahoma, commenting in one report to the secretary of the interior that the territory was the "most progressive of any Western Commonwealth" and that "a story what would sound like a fairy tale might be truthfully written of the progress and advancement of the Territory of Oklahoma, the 'land of the Fair God.'"

Statehood might have been attained by Oklahoma during Ferguson's term had he not been opposed to joint statehood with the Indian Territory. He believed that consolidation of the two "would make Oklahoma a southern state" and "would fill her with southern people, a civilization many years behind our own." He might have been reappointed governor by Roosevelt had not an old friend of the president, Frank Frantz, wanted the job. Ferguson thus returned to private life on January 13, 1906, and continued to run his newspaper at Watonga until his death in 1921.

Frank Frantz, Oklahoma's last territorial governor, was also its youngest, coming to office at age thirty-seven. Born in Illinois in 1869, he had attended Eureka College in Illinois before moving to Oklahoma in 1894 to operate a lumber and hardware store at Medford. He subsequently moved to California and then to Arizona, enlisting in the Rough Riders in 1898. During the Spanish American War he so distinguished himself at San Juan Hill that he was given a battlefield promotion to captain—and earned the friendship of Theodore Roosevelt. Moving to Oklahoma in 1900, he settled at Enid to operate a hardware store and then, with Roosevelt's sponsorship, became postmaster there. In 1904 he became Indian agent to the Osage, a position involving great difficulties because oil and gas had been discovered on their lands, and many people sought entry onto their rolls to share in the wealth. In November 1905, because of his praiseworthy handling of this situation, Frantz was named governor.

Inaugurated on January 13, 1906, Frantz commented, "The lesson of the present day is progress with honor. The spirit in the very air is for fair play . . . . I shall try to be governor of all the people of the territory." No legislative sessions were held during his term, but he used the time to advantage. In one way or another he saved an estimated $200 million for the common school fund. At his urging the territory filed suits against the Rock Island and the St. Louis and San Francisco railroads to force them to lower their freight rates by 12 percent, and then he moved to prevent drilling for oil on school lands. Naturally these actions raised storms of political protest, and his last months in office were marked by bitter charges and denunciations. With passage of the Omnibus Statehood Bill on June 14, 1906, popular election of a governor was on the horizon, and Frantz was defeated as voters chose an almost totally Democratic slate. Frantz moved to Colorado to enter the oil business, returning to Tulsa in 1915 as head of the land department of Cosden Oil Company. (When Frantz was elected a member of the Oklahoma Hall of Fame in

1932, other inductees included Charles N. Haskell, who succeeded him as governor of Oklahoma, and William M. Jenkins, who had been removed as governor in 1901.)

The other office of importance to the entire Oklahoma Territory was the delegate to Congress. Territorial delegates could participate in debates but not vote. When Republicans convened in 1890 to nominate a candidate for this position, their choice was David A. Harvey, who would defeat his Democratic challenger on November 4. A little more than a year later, on January 25, 1892, Harvey introduced the first bill in Congress to make Oklahoma a state.

In 1892 Dennis T. Flynn won the Republican nomination for delegate to Congress and in the general election he defeated two others, nominated by the Democrat and Populist parties. Flynn had come to the territory during the run of 1889 to settle in Guthrie, and there he helped write the city charter. He would serve four terms as delegate to Congress and would be the dominant figure in one faction of the Republican Party in the territory. In 1893 Flynn quickly secured passage of an act giving Oklahomans more time to pay the government for their lands; poor crops and low prices had made it difficult for them to make their land payments in the allotted five years.

This measure made Flynn extremely popular, and he was easily reelected in 1894. Yet the growing discontent of farmers two years later at their hard lot and the depression then gripping the nation caused them to turn against Flynn. That year the Populists and the Democrats both nominated James Y. Callahan for territorial delegate, and he defeated Flynn. Callahan's service was undistinguished, and in 1898, following a return of general prosperity, Flynn was reelected.

Early in 1900 Flynn secured passage of a "Free Homes Bill," which allowed settlers in much of western Oklahoma to avoid paying a dollar twenty-five to a dollar fifty an acre for their homesteads. Thus in November that year he easily won reelection. Two years later Flynn chose not to seek reelection, whereupon Republicans nominated Bird S. McGuire of Pawnee. McGuire served as territorial delegate until statehood in 1907, winning reelection in 1904 and 1906, but his term was marked by bitter quarreling as statehood approached. McGuire, a Republican, favored the creation of a state out of Oklahoma Territory alone, while the Democrats favored joint statehood with the Indian Territory. When statehood became a reality, McGuire was elected to Congress from the First District, one of the

few Republicans to win office in that election.

The sessions of the Oklahoma territorial legislature reflected the national struggle between Republicans and Democrats. During most of these years the Republicans controlled the legislature. However, when Democrats and Populists joined forces, the Democrats were able to control both houses of the legislature from 1896 to 1900, the lower house from 1900 to 1902, and the upper house from 1902 to 1904. During the seventeen years the area was a territory, there were several recurring issues: the location of the charitable or educational institutions, the permanent location of the capital, and school financing.

In the first territorial legislature the spoils were divided among several towns: Stillwater received the agricultural and mechanical college, Norman was granted the university, and Edmond received the normal school. No penitentiary was created because Ira N. Terrill, a Populist member of the first legislature (described by a fellow member as "A wild-eyed, vicious, beastly anarchist"), secured passage of a bill sending Oklahoma's prisoners to the Kansas State Penitentiary at Lansing. This was intended to save money for the territory. Ironically Terrill was among the first Oklahomans sent to Lansing, for on January 3, 1891, he was convicted of killing George M. Embrey, who had called him a Sooner. After serving his sentence, Terrill wrote a long poem whose title told what he thought had happened to Oklahoma: "A Purgatory Made of Paradise."

The permanent location of the capital was a continuing fight. The Organic Act of 1890 creating the territory had stated that the capital would temporarily be at Guthrie. In the first legislative session Guthrie naturally sought to retain this plum, but after a bitter fight the legislature in 1890 voted to move to Oklahoma City, an action vetoed by Governor Steele. The following year Congress passed an act prohibiting the Oklahoma legislature from moving the capital from Guthrie, but also forbidding the building of a capitol building. For the remainder of the territorial years the capital stayed at Guthrie, operating out of rented business buildings.

The Organic Act of 1890 made no provision for opening a public school system, however it did carry a federal appropriation

James Y. Callahan was elected territorial delegate to Congress on a Democratic-Populist fusion ticket in the election of 1896. He served a single term of office. OHS

of $50,000 for use in erecting a temporary system, and the Organic Act provided that two sections in each township were to be reserved for the support of education. In December 1890 the legislature used the $50,000 to create a system of elementary and high schools, and it authorized the election of local school boards to oversee the various school districts. The people who had rushed to Oklahoma held the traditional frontier view that education was valuable, and by the fall of 1891 more than 400 school districts were active with almost 10,000 students enrolled. In 1893, when the school lands were leased, more than $100,000 was secured, and with this money local school districts began making improvements.

These schools at first were raw and crude. Georgia Coffey Camp later recalled that her father, George Coffey, in 1893 opened a school in the Cherokee Outlet "in a one-room dugout .... with only a dirt floor and no furniture, no books, and no other supplies." He did this "with a few books of his own, Bibles, almanacs, and old papers

brought by some fourteen students . . . ." In Kay County in 1894 Cora Waugh was persuaded to teach local students for three months for seventy-five dollars in a sod smokehouse loaned by a local farmer. Her daughter later recalled:

Seventeen pupils in grades one through eight sat on homemade benches. Slates and textbooks from Kansas schools were used. The March wind blew so much dirt into the schoolroom that the teacher and pupils could not remove their sunbonnets and straw hats. Outside, they played ball. A mother had sewn a string ball. A flat board was their bat.

Despite the hard conditions, these schools trained young Oklahomans to read and write, to do arithmetic, to mind their manners, and to perform as useful citizens. Improvements gradually were made, and soon a stream of young men and women were graduated from these early institutions.

While the lands of the Oklahoma Territory were being opened, while farms and

As Oklahoma Territory continued to grow and prosper, new businesses were established to provide services to the expanding population. D.I. Brown's store sold most goods that farmers would need, and his grain elevator provided storage for wheat to be shipped to market. Courtesy, Western History Collections, University of Oklahoma Library

ranches were being developed, while railroads were transporting agricultural produce out and manufactured goods in, while schools and churches were doing their work, and while territorial, county, and city officials were overseeing the growth of industry, roads, and farms, the residents of the Indian Territory were seeing an end to their dreams. No longer were the tribes independent nations existing within the boundaries of the United States and protected by treaties that guaranteed them sovereign status. Many Indians resisted these changes, but the federal government was dedicated to bringing them into the mainstream of American national life. Nevertheless by 1890 the various tribes still owned all the lands in the Indian Territory, and Indians held all political offices.

Passage of the Dawes Severalty Act of 1887 caused many non-Indians to believe that the reservations would soon be broken up by allotment and that surplus lands then would be available for settlement (although this act expressly exempted the Five Civilized Tribes from its provisions). The result was that by 1894 there were 250,000 non-Indians living in the Indian-Territory—with no schools of their own, no legal title to land, and few legal protections or restraints. In cities such as Tahlequah and Muskogee the tribal governments could maintain order, but in rural areas crime was rampant. Moreover, within each tribe a few dozen individuals controlled thousands of acres of the best land, while the remainder of the Indians lived at the subsistence level. Yet when the Jerome (or Cherokee) Commission, created in 1889, tried to discuss allotment of lands, the leaders of the Five Civilized Tribes expressed no interest in negotiating.

Congress responded in 1893 by creating the Dawes Commission (named for its chairman, Henry L. Dawes of Massachusetts) to negotiate allotment with the Five Civilized Tribes. The other members of this commission were A.S. McKennon and M.H. Kidd. When this commission arrived in the Indian Territory in February 1894 and met with delegates of the tribes at Checotah, the Indians flatly rejected allotment, feeling that this would lead to white domination of the lands promised to them by treaty and an end to their way of life. Subsequent meetings with individual tribal leaders also accomplished nothing, whereupon Congress in 1895 increased federal authority by enlarging the number of federal courts in the Indian Territory to three. These courts were given authority over whites in the territory, as well as in cases involving the death penalty or long imprisonment. Sitting together in McAlester, these three judges also constituted an appellate court. Congress in March 1895 also provided for the surveying of the Indian Territory by the United States Geological Survey, a move obviously made in anticipation of allotment of individual homesteads.

Still the Five Civilized Tribes resisted. When the Dawes Commission met with tribal leaders at Eufaula in June of 1895, nothing could be accomplished. A year later Congress took more drastic action, authorizing the Dawes Commission to compile tribal rolls for the purpose of making allotments—with or without the help of the tribal governments. Included in this act was a statement that the United States would "establish a government in the Indian Territory which would rectify the many inequalities and discriminations now existing in said Territory and afford needful protection to the lives and property of all citizens and residents thereof." This was an obvious reference to the status of the many whites living in the territory.

The strong stance taken by Congress stimulated some tribal leaders to begin serious negotiations. First to accept the inevitable were the Chickasaws and Choctaws. Their leaders made one agreement in December 1896 at Muskogee. When this proved unacceptable to their followers, they negotiated another at Atoka the following April 23. This Atoka Agreement, the first break in the solid front of the Five Civilized Tribes, provided that timber and mineral-bearing tribal lands might be reserved for the benefit of the tribes and the remaining lands surveyed for allotment into homesteads and city lots. Moreover, it stipulated that tribal governments would survive for only an additional eight years past March 4, 1898, after which tribal members would be citizens of the United States. By this agreement the two tribes would lose both their reservations and their governments. The members of both tribes resisted ratifying the Atoka Agreement for a time, but eventually it was accepted—and spelled the end of separate Indian Nations and a separate Indian Territory. A similar agreement was reached with the Seminoles shortly afterward, and it

The Dawes General Allotment Act required that members of the Five Civilized Tribes be listed on tribal rolls and that each member of the tribes be allotted land in severalty to prepare the Indian Territory for statehood. This commission camp near Okmulgee was enrolling members of the Creek Nation prior to issuing them allotments. OHS

The Dawes Commission enrolled members of the Five Civilized Tribes prior to issuing them allotments. Taking to the field near Okmulgee to enroll members of the Creek Nation, the commission members posed for this photograph. OHS

was quickly ratified. Congress on July 1, 1898, accepted the Seminole settlement, making it the first fully implemented.

While the Choctaws and Chickasaws were dragging their heels at adopting the Atoka Agreement and while the Creeks and Cherokees were resisting allotments totally, Congress passed yet another measure signaling the end of the Indian Territory. The Curtis Act of June 28, 1898, was named for

its author, Charles Curtis, a mixed-blood Kansa Indian (who later would be vice-president of the United States). This legislation destroyed the powers of the tribal governments by stipulating that the payment of tribal funds thereafter would be made directly to individual tribal members, and it ended the system of tribal courts by providing that everyone—red, black, and white—was subject to the laws of the United States or of the state of Arkansas. In addition, it called for a survey of tribal lands, the allotment of lands to individuals on the basis of tribal rolls compiled by the Dawes Commission, the erection of a system of schools open to all children, the leasing of tribal mineral lands by the secretary of the interior, the incorporation of towns in the territory, and voting by all citizens in these towns. All these provisions were to be fully effective at the end of eight years, and tribal government would cease on March 4, 1906.

Members of the Five Civilized Tribes fully understood the importance of the Curtis Act. In August 1898 the Choctaws and Chickasaws ratified the Atoka Agreement, and the Creeks and Cherokees conceded defeat in 1900. Agreements made with the last two tribes were ratified in 1901. These provided for an end to tribal government on March 4, 1906, ended tribal courts, and began liquidating tribal holdings. Some diehard members of the Cherokee tribe, organized as the Keetoowah Society, refused to appear to be enrolled by the Dawes Commission; claiming 5,000 members, the Keetoowah Society was composed largely of descendants of the anti-treaty party. It continues to be a force in northeastern Oklahoma to the present, although it has gradually become somewhat akin to a religion (or to a fraternal organization).

Using United States marshals and their deputies for protection, the Dawes Commission proceeded with the work of making tribal rolls. Henry L. Dawes was the nominal head of this commission until his death in 1903, but Tams Bixby, who became a member in 1897, actually directed most of the commission's work. The opposition was most violent among a faction of Creeks led by Chitto Harjo (also known as Crazy Snake). Harjo called a general council to meet late in 1900 for rebellious Creeks intent upon establishing their own Creek Nation and government, but Creek Chief Pleasant Porter used United States marshals to disperse the group. Then in January 1901 Harjo held his council and his followers tried to coerce tribal members not to accept allotments. This "Crazy Snake Rebellion" ended when the United States cavalry arrived and arrested ninety-four of the ringleaders. Tried at Muskogee, they were released after promising to accept allotment.

With or without Indian cooperation, the Dawes Commission proceeded in making

Pleasant Porter, Creek principal chief, served as president of the Sequoyah Statehood Convention in 1905. Although the movement to create the state of Sequoyah did not succeed, the Indian leadership of the Indian Territory did join the bandwagon to support single statehood for Oklahoma. OHS

tribal rolls in order to determine which individuals legally were entitled to land allotments. In 1905 Congress abolished the Dawes Commission, replacing it with the Commission to the Five Civilized Tribes, which operated until 1914. Between June 1898 and March 1907, when work was completed, this commission established that the Five Civilized Tribes held 19,525,966 acres (the Cherokees had 4,420,068 acres, the Choctaws 6,953,048, the Creeks 3,079,095, the Chickasaws 4,707,903, and the Seminoles 365,852). A total of 101,526 were enrolled (41,693 Cherokees, 25,091 Choctaws, 18,812 Creeks, 10,955 Chickasaws, 3,119 Seminoles, plus individuals from other tribes in that area), while more than 200,000 whites and blacks who sought enrollment—and land—were rejected. Almost sixteen million acres were allotted to those enrolled, and the remaining three-and-a-half million acres were opened to sale at public auction. Some tribal mineral lands were reserved, and the funds derived from the auction of mining rights were held in trust for the tribal members.

By March 4, 1906, when tribal government ceased among the Five Civilized Tribes, the Indian Territory was approaching a point where statehood seemed possible, as was the case in the Oklahoma Territory. The only question involved was whether there would be two states or one.

Soon to become citizens of the United States, the people of Oklahoma City are preparing for a genuine Fourth of July celebration

THE DAILY OKLAHOMAN

12,992 DAILY AVERAGE FOR MAY

LARGEST DAILY NEWSPAPER IN GREATER OKLAHOMA

VOL. 18. NO. 55   OKLAHOMA CITY, OKLAHOMA, SUNDAY, JUNE 17, 1906.   PRICE 5 CENTS

THE PRESIDENT HAS SIGNED THE STATEHOOD BILL

The Final Chapter of the Six Year's Legislative Battle to Make Oklahoma and Indian Territory a State Was Enacted Yesterday Afternoon at 3 O'clock in the Cabinet Room of the White House.

Chief Executive Signed the First Name "Theodore" With Gold Pen and "Roosevelt" With an American Eagle's Quill.

KOREA REVOLTS

JAPS ATTACK THE CITY BLOWING UP THE GATES AND RUSH IN TOWN

MANY PEOPLE KILLED

Koreans Appear to Be Well Armed and Offer Stiff Resistance to On slaughter.

SEE OWNERSHIP

ADVOCATES OF PUBLIC UTILITIES FIND BOAST IN GOVERNMENT OWNERSHIP OF CANALS

CALLS IT JOBBING SCHEME

Warm Debate Is Precipitated in Congress—La Follette Throws Out Warning By Arrangement of Republicans.

GERMANY REPRESENTED

MEN PROMINENT IN THE TWO TERRITORIES WITNESSED THE SIGNING OF THE BILL

LAST CHANCE FOR ARIZONA

IT IS FREE TRADE

REPUBLICAN PARTY MUST ACCEPT THE DOCTRINE OF TARIFF FOR REVENUE ONLY.

DEMOCRATS ARE VICTORIOUS

CLOTH ASSAULTED

DASTARDLY DEED OF JAP SOLDIERS IN CATHEDRAL AT SEUL

WILL CAUSE TROUBLE

HOUSE SUMMARY

SENATE SPECIFIES WHAT AND HOW MATERIALS ARE TO BE BOUGHT

CANTEENS ARE DISCONTINUED

President Is the Arbiter in Matters Pertaining to Canal Supplies—Debate Limited

OKLAHOMAN INDEX

WEATHER FORECAST

CHAPTER XII

The Forty-Sixth Star

The Daily Oklahoman
proudly announced Oklaho-
ma's statehood in this
front-page banner headline
published on Statehood
Day, November 16, 1907.
OHS

A standing joke on the American frontier was that when five people met in the wilderness they immediately began demanding territorial status, and when the population reached 100 they wanted statehood. Oklahoma's population was far more than this: 258,657 by 1890 and 790,391 by 1900. Thus the area qualified in number of residents for statehood at an early date. It was politics, not population, that delayed Oklahoma's admission to statehood.

In the Indian Territory there was little sentiment for joint statehood with the Oklahoma Territory. Indian leaders feared that whites would dominate all offices in a single state government, but when they became convinced that allotments and an end to tribal governments would be forced on them they began work about 1902 to have the Indian Territory become the state of Sequoyah. In the Oklahoma Territory there were no such worries, for the people there definitely wanted statehood. In December 1891 the first Oklahoma Statehood Convention was held in Oklahoma City, and Sidney Clarke prepared a memorial to Congress asking that the two territories be admitted as one state. Introduced in Congress the following month the measure quickly died— but the dream lived on.

During the 1890s several plans concerning statehood were discussed: single statehood for each territory; joint statehood for the two; immediate statehood for Oklahoma with the Indian Territory to be joined later; statehood for Oklahoma with continued territorial status for the Indian Territory; and postponing statehood for both territories until some future date. Partisan politics were heavily involved in these debates because, although the Republicans generally held a majority of offices in the Oklahoma Territory, most observers felt that with the coming of statehood the Democrats would win control of both territories. Thus national Republican leaders were not enthusiastic about

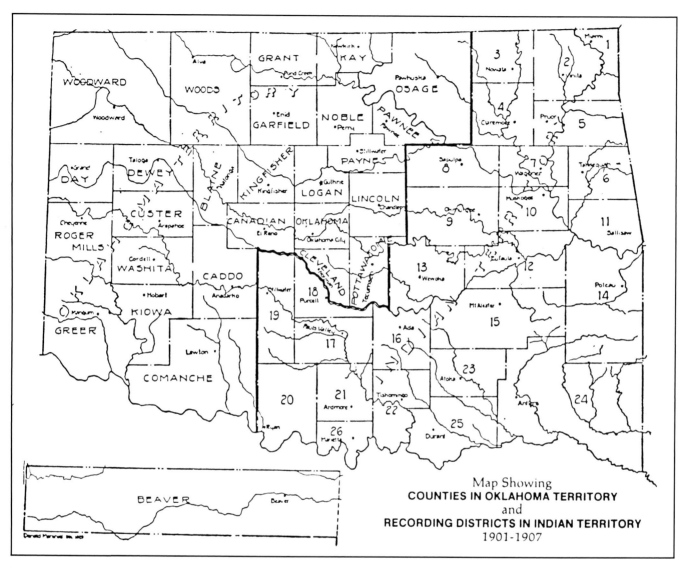

Map Showing
COUNTIES IN OKLAHOMA TERRITORY
and
RECORDING DISTRICTS IN INDIAN TERRITORY
1901-1907

At statehood Oklahoma Territory was divided into twenty-six counties (the Osage Indian Reservation would make an additional one), and the Indian Territory was divided into twenty-six districts. OHS

statehood for Oklahoma, while some Democrats tended to favor separate statehood in order that their party might gain four new seats in the Senate along with several new representatives in the House. A growing number of Republicans argued that with both territories as a single state their party might maintain its power, but party leaders listened to the debate and did nothing.

The pro-statehood forces in Oklahoma Territory annually pushed the introduction of bills in Congress calling for action. These bills usually died in committee as opponents pointed out how small Oklahoma was; however, this argument lost force as additional land was added to the territory with each new run, lottery, and auction. Opponents of Oklahoma statehood then killed the measure by noting the reluctance of the Indians toward joint statehood. As long as the tribes clung to their reservations and their tribal governments, little progress could be made

toward single statehood. The action of the Five Civilized Tribes Commission gradually reduced this argument, and by the early 1900s most Oklahomans favored single statehood as the best means of achieving a quick entrance into the Union.

In 1902 proponents of Oklahoma statehood tried to join their cause with Arizona's and New Mexico's push for admission, and an Omnibus Statehood Bill was introduced in Congress calling for the admission of all three as states. This failed, as did similar attempts in 1903 and 1904. Yet the persistence of this effort gradually convinced leaders in the Indian Territory that they must act quickly if they were to prevent unification of their area with Oklahoma.

At a meeting in Eufaula in 1902, representatives of the tribes formed an executive committee to study alternatives, but nothing came of the effort. Then in July 1905 tribal leaders issued a call for the election of dele-

This was the homestead allotment of Alexander L. Posey, a Creek Indian poet who served as secretary of the Sequoyah Statehood Convention. Courtesy, The Thomas Gilcrease Institute of American History and Art, Tulsa, Oklahoma

ALLOTMENT DEED.   Creek Indian ROLL. NO 3671

THE MUSKOGEE (CREEK) NATION,
INDIAN TERRITORY.

To all Whom These Presents Shall Come, Greeting:

WHEREAS, By the Act of Congress approved March 1, 1901 (31 Stats., 861), agreement ratified by the Creek Nation May 25, 1901, it was provided that all lands of the Muskogee (Creek) Tribe of Indians, in Indian Territory, except as therein provided, should be allotted among the citizens of said tribe by the United States Commission to the Five Civilized Tribes so as to give to each an equal share of the whole in value, as nearly as may be, and

WHEREAS, It was provided by said Act of Congress that each citizen shall select, or have selected for him, from his allotment forty acres of land as a homestead for which he shall have a separate deed, and

WHEREAS, The said Commission to the Five Civilized Tribes has certified that the land hereinafter described has been selected by or on behalf of _____

____Alexander L. Posey_____, a citizen of said tribe, as an allotment, exclusive of a forty acre homestead, as aforesaid,

NOW, THEREFORE, I, the undersigned, the Principal Chief of the Muskogee (Creek) Nation, by virtue of the power and authority vested in me by the aforesaid Act of the Congress of the United States, have granted and conveyed and by these presents do grant and convey unto the said

_____Alexander L. Posey_____

all right, title and interest of the Muskogee (Creek) Nation and of all other citizens of said Nation in and to the following described land, viz:___ The West Half of the North East Quarter, and the South East Quarter of the North East Quarter of Section Seventeen (17), Township Ten (10) North, and Range Fifteen (15) East,

of the Indian Base and Meridian, in Indian Territory, containing___ One Hundred and Twenty (120) _____ acres, more or less, as the case may be, according to the United States survey thereof, subject, however, to all provisions of said Act of Congress relating to appraisement and valuation, and to the provisions of the Act of Congress approved June 30, 1902 (Public No.200).

IN WITNESS WHEREOF, I, the Principal Chief of the Muskogee (Creek) Nation, have hereunto set my hand and caused the Great Seal of said Nation to be affixed this____ 3rd

day of____ September, A. D. 1902.

P. Porter
Principal Chief of the Muskogee (Creek) Nation.

Department of the Interior,

Approved   DEC 22 1902 .190 .

Thos. Ryan
Secretary,
Acting.

Right
Green McCurtain, principal chief of the Choctaw Nation, also served as a vice-president of the Sequoyah Statehood Convention. OHS

Far right
Charles Nathaniel Haskell, a recently arrived resident of the Creek Nation, represented the Creek Indians at the Sequoyah Statehood Convention. He later served as delegate to the Oklahoma Constitutional Convention and was elected as the first governor of Oklahoma. OHS

gates to a constitutional convention, known as the Sequoyah Convention, to meet at Muskogee on August 21. Both white and red residents of the Indian Territory elected 182 delegates, the first time the two races had worked in harmony to achieve any major goal. Chief Pleasant Porter of the Creek Nation was elected president, and Alexander Posey, the noted Creek poet, was chosen its secretary. Five vice-presidents represented the various tribes: W.C. Rogers, for the Cherokees; Green McCurtain, for the Choctaws; John Brown, for the Seminoles; William "Alfalfa Bill" Murray, for the Chickasaws; and Charles N. Haskell, for the Creeks.

Haskell was a non-Indian railroad promoter and attorney who had moved to Muskogee in 1901 and who believed that statehood would benefit his commercial interests as well as those of the people of both territories. Thus he worked to convince the delegates that if separate statehood failed they should drop their opposition to single state-

hood with the Oklahoma Territory, thereby clearing the way for the area's admission to the Union. Murray, a thirty-six-year-old non-Indian who had moved to Tishomingo in 1898 and had married into the Chickasaw Nation, promoted the same ideas.

W.W. Hastings, a Cherokee, chaired the committee that drafted the proposed constitution. The document was a statement of Indian hopes and aspirations couched in terms similar to those of the American Constitution and the Bill of Rights. It called for creation of a state named Sequoyah with forty-eight counties, a two-house legislature, a supreme court and judicial system, and Fort Gibson as the capital (despite the fact that Muskogee offered to erect a capitol costing one million dollars if it was named the capital). After the convention adjourned Haskell and Murray led the campaign for popular ratification of the document, and in an election held on November 7, 1905, residents of the Indian Territory accepted the Sequoyah constitution by a vote of 56,279

Guthrie was to be the territorial capital until 1913, and the new state constitution had to provide for a system of public schools, to exclude alcoholic beverages from what had been the Indian Territory and the Osage Nation for twenty-one years, to accept the Fifteenth Amendment to the Constitution, and to submit the proposed state constitution to a popular vote. It also provided that the new state would have five seats in Congress until the next census (1910), and the federal government committed itself to paying Oklahoma five million dollars to help establish a public school system because no lands had been set aside in the Indian Territory for this purpose.

When the delegates convened in Guthrie on November 20, the Democrats were jubilant that they had won 100 of the 112 seats. When they organized, Alfalfa Bill Murray, also known as "Cocklebur Bill" Murray, was elected president, while Pete Hanraty of McAlester, representing the coal miners

William Henry "Alfalfa Bill" Murray, an inter-married Chickasaw Indian citizen, served his tribe at the Sequoyah Statehood Convention, then was elected president of the Oklahoma Constitutional Convention, voted the first Speaker of the Oklahoma House of Representatives, and later became governor of Oklahoma. OHS

Depicted is a panoramic view of the Oklahoma Constitutional Convention in Guthrie, with President William H. Murray standing at the podium on the left. OHS

to 9,073. Yet this document found little support in Congress, for the president and leaders in Washington had determined on single statehood. The movement for the state of Sequoyah had been worthwhile, however, for afterward Indian leaders honored their commitment not to oppose joint statehood further.

In December 1905, during the debate over the admission of the state of Sequoyah, five separate bills were introduced in the House of Representatives to admit the Oklahoma territories as a single state. When the bill to admit Sequoyah was killed, action began in earnest to pass an enabling act for single statehood, culminating in the Oklahoma Enabling Act on June 16, 1906. This provided for a constitutional convention consisting of fifty-five delegates from the Indian Territory, fifty-five from the Oklahoma Territory, and two from the Osage Nation.

there, was elected vice-president.

Kate Barnard, a young woman who had moved to Oklahoma in 1892 from her native Nebraska, significantly influenced the work of the convention, although she was not a delegate. An ardent reformer, she had fought for and secured higher wages for street workers in Oklahoma City and had helped organize them into the Federal Union, which affiliated with the American Federation of Labor. She also was closely identified with the progressive movement in Oklahoma. Because of her strong political base, she was able to exert pressure on the delegates to include provisions in the constitution such as compulsory education and a clause abolishing child labor in Oklahoma.

The debates and work of the convention lasted until March 1907 and touched on several burning issues that confronted the delegates: Jim Crow laws were not included

Above
The Oklahoma Constitu-
tional Convention was
convened in Guthrie in November 1906. Meetings
were held in the Guthrie
City Hall, pictured in
1906. OHS

Opposite page, left
Peter Hanraty served as
vice-president of the Oklahoma Constitutional Con-
vention, and was later
elected the first chief mine
inspector of Oklahoma.
OHS

Opposite page, right
"Our Kate," Kate Barnard,
influenced the members of
the constitutional convention to pass provisions for a
department of charities and
corrections. She later
served as the first commissioner of that department.
OHS

in the constitution for fear that these might cause it to be rejected by Congress or the president. Nothing was included concerning prohibition. Instead, a rider was attached calling for a referendum on the issue. Congressional districts were gerrymandered to the benefit of Democrats, for the few Republican delegates realized the new state probably would vote overwhelmingly Democratic. As a whole the constitution was designed to limit the power of governmental officials, to strengthen the hand of private citizens through the use of the initiative and referendum, to maintain some balance between the suppliers of governmental services and their users, and to exact the maximum amount of tax revenues from business and industry, while maintaining tight control over their activities.

The constitution contained provisions for a two-house legislature, a governor and other state officials who would serve four-year terms, and a judicial system with a five-member (later a nine-member) supreme court. Lingering memories of the appointment of carpetbaggers insured a provision for the popular election of almost every state official, including the secretary of state, clerk of the supreme court, state mine inspector, and even the state auditor. Because Oklahomans distrusted railroad officials, as did residents of many western states, the constitution provided for a strong

William Jennings Bryan, the Great Commoner, spoke on behalf of the progressive constitution passed by the constitutional convention. When submitted to a vote of the people of Oklahoma, the constitution passed overwhelmingly. OHS

and another for Murray), this committee also subdivided the five large western counties of Woodward, Beaver, Woods, Comanche, and Greer. Subsequently two additional counties were created (Harmon County out of southwestern Greer County in 1909 and Cotton County in 1914 out of the southern part of Comanche County), bringing the total to seventy-seven counties in Oklahoma.

When the convention adjourned on March 15, 1907, everyone expected that Governor Frantz would call for a vote on the constitution within twenty days, but he delayed, saying the work of the convention would not be complete until an official copy of the document had been filed with the secretary of the territory. Murray continued to hold the constitution—he claimed—in an iron strongbox in his home; apparently he wanted to gauge public reaction to the document, and particularly the reaction of President Roosevelt, before filing a final copy with the territorial secretary.

There were many Republicans at the state and national level who were displeased with the constitution. In fact, some minority members of the convention drafted a second constitution that omitted many of the reform features of the majority document. President Roosevelt, when he saw the original, had comments that reportedly were unprintable and suggested several changes in the document. In addition, Woods County citizens who were unhappy at the way their county had been carved into smaller counties filed suit and persuaded a judge to issue an injunction halting ratification.

In the midst of this turmoil Alfalfa Bill Murray called the convention back into session to make some of the changes suggested by President Roosevelt. Meanwhile, the Oklahoma Territorial Supreme Court voided the injunction against a ratification vote, and Murray filed the original copy of the document. At last Governor Frantz called for an election to be held on September 17.

For almost two months the campaign raged. Murray and Haskell, aided by the Great Commoner, William Jennings Bryan, spoke for ratification, saying the vote would be a pronouncement of the people's will. Republicans opposed the document, fearing that it threatened their political dominance in the state, and they were critical of provisions calling for regulation of business and industry. Roosevelt even sent Secretary of War William Howard Taft to Oklahoma to

Corporation Commission popularly elected; it would grant corporate charters and would have the authority to regulate businesses, such as railroads and utilities, with the public interest in mind. Moreover, the popular belief in the value and utility of education led the delegates to include a provision requiring vocational education in the public schools. The delegates also included a popularly elected statewide office, Commissioner of Charities and Corrections, which everyone understood would be filled by the reformer Kate Barnard.

Dividing the Indian Territory into counties and naming the county seats proved one of the most time-consuming duties of the convention, because almost every town aspired to be the seat of some county. Finally Bill Murray exerted his influence, obtained the resignation of several members of this committee, and then named Charles Haskell to chair it. Haskell and Murray had formulated the county boundaries in the Sequoyah Convention, so they used much of their work from that effort to draw Oklahoma's counties. In addition to creating the counties in the eastern half of the new state as they exist today (naming one county for Haskell

campaign against the constitution, hoping after a defeat to call a convention that would write a "good" document. Some conservatives stated that ratification of the proposed constitution would lead to economic and social unrest and to the collapse of the financial system of the area.

Unfortunately for the Republicans, theirs had been the dominant party in national politics during the territorial years, and they were associated with carpetbaggers and oppression. Moreover, it had been Republicans who were viewed as having destroyed the Indian nations. In addition, many settlers in Oklahoma had come from the South and were staunchly pro-Democratic, while most newcomers to the territory favored the social reforms and the anti-business features of the progressive constitution. In short, Oklahomans were weary of politicians in Washington making decisions for them, and they wanted statehood in order to end this practice. In nineteenth-century terms, "They were full of roast beef and ice cream,

and spoiling for a fight." They approved the new constitution by a vote of 180,333 to 73,059. The sobs and wails of mourners for the Indian Territory were lost among the hoorays and cheers of those celebrating the coming of statehood.

In that same election the voters chose new state officials. Democrat Charles N. Haskell defeated Republican Frank Frantz for the governorship; four of the five congressional seats were won by Democrats; and both houses of the legislature had a Democratic majority, while members of that party won almost all other state offices. In addition, the voters, by a majority of 130,361 to 112,258, chose statewide prohibition—the same day Oklahoma entered the Union, its saloons would close at midnight. Teddy Roosevelt might not have liked the new constitution, but he had to admit that it met all terms of the Enabling Act. On November 16, 1907, Oklahoma entered the Union, and the forty-sixth star was added to the national flag.

Governor Charles Nathaniel Haskell took the oath of office as Oklahoma's first governor on the steps of the Carnegie Library in Guthrie on November 16, 1907. OHS

CHAPTER XIII

I Promise if Elected

Alice M. Robertson was elected United States representative from Oklahoma in 1921. The descendant of Samuel A. Worcester and a missionary teacher herself, she was the only woman elected to national office from Oklahoma. OHS

*G*uthrie was filled with celebrating people on the morning of November 16, 1907, as citizens gathered from all parts of the new state to see Charles N. Haskell inaugurated as Oklahoma's first governor. A platform had been built on the steps of the Carnegie Library, and thousands crowded in to view the historic event. The ceremony began with the mock wedding of an Indian girl, dubbed Miss Indian Territory, and a cowboy, representing Mr. Oklahoma Territory. This marriage symbolized the arrival of statehood for the two territories and the union of the two cultures. After Haskell's inaugural speech everyone went to the city park for a barbecue, and then many men swarmed into nearby saloons to drink as much whiskey and beer as they could hold. At midnight all saloons had to close, seal their alcoholic beverages, and ship them out of the state.

Haskell had been a lawyer and railroad promotor in Muskogee prior to his election. At the constitutional convention he was a major force, highly respected by the other delegates. His popularity garnered him over 53 percent of the vote in the gubernatorial election, while opponents Republican Frank Frantz and Socialist C.C. Ross took 42 and 4 percent, respectively.

Haskell, although a businessman and somewhat conservative personally, recognized the political mood of Oklahoma's citizens at the onset of statehood. During the first decade of the twentieth century Oklahomans, along with perhaps a majority of American voters, were caught up in a so-called "progressive" mood that called for an increasingly activist government. Moreover, many Oklahomans were still filled with the zeal of Populism, an agrarian movement of the 1880s and 1890s filled with hatred of business and dedicated to the graduated income tax and to government regulation of railroads and grain elevators. Moreover, there was a significant percentage of Oklahomans in 1907 who were voting the Social-

The first two governors of Oklahoma took their oaths of office on the steps of Carnegie Library in Guthrie. Ironically, the last piece of legislation signed in Guthrie was the bill removing the capital to Oklahoma City, although Lee Cruce took his oath of office in Guthrie to avoid any legal difficulties. Photo by Jim Argo

ist ticket to demand government ownership of banks, railroads, and grain elevators—perhaps even telephone and telegraph companies.

In keeping with this reality, Haskell asked the first legislature to regulate trusts and monopolies, to provide for a compulsory primary election system, and to enforce prohibition. The legislature complied with a host of Populist-Progressive legislation. To pay for running state government, it enacted a 2 percent gross revenue tax on coal mines, oil pipelines, and telegraph lines; a tax of one percent on oil, railroads, and utilities; and a graduated income tax ranging from

one-half of one percent on incomes from $3,500 to $10,000 to three and one-half of one percent on incomes of more than $100,000. It drafted a broad labor law that included a safety code and restrictions on the use of child labor, provided a system for inspecting workplaces, and established an employers' liability fund. To protect Oklahomans from bank failures, such as had happened during the Panic of 1907, a bank guaranty system was established (similar to the Federal Deposit Insurance Corporation of today). In addition, the legislators provided for compulsory free public education, the certification and training of teachers, a

textbook commission, and additional funding for an expanding number of institutions of higher learning.

Despite their absence from the constitution, Jim Crow laws were enacted by the legislature to curtail the rights of non-white citizens. These were mandated due to the large number of former Southerners in the state, and because some whites disliked Indians. In 1910 the state would adopt the "Grandfather Clause" used in Southern states to prevent voting by those whose ancestors could not vote as of January 1, 1866, unless he could pass a literacy test. These laws, however, led to discontent and even to riots, for blacks did not submit tamely to this discrimination. (Oklahoma at this time was unique in that it contained more than twenty all-black towns.) Finally, after Commissioner of Charities and Corrections Kate Barnard inspected the Kansas State Penitentiary at Lansing and publicized the brutal conditions under which Oklahoma's felons were suffering, the legislature provided for the construction of a state prison at McAlester—which was built with convict labor to save money.

The most controversial issue in Haskell's term as governor was the permanent location of the capital. In the first two meetings of the legislature there was endless argument about where the capital should be located, although most agreed it should be near the geographical center of the state. Some lawmakers wanted to remove it to a point just west of Oklahoma City and start

a new community, to be called New Jerusalem. Democrats were especially anxious to remove the capital from Guthrie, which they believed to be a "Republican nest," while Governor Haskell agreed to move the capital because he was angry with the continued attacks on him by Republican newspapermen in Guthrie, particularly Frank Greer.

In 1910 a petition was circulated and received sufficient signatures to call a referendum on the issue. Voting on July 11 of that year, Oklahomans overwhelmingly chose Oklahoma City as their capital. That city's 96,261 votes easily beat Guthrie's 31,301 and Shawnee's 8,382. That night Haskell sent his secretary of state to Guthrie to get the state seal, and the next morning, the seal in his possession, Haskell declared the Lee Huckins Hotel in Oklahoma City to be the temporary capitol. The state supreme court would remain in Guthrie for a time, and residents of that city would protest mightily, but no one could find a legal way to force the governor to move from Oklahoma City. Thereafter the capital remained.

In 1910 came the election of a new governor. Lee Cruce, a forty-seven-year-old native of Kentucky who had moved to Ardmore in 1891 to practice law and then to work as a cashier in a local bank, had unsuccessfully contested Haskell for the Democratic nomination in 1907. Yet in this election he won despite a spirited primary contest with Alfalfa Bill Murray. In the general election Cruce received 120,318

This billboard appeared in Oklahoma City, calling for support of the effort to remove the capital from Guthrie to Oklahoma City in 1910. OHS

votes to Republican Joseph W. McNeal's 99,527. During his term he emphasized economy in state government, and pushed for creation of boards of regents for state colleges and the University of Oklahoma to avoid duplication (at this time the Agricultural and Mechanical College and other agricultural schools were administered by the State Board of Agriculture). The Oklahoma State Highway Department was created during Cruce's administration to be financed by a one dollar license on all vehicles.

On two issues Cruce held strong convictions: he opposed capital punishment, and he favored the so-called blue laws. Although he could not convince the legislature to abolish capital punishment, he did commute the sentences of twenty condemned men to life imprisonment. When criticized for these actions, he responded, "I have received thousands of letters praising my actions. I'm perfectly pleased with the result." During his term unruly mobs lynched fifteen murderers before they could be brought to trial or before he could commute their sentences. In 1915, after Cruce left office, the legislature changed the method of execution in the

state from hanging to electrocution, which was considered more humane. In enforcing blue laws—closing businesses on Sunday, outlawing horse racing, enforcing prohibition, and ending prizefighting—Cruce was more successful. When local law enforcement officials could not or would not effect these measures, the governor sent in the state militia to help.

The census of 1910 showed that Oklahoma rated three additional seats in Congress, bringing its total to eight. Democrats wanted to gerrymander the state to allow the election of three additional members of their party, but Cruce said he would veto such a partisan measure. Thus the three seats were elected statewide. This, along with his economizing, led to Cruce's near impeachment in 1913 by an unhappy legislature—and began a period of intense political rivalry between the legislature and subsequent governors.

In 1914 the Democrats nominated Chief Justice of the state supreme court Robert L. Williams for governor after a primary in which he defeated Al Jennings, a former train robber who had served time in prison. Williams, born in 1868, had moved to Du-

Opposite page, top
Governor Charles N. Haskell met with Secretary of State William Cross at the governor's Oklahoma City hotel suite following the removal of the capital from Guthrie in 1910. A vote of the people relocated the capital to Oklahoma City on June 11, 1910. OHS

Opposite page, bottom
As Oklahoma City continued to grow, transportation became one of the city's most important necessities. An interurban line of streetcars was initiated soon after the turn of the century. Courtesy, Oklahoma County Metropolitan Library

Below
When the capital was removed from Guthrie in 1910, Oklahoma City had already experienced a growth in population from 32,000 in 1907 to over 65,000 in 1910. Courtesy, Bob L. Blackburn

rant, Indian Territory, in 1896 from his native Alabama and had been a member of the constitutional convention. In the 1914 general election, Williams defeated Republican challenger John Fields by only 5,000 votes, while Socialist candidate Fred Holt received more than 50,000 votes. During Williams' administration laws were passed to protect the working class, including a labor code for women that contained social welfare provisions and set the maximum number of hours they could work. The state supreme court in 1915 struck down the Grandfather Clause, which prevented some blacks from voting, but the legislature found a new way, a shrewdly devised registration law, to keep most blacks from the polls.

With the outbreak of World War I in 1917, Socialists and radical labor groups began open rebellion against the drafting of

young men, and property was destroyed in several counties. This so-called "Green Corn Rebellion" was ended by mob and posse action, and many Oklahomans joined the conservative American Protective League to use extralegal and illegal methods to end what they saw as anti-Americanism.

Perhaps the most famous event of Williams' term was moving the state government into the new capitol building in 1917. Because of the wartime shortage of materials, no dome was put atop this building, although the plans called for one (to the present time no dome has been added).

In 1918 Democratic candidate James B. Robertson defeated Republican Horace G. McKeever by a vote of 104,132 to 82,865 following a hard-fought primary against Alfalfa Bill Murray. During Robertson's term more than 1,000 miles of modern highways were constructed, and the colleges were given separate boards of regents, rather than operate under the centralized Board of Education that Governor Williams had secured. Substantial state support for public schools began during Robertson's term. Many new schools were constructed, reforms were made in curriculum and teach-

ers certification, and appropriation of $100,000 was made for public instruction. Also during Robertson's term Oklahoma experienced a serious conflict with the state of Texas over ownership of the Red River bed. Federal courts ruled that the Treaty of 1819 with Spain had set the boundary at the *south* bank of the river and thus the state of Oklahoma owned the entire riverbed, but Texans insisted they owned half of the riverbed. Units of the national guard of both states faced each other across the river, and shooting was about to begin before cooler heads prevailed.

The latter part of Robertson's term was marked by an economic depression at the end of World War I, and in the election of 1920 Republicans swept five of the eight congressional seats, won a majority in the state House of Representatives, and secured a strong minority in the state Senate. Republicans in the House then brought impeachment charges against Lieutenant Governor Martin Trapp (and tried to impeach Robertson), but Democrats in the Senate refused to convict Trapp.

In 1922 John C. "Jack" Walton captured the governor's mansion, defeating Republi-

Above
The Oklahoma State Capi-
tol was dedicated in 1917.
OHS

Far right
Robert Lee Williams was
governor of Oklahoma from
1915 to 1919. OHS

can John Fields by approximately 50,000
votes out of more than half a million votes
cast (women voted for the first time in this
election). Born in Indiana in 1881, Walton
moved to Oklahoma in 1903 as a sales engineer. He was elected commissioner of public
works in 1917, mayor of Oklahoma City in
1919, and won the governorship in 1922
with support from the Oklahoma Farm
Labor Reconstruction League, a liberal (almost radical) organization formed the previous year by former Socialist Party members
and various labor and small farmer organizations. The league favored public ownership of utilities and heavy land taxes based
on improvements to property (and thus
hardest on city land owners).

Walton opened his inaugural ball to the
entire public—the last event of his term
where he found much reason to smile. He
had risen in politics by his ability to work
compromises, but in office this was per-
ceived as vacillation. In addition, wholesale
appointment of friends to positions of authority at the university and at the Agricultural and Mechanical College brought
strong hostility from the legislature and
alumni of these institutions. The wheels of
state government almost came to a halt due

to Walton's unsure hand, and then came
public excesses, including activity by the Ku
Klux Klan. A grand jury was called in
Oklahoma City to investigate the governor's
actions, whereupon Walton proclaimed martial law in the state, saying the "deadly Invisible Empire" (the Klan) was attempting
to destroy Oklahoma. This excess led to

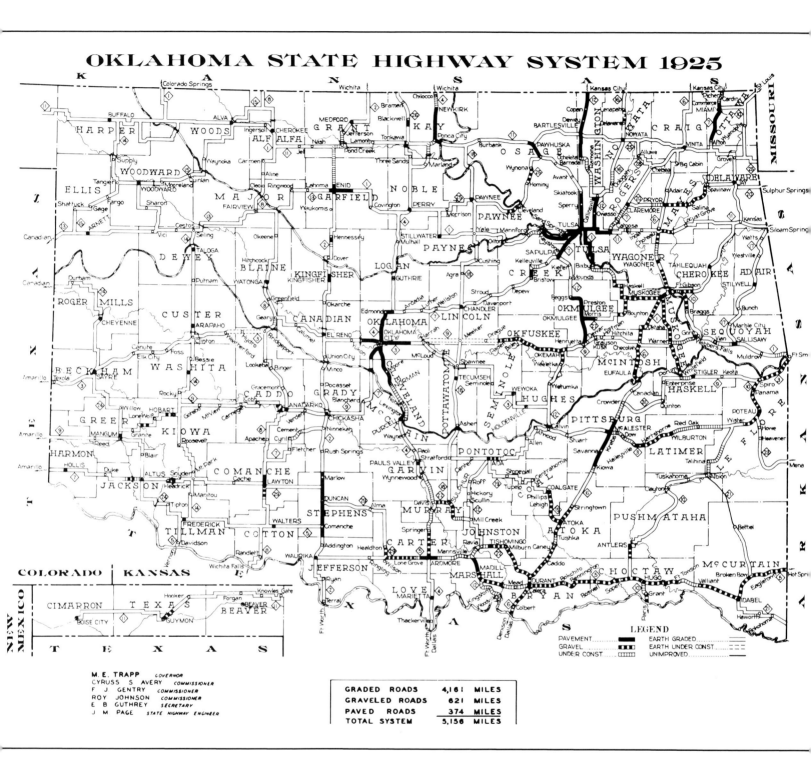

OKLAHOMA STATE HIGHWAY SYSTEM 1925

M. E. TRAPP GOVERNOR
CYRUSS S AVERY COMMISSIONER
F J GENTRY COMMISSIONER
ROY JOHNSON COMMISSIONER
E B GUTHREY SECRETARY
J M PAGE STATE HIGHWAY ENGINEER

GRADED ROADS	4,161	MILES
GRAVELED ROADS	621	MILES
PAVED ROADS	374	MILES
TOTAL SYSTEM	5,156	MILES

Walton's impeachment and removal by the Democratic legislature on November 19, 1923. Next year, however, Walton won the Democratic nomination for the United States Senate—only to lose to W.B. Pine, a wealthy Republican businessman from Okmulgee.

Lieutenant Governor Martin Trapp served the remainder of Walton's term. He had served in various offices before becoming lieutenant governor in 1915, and had survived an impeachment vote in 1921. His tenure as governor was marked by little activity, although state spending was cut by one-third, and an anti-mask law severely curtailed Klan activities in the state.

In 1926 Democrats recaptured control of the Oklahoma legislature and continued their monopoly on the governorship. Henry S. Johnston easily defeated Republican Omer Benedict for the governor's seat, although his use of the governor's patronage power in the Highway Department brought his downfall. After his inauguration on January 10, 1927, Johnston quieted the political waters with strong support for hospitals and schools. However, his executive secretary, Mrs. O.O. Hammonds, was fond of ordering legislators out of the governor's office, and some legislators charged that she made all executive decisions—and there were semi-public allegations by Johnston's political enemies that he and Mrs. Hammonds were having an affair. Johnston defended his secretary by saying she was as gentle as a "ewe lamb." Legislators convened in a special session in late 1927 at the Huckins Hotel in Oklahoma City in an attempt to impeach the governor, a move the newspapers called "the ewe lamb rebellion," but the state supreme court ruled the session illegal.

Johnston thus survived this first effort to unseat him, but he angered many legislators by campaigning in 1928 for Democratic presidential nominee Al Smith, a Catholic who favored the repeal of prohibition. When Herbert Hoover and the Republicans swept national offices, Johnston lost control of the state Democratic Party. The legislature, meeting in regular sessions early in 1929, quickly voted articles of impeachment against Johnston, and on March 20 he was removed from office solely on the general charge of "incompetency," his impeachment caused more by political error than any criminal activity.

Lieutenant Governor William J. Holloway had been acting governor since January when impeachment proceedings began against Johnston. During Holloway's years as governor, several educational reforms were enacted, the mining code was strengthened, and the Highway Commission was restructured. Holloway appointed Republican Lew Wentz to the Highway Commission in an effort to promote bipartisanship in that body, leading to some criticism of the governor by fellow Democrats. During his term also came adoption of the runoff primary; this provided that a candidate in a primary election had to receive a majority vote, otherwise a runoff between the top two candidates would be necessary. The beginning of the Great Depression in 1929 did not affect Oklahoma greatly for some months, but Holloway nevertheless tried to keep state spending to a minimum.

Because of the Depression, which hit

Oklahoma by the summer of 1930 and which was associated nationally with the Republican Party, the Democrats eyed the 1930 elections confident of victory. Contending for that party's nomination was former governor Martin Trapp, who argued that the constitution did not prevent his candidacy since his previous three-year term came as a result of Walton's impeachment. He was defeated, however, in the primary by Alfalfa Bill Murray, who went on to defeat Republican Ira Hill in the general election by almost 100,000 votes. Murray's candidacy was ridiculed in most state newspapers, for he was crude and dressed poorly. He was born in the community of Toad Suck, Texas, in 1869. After serving as president of the constitutional convention, he had been speaker of the state House of Representatives and then was elected to Congress. In 1924 he went to Bolivia to found an agricultural colony, but when that failed he returned to Oklahoma to reenter politics. Despite Murray's occasionally dishevelled appearance, the common people identified with him and gave him their votes.

When Murray took office on January 12, 1931, Oklahomans faced severe difficulties caused by the Depression. Jobs were disappearing, banks were failing, and individuals were facing bankruptcy—and some of them hunger. Moreover, the state was five million dollars in debt and could find few banks that would honor its warrants. Murray economized by cutting appropriations, and he established a Tax Commission to halt tax evasion. In addition, he raised taxes on gasoline and petroleum products, which increased state revenues by more than two million dollars, and he tried to shift the tax burden away from individuals more heavily onto corporations. His one luxury was to reinstate free textbooks for the public schools, a practice halted during Governor Trapp's administration. Because of Murray's demands for spending cuts, legislators began muttering about impeachment, to which Murray snorted, "It'll be like a bunch of jack rabbits tryin' to get a wildcat out of a hole." Talk of impeachment ceased.

Murray was equally forceful in dealing with other problems. When overproduction caused petroleum prices to fall drastically, he called out the National Guard to force producers to stay within the production limits set by the Corporation Commission.

167

When the state constructed a free bridge across the Red River to compete with a toll bridge owned by Texans, Murray again used the National Guard to keep the free bridge open—even in the face of a federal court ruling against the free bridge.

In 1932 Murray had visions of getting the Democratic nomination for president, but that prize went to Franklin D. Roosevelt, who instituted the New Deal after he took office. Murray frequently voiced his dislike both for Roosevelt and the New Deal, although in 1933 he did agree to the repeal of prohibition by signing a bill allowing the sale of light beer (3.2 percent alcoholic content). Yet his antics angered voters, and in 1934, despite his support of Tom Anglin of Holdenville for governor, the Democratic nomination went to Ernest W. Marland.

Marland was a former multimillionaire, who lost his fortune in 1929 due to lavish living and free spending. He entered politics and was elected to Congress in 1932 prior to his Democratic nomination for governor. In the general election he defeated Republican candidate W.B. Pine by more than 120,000 votes in a contest in which Marland asked the voters to "Bring the New Deal to Oklahoma."

In office Marland fully embraced New Deal programs, pushing many of them through the legislature despite intense opposition from conservatives led by Speaker of the House Leon C. "Red" Phillips. This bloc argued against deficit spending for New Deal measures. Despite Marland's successes, however, federal relief programs, such as the Works Progress Administration, Civilian Conservation Corps, and Federal Emergency Relief Administration, were continually under-funded. However, in the 1935 legislative session, he secured passage of a 2-percent general sales tax earmarked to aid the aged, the blind, and the indigent. This marked the beginnings of the Department of Human Services, a state agency that would operate as a semi-independent barony, its director secure so long as he dutifully doled out jobs to those recommended to him by legislators.

In the election of 1936 Governor Marland failed to win the United States Senate seat he sought, but his followers did win control of the state legislature. In the legislative session of 1937 this branch of the Democratic Party appropriated millions for relief and reform. Unfortunately, revenue-raising

measures to finance the increased spending were not passed, leaving the state with a massive debt. Lawmakers that year also created the Oklahoma Highway Patrol, a move heavily opposed by many citizens for fear that the organization would be a statewide police force subject to political appointments and political pressures.

In the election of 1938 Marland was succeeded by his principal enemy, Leon C. Phillips. There was some question about the legality of his nomination, for the primary runoff election had been abolished by the legislature in 1937, and Phillips had defeated his closest Democratic opponent, General William S. Key, by only 3,000 votes. His victory in November, however, was unquestioned; he had 355,740 votes to Republican Ross Rizley's 148,861.

Robert S. Kerr, founder of Kerr-McGee Petroleum Company, was governor of Oklahoma from 1943 to 1947 and United States senator from 1949 to 1963. OHS

Due largely to the influence of Senator Robert S. Kerr, the McClellan-Kerr Arkansas River Navigation System was developed to open the Arkansas River to barge traffic. Head of navigation is Catoosa, on the Verdigris River northeast of Tulsa. Photo by Jim Argo

As governor, Phillips demanded that the state budget be balanced, and in 1941 he secured an amendment to the constitution prohibiting the legislature from appropriating more money than there were funds available in any given fiscal year. To cut spending and retire the debt, Phillips halted construction of many projects begun during the Marland years. Budgets for institutions of higher learning were cut by 20 percent, and additional taxes were imposed on tobacco and gasoline. Bonds in the amount of thirty-five million dollars were issued to retire the public debt. With the outbreak of World War II, prosperity returned to Oklahoma, ending the hardships of the Depression and easing the financial posture of the state, but the war placed a heavy burden on Phillips to meet the state's responsibilities in the war effort.

Another feature of the Phillips' years was the intense fighting between factions of the Democratic Party. Several of Marland's friends, among them Dr. Henry G. Bennett, president of Oklahoma A. & M. College, feared prosecution for alleged irregularities in the state textbook commission. In return, there were ugly accusations against Phillips, but the state's preoccupation with the war effort reduced this feud somewhat.

In 1942 Robert S. Kerr became the state's first native son to be elected governor. Born near Ada, Indian Territory, in 1896, Kerr studied law and, in 1926, founded what was to become the Kerr-McGee Oil Company. After a difficult primary battle, he was nominated by the Democrats, and in the general election defeated Republican

The Oklahoma state legislature met in joint sessions to hear the annual "State of the State" message from the governor. Since 1968 annual sessions of the legislature have been held, although the state constitution prohibits sessions from exceeding ninety working days. Special sessions of the legislature may be called by the governor or by the legislature itself. OHS

William J. Otjen. Kerr was also committed to reducing the state's debt and was aided in this effort by the wartime boom that brought greater state revenues from rising personal incomes and increased petroleum production; so great was the flood of revenue that the entire thirty-seven million dollar debt was paid off by 1947.

Kerr also pushed for and secured creation of the Pardons and Parole Board, and he convinced the voters to approve a constitutional amendment establishing separate boards of regents for the University of Oklahoma and for the Oklahoma A. and M. system. The runoff primary was reinstated, and free textbooks were again made available in the public schools (which had been halted after a textbooks scandal that had led to the near impeachment of some officials several years before). As wartime governor, Kerr also fought to attract military bases to the state. A total of twenty-eight Army, thirteen Navy, and many Army Air Corps installations were opened during these years and provided employment to tens of

thousands of Oklahomans. By 1946, as the general elections approached, Kerr could look back on a record of solid accomplishment—and a growing national reputation for himself.

Kerr was followed in office by another oil man, Roy J. Turner, who also was a successful rancher. Campaigning for the Democratic nomination, Turner defeated Republican Olney J. Flynn, son of Territorial delegate to Congress Dennis Flynn.

Turner, continuing the tradition of stressing economy in state government, vetoed several bills increasing welfare spending (although he did raise old-age pensions to fifty-eight dollars a month). Moreover, he pushed for reorganization of several state boards and commissions, such as the Planning and Resources Board, the Oklahoma Tax Commission, and the Oklahoma Highway Commission. This move was brought on by the discovery that much state highway money had been wasted through mismanagement and political patronage. To combat this, the department was placed under the state merit system, and turnpikes were authorized to reduce state spending on highways. Another major problem during Turner's administration was skyrocketing enrollment in state colleges caused by World War II veterans returning home and enrolling under the GI Bill. To alleviate the overcrowding that resulted, Turner, working with legislators, financed a building program for colleges by issuing thirty-six million dollars in bonds to be repaid from an increased tax on cigarettes. During Turner's term, the state supreme court ordered integration in some college programs, ending decades of discrimination.

In 1950 Johnston Murray, the son of Alfalfa Bill Murray, became governor. Running for office on a plank of being "just plain folks," Murray won the Democratic primary in a bitter contest, then defeated Republican Jo O. Ferguson in an extremely close contest.

His administration was one of contrasts: stringent economy in some areas, especially welfare (where there was strict enforcement of eligibility), and proposed massive spending in other areas, such as one plan to build a series of canals to move water from the eastern part of the state to the arid western area. He did secure passage of a plan to consolidate rural schools, but a constitutional amendment to allow eighteen-year-olds to vote failed. Murray also tried to reorganize state government by establishing a Governor's Joint Committee on State Government and by forming a "broom brigade" whose task was to rid state government of unneeded personnel. He fulfilled his promise to be just plain folks by maintaining an open-house policy at the governor's mansion, and his elderly father again became a familiar figure in the state capitol as he wandered the corridors and sat in offices.

In 1954 came the election of the first governor born since statehood. Raymond D. Gary, a former teacher, salesman, oil businessman, and senator, defeated Republican Reuben K. Sparks by more that 100,000 votes. In that election Governor Johnston Murray angered many Oklahomans by declaring martial law in several counties and using the National Guard to watch polling places to prevent irregularities.

Gary's administration saw a marked increase in appropriations for both public and higher education, as well as for mental institutions. During his term the public

Henry Louis Bellmon was the first Republican elected governor of Oklahoma, serving from 1963 to 1967. He later became United States senator from 1969 to 1981. OHS

schools were integrated, more than 3,000 miles of highways were constructed (including the start of the Interstate Highway system), the Department of Commerce and Industry was created to stimulate economic growth, and a water code was passed allowing dams to be built to conserve water.

In 1958 J. Howard Edmondson became the youngest man ever to hold office of chief executive. Just thirty-three when he took office, Edmondson received his law degree from the University of Oklahoma, and entered politics after moving to Tulsa. He brought to the statehouse many young and aggressive assistants, and with him they antagonized veteran politicians by trying to accomplish what old-timers saw as "too much too fast." Edmondson's most pronounced victory was the repeal of prohibition in 1959. This was accomplished by strict enforcement of the law, causing many thirsty Oklahomans to decide to vote for repeal. Edmondson also pushed vigorously for county consolidation, a merit system for state employees, centralized purchasing for state agencies, a withholding plan for state income taxes, and expanded construction of turnpikes. While some of these programs were passed, Edmondson failed to win acceptance of legislative reapportionment or a constitutional Highway Commission.

When United States Senator Robert S. Kerr (the former governor) died on January 1, 1963, Edmondson resigned as governor and five days later was appointed to fill the remainder of Kerr's term in the Senate. There were cries that Edmondson had made a "deal" with George P. Nigh, who had been elected lieutenant governor in 1958 and who had been colorful and outspoken during his four years in that office. Nigh served as governor for nine days before Henry L. Bellmon, Oklahoma's first Republican governor, took over the office.

Bellmon, born at Tonkawa, Oklahoma, in 1921, had farmed at Billings and served in the state legislature before winning the Republican nomination for governor in 1962. In a general election that surprised most political observers, Bellmon, thanks to the best organization ever put together by a Republican, defeated Democrat William P. "Bill" Atkinson.

Facing a legislature dominated by Democrats, Bellmon pledged to veto any measure calling for increased taxes. This split the legislative and executive branches and threatened to halt all activity by the state government, but Bellmon managed to secure legislation improving the retirement system for state employees, and additional bonds were authorized for additional turnpike construction. After prolonged debate about teachers' salaries—and the threat of a teacher strike—Bellmon and the legislators agreed to raise the state appropriation for both public and higher education through an increased tax on cigarettes. One scandal marred the Bellmon administration, although neither he nor his staff was touched by it. The scandal involved certain judges who were accused of taking bribes, and Associate Justice N.B. Johnson of the state supreme court was impeached in 1965.

In 1966 voters chose a second Republican governor, former state senator Dewey F. Bartlett. After defeating Democrat Preston J. Moore by more that 80,000 votes in the general election, Bartlett took office on January 9, 1967. During his administration he stressed pride in Oklahoma, encouraging everyone to wear "Okie" pins to demonstrate that this once derisive term had become a proud name. His tenure was marked by rapid increases in population and growth in industry, as he fought to reverse Oklahoma's anti-business attitude.

Bartlett was the first governor eligible to succeed himself, for state voters had recently passed a constitutional amendment removing the old clause restricting governors to one term. Bartlett, however, lost the election by slightly more than 2,000 votes to Democrat David Hall.

Born in Oklahoma City in 1930, Hall had earned a law degree from the University of Tulsa and had been county attorney in Tulsa County before his election. During his early years in office, Oklahoma continued to grow in population and the number of people employed in manufacturing rose to an estimated 200,000 by 1971. However, Hall angered many voters because he pushed for a large tax increase in 1971, part of it on oil and gas and the other on personal income and liquor. Although he argued that these increases would hit only "fat cats," the result was higher taxes for an overwhelming majority of Oklahomans. Much of this revenue went to support public education, including free public kindergartens, and the remainder to the construction of state highways. Late in his term, as Hall campaigned for reelection, rumors circulated that he was involved in a bribery attempt, and shortly after he left office he was arrested and convicted on charges of soliciting a kickback, and was sentenced to three years in federal prison.

Defeating Hall in the Democratic primary was David L. Boren, son of Lyle H. Boren, a former member of Congress from the fourth Oklahoma district. After graduating from Yale University and then studying in England, Boren had returned to Oklahoma to earn a law degree from the University of Oklahoma. While teaching at Oklahoma Baptist University, he also had served in the state House of Representatives. His opponent in the general election was Republican James Inhofe of Tulsa. Elected on a reform platform that utilized Johnston Murray's theme of the "broom brigade," Boren began working to reorganize the state government by making fewer state offices elective, thereby shortening the ballot for state officials, and he was concerned with restoring confidence in state government lost during the Hall administration. He also increased funding for public and higher education, and promoted a better public understanding at the national level for Oklahoma's petroleum industry. The teacher retirement sys-

Governors Dewey Bartlett and David Hall spent extensive effort to attract industry to Oklahoma during their terms of office. This effort was rewarded when the General Motors Assembly Plant was located in southeastern Oklahoma City during the administration of Governor Hall. Photo by Jim Argo

tem was overhauled, and a beginning was made on ending the earmarking of state sales tax revenues for the Department of Human Services.

The 1978 Democratic gubernatorial nomination went to George P. Nigh. A native of McAlester, Nigh taught Oklahoma history in the public schools before serving in the legislature and then becoming lieutenant governor in 1958. He proved extremely popular with state voters because of his wit and his outspoken candor, but failed to win election as governor in 1962. Reelected lieutenant governor in 1966, he continued to hold this office until his 1978 election as governor. Four years later in an era of economic prosperity almost unparalleled in Oklahoma

history, Nigh became the first governor reelected to that office in a victory of stunning proportions. In defeating Republican Tom Dixon, Nigh carried all seventy-seven counties in Oklahoma, a feat never before accomplished.

Nigh's first term in office was marked by an economic boom, high employment, tax cuts, and swelling revenues. Money was appropriated for salary increases of high proportions for state employees and public and higher education, road construction, and the Department of Human Services were appropriated large budget increases. This was possible because of the boom in oil and gas production, swelling state coffers thanks to the tax increases voted during the

administration of David Hall. Oklahoma's economy heated to the point that for several months the state had the lowest unemployment rate in the nation, and job seekers flowed into the state at a rate that triggered a spree of construction—and a reversal of the out-migration of the Depression years. At the end of Nigh's first term, the boom collapsed, and appropriation exceeded state revenues. Cuts in state spending were matched by cries for tax increases by those affected by the reductions. Even longtime director of the Department of Human Services, Lloyd Rader, caught in this dilemma and facing charges of administering a system in need of overhaul, was forced to resign. Early in 1984 the legislature responded to the problem of declining revenues by enacting a "temporary" one-cent increase in the state sales tax and by passing tax hikes in several other areas; in 1985 the "temporary" tax became permanent, and there were other increases in state levies.

Nigh, like his twenty-one predecessors in office as state governor, has received credit for the good things that happened during his administration and has been blamed for the hard times and the scandals. In truth, Oklahoma's chief executive has little real power, for the state has been dominated by its legislature (some observers have argued that the speaker of the House has more real

power than the governor). Like the governorship, the legislature, consisting of forty-eight senators and 101 representatives, has been almost exclusively controlled by the Democratic Party. Republicans have won significant numbers of seats only during years in which their party did well at the national level, as in 1920. In more than seventy-five years of statehood, there has been only one Republican Speaker of the House.

Republicans have been numerous among Oklahoma's representatives in the United States Senate, however. At statehood there was an informal agreement that one senator would be chosen from what had been the Indian Territory, the other from the Oklahoma Territory. Although senators then were appointed by the legislature, there was a referendum in 1907 in which the people voted for their choice. Democrats Robert L. Owen from Muskogee and Henry M. Furman from Ada came in first and second, but, honoring the agreement made earlier, Furman stepped aside to allow Democrat Thomas Gore of Lawton, who had finished third, to be appointed. Gore, who drew the short term, was blind, but he proved to be one of the most colorful and energetic representatives to Washington ever produced by the state. He was succeeded in 1920 by J.W. Harreld, a Republican who held office only one term. In 1926 Democrat Elmer Thomas won election and held the office for twenty-four years. He was succeeded in 1950 by Mike Monroney, also a Democrat, who stayed in office until 1968 when Republican former governor Henry Bellmon won the office. In 1980 Republican Don Nickles, a young businessman from Ponca City, won election.

The other line of succession in the United States Senate has been filled by several men: Robert L. Owen, a Democrat who served from 1907 to 1924; W.B. Pine, a Republican who served one term; Thomas P. Gore, the blind former senator from Lawton, served from 1930 to 1936; Josh Lee, a Democrat, 1936 to 1942; Ed H. Moore, a Republican, held office from 1942 to 1948; Robert S. Kerr, the former governor, served from 1948 until his death on January 1, 1963; J. Howard Edmondson, the Democrat who resigned as governor to assume the office on January 6, 1963, and who served until the general election in 1964; Fred R. Harris, a Democrat, who won the seat for two years in 1964 and then was reelected in 1966 to a full term; Dewey F. Bartlett, the former Republican governor who won office in 1972; and former Democratic Governor David Boren, who was elected to the office in 1978.

At the time of statehood Oklahoma received five seats in the United States House of Representatives. Four of the five elected that year were Democrats. After the census of 1910 the state received three additional seats, which were filled at large until redistricting in 1914. After the census of 1930 the state was given yet another congressional seat, which was elected at large. During the Dust Bowl years, however, Oklahoma's population declined, and in 1940 the state lost one seat, leaving it eight. This was followed by the loss of two more seats in 1950. Today Oklahoma is still represented by six congressmen. Notable among those who have served in this capacity are Alice M. Robertson of Muskogee, elected in 1920 as a Republican (she was the second woman in history to serve in Congress); Carl Albert, born in 1908 and a Rhodes scholar who served as a Democrat in the House from 1946 to 1976 and who in 1971 became speaker of that body; and Tom Sneed, a Democrat first elected to the House in 1950.

Oklahoma today is still divided into seventy-seven counties, each of which by law must be at least 400 square miles of taxable land in area, contain a population of at least 15,000, and have a minimum of four million dollars in taxable wealth. The powers of these counties are only those delegated by the state, and consist almost wholly of administering state laws. The voters in each county select three county commissioners (by district), a county clerk, an assessor, a treasurer, a sheriff, and a surveyor. In addition, many counties still elect a county school superintendent (although most counties no longer have any rural schools to be administered). Prior to 1965, when the legislature created a statewide system of district attorneys, each county also elected a county attorney. In counties other than Oklahoma and Tulsa (where the municipal government provides most services) the county commission is still an influential body controlling local law enforcement and taxation.

A major task of county commissioners is overseeing roadwork in their districts, which involves the expenditure of large sums of

Carl Albert was United States representative from the Third District of Oklahoma from 1947 to 1977. He was named Speaker of the United States House of Representatives in 1971, serving until his retirement from the House in 1977. OHS

money. In the early 1980s came a scandal, prosecuted by the federal government, in which more than 230 persons—commissioners and suppliers—were convicted of taking or giving kickbacks, but despite the widespread proof of corruption the legislature enacted few meaningful reforms. Thanks to the automobile and improved roads, there is no real reason today to have seventy-seven counties in a state the size of Oklahoma, but county officials constitute the second largest lobby (behind teachers) in the state, and no political leader talks seriously about county consolidation. The only modern governor to discuss such reform, J. Howard Edmondson, was unable to accomplish the task and was hurt politically for even talking about the subject.

Oklahoma's politics have been colorful—and promise to remain so in the future. Although the Republican Party in the 1960s managed to elect two governors and to win the presidential race in every contest since 1952, Democrats still dominate among registered voters by a wide margin. Requirements for voting in the state are simple: the citizen must register at least ten days prior to the election. Today the voters seem little concerned with party affiliation, looking instead at the personality and philosophy of candidates. Those who register and go to the polls apparently are as independent as their ancestors who settled the region.

CHAPTER XIV

Riches From the Land

Oklahoma is a land of great contrasts in climate, soils, and elevation. East of U.S. Highway 81 the annual rainfall increases dramatically, approaching forty and even fifty inches a year. To the west of this line, however, the annual rainfall decreases rapidly, often falling below ten inches a year moving west into the panhandle. In the southeastern corner of the state the growing season approaches 230 days, while in the panhandle it can be less than 180 days. In the east the soil often is thin and lacks fertility, while in the west it is rich and deep. These factors make for a diverse agriculture.

Since the days of prehistory there has been farming in eastern Oklahoma by the Indian inhabitants. With the removal of the Five Civilized Tribes to the area, the federal government sent agents to urge the newcomers to plant and harvest, like they had been doing in their old homeland. Through their own hard labor, and that of their slaves, these tribes soon had surpluses of corn and cotton for sale. Because of their methods of farming, however, they soon exhausted the fertility of the soil, and by the post-Civil War period much of the land had been returned to grass used to fatten cattle. The arrival of the railroad made farming profitable once again by expanding the marketplace, and new land was cleared for a return to some cash crop production by the 1880s.

Then came the land runs, auctions, and lotteries, and western Oklahoma was filled with new settlers, most of them farmers. They usually established farms on 160-acre tracts. Their first chore was to break the thick topsoil, usually matted with grass roots. Frequently they plowed open spaces around their quarter sections for protection from prairie fires and as a place to plant fruit trees. Most of the crops they planted had already been tested in Kansas or north Texas. By 1891 Oklahoma's white settlers

were growing wheat, corn, oats, sorghum, and cotton, along with potatoes, peanuts, watermelons, turnips, and many varieties of fruit. The territorial legislature created a Board of Agriculture in 1901 to assist these farmers, while scientists at the Oklahoma Agricultural and Mechanical College introduced new techniques and crops. Working together, the board and the scientists provided much appreciated assistance to farmers, ranchers, and dairy operators.

In 1909, the first year after statehood, the census bureau began gathering information concerning Oklahoma agriculture. In that year there were twenty-nine million acres in cultivation, about 65 percent of the state's total of 44,424,960 acres. The average size of Oklahoma's approximately 190,000 farms in 1909 was 151.7 acres—of which only 137 (or .1 percent) were irrigated. Farm land was valued at twenty-two dollars and forty-nine cents per acre, an increase from six dollars and fifty cents per acre in 1899. More than eight million acres were planted in corn, producing slightly less than seventy-two million dollars in income. The third most significant crop was hay and forage grasses, totaling 1.3 million acres and producing $9.5 million in income. The total value of all crops that year in Oklahoma was estimated at $133,454,405.

The livestock industry, which had flourished in Oklahoma since the days of the Cherokee Strip Live Stock Association, was

even more valuable than farming to residents of the state. Ninety-seven percent of all farms reported domestic animals. Together with ranchers, this totaled almost two million cattle, almost a million horses and mules, and 135,000 hogs. The total value of these animals was $150 million.

By 1910 life on many Oklahoma farms had improved considerably. Few people still lived in dugouts, and for the wealthy there were ornate, comfortable wooden houses with wide porches, stuffed furniture, and many luxuries. For the poor there were log cabins or frame "shotgun shacks." Schoolhouses had been built in most rural areas, and there the children received several months of education throughout the year. Classes were dismissed in the fall during harvest season because everyone, even children, was needed in the fields. The schoolhouse usually served as a church on Sunday, with some untrained but fervent farmer in the area contributing the preaching. Despite gatherings for church, school recitals, all-night sings, and lectures by professors about agriculture, rural life still was lonely—the winters cold, the summers hot.

Machinery, mostly steam powered, some powered by gasoline motors, gradually was introduced to end some of the hard drudgery, making it possible to break the thick prairie sod or harvest wheat or sow grain with fewer laborers and less hand work. Yet farmers needed credit to buy machinery,

This team of oxen prepares to break the prairie sod in western Oklahoma. Oftentimes crews would contract out to individual farmers to break the sod so that farms could be improved. OHS

and interest rates at banks ranged to a legal high of 24 percent. In years when cotton and corn prices dropped, some farmers were unable to pay their debts and lost their land through mortgage foreclosure. Because of this, tenant farming increased steadily in the state. In 1910, 54 percent of all farms were operated by tenants, a figure that rose to 60 percent by 1935.

In addition to mortgages and debts, farmers were also burdened by the freight rates charged by railroads and the storage charges of grain elevator owners. Many farmers came to believe there was a conspiracy among bankers, railroaders, and elevator operators to keep them poor, especially in years of good harvests when prices fell. It seemed the more the farmer produced, the less money he had. Therefore some farmers flirted with the Socialist Party for several years after statehood. In 1907 the Socialist candidate for governor received 9,740 votes, a figure that grew to 52,703 votes in 1914. The prosperity generated by high prices during World War I and repressive policies by government officials caused the Socialist vote to decline to 7,428 in 1918, and thereafter it became insignificant.

The quality of farm life gradually improved as farm-to-market roads were graded, as schools were consolidated, and as Model T Ford automobiles became commonplace. Moreover, county agents and agricultural experiment stations demonstrated the value of scientific farming, and dairy herds were slowly upgraded, better types of seed were used, and marketing cooperatives were formed. Soon there was an Oklahoma Grain Growers Union, an Oklahoma Poultry Improvement Association, an Oklahoma Co-Operative Creameries Association, an Oklahoma Cotton Growers Association, an Oklahoma Livestock Growers Association, and even an Oklahoma Pecan Growers Association. These groups spread knowledge and urged cooperative marketing to achieve better prices. Organizations for youngsters—for boys the Future Farmers of America, for girls the Future Homemakers of America, and for both the 4-H clubs— encouraged scientific farming.

For these reasons the number of farms in Oklahoma, along with the total number of residents in the state, steadily grew. At statehood the population stood at 1,414,177. This increased to 1,657,155 by 1910, to

Right
Oklahoma schoolhouses went through a series of changes as they progressed from untamed frontier to settled countryside. This sod school in northwestern Oklahoma was established in 1893. OHS

Opposite page, top
Cotton emerged as a major cash crop after statehood. It required intensive manual labor, and many families turned out all members to help with the harvest. OHS

Opposite page, bottom
Use of farm machinery increased acreage under cultivation and improved harvests. This early tractor and combine operated in western Oklahoma in the 1920s. OHS

Bottom
The two-story school in Amber marked the beginning of the consolidation of school districts that accelerated during the 1930s. OHS

2,028,283 by 1920, and to 2,396,040 by 1930. One dramatic change during this period was a drop in acreage devoted to cotton farming after 1925 and an equally dramatic rise in the acreage on which wheat was grown.

Then state farmers experienced two major disasters in close succession: the Great Depression and the Dust Bowl. The Depression that began in 1929 caused a sudden drop in prices paid for farm commodities. Prime cotton fell below five cents a pound (and low grade cotton to two cents), while cattle and hogs had little market at any price. The Agricultural Adjustment Act of 1933 paid farmers for limiting production, but was declared unconstitutional by the United States Supreme Court in 1936. In 1938 Congress passed another act of the same name, providing for federal control of acres planted and prices paid for commodities, and it established a form of federal crop insurance. Moreover, the federal government passed legislation designed to extend credit to farmers as well as to tenants who wanted to buy their land.

Yet the greatest disaster for farmers in western Oklahoma was the Dust Bowl. This was the popular name given to a five-state region that included parts of Oklahoma, Texas, New Mexico, Colorado, and Kansas—the Great Plains region originally covered by grass and grazed by buffalo. During World War I millions of acres in this region had been plowed for the first time in order to produce wheat. Much of this area consisted of a thin layer of topsoil that was bone dry, except during the spring and fall rains. Worse still, the farmers or absentee landowners did little to conserve moisture or rebuild the soil. When drought came, as it did periodically, the winds whipped soil loose from plowed land to settle in streambeds crossing the region. Rivers such as the Beaver and Cimarron became sluggish and muddy, flowing over wide, sandy beds. For example, the Washita River during the latter part of the nineteenth century had supported navigation by small boats. After its channel filled with sand, it became useless for commerce.

During 1932 there were dust storms during the spring followed by dry, hot summer days when the temperature often hit 100°—but no rain fell. That fall farmers plowed and planted winter wheat, after which came winds that whipped up dust clouds through a process known as "saltation." Small particles of soil were dislodged by the wind, displacing other particles until the air was filled with flying topsoil and dust. These blew until they found protection from the wind in a ditch or against the side of a building; there the dust piled up in mounds many feet thick.

As the dust worked loose, plants on the windward side of a field had their roots bared, to then blow over and tangle with an adjoining row, hastening the tearing out of yet more plants. Entire fields were stripped in a day in this manner. Farmers soon came to dread the clouds of dust they saw approaching, some as tall and dark as thunderheads. By the spring of 1934 dust storms were so intense that daylight hours became as black as night. Nowhere was there protection. Dust seeped through cracks around doors and windows, coating everything in houses, killing birds and rabbits, even cattle and horses, by suffocation. Humans kept damp cloths over their noses and mouths. After such a storm passed, the dust would swirl about in small eddies for several more days—as farmers cursed or wept and looked in helpless frustration at what had been their fields.

When the winds came from the west, as they did in the spring of 1934, the dust of Oklahoma was carried eastward, sometimes as far as the Atlantic coast. That year Secretary of Agriculture Henry A. Wallace commented, "On May 12, 1934, for the first time since white men came to America, we had a great dust storm that originated in the plains country near the foot of the Rocky Mountains and swept across the continent and far out to sea."

From 1932 to 1938 farmers in Oklahoma fought the dust. As they plowed and planted, they met dry summers, hot winds, dust storms, and plants that were stripped away by the wind. Tenant farmers and migratory workers were the first to leave, some moving east to join relatives where it still rained, others heading for California and the "Golden West" they had heard about. These were the "Okies" celebrated by John Steinbeck in his *Grapes of Wrath*. Farm values tumbled to near five dollars an acre, while several western counties lost residents. Attendance at Panhandle Agriculture and Mechanical College at Goodwell dropped to ninety-two students—who studied soil conservation through dust-choked eyes. The region lost fewer people, however, than exaggerated newspaper accounts indicated. Nor were all those moving to California actually from Oklahoma. Because the Sooner State charged less for its license plates than any surrounding state, migratory farm laborers usually registered their automobiles in Oklahoma. Thus when they arrived at the California border, to be halted there by state police unless they had proof of a waiting job, reporters saw Oklahoma license tags and mistakenly called these people "Okies," a name that came to be used in derision about the hard-working and proud people displaced by the whims of nature.

Those people who remained in western Oklahoma faced their dilemma armed with a sense of humor. Beaver County residents tested the strength of the wind by nailing a chain to a fence post; the wind could not be

despite such efforts, the dust continued to blow. The federal government would later distribute films and millions of printed words to show that the Dust Bowl had been transformed, but such was not the case. Only when it began to rain again did the Dust Bowl end. In 1938 a little rain fell, enabling some farmers to raise a small crop. Then early in 1939 came a fourteen-inch snow, followed by good rains in April, and the drought at last was broken. The 1939 wheat crop, first estimated at twenty-five million bushels, jumped to 46,763,000 bushels when it was harvested. Farmers thereafter did practice methods of retaining moisture in the soil. New, drought-resistant types of seed helped, as did better techniques of soil management and a method of plowing known as stubble-mulching. Of greater help, however, were years of good

Dust storms, such as this one approaching Keyes in the Oklahoma Panhandle during the 1930s, literally blotted out the sun. Courtesy, Donovan L. Hofsommer

called a stiff breeze until the chain blew straight out. Another story told of a New Mexican farmer who sued an Oklahoman for his farm, which had blown east and settled at Guymon; reportedly the Oklahoman filed a countersuit, saying he had just planted a crop on this land when the wind blew it back to New Mexico. One humorist told—with a straight face—that he had seen a prairie dog digging a hole up in the air ten feet off the ground.

The New Deal administration of Franklin D. Roosevelt established programs to help farmers in affected areas. The Soil Conservation Service and local soil conservation districts demonstrated methods to prevent wind erosion, such as contour plowing and land terracing. The Shelterbelt Project was born, in which rows of trees were planted at government expense to slow the wind and hold down the soil. Farmers were asked to allow half their land to lay fallow each year, allowing moisture to store in the soil, but,

rains and high prices during World War II. These brought prosperity—and the breaking of yet more land and planting it in wheat. Then came dry years during the 1950s that saw a return of blowing dust as great as that of the 1930s—and a growing realization that this area could be productive only if man respected nature's periodic spells of drought.

By 1940 the number of farms in Oklahoma had dropped to 179,687, and the population had fallen to 2,336,434. There the population stabilized, but the number of farms continued to decline to fewer than 143,000 in 1950, fewer than 120,000 in 1960, to fewer than 90,000 in 1970, and to approximately 85,000 by 1980. Yet the number of acres under cultivation grew from some twenty-nine million in 1910 to 36.9 million in 1979, and the average size of a farm increased to almost 450 acres during the same period. There were, however, no corporate farms in Oklahoma because a

Public works projects in the New Deal provided jobs for destitute laborers and helped to reduce erosion caused by a prolonged drought. OHS

rural-dominated legislature early enacted laws allowing only family-owned corporations to engage in agriculture.

During this period a major shift occurred from cotton cultivation to wheat. In 1930 more than four million acres of cotton were cultivated, producing 1,130,415 bales valued at $106,992,573. By 1935 this had dropped significantly to 333,595 bales and by 1974 to 310,000 bales. The annual wheat crop rose as cotton decreased: in 1930 almost forty million bushels were produced, in 1940 more than fifty million bushels, in 1950 more than seventy-eight million bushels, and by 1980 some 175 million bushels. Today wheat is the state's largest cash crop, ranking third nationally and worth more than $300 million annually. The reason for this dramatic change was the introduction of man-made fibers to end the nation's—and the world's—dependency on cotton for clothing. In the early 1980s, however, as denim "blue jeans" became fashionable and cotton prices climbed, farmers began increasing their acreage of that crop while reducing wheat acreage, in line with the federal government's policy to reduce its stockpile of surplus grain.

Farmers at the same time were participating in one of the greatest agricultural revolutions in world history. No longer was the fertility of the soil or the amount of annual rainfall related to the abundance of their harvest. Irrigation wells perforated the land of western Oklahoma, and water could be pumped to the surface and dumped on crops as needed. Chemicals derived from petroleum were used as fertilizers and insecticides. Farm machinery of great sophistication—and cost—enabled one man to do the work that took dozens only a few years before (one man with a two-bottom plow pulled by four horses might, on a good day, plow twenty-five acres. Today a combine operated by one man can move through 100 acres in a day). Oklahoma thereby has become one of the great food-producing states of the Midwest—and will remain so as long as petrochemicals and underground water remain available, and if crop prices allow farmers a decent profit. Unfortunately the water table in western Oklahoma has begun to drop significantly, causing some state politicians and agricultural experts to call for a series of canals to move water from wet eastern Oklahoma to the arid western part of the state.

Livestock production kept pace with farming during these years—and actually brought more income to the state. Okla-

Above
During World War II wheat acreage and harvests increased impressively as Oklahomans sought to combat the Axis powers on the home front. OHS

Right
Irrigation helped offset the unreliability of Oklahoma's precipitation pattern. In Custer County an irrigation well helped this farmer produce bumper crops. Courtesy, United States Bureau of Reclamation

homa ranks fifth nationally in income from cattle and calves, and second in number of head. By 1980 there were six and a half million head of cows and calves on Oklahoma ranches, valued at almost one billion dollars; some 100,000 head of sheep and lambs valued at two and a half million dollars; and 350,000 hogs valued at fifteen million dollars. In addition, Oklahoma ranchers are major producers of the nation's quarter and riding horses, a number that may increase because of a referendum passsed in 1982 allowing pari-mutuel betting at legal racetracks in the state. There are also some 140,000 milk cows producing almost 1.2 bil-

barrels a day—began at Neodesha, Kansas, in 1893. Drillers, however, were slow to enter the Indian Territory because of uncertainty about the ownership of Indian lands. Speculators found oil near Chelsea in 1889, near Muskogee in 1894, and near Bartlesville in 1897, but none of this could be exploited because there was no way to get the petroleum to market. After the Dawes Commission began alloting land to individual Indians, leases could be signed with certainty, and the result was a significant strike in 1904 at Red Fork (just south of Tulsa) on land belonging to a Creek Indian. Although the Red Fork Pool was small,

This Oklahoma livestock operation was located near Chickasha. The photographer of this picture noted that a record price was received by these cattle when sold at the feedlot—450 head sold for $100 per head. OHS

lion pounds of milk annually, valued at more than $100 million.

Oklahoma's forestry industry annually produces products valued at some seventy-five million dollars. Approximately 23 percent of the state, some ten million acres, is covered with forests, one-half of it of commercial quality. This mainly centers in seventeen southeastern counties where loblolly pine, short-leafed pine, sweet gum, various oaks, cottonwood, pecan, and walnut trees are grown for commercial use. Lumbermen quickly learned the value of replanting trees cut for timber, and thus forestry has an excellent future in the state.

Life for Oklahoma's farmers and ranchers of today is immeasurably better than for their ancestors. Today, the soil for which the Boomers and Sooners fought has delivered the rich promise they saw, and their descendants help feed a hungry world. Making much of this prosperity has become possible due to chemical fertilizers manufactured from petroleum. Oil men knew early that the Mid-Continent region contained petroleum, for commercial production—twelve

Prairie Oil and Gas Company, a subsidiary of Standard Oil Company, built a pipeline to carry the production to a refinery in Kansas. This strike spurred others to search in the region, and the same year another field was opened near Cleveland, followed in 1905 by a discovery at Glenn Pool. Opened by Robert A. Galbreath and Frank Chesley, Glenn Pool was a major stike that made several millionaires and triggered the modern oil boom in Oklahoma. Another strike at Okmulgee in 1906 further encouraged oil speculators. Tulsa became the center of this activity, and soon what had been a small cattle town and Indian trade center was transformed into the self-proclaimed "Oil Capital of the World." In 1907, thanks largely to Glenn Pool's output, Oklahoma produced forty-three and a half million barrels of oil. The Texas Company (Texaco) and Gulf built pipelines to carry crude to refineries on the Gulf Coast, while Prairie Oil and Gas constructed another pipeline to take Oklahoma oil to a Standard refinery in Louisiana.

The next major strike came in 1912 at

the Cushing Field, because of the determination of several men who believed oil was there. Chief among them was Tom Slick, a Pennsylvanian who learned the oil business in his home state and who boasted that he could smell oil-laden sands before a drill bit touched the earth. For several months he suffered disappointment as he tried to drill a producing well, but finally he and his backers tapped what eventually would prove to be the second largest field in Oklahoma's history.

In the weeks and months that followed Tom Slick's initial discovery, Cushing experienced what other towns would come to know when oil was found nearby. Before Slick's success, Cushing had been a dusty, sleeping village. A few businessmen along the main street kept their doors open by extending liberal credit to farmers who hoped to pay their bills at harvest time. When crops failed, so did some businesses. There was not a single telephone, electric line, paved street, or automobile in town.

Oil brought dramatic and almost immediate change. Telephone lines were quickly strung, while the noise and fumes from automobiles soon could be heard along dusty streets, scaring horses and starting grass fires. All over town new businesses sprang into existence: storage yards for pipe and the assorted machinery needed to drill oil wells, lumber yards filled with massive derrick timbers, wagons used to transport all this to sites in the countryside, restaurants and hotels catering to the mass of humanity bustling about town, and supply houses carrying a wide assortment of merchandise at inflated prices. Other businesses opened for the sole purpose of separating the newly wealthy from their money: automobile dealerships, jewelry stores carrying a wide assortment of glittering gewgaws, and gift shops carrying "presents" for loved ones left behind. All the businessmen seemed to be doubling their prices almost every hour.

Because of the rapid growth, there was confusion, disorder, and uneven progress. For example, at the height of the boom, Cushing still had no sewer system, nor did it have suitable housing, and food often was in short supply. Housing was in such de-

Livestock production in Oklahoma remains one of the leading cash producers for the state's economy. Cattle still outnumber humans in the state. While technology has improved, roundups on horseback are still necessary. Photo by Jim Argo

Tulsa, pictured in the late 1920s, was the Oil Capital of the World. OHS

mand that enterprising pool hall owners allowed men to sleep on and beneath billiard tables from midnight to sunup for fifty cents (even chairs were rented for sleeping space). More enterprising men erected shanties from packing crates, cardboard, tree limbs, or anything else available on any plot of ground they could defend.

Conditions were made worse by the horde of tramps, vagrants, and hangers-on who swarmed into Cushing, as they did to every boomtown in Oklahoma. Unable to find work, they stood along the streets, sleeping in alleys and begging for food. There were also camp followers of a less desirable nature: gamblers who kept games going at all hours, women with no visible means of support, and whiskey peddlers. One writer referred to this class as "vultures, harpies, and the riffraff of the country . . . ." Crime became rampant, as did disease spread by cramped living conditions, poor food, impure water, and lack of proper sanitation. Meningitis became a dreaded killer, and typhoid was common.

Cushing was no quiet, sober community. It was boisterous and alive, its streets a jumble of humanity. Restaurants, hotels, stores, barbershops, illegal saloons, all brightly lighted, kept open house on both sides of the main street late into the night, while down at the freight yards men could be heard swearing as they sweated to load wagon after wagon with pipe or steam boiler or lumber or wire. The "roughnecks," as oilfield workers were known, arrived at the end of their shift of work and began to spend. And spend they did, for their wages ranged from six to fifteen dollars a day. Oklahoma was officially dry, but in the first week of the boom whiskey peddlers seemed to be on every corner doing a brisk business.

Theirs was a raw, potent product that seared the throat, warmed the stomach, and inflamed the head. One teetotaler commented in disgust, "Every bottle sold seemed to contain a thousand curse words, several arguments, and at least one fist fight."

The countryside around Cushing changed as much as the city during the oil boom. Dirt roads suddenly were crowded with flashy automobiles carrying agents offering fistfuls of money for drilling rights. Farmers and their sons, to whom $100 cash had once seemed a fortune, suddenly were exposed to fast-talking city slickers from Houston or Chicago offering thousands of dollars in return for a signature on a lease. Once the lease was signed, heavy wagons carrying steel, pipe, and timber cut deep ruts into roads that became impassable when it rained, while makeshift roads were torn across once-barren pastures. Such was life in and around a booming Oklahoma oil town.

The year after the discovery at Cushing, another major field opened at Healdton (near Ardmore). The combined production of the two fields swamped the national oil market as tens of thousands of barrels were brought to the surface daily, dropping the price of crude to forty cents a barrel. In fact, when a great fire destroyed more than 500,000 barrels of oil at Cushing, some producers were relieved to be rid of the excess. Eventually some producers tried self-regulation to slow production and stabilize oil prices. When this "gentlemen's agreement" failed to work, the Oklahoma Corporation Commission undertook regulation of the new industry in 1914. Although this attempt was largely a failure, the legislature passed laws the following year to stop the waste and try to bring order to the industry. Thereafter the Corporation Commission exercised some control in the oilfields, although several governors found it necessary to call out the National Guard to enforce the stop-production rulings of the commission to protect oil prices.

The outbreak of World War I increased oil prices after 1914, which, in turn, stimulated the search for new oil. Fields were now being located through geological analysis rather than by evaluating surface formations. Using this new method, three fields were discovered at Tonkawa (Three Sands) and Burbank by E.W. Marland.

In 1926 came the opening of the Greater Seminole Oil Field. The first discovery in this area had been made at Wewoka in 1923, but little development had taken place. When the extent of the field was realized in 1926 and serious production started, more than eight million barrels of oil were pumped within one year. The strike had a dramatic impact on the estate of O.D. Strother, a shoe salesman thought to be "land and lease poor." Regardless, Strother believed that oil was in the area, and when he died in March 1926, oil had been discovered and his estate was conservatively valued at seven and a half million dollars.

Then in December 1928 came the opening of the Oklahoma City Field when, "with a roar like thunder, . . . black gold flowed," as one newsman wrote. As early as 1915 oil men had learned that small deposits of oil and gas were underground in the area, however, most producers believed these were too small to be of commercial potential. In 1928 the Indian Territory Illuminating Oil Company drilled below the first level of production, and the main pool was located. Soon the output of the Seminole and Oklahoma City fields threatened to outdo the disastrous results of overproduction at Cushing and Healdton. To prevent a glut of oil and disastrously low prices, the Corporation Commission attempted to enforce the 1915 laws limiting overproduction—only to find itself disregarded and production increasing. Just at this time came the onset of the Great Depression—and the discovery of the East Texas Oil Field, one of the largest in the nation's history. The Depression slowed industry and slackened oil consumption just when production was greater than ever, and prices tumbled below fifteen cents a barrel. Governor Bill Murray twice declared oil wells under martial law to enforce Corporation Commission rulings. Certain wells were not allowed to produce again until the price of oil reached a dollar a barrel. There was open violence between the National Guard

The Cushing Oil Field was discovered by Tom Slick in 1912. This road ran from Cushing to Oilton through the heart of the field, showing the density of wells in the field, as well as the haphazard development of transportation routes and communication networks. Courtesy, Western History Collections, University of Oklahoma Library

The Greater Seminole Oil Field east of Oklahoma City was one of Oklahoma's largest producing fields from 1925 to the mid-1930s. Over-production from this and other Oklahoma fields led Governor "Alfalfa Bill" Murray to order the Oklahoma National Guard to close Oklahoma's oil fields to enforce proration. Courtesy, Western History Collections, University of Oklahoma Library

and roughnecks during the second period of martial law (1932), and some "hot oil" (illegally pumped) continued to flow through clandestine pipelines.

To remove the need for future declarations of martial law, the legislature in 1933 passed a proration law that provided a staff to oversee production and to halt illegal production. Although this law was imperfect, as when it relied on production potential rather than acreage to determine how much oil could be pumped from a well, it nevertheless became a model followed by other oil-producing states.

After 1935 the Oklahoma oil business began to settle down. The search for new fields became more orderly, as did the conduct of oilfield workers in towns where booms occurred. Major finds were made in the southern and northwestern areas of the state, including the Panhandle Field near Guymon. The discovery of the West Edmond Field in 1943 showed that unknown large pools were still underground, and technical innovations allowed secondary and tertiary methods of oil recovery in fields thought exhausted. When the Organization of Petroleum Exporting Countries (OPEC) embargoed oil shipments to the United States in 1973, intensified efforts to find additional petroleum in the United States led to a drilling rush in Oklahoma, especially

after 1981 when President Ronald Reagan signed legislation deregulating petroleum prices, allowing free market prices to prevail. In addition, this legislation allowed a free market on natural gas discovered at depths greater than 15,000 feet.

When the price of oil soared toward forty dollars a barrel, a boom of historic proportions developed in Oklahoma. This was especially true in the Anadarko Basin where drilling reached record depths of more than 25,000 feet to bring in gas wells of incredible richness. The state's unemployment rate dropped to the lowest in the nation, and migrants flowed into the state at such a rate that some Oklahoma towns experienced growth that rivaled the boom era of the 1920s. Elk City, Woodward, Clinton, and other cities in the western and northwestern portions of the state saw explosive growth with workers living in tents and trailers, while municipal services were stretched almost beyond their limits.

The oil men who created this boom were so successful and their wells so productive that the world price of oil was forced below thirty dollars a barrel, causing the boom to collapse late in 1982. This left in its wake a multitude of bankruptcies and the closing of Penn Square Bank in Oklahoma City, a financial institution that had specialized in financing oil men in their quest for black gold. Its collapse sent shock waves through financial circles across the United States, while the lower prices commanded by oil and gas forced the state of Oklahoma into painful economic retrenchment when the taxes on petroleum production dipped below anticipated levels.

Several giant firms emerged out of the boom-and-bust cycle of Oklahoma's petroleum industry: Phillips Petroleum of Bartlesville, Continental Oil Company (Conoco) at Ponca City (formerly Maryland Oil Company), Champlin at Enid, Skelly at Tulsa, and Kerr-McGee of Oklahoma City. These were large, integrated firms involved in producing, refining, and marketing petroleum products. There were also dozens of independent producing companies in the state involved only in drilling and developing wells, and selling their output to major corporations or to independent refiners and marketers. In the late 1970s and early 1980s, as the consolidation of small firms into larger ones occurred at a rapid pace, some of Oklahoma's better-known companies disappeared. For example, Skelly merged with Getty Oil, which in turn was bought by Texaco. There were, in addition, takeover attempts by other major oil companies that produced headlines across the nation. These firms, large and small, have written a significant portion of the history

of petroleum in both the United States and the world, for the majors and independents who pioneered in Oklahoma took their knowledge and expertise to other states and nations, even to the oceans with offshore drilling technology.

The impact of the petroleum industry in

Above
The Indian Territory Illuminating Oil Company's Oklahoma City discovery well, brought in during 1928, was located near present-day S.E. 59th Street and Shields Boulevard. OHS

Left
Elk City, pictured in the 1950s, became the center of a modern-day oil and natural gas boom during the late 1970s. OHS

Oklahoma cannot be over-emphasized. The total value of petroleum products, in terms of jobs, wages, dividends, and lease payments, grows each day, amounting to more than forty billion dollars since statehood, while the taxes taken by the state from both production and wages have enabled all Oklahomans to enjoy a far higher standard of living than otherwise would have been possible in a state whose tax structure has not always been favorable to business. Still the search for petroleum proceeds in Oklahoma—the history of the industry is such that other booms doubtless lie ahead.

Oklahoma's petroleum energy has been made available to both residential and business customers by natural gas pipeline companies, and it has been used to fuel electric generators. Many cities in the first years of the twentieth century used diesel generators to produce electricity, but later switched to coal-fired generators. With the building of great dams in eastern Oklahoma, particularly in the 1950s and 1960s, electricity generated by waterpower became widely available through such organizations as the Grand River Dam Authority (GRDA), which sold much of its output to rural electric cooperatives. In the early 1980s, as the cost of energy soared, plans to build a nuclear generator, the Black Fox project in eastern Oklahoma, were abandoned because of soaring costs and public disapproval. A less conventional source of power is also widely available in Oklahoma: wind-turned electric generators. One pioneering firm in Norman specialized in manufacturing "wind-chargers," as these were known to farmers as early as the 1930s, and were used to power a radio and a few lights.

Other mineral resources of great value to Oklahoma include lead, zinc, coal, copper, cement, granite, gypsum, helium, limestone, sand and gravel, and stone. Oklahoma stands fourth among all states in the production of lead and zinc. This is in a region known as the Tri-State Zinc-Lead Mining District, which encompasses producing centers in southeastern Kansas, northeastern Oklahoma, and southwestern Missouri. Oklahoma coal mining began in the 1870s when J.J. McAlester, an intermarried citizen of the Choctaw Nation, established the Oklahoma Mining Company. Production also occurred at Krebs, Coalgate, and other towns in the Choctaw and Creek regions. Many of the early coal miners were immi-

grants from Czechoslovakia, Hungary, Germany, and Italy, and the result was the development of towns with a European flavor that has been retained to the present. By 1900 almost two million tons of coal were being mined each year, an amount that grew to almost five million tons by 1920. Production since that time has varied, but by the 1970s, as the energy needs of the nation grew and the price of petroleum soared, Oklahoma's coal reserves increased in importance. Dozens of small strip-mining corporations were formed in Muskogee, Okmulgee, and surrounding counties, but because of the coal's high sulphur content the federal Environmental Protection Agency refused to allow it to be burned in the area. Thus Oklahoma's coal often is exported to foreign countries (by way of the McClellan-Kerr waterway), and electricity is generated in the area with low-sulphur coal from Wyoming and other states.

Oklahoma's rich soil has also been used as a raw resource for two other important products: bricks and glass. Long before statehood, bricks were being made from Oklahoma clay. Mormons who arrived in Tahlequah in 1844 showed the Cherokees how to make the bricks that were used to erect their Male and Female Seminaries. After the land runs, scores of plants in the Oklahoma Territory fired the deep red bricks needed to erect buildings and homes. Today the low cost of bricks in the Sooner State means that even modest homes are attractively faced with Oklahoma-fired bricks. Sand of high quality for glass-making plants is available at many locations, and the abundance of cheap natural gas brought many firms to the state to produce canning jars (at Sand Springs and Okmulgee), sheet glass (at the Ford float plant in Tulsa), bottles and bakeware (at the Corning and Brockway plants in Muskogee), and other types of specialty glass at Sapulpa and Henryetta.

Since statehood the total value of Oklahoma's mineral production, including petroleum, has moved far beyond sixty billion dollars in value. Most experts agree that the amount of oil and natural gas still underground is greater than that taken out in the past. The future promises even greater riches from the soil, and as technology advances Oklahomans will again discover how generously endowed their state is in natural resources.

A celebration commemorating the capitol dome project,
which was finally completed on November 16, 2003.
When construction originally began in 1914, funds were
diverted to World War I. Courtesy, Terry Zinn

A lone buffalo grazes in the Wichita Wildlife Refuge near Lawton, Oklahoma. Courtesy, William D. Welge

The historic capitol building for the Chickasaw Nation, located in Tishomingo. Built in 1898, it is on the National Register of Historic Places and is used as a museum depicting Chickasaw tribal history. Courtesy, William D. Welge

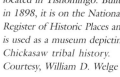

Mount Scott, located in the Wichita Wildlife Refuge near Lawton. Courtesy, William D. Welge

Remains of the old Fort Washita near Madill. Established in 1842, it served as a buffer against nomadic plains tribes such as the Comanche and Kiowa raiding the Choctaw and Chickasaw tribes who were peaceful farmers and ranchers. Courtesy, William D. Welge

Along many of Oklahoma's highways one can see rustic settings such as this wooden barn located south of Chickasha along Highway 81. Courtesy, William D. Welge.

*One-hundred-sixty-eight
empty chairs signify the loss
of lives during the Oklahoma
City bombing in 1995.
Oklahoma City National
Memorial. Courtesy, Terry
Zinn*

An interior view of the new rotunda at the state capitol, circa 2004. Courtesy, Terry Zinn

197

Spirit of Red Earth, *a double exposure of Joy Anderson, Sioux tribal member. Courtesy, Terry Zinn, © 1989*

Above:
A herd of Buffalo at the
Wichita Wildlife Refuge.
Courtesy, Terry Zinn, ©
1989

Left:
Kiowa Black Leggings
Society (Kiowa Warriors) at
the inauguration of Governor
Brad Henry in 2003.
Courtesy, Terry Zinn

A pasture near Milburnay.
Courtesy, William D. Welge

The Falderal String Band
entertains guests at the
National Cowboy and
Western Heritage Museum
with old folk songs from the
pioneer past. Courtesy,
William D. Welge

Pictured here are patches of azaleas in Muskogee, where the Azalea Festival is held each April. Courtesy, William D. Welge

A Spanish-style home which is now used by the Philbrook Museum of Art in Tulsa. Courtesy, William D. Welge

The reflecting pool at the Oklahoma City National Memorial. Courtesy, Oklahoma City National Memorial

One of the MAPS projects, enhancing the cultural life of those in Oklahoma City. The SBC Bricktown Ballpark has a statue of Oklahoma native Johnny Bench, who played for the Cincinnati Reds. Courtesy, William D. Welge

Colorful buffalo statues can be spotted all over Oklahoma City. Sponsored by the Oklahoma Centennial Commission, this piece is in front of the SBC Bricktown Ballpark near downtown. Courtesy, William D. Welge

The Bethany Balloon Festival is held each August by local businesses and civic organizations. Courtesy, Oklahoma Historical Society (OHS)

The Oklahoma City Festival of the Arts is held near downtown Oklahoma City each April. Courtesy, Terry Zinn

The dedication of the
Meinders School of Business
at Oklahoma City University
in 2004. Courtesy, Terry
Zinn

Chandelier, an exquisite glass
work by world renowned
artist Dale Chihuly, is on
permanent exhibit at the
Oklahoma City Museum of
Art. Courtesy, Terry Zinn, ©
2003

The Buffalo Bill statue at the
National Cowboy Museum
and Western Art Center in
Oklahoma City. Courtesy,
Terry Zinn

The Oklahoma state capitol building in Oklahoma City, circa 2004. Courtesy, Terry Zinn

A High Quality of Life

*I*n 1889, on the eve of the first land run, Oklahoma was still largely the way nature had shaped it. Some Indians in the eastern part of the territory were farming and some railroad tracks had been laid, but most of the region was still undisturbed by man. Moreover, the population was small, amounting to fewer than 200,000 people. In the decades that followed towns were built, railroads were joined by highway, river, and air transportation systems, communications improved dramatically, newspapers grew in number, and a modern educational system was erected. The people of the state showed their love for the arts and music, just as they demonstrated an appreciation and awareness of their heritage by establishing museums and joining historical organizations to preserve their unique heritage.

By the date of the first major land run, there were only seven incorporated towns in what would become Oklahoma. The first was in 1873 when the Cherokee Nation approved the incorporation of Downingville (now Vinita)—although residents of Tahlequah claim that their town was incorporated in 1852. Webbers Falls was incorporated in 1885; Mangum, in Greer County, was incorporated under the laws of Texas in 1886; and Chelsea, Chouteau, and Claremore were incorporated in 1889.

Today the most populous city in the state is Oklahoma City, which was born in a single hour on April 22, 1889. Where only a small railroad depot and hotel rested on the prairie that morning, more than 10,000 people had gathered in thousands of tents and wagons by that evening. Confusing the situation were two competing township companies trying to develop the city. Moreover, the federal act opening the Oklahoma District had not authorized city government. Yet the settlers did not worry about the niceties of the law, and on their own initiative organized a local government, elected officials, passed ordinances, and enforced their

Oklahoma City, the largest city in the state and the financial and governmental capital of Oklahoma, has burgeoned from a born-grown town of less than 10,000 in 1889 to a metropolitan area with almost one million inhabitants. Photo by Jim Argo

laws. One township company, the Oklahoma Colony Company, made the run from the south and surveyed south of the railroad tracks. The second, the Seminole Land and Improvement Company, came from Kansas and platted from Clarke (now Sheridan) Avenue northward. After the organization of the territory, the two plattings merged into a town called Oklahoma. The word "City" would not be recognized by the post office for thirty-four more years.

When Oklahoma City was founded, it had no real geographical advantages. Yet because of solid leadership and initiative it grew and prospered, and its future was assured when it became the state capital in 1910. Gradually, thanks to good rail service, it became the wholesaling and jobbing center for much of the state, as well as the major livestock market in the region. The drilling of an oilfield in 1928 inside its corporate limits brought yet another major industry there, while the location of Tinker

Field on its eastern outskirts during World War II provided permanent employment for thousands (and Tinker remains the largest single employer in the state). The Commercial Club, later the Chamber of Commerce—for many years under the leadership of Stanley Draper—played a leading role in attracting industry, securing conventions, and providing cultural activities. Today the city has more than 500,000 residents, while its satellite communities constitute a metropolitan area of approximately 850,000. A pioneering spirit is still evident in Oklahoma City, for in the late 1960s when the downtown area began to deteriorate with age, local leaders began a major urban renewal program that is transforming the face of the city. This rebuilding is scheduled for completion in 1989, the centennial of the run that brought the city into existence.

Oklahoma City's major competitor has been Tulsa, a city started by Creek Indians migrating from the southeastern United

States. In 1836 they founded the community they named Talsi, later called Tulsey Town and then Tulsa. For almost fifty years the community existed as an Indian village. Then in 1882 the Frisco Railroad arrived, and Tulsa became the center of cattle trade in eastern Oklahoma. Under the terms of the Curtis Act of 1898, Tulsa was incorporated and a town survey was made in 1900. Four years later came the discovery of oil at nearby Red Fork, followed in 1905 by drilling at Glenn Pool, and Tulsa changed within a few short years from a sleepy cow town into the "Oil Capital of the World." As a result, the population, which had reached 18,182 in 1910, boomed to 72,075 by 1920. City fathers made a concerted effort to attract oil company corporate headquarters, as well as oil-related manufacturing concerns and refineries. The International Petroleum Exposition, which began in 1923, made oil men everywhere aware that Tulsa, unlike some other cities, wanted their business, and more of them moved to Tulsa. Building on this base, the city grew and prospered, while oil-millionaires-turned-philanthropists beautified and enriched life in the city through selected gifts and donations of parks, museums, and municipal structures. In 1954 *Reader's Digest* named Tulsa "America's Most Beautiful City," and in 1974 *Harper's Magazine* rated it the second-best city in America for livability.

During World War II Tulsa's economy diversified when several non-petroleum-related industries moved to Tulsa, diversifying the area's economic base into aviation (later aerospace) and other concerns. Then in 1971 the McClellan-Kerr Arkansas River Navigation System was opened and provided barge transportation that, in effect, made Tulsa a seaport. All these changes promised to change Tulsa yet again, making it not only a major oil center but also a manufacturing and transportation hub for much of mid-America. Today its population has surpassed 400,000 and its metropolitan area includes almost 600,000.

Another major metropolitan area in Oklahoma is Lawton, born on August 6, 1901, when the Kiowa-Comanche lands were opened to white settlement. Lawton has benefited from the presence of nearby Fort Sill, as well as from the businesses and industrial firms that have located there. Today its population exceeds 80,000, and its future looks bright. Other prominent Oklahoma cities include Norman, home of the University of Oklahoma and aircraft and wind-powered generator industries; Midwest City, a suburb of Oklahoma City and the actual site of Tinker Field; Enid, for many years the home of Champlin Oil Company and now a regional trade and distributing center; Muskogee, former premier city of the Indian Territory and now a center of glass and optical manufacturing; Stillwater, home of Oklahoma State University; Bartlesville, the location of Phillips Petroleum Company; and Ponca City, home of Conti-

Lawton, home of Fort Sill, county seat of Comanche County, and the largest city in southwestern Oklahoma, grew dramatically from a tent city following the lottery of 1901 into Oklahoma's third-largest city in 1980. OHS

Above
Participants at the International Petroleum Exposition met with members of Indian tribes whose lands produced oil and natural gas. Oklahoma's Osage Indians were numbered among the world's wealthiest people in the 1910s and 1920s during the height of the oil boom in Osage County. Courtesy, Tulsa County Historical Society

Right
Depicted circa 1905 is the print shop of the Cherokee Advocate, staffed by Cherokee Indians. Courtesy, Western History Collections, University of Oklahoma Library

nental Oil Company (Conoco).

Within weeks of the establishment of most towns in newly-opened territories, local newspapers began publication to predict an unlimited future for each community. These joined the *Cherokee Advocate,* which for decades had been the only newspaper in Oklahoma except for religious tracts published by missionaries, and about ten weeklies that began publication in the 1880s with the arrival of the railroads. Most of these early efforts were small and had limited circulation, but gradually a few newspapers emerged to dominate the state. The *Indian Chief* began publication in Tulsa in 1884, and in 1893 came the *Indian Republican;* in 1905 came the *Tulsa Daily World,* which traces its lineage to both these earlier papers. The *World's* major rival, the *Tulsa Tribune,* traces its founding to the *New Era,* a weekly which eventually became the *Tulsa Democrat* and then in 1919 was acquired by Richard Lloyd Jones and renamed the *Tulsa Tribune.* Today the *Tribune* and the *World* are the major daily papers of eastern Oklahoma.

In the Oklahoma District one of the first newspapers was the *Edmond Sun,* founded by Milton Reynolds, but after his death in 1890 it diminished in importance. The *Oklahoma City Times,* later to become the *Oklahoma Journal,* then the *Oklahoma City Times-Journal,* and finally the *Oklahoma Times,* began publication on May 9, 1889, as a weekly under the editorship of Angelo Scott and his brother Winfield W. Scott. The *Daily Oklahoman* began publication in 1889 under the editorship of the Reverend Samuel Small, ceased for a time, and then was reissued by a stock company headed by Whit Grant. Both the *Daily Oklahoman* and the *Times* eventually became part of the Oklahoma Publishing Company of E.K. Gaylord, who arrived in Oklahoma City in 1902 and for more than seventy years was a major force in journalism in the state (in 1984 the two papers were combined into one daily published by E.L. Gaylord, son of the founding publisher).

By 1900 Oklahoma Territory was the home of nine daily papers, 139 weeklies, eighteen monthlies, and four semi-monthlies. These publishers realized early the need for some central organization to represent their interests, and in 1888 at Muskogee they had formed the Indian Territory Press Association, a name changed to the Oklahoma

Press Association after statehood.

The roads over which these first newspapers were delivered were little more than wagon tracks. These had evolved as Indians, especially members of the Five Civilized Tribes, wound through the countryside looking for the easiest way to drive a wagon from one settlement to the next. When they came to rivers and creeks, they sought a place to ford the stream or, failing that, a place where a ferry might profitably be started. These roads usually began in Arkansas and proceeded to Texas or, in the case of the famed Texas Road, started in Kansas and proceeded through eastern Oklahoma to the Lone Star State. Other roads were laid out by soldiers connecting major posts in the territory.

The coming of the railroads eased transportation problems in Oklahoma. The Katy, the Frisco, the Santa Fe, and the Rock Island would remain the principal carriers of freight, mail, and people well into the twen-

Edward K. Gaylord arrived in Oklahoma City after the turn of the century, becoming the business manager of the Daily Oklahoman. *He used this position to build the newspaper into the most widely read tabloid in the state, and expanded his empire into radio, television, and transportation. Courtesy, Bob L. Blackburn*

tieth century. Despite the appearance of automobiles at the start of the twentieth century, little was done to build roads, other than city streets, for a decade. Then in 1909 representatives from six states and Canada gathered at Guthrie to map out a highway to run from Canada to the Gulf (eventually this would become U.S. 77). The immediate effect of the proposed highway was to cause the legislature to create the State Highway Department in 1911—but only after intense lobbying by Governor Lee Cruce. To fund this department the legislature authorized a license fee of one dollar for each automobile in the state. Three years later state records show there were 6,524 automobiles in Oklahoma although only 2,241 owners had paid

geles by way of Tulsa and Oklahoma City; and U.S. 77 crossed the state from north to south, going from Wichita, Kansas, to Dallas, Texas. In addition, the state gradually built hard-surfaced farm-to-market roads in every county. Progress could be seen in the number of highway miles in Oklahoma: in 1916 there were twenty-five and a half miles of surfaced roads; in 1939 the number had grown to 4,804 miles of paved highways and 2,470 miles of graveled roads.

Little could be done during the war years, but in 1947 the legislature authorized the construction of the first turnpike in the state—the Turner Turnpike connecting Oklahoma City and Tulsa. Other turnpikes followed until much of the state was cov-

The Turner Turnpike, linking Oklahoma City with Tulsa, was completed in 1953. Courtesy, Oklahoma Turnpike Authority

the annual fee. In 1915 the legislature enlarged the State Highway Department, authorizing a highway commissioner, a state engineer, an assistant engineer, and a secretary, and it increased the automobile license fee and authorized a tax earmarked for highway construction. Nevertheless, the bulk of all highway construction remained in the hands of the three county commissioners in each of Oklahoma's seventy-seven counties—231 fiefdoms with needless duplication of expensive machinery, haphazard planning, considerable waste, and some corruption.

In 1916 the Federal Aid Road Act was enacted, providing federal matching funds for building national highways, and Oklahoma received $115,139. This was augmented seven years later by passage of a one-cent-per-gallon state gasoline tax. The result was an inflow of sufficient revenue to build national highways across the Sooner State: U.S. 66 ran from Chicago to Los An-

ered, several of them unprofitable because they were born out of intense political pressures rather than sound fiscal analyses. Likewise, automobile tax collection was turned over to private tag agents appointed through senatorial patronage. This also led to waste and some corruption.

Meanwhile the Federal-Aid Highway Act, also known as the Interstate Defense System, became law in 1956, providing 90 percent federal financing for multiple-lane, access-controlled roads. Today this system is virtually complete in Oklahoma. I-35 runs south from the Kansas border to Oklahoma City and Ardmore, then crosses into Texas to Dallas-Fort Worth, while I-44 has replaced old U.S. 66 from the Missouri border to Tulsa and Oklahoma City, and I-40 carries traffic from Fort Smith westward to Oklahoma City and on to Amarillo, Texas.

The Department of Transportation is controlled by an appointive eight-member board funded by earmarked road-user taxes, appropriations from the state general fund, and monies derived from the Federal Highway Trust Fund (which comes from federal taxes on gasoline and other sources). The department cares for a state highway system of more than 12,000 miles of hard-surfaced roads and employs more than 3,000 people, while the Oklahoma Turnpike Authority, a six-member board, oversees six turnpikes of 488 miles.

Another form of transportation as old as the early European exploration of Oklahoma is by way of the Arkansas River. Where Frenchmen once traveled by pirogue and flatboat, the first American settlers moved by steamboat. By the late nineteenth century, however, railroads had supplanted steamboats because of the fickle nature of the Arkansas, which rose and fell depending on each spring's snow melt and rain fall. In 1971, however, after twenty-two years of work, the McClellan-Kerr Waterway opened the Arkansas to barge navigation. Thanks to dredging and an intricate system of locks, river traffic was possible for the 440 miles from the port of Catoosa outside Tulsa to the Mississippi River (and from there to New Orleans and the Gulf of Mexico). Down this artery of commerce passed coal and agriculture commodities, as well as many industrial products. To keep the proper level of water in this waterway, the Corps of Engineers created a series of man-made

lakes: Heyburn (1950), Huhlah (1951), Tenkiller (1952), Fort Gibson (1953), and Robert S. Kerr and Webber Falls (1970). These lakes not only provided water to the largest single civil works project ever undertaken by the Corps of Engineers, but have also become major recreation sites.

Today much of the interstate travel by Oklahomans is done by airplane. The first recorded flight in the state was made in Oklahoma City in 1910 by exhibition pilot Charles F. Willard. For this effort he received $1,000—and crashed. Aviation remained a curiosity until World War I, when a military flying field was created in Oklahoma at Fort Sill. Even after the war ended there was little interest in aviation except among former military fliers, many of whom "barnstormed" across the state, landing in pastures near towns to give local residents a brief flight over the countryside for three to five dollars each.

Then in 1926 Oklahoma City was placed on a transcontinental air mail route, which ran from Dallas to Chicago. To secure this, Stanley Draper of the Oklahoma City Chamber of Commerce guaranteed that an average thirty pounds of air mail would originate in Oklahoma City daily. To meet this quota Draper, on occasion, had to send bricks by air mail to friends in distant parts of the United States. Following Charles Lindbergh's solo flight across the Atlantic

This aerial view pictures the Tulsa Port of Catoosa at the head of navigation on the McClellan-Kerr Arkansas River Navigation System. The system opened the heartland of Oklahoma to river transportation and new economic ties with foreign markets. OHS

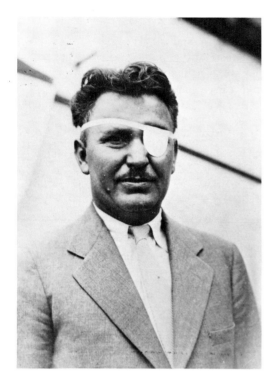

the following summer, interest in aviation soared, and National Air Transport began a passenger and express service from Oklahoma City to Chicago. Tom E. and Paul Braniff began operating what would become Braniff Airways between Oklahoma City and Tulsa in June 1928, while the following November Earle P. Halliburton of Duncan started SAFEway Airlines. Oil men such as Halliburton played an important role in early aviation because they were constantly fighting time and distance, and they learned that airplanes could get them where they needed to go quickly. Frank and L.E. Phillips made important advances in high-test aviation gasoline and pioneered high altitude flying. In 1928 William G. Skelly assumed ownership and management of Spartan Aviation in Tulsa; this firm built airplanes, and its school trained thousands of pilots and mechanics. Aviation in Oklahoma was also aided by the federal Civil Works Administration, which helped finance landing fields, lights, and radio equipment. Oklahoma pilot Wiley Post captured world headlines by setting an around-the-world speed record in 1930 and again in 1933, while Bennett Griffin and James J. Mattern set records in their around-the-world flight that ended in Russia in 1932.

Farmers and ranchers found the airplane to be an excellent tool, and in August 1944 they organized a statewide group known as the Oklahoma Flying Farmers. This soon expanded into the National Flying Farmers Association and then into the International Flying Farmers Association.

World War II brought many military airfields and thousands of young pilot trainees to Oklahoma, further stimulating aviation in the state. Airplane factories were opened in Tulsa, Oklahoma City, and Norman, and these continued to function after the conflict ended, while military airfields and auxiliary landing fields became municipal airports. During the Korean War, when Oklahoman Harold C. Stuart was assistant secretary of the Air Force, bases at Enid and Altus became permanent Air Force fields, and Tinker Field assumed a major role in Air Force planning. Rockwell and McDonnell-Douglas, both at Tulsa, continue to win major military aviation and aerospace contracts employing thousands, while Aero-Commander manufactures corporate aircraft at Bethany (a suburb of Oklahoma City). Oklahoma is in the vanguard of pioneering the next chapter in flying—the move into space. The Sooner State has contributed more astronauts to the efforts of the National Aeronautics and Space Administration than any other state.

The telegraph arrived in Oklahoma around 1871 with the railroad, and it drastically improved links with the outside world. As tracks were laid, additional lines were strung until every railroad station in both Indian and Oklahoma territories had telegraph service. News came over the wires to fill newspapers, and at times of great national sporting events, or national emergency (as during the Spanish-American War and World War I), the telegraph office in each city posted news and game results for the throngs of people gathered outside.

The telephone gradually replaced the telegraph as the main instrument of communication. Apparently the first telephone line in Oklahoma was a military one, strung between Fort Reno and the Darlington Agency. The first commercial telephone service in Oklahoma was organized in 1886 by a twenty-year-old Cherokee, E.D. Hicks, who, after seeing the instrument demonstrated in St. Louis, organized a firm and strung lines between Tahlequah and Fort Gibson, then on to Muskogee. By the time his switchboard opened, he had eighteen customers. Service came slowly to other towns and cities as local firms opened exchanges. For example, the Missouri and Kansas Telephone

Telephones were a recent invention when Oklahoma was opened to non-Indian settlement, but they quickly became indispensable for early settlers. The first telephone line constructed in Tonkawa in the Cherokee Outlet was completed in 1902. Courtesy, Western History Collections, University of Oklahoma Library

Company began service in Oklahoma City in 1893, seven years after Hicks' exchange opened. By 1906 there were a reported 162 telephone companies in Oklahoma, a number that in just two years expanded to 275. The largest of these was Pioneer Telephone Company, which in 1917 joined the Bell System as Southwestern Bell Telephone Company.

The generally accepted date of the first radio broadcast in Oklahoma is November 2, 1920, when Earl Hull, using a twenty-watt transmitter installed in his garage in Oklahoma City, went on the air using call letters WKY. His was the first radio station west of the Mississippi River and the third in the nation to broadcast on a regular basis. Receiving a license in 1923, Hull operated WKY with H.S. Richmond as a partner. In 1928 the station was purchased by the Oklahoma Publishing Company, which has continued to operate it. Next to go on the air was WMAB, which no longer operates; followed by KFJZ (now KOMA) in Oklahoma City; and WNAD, operated in Norman by the University of Oklahoma. Other stations went on the air when individuals across the state decided that a radio

station could do much to promote a city. For example, R.H. Rollestone started KFRU in 1924 in Bristow, telling the audience that the station's letters stood for "Kind Friends, Remember Us." Moving to Tulsa, KFRU was acquired by oil man W.G. Skelly in 1928, and its call letters changed to KVOO (Voice Of Oklahoma). Other pioneers in the field of radio included J.T. Griffin of Muskogee, also known for his food processing and grocery wholesale business; eventually he owned several stations and brought numerous innovations to the radio business.

When these early radio stations went on the air, their audience was small. Few Oklahomans in the mid 1920s had the money (and, in many cases, no available electricity) to purchase expensive radio sets which, at best, picked up little more than static occasionally interrupted by a scratchy voice or a bit of music. By the 1930s, however, most urban Oklahomans had radios in their homes, while rural residents waited for rural electric cooperatives to arrive and power their homes so they could listen to the outside world. A few hardy farmers used "windchargers" (wind-driven generators re-

217

The first commercial radio station in Oklahoma was WKY of Oklahoma City. This is an early sound effects booth of this communications and entertainment pioneer in the state. Courtesy, WKY Radio

sembling windmills) to operate a radio. By this time Oklahoma's stations had affiliated with national networks, and local residents each evening eagerly awaited a favorite program of news, music, comedy, or drama. There were locally produced programs, many devoted to country music, which might have made Tulsa or Oklahoma City the center of this industry, had there not been a feeling that listening to this music showed a lack of "culture."

The first television station in Oklahoma was owned by the Oklahoma Publishing Company, the same firm that owned the state's first radio station. It also had the call letters WKY, and its 1949 debut was shortly followed by station openings in Tulsa. Not until 1952 were these connected by telephone cable to national network programming, and even in this area Oklahomans

pioneered. For example, KWTV in Oklahoma City began telecasting from a 1,572-foot broadcast tower on January 1, 1954, at that time the tallest man-made structure in the world. Later that same year WKY-TV became the first non-network station in the United States to broadcast color programming. Today the educational potential of television is realized through the Oklahoma Educational Television Authority. Funded by the state and by private donations and using four broadcast towers, this network provides educational programming to all parts of the state.

When Oklahomans, along with other Americans, began listening to radio in large numbers, some educators said that children would stop reading. Similar cries were heard when television stations went on the air. In reality, the number of books circulating from Oklahoma's libraries has increased every year. When the Oklahoma Library Commission was created in 1919, fifty-two of the seventy-seven counties had no public library within their jurisdictions. Now named the Department of Libraries and governed by a seven-member board, this central agency has assisted in promoting public, school, and institutional libraries. Today every county has at least one public library, and many belong to multi-county or city-county library systems supported by a special ad valorem tax.

Oklahoma's public school system has struggled through a difficult infancy. At statehood the rural schools of the Indian Territory were merged with those in Oklahoma Territory to form one system—with scant funds, ill-prepared teachers, and students often kept home to help with planting and harvesting. In what had been the Oklahoma Territory, two sections in each township were reserved as school lands, to provide income to help fund public schools. Such had not been the case in the Indian Territory, and Congress at statehood appropriated five million dollars for the territories' school fund in lieu of such land. This, combined with the value of the reserved school lands, totaled twenty-two million dollars for the state. Very quickly legislators realized that the income from the reserved school lands was inadequate, so annual appropriations for public education were made from the general operating fund, in addition to local property tax assessments. By 1921 this sum had reached $100,000, plus the income derived from school lands.

At first the school term was short, but gradually the length of sessions increased until it reached a full nine months statewide. Moreover, state law, which originally prescribed free public education for all Oklahomans aged eight to seventeen, was changed to guarantee the same right to all citizens from age six to twenty-one, and then free public kindergarten was added.

In the early years after statehood, conditions varied widely from district to district. Some were rich because of valuable property or oil deposits, while some rural districts had only a small tax base. Others had residents unwilling to approve high taxes to support local education. The state founded normal colleges and gradually increased the educational requirements for teacher certification, but in the early years most teachers

began their careers in small, one- or two-room schools that were short of supplies and books. Teachers often had to serve not only as instructors, but also as janitors, nurses, lunch makers, and counselors—all for a salary as low as forty dollars a month. Jennie Hays Higgins of Coweta later recalled her experiences in one school. Although only twenty years old, she had been teaching four years when she arrived there:

I was to get sixty dollars a month for eight months. But they told me it was a "cotton school." I asked what a cotton school was. My schedule included teaching two months during the summer, July and August, then dismissing for three months [so the children could pick cotton] and beginning again in December . . . . Monday morning my father took me to school. When we arrived, the yard was full of children and some grown people. I asked, "Why are all these men and women here?" Father thought they had walked with their children for the first time. When I rang the hand bell, all the children and grown folks came in . . . . I found that I had nine grown girls and seven grown boys [in grades one to eight].

During the next eight years, conditions became worse. Elizabeth Howard of Sapulpa later remembered her teaching experience in that school in 1931:

During the depression, before the federal or state lunch programs were started, mothers would bring vegetables and meat to the school to prepare soup for those children whom the principal found to be in need of food. There were those who fainted in school and who came without lunches.

In 1946 residents of the state approved a constitutional amendment providing for free textbooks (which had been discontinued because of a scandal during the 1930s), and three years later the legislature drafted a school code making all regulations uniform throughout the state. Yet the big crises of the postwar years were school consolidation and desegregation. Governor Roy Turner attempted to consolidate 500 rural schools into several larger districts, but local communities furiously fought to retain their schools' autonomy. Gradually the smaller ones were closed and the children bussed to bigger schools, but to the present day the consolidation of all small schools has not been achieved.

During Turner's administration desegregation came to the forefront in higher education. Ada Lois Sipuel (Fisher), a graduate of Langston University, applied for admission to the University of Oklahoma Law School in January 1946, but was refused admission on the basis of her color. The state supreme court refused to hear her appeal, but the United States Supreme Court ruled on January 12, 1948, that Sipuel had to be admitted. In 1949 the legislature then said that blacks could be admitted to graduate programs in state educational institutions. Then came the Supreme Court ruling in 1954 which ended desegregation in public schools, whereupon such discrimination was dropped not only in colleges and universities, but also in the public schools. Subsequently the state saw the advent of bussing to achieve racial balance in urban schools—along with white flight from urban to suburban areas. This nationally mandated attempt to achieve racial balance also brought skyrocketing costs to public education as well as some public outcries about the courts tampering with what was seen as the sole concern of individual school districts.

Today there are more than 600 school districts in Oklahoma, most of them independent (serving a population base of more than 1,200 students and required to maintain a high school), providing free public education for more than 650,000 students. The teachers who operate this system have developed what many observers agree is the most effective lobby in the state, and, more than 40,000 strong, they annually pressure for more money to be appropriated for education. Changes are coming to Oklahoma's public school system, some of them due to concerns of teachers, some of them a result of public demand. In 1981 the legislature mandated competency testing for all new teachers, and national trends indicate that the concept of merit pay for outstanding teachers may soon become commonplace.

A statewide system of vocational training has been closely connected with the public schools. Authorized by Congress in 1917 in the Smith-Hughes Act, this system provides education for high school students and adults who learn by doing and who usually qualify for jobs immediately after graduation. In 1968 the legislature consolidated this system by creating the State Board of

Vocational and Technical Education, which oversees the training of more than 250,000 Oklahomans each year through area "votech" schools. Under Governor Dewey Bartlett, the vo-tech system made a concerted effort to work with prospective manufacturing concerns to train workers for factories, thereby attracting more industry to Oklahoma. The vo-tech system has been one of the bright spots in the state's educational effort.

In the field of higher education, Oklahoma can lay claim to excellence in several fields. The University of Oklahoma, created by an act signed by Governor Steele on December 19, 1890, is recognized worldwide for its efforts in the area of energy, especially in geology and petroleum-related fields. Opening its doors in 1892 on a donated forty-acre tract one-half mile south of Norman, the university today covers more than 1,000 acres and includes the Health Sciences Center in Oklahoma City, the College of Medicine in Tulsa, the Dental College in Oklahoma City, and the State Geological Survey. Its athletic teams have brought national renown to the Sooner State and provided its citizens with many thrills—along with reasons for feeling pride in the accomplishments of its young people. The university is governed by a separate seven-member board of regents appointed by the governor, and today has an enrollment in excess of 20,000 on its main campus.

To the north in Stillwater is Oklahoma State University (OSU), created by an act of the First Legislature which was signed into law by Governor Steele on December 25, 1890. First named Oklahoma Agricultural and Mechanical College, it was the land grant institution in the Sooner State and opened its doors on December 14, 1891, on a donated 200-acre tract. With more than 20,000 students today, it covers 415 acres on its main campus and has one Technical Institute at Okmulgee and another in Oklahoma City, along with a College of Veterinary Medicine in Stillwater and Agricultural Experiment Stations across the state. In addition, all Oklahoma County Agents and Home Demonstration Agents are part of its faculty.

The A & M Board of Regents, appointed by the governor, oversees OSU, Langston University (which began as The Colored Agricultural and Normal University), Cameron University at Lawton, Connors State College at Warner, Northeastern Oklahoma

Agricultural and Mechanical College at Miami (originally the Miami School of Mines), and Oklahoma Panhandle State University at Goodwell.

The third college created in the Oklahoma Territory was originally known as the Territorial Normal School and located at Edmond. This institution is today Central State University. It began classes on November 9, 1891, more than one month before OSU, allowing it to claim to be the oldest public institution of higher learning in the state. In 1897 two additional normal schools were created: Northwestern at Alva and Southwestern at Weatherford. After statehood the legislature determined the former Indian Territory should have an equal number of normal schools, and three new ones were opened: Northeastern at Tahlequah, East Central at Ada, and Southeastern at Durant. The names of each was changed to "Teacher College" in 1919, to "State College" in 1949, and then to "State University" in 1974, and they were placed beneath one board of regents under the title, "Regional State Universities." In

addition, in 1908 the state opened the Oklahoma College for Women. Today called the University of Science and Arts of Oklahoma, it is located in Chickasha and is an "innovative institution."

In the 1920s and 1930s some cities began establishing junior colleges, financed through local taxes, as an extension of their high schools. In the 1960s, however, the legislature moved to create a system of state-financed junior colleges: in Tulsa and Oklahoma City in 1968, in Altus in 1969, and again in Oklahoma City in 1971. Two years later, tired of the annual fight to create yet another state junior college, the legislature enacted a law allowing existing municipal junior colleges at Claremore, Poteau, Seminole, El Reno, and Sayre to join the state system.

Governing all these state institutions and coordinating their budgets, programs, and efforts are the State Regents for Higher Education, a nine-member body established by constitutional amendment in 1941. The regents, in turn, appoint a chancellor to serve as their administrative officer.

In addition to a network of state-supported colleges and universities, Oklahoma also boasts several fine private institutions of higher education. Oklahoma City University was founded in 1904 and has remained in Oklahoma City since a brief stay in Guthrie from 1911 to 1919. Courtesy, Oklahoma City University

Oklahoma Baptist University in Shawnee is supported by the Baptists of Oklahoma. OHS

In addition, the state has fifteen private institutions of higher learning, most of them affiliated with a religious denomination. Oklahoma City University, a Methodist institution, opened in 1904 as Epworth University. Moved to Guthrie in 1911, it returned to Oklahoma City in 1919 and has grown to a position of prominence. Henry Kendall College, which was opened in Muskogee in 1894 by Presbyterians, traces its origins to mission schools for Creek Indians maintained by missionaries from New England. Moved to Tulsa in 1907, it changed its name thirteen years later to the University of Tulsa. Generously supported through the years by Tulsans, this institution has made important contributions, especially in fields related to petroleum.

The Baptists likewise wanted a denominational institution of higher learning, and in 1915 they opened a school in Shawnee. Other Baptist colleges opened in Oklahoma City, Blackwell, and Mangum, but eventually all united with the institution in Shawnee to become Oklahoma Baptist University. The Disciples of Christ founded Oklahoma Christian University in 1906 at Enid, changing the name to Phillips University in 1913 to honor a generous donor. Other private institutions include Oral Roberts University in Tulsa, Bethany Nazarene College in Bethany, Oklahoma Christian College in Oklahoma City, St. Gregory's College in Shawnee, and Bacone College in Muskogee.

Each year approximately 70 percent of Oklahoma's high school graduates enroll in college, public or private, placing the state near the top nationally in this category and reflecting a belief among Oklahomans that education is valuable. Although the Sooner State has more than 175,000 students attending colleges and universities, because of its tax structure and the large number of educational institutions, the state has been unable to support any of these schools at a high level of funding. It has, however, proven politically impossible to close those schools with too few students for efficient operation. In fact, the opposite has been the case. In 1982, owing to a continuing quarrel with federal officials because Langston University still was predominantly black, the state created a University Center at Tulsa, its faculty provided jointly by Langston, the University of Oklahoma, Northeastern State University, and Oklahoma State. Eventually the center at Tulsa may become a free-standing state university due to Tulsan demands for a state-supported institution of higher learning in their city.

Oklahoma's artists and musicians, historical societies and organizations, and public and private museums also serve to educate the public, but in a less structured way than the classroom. Art has always been part of the region. Prehistoric Indians decorated their weapons, pottery, and skin tepees with drawings of animals, battles, and hunts, or with designs of mystical or esthetic appeal. Later, the horse and the buffalo dominated their art, for on these two beasts their culture rested. In 1929 Professor Oscar B. Jacobson at the University of Oklahoma attracted five young Kiowa artists to attend the university: Monroe Tsa-to-ke, Spencer Asah, Steve Mopope, Jack Hokeah, and Bou-ge-tah Smokey. This group gradually attained national acclaim and recognition, holding exhibitions in many parts of the United States and Europe.

Likewise promoting pride in the Indian heritage was the Art Department at Bacone College, where talented instructors and brilliant students began a tradition of excellence in the 1930s. Among those participating in this program were Acee Blue Eagle, Solomon McCombs, C. Terry Saul, Dick West, Fred Beaver, Willard Stone, Dennis Belindo, Enoch Kelly Haney, Jerome Tiger, Ruthe Blalock Jones, Virginia Stroud, and David Williams. Other Indian artists of note include Woodrow Crumbo, Carl Sweezy, Archie Blackowl, Black Bear Bosin, and Troy Anderson. Their styles in one way or another represent a two-dimensional perspective of a world not dominated by technology, and their work has had a two-fold result: it has given Native Americans strength to face the changes that have come into their lives, and it has inspired non-Indian people who are no longer so impressed by the endless conquest of nature.

The first non-Indian artists in Oklahoma were Easterners who paused to use brush and canvas while in the area. In 1834 George Catlin recorded scenes of Indian activity, while Frederick Remington came to Fort Reno and the Darlington agency in 1882 and there made many sketches. The first Oklahoman to attain success with his canvases was John Noble who, after making the run into the Cherokee Outlet, painted *The Run* to capture the excitement of that day. Howell Lewis and Nellie Shepherd did landscapes in an impressionistic style in the early years of the twentieth century, while primitive (untrained) artists such as Augusta Metcalf painted the scenes of ordinary Oklahoma life: fighting a prairie fire, herding cattle, a frontier wedding. Among Oklahoma's modern artists to achieve renown are Charles Banks Wilson, whose work adorns the state capitol; George Miksch Sutton, whose paintings of birds rival (or excel) those of Audubon; Fred Olds, who blends his heritage as a cowboy with his artistic gifts to depict that aspect of the state's past; and James Boren, whose work is nationally known.

Oklahoma's first musicians, like its first artists, also were Indians. Using the flute and drum, they produced a music of complexity and beauty that is understood and appreciated by few non-Indians. In recent years members of the various tribes have rediscovered their rich musical heritage and are preserving it for their children.

Among non-Indian immigrants to Oklahoma, music was usually made with a fiddle or other stringed instrument and used for dances and hoedowns or gospel music sung in church and brush arbor. From this rural tradition sprang the state's rich tradition in country-western folk music. Among the greats in this field have been Woody Guthrie, a native of Okemah who never gained wealth, but whose songs have become part of the American tradition; Bob Wills, known as the "Father of Western Swing," who gained fame over radio station KVOO in Tulsa in the 1930s and 1940s; and Gene Autry, who also performed over KVOO before going on to a great career as a movie star and recording artist.

Less well known is Oklahoma's rich contribution to the field of gospel and jazz music. Alexander Reid, a minister, published two great gospel songs from former slaves in the Choctaw Nation, Wallis Willis and "Aunt" Minerva: *Swing Low, Sweet Chariot* and *Steal Away to Jesus.* The Oklahoma City Blue Devils were performing songs in the genre of jazz and blues before these were popularized in New Orleans and Memphis, and one member of that group went on to world renown as Count Basie. Charles Christian, whose skill on the electric guitar brought him national prominence, and Barney Kessel, a jazz guitarist, made solid contributions in these fields, while Leon Russell, a pianist-singer, cut records that sold in the millions.

Also less known has been Oklahoma's rich tradition of appreciating—and performing—classical music, opera, and ballet. The Tulsa Opera is among the best in the nation, while symphony orchestras perform in Tulsa, Oklahoma City, and Lawton. Five great ballerinas have come from Oklahoma: Maria Tallchief and her sister Marjorie, Yvonne Chouteau, Rosella Hightower, and Moscelyne Larkin. The Tri-State Music Festival at Enid each year attracts thousands of youngsters and encourages an interest in music.

Today the various tribes in Oklahoma celebrate their heritage by holding powwows and dances that attract thousands of Native Americans as well as non-Indian spectators. In some nineteenth-century towns of the Five Civilized Tribes (such as Tahlequah)

223

Spokesman for the victims of the Great Depression was Okemah's Woody Guthrie. Courtesy, Western History Collections, University of Oklahoma Library

government in 1895 and, after moving several times, assumed its present home in the Wiley Post Building in the state capitol complex in 1930. Its museum interprets the history of the state, its publications preserve that record in print, and its educational division aids Oklahoma teachers of history in myriad ways; moreover, its library is an excellent repository of newspapers, research materials, and genealogical records devoted to the state's past and its people.

It was Joseph B. Thoburn, director of the Historical Society, who in 1924 initiated a statewide contest to change the state flag. In 1911 the legislature had adopted a red banner with a blue-bordered white star in the center. In the middle of the white star were the blue numerals "46" to indicate that Oklahoma was the forty-sixth state. Thoburn thought the order of Oklahoma's admission to the Union was incidental and began a contest to select a better design. Louise Fluke, a thirty-five-year-old artist in Oklahoma City, visited the Historical Society and was impressed by a buffalo-hide war shield with a pendant of eagle feathers and a pecan peace pipe. These she placed on a blue background to represent loyalty and devotion, and the legislature subsequently adopted her design.

Another organization devoted to preserving the past has been the Oklahoma Heritage Association, started in 1927 as the Oklahoma Memorial Association with the legislatively-mandated task of operating the Oklahoma Hall of Fame. Its headquarters, formerly the home of Judge and Mrs. Robert A. Hefner, is a living museum, and its publications program is devoted to preserving in print the lives of Oklahoma's "Trackmakers" and the story of the state's institutions.

Major museums are also operated in Oklahoma by public and private trusts. The National Cowboy Hall of Fame and Western Heritage Center in Oklahoma City, in many ways a testament to its former director, Dean Krakel, is funded by seventeen western states, while the Thomas Gilcrease Institute of American History and Art is owned by the city of Tulsa. Both are national in stature—and deservedly so. Other noteworthy museums include the Museum of the Great Plains at Lawton, the Cherokee Strip Museum in Alva, the Southern Plains Indian Museum and Crafts Center in Anadarko, Woolaroc Museum near Bartles-

there were theaters where stage productions were regularly presented. The white settlers who participated in runs, lotteries, and auctions likewise had "opera houses" where touring theatrical troupes performed both classical and contemporary plays. Notable among Oklahoma playwrights has been Lynn Riggs, whose *Green Grow the Lilacs* was the basis for the modern stage hit *Oklahoma!* Well-known productions in Oklahoma include the Wichita Mountain Easter Pageant and the reenactment of the Trail of Tears in the Cherokee production at Tsa-La-Gi each summer in Tahlequah. High school, university, and little theater troupes likewise present an annual diversity of drama and comedy in virtually every town and city in Oklahoma, while touring companies bring the latest hits from Broadway to Tulsa and Oklahoma City.

The oldest organization in Oklahoma dedicated to preserving its past is The Oklahoma Historical Society, founded in 1893 by the Oklahoma Territorial Press Association. This became an agency of the territorial

The Oklahoma Historical Society was founded in 1893 to "preserve and perpetuate the history of Oklahoma." Its headquarters are in the Wiley Post Historical Building, Oklahoma City. OHS

ville, the Will Rogers Memorial and the Davis Gun Collection at Claremore, the Fort Sill National Historical Landmark and Museum at Lawton, the Five Civilized Tribes Museum at Muskogee, the Stovall Museum of Science and History at Norman, the Oklahoma Firefighters Museum and the 45th Infantry Museum in Oklahoma City, Enterprise Square (operated by Oklahoma Christian College to educate the public about free enterprise), the Pioneer Woman Statue and Museum and the Marland Mansion in Ponca City, the Territorial Museum in Guthrie, the Cherokee Cultural Center at Tahlequah, and the Philbrook Art Center in Tulsa. More recently the Kirkpatrick Center in Oklahoma City (also called the Omniplex) has gained renown as a complex of museums; of special note there is the Oklahoma Air Space Museum, largely the handiwork of pioneer aviator Clarence E. Page.

For most Oklahomans, however, the out-of-doors continues to hold the greatest appeal. For their enjoyment, the Tourism and Recreation Department operates almost eighty recreational properties, including

parks, recreational areas, monuments, museums, and historic lodges, which in 1980 were visited by more than twenty million people. The department also operates seven state resort hotels, all located in state parks (although in 1984 two of these hotels were put up for sale). The department also promotes tourism in Oklahoma, which has become the third-largest source of income for the state (behind agriculture and industry).

A modern Oklahoma wonder is its many man-made lakes. In 1957 the legislature created the Water Resources Board to develop and regulate water reserves. The result has been the building of a huge number of lakes to supply water to the population and for agricultural, industrial, and power generation uses. Oklahoma's 1,137 square miles of lakes are also major recreational sites. Hunting, fishing, boating, and camping are pastimes for many state residents, and the Department of Wildlife Conservation oversees 650,000 acres of public hunting lands. Oklahomans find the climate attractive, fish and game abundant, cultural and recreational activities widely available, and the good life within reach of all.

CHAPTER XVI

Turning
Toward
Tomorrow

The Oklahoma petroleum industry is one of the important aspects of the state's economy. In the 1970s and 1980s the Arab oil boycott and rapidly rising prices for crude encouraged exploration and production. Courtesy, Western History Collections, University of Oklahoma Library

*O*n the morning of November 17, 1907, the journey home began for the thousands who had jammed into Guthrie the day before to participate in the ceremonies marking statehood. Most Oklahomans felt confident about their future. The land had been settled, farms and ranches were prospering, oil had been discovered, and statehood had been achieved—all in just eighteen years. Through energy and hard work, Oklahoma's settlers had changed the face of the region dramatically—although much remained to be done.

Despite the hard times created by the Panic of 1907, which caused a great scarcity of cash and the issuance of scrip by some banks, the new state government quickly began erecting the machinery necessary to provide services—and to collect the taxes to pay for them. In the next decade Oklahoma witnessed vast new changes as public schools were funded at a higher level, colleges were opened, public buildings were erected, and roads were graded and paved. The new state passed a bank guaranty law to protect depositors from loss in case of bank failure, established an insurance board to protect people from fraud, started a public health service, opened the State University Hospital in Oklahoma City to train physicians, set standards for workman's compensation, and regulated the number of hours and conditions under which women and children could work. Naturally, state expenditures rose accordingly: from $3.9 million in 1907 to $10.5 million in 1913 and $20.5 million by 1921.

During this same period, Kate Barnard, Commissioner of Charities and Corrections, personally inspected conditions at Kansas State Prison at Lansing, where Oklahoma had by contract been sending its prisoners. Her report of the abuses heaped on Oklahomans jailed there was so shocking that in 1909 the legislature appropriated funds to

OKLAHOMA: A RICH HERITAGE

establish a prison system at McAlester. Oklahoma's prisoners came home by special train under the watchful eyes of heavily armed guards, and they did most of the work of constructing the walls and buildings at the new site. Barnard was also influential in getting other major state institutions established, including schools for delinquents, orphans, the blind, the deaf, and the insane.

Many Americans not familiar with the new state saw it as the home of cowboys and Indians, and the exploits of Jim Thorpe in the 1912 Olympics, which thrilled all Americans, contributed to this image. Born in 1888 at Prague, Oklahoma, Thorpe attended the Indian school at Carlisle, Penn-

sylvania, from 1907 to 1912, interrupting his education to play semi-professional baseball. At Carlisle he became a national sensation as a football player, but his reputation became international when he won the decathlon and pentathlon in Sweden at the 1912 Olympic Games. King Gustav, in presenting his medals, called Thorpe "the greatest athlete in the world," but later, because he had taken fifteen dollars a week to play baseball, Thorpe was forced to return his medals. Afterward he became a major league baseball player and then a professional football star. Three years before his death in 1953 the Associated Press named Thorpe the best athlete during the first half of the twentieth century. Finally, after years of popular protest, the International Olympic Committee returned Thorpe's medals to his family in 1982 and reinstated him in the record books.

Because many Americans believed the myths about lawlessness and wildness in Oklahoma, as portrayed in dime novels and silent movies, a few enterprising Oklahomans in the first two decades after statehood took Wild West shows on tour in the East and in Europe. Most of the performers in these "exciting extravaganzas" were actually cowboys, as some of Buffalo Bill Cody's employees found out to their sorrow on one occasion. That occurred when both Buffalo Bill's show and that of Colonel Zach Mulhall were performing at the same time but at different locations in New York City. Cody's cowboys decided to "show up them Mulhall fellers" in a contest of cowboy skills. Cody's performers failed to realize that Mulhall's people worked as cowboys all year round, and they were totally outclassed. By the 1920s this kind of show was declining as movies filled part of the public's appetite for knowledge about the "real West." The rodeo gradually became popular, however, and Oklahoma would be home to the top two rodeo events in the nation: the National Finals Rodeo, staged for years in Oklahoma City by the Professional Rodeo Cowboys' Association, and the International Finals Rodeo, staged in Tulsa each year by the International Rodeo Cowboys' Association. Moreover, Oklahoma is home to the Rodeo Historical Society and the Rodeo Hall of Fame, housed in the National Cowboy Hall of Fame in Oklahoma City.

In the years between statehood and World War I Oklahoma was a curious

The Miller Brothers 101 Ranch Real Wild West Show was popular during the 1910s and 1920s. Hard times during the Great Depression finally forced the show out of business, after years of entertaining millions with rodeo and wild west action. Courtesy, Western History Collections, University of Oklahoma Library

A cavalry troop of the Oklahoma National Guard was assembled to be transported from Okemah to the Mexican border during the Pancho Villa uprising of 1914. OHS

blend of wild frontier and social reform. Prohibition was written into the constitution, but alcoholic beverages were freely available. Gambling was illegal, but horse races, dog fights, and prizefights were scenes of wild betting. On April 14, 1914, Governor Lee Cruce called out the National Guard, after declaring martial law, to halt a horse race in Tulsa, so avid were the fans who wanted to gamble. Almost every town had saloons and a "red light district," but an overwhelming majority of the state's residents belonged to and regularly attended fundamental Protestant churches.

The outbreak of World War I in Europe in 1914 went largely unnoticed in Oklahoma. The following year, however, Oklahomans did take notice when President Wilson called out the Oklahoma National Guard to pursue Mexican bandit-patriot Francisco "Pancho" Villa for his raid on Columbus, New Mexico. The Oklahoma National Guard, commanded by Colonel Roy Hoffman, traveled to Mexico on what proved to be a fruitless exercise, but thereby Oklahomans gained valuable military experience that helped them in the great war that followed.

When the United States entered the global conflict on April 16, 1917, many of Oklahoma's young men rushed to volunteer for service, while those in the National Guard were mobilized for service immediately. Together these numbered more than 91,000 men, a figure that included Indians from most tribes along with some 5,000 blacks. These men fought as part of the famed 36th and 90th divisions, while the Tulsa Ambulance Company was organized within the state. Oklahomans fought in such battles as St. Etienne, Forest Ferme, St. Mihiel, and the Meuse-Argonne. As Louis W. Duncan, who later would enjoy a distinguished banking career in Muskogee, wrote home from the front in the fall of 1918:

To me it seems almost unbelievable that an army that only a few weeks ago were farmers, clerks, lawyers, etc., could come over here and make all of the armies of the world sit up and take notice; but this is just what they did.

Of the Oklahomans involved, 1,064 died in combat, 4,154 were wounded, 502 were missing in action, and 710 died from disease. Oklahoma's surviving servicemen returned to Oklahoma at the end of the conflict to parade in cities and towns across the state—and then to join the American Legion and the Veterans of Foreign Wars.

The draft in Oklahoma was first administered by Adjutant General Ancel Earp, but he resigned in December 1917 to go to Europe to fight. He was succeeded by Adjutant General E.H. Gipson, who was aided by Major Eugene Kerr. Together they saw to the induction of approximately 70,000 Oklahomans. Not everyone in the state believed the government had the right to draft Americans. There were large numbers of Socialists who opposed the draft, as did members of the radical labor union, the International Workers of the World (the IWW or "Wobblies"). These people argued that the conflict in Europe was "a rich man's war," which poor men had to fight. In early August 1917 these protesters, centered in Pottawatomie, Seminole, and Hughes counties, began burning bridges and barns, firing at law officers, and threatening to raid banks, train stations, grain elevators, and stores. Local citizens armed themselves and fought the so-called "Green Corn Rebellion," and hundreds of the protesters

were captured, imprisoned at McAlester for trial, convicted, and sentenced to prison.

For Oklahomans who stayed at home during the war, there was much to be done on the farm, ranch, mine, and oil derrick, for industry was not yet a significant factor in the state's economy. Oklahoma, along with other states, had its Council of Defense, a branch of the National Council of Defense. This agency coordinated Liberty Bond sales and recruited support for the Red Cross. Feelings ran so high in favor of the war effort that many Oklahomans joined the American Protective League or the Knights of Liberty. Sometimes wearing white robes, these patriots watched for people who failed to buy Liberty Bonds, using tar and feathers on "slackers," as they were called. Oklahoma also had its branch of the Food Administration. Headed by Dr. Stratton D. Brooks, it urged food conservation through such devices as "wheatless" and "meatless" days, and by advocating home gardens to conserve food "for the boys at the front." There was some sugar, beef, and flour rationing, and hoarders were visited by members of the American Protective League—or even by angry neighbors.

The war months were especially difficult for Oklahomans of German descent, particularly the Mennonites who conducted church services in the German language. They were warned to speak only English, even in church. Anyone who spoke out for Germany was tarred and feathered, whipped, and even killed on occasion. Civil rights were violated, but opposition to the war ceased, and the state's soldiers were enthusiastically greeted when they returned home.

Most of Oklahoma's 710 servicemen who died of disease had contracted Spanish influenza. This flu epidemic spread into the state in October 1918—at a time when a third of all doctors and half the nurses were away with the armed forces. Within a short time there were reportedly 125,000 cases in the state, and eventually some 7,000 died from it. In an attempt to halt the spread of the epidemic State Health Commissioner John W. Duke ordered all churches, schools, and movies closed, and gatherings of more than twelve people were forbidden—even for funerals. Almost every family had at least one member sick, and soon business activity virtually ceased in the state. Just as the first epidemic eased, a second outbreak came in late November and early December, but it proved less deadly. Then in the spring of 1919 came an epidemic of smallpox, at that time a dreaded killer, and doctors again were called upon to make heroic efforts. In Okmulgee, for example, Dr. Fred S. Watson established a "Pest House" that gained national attention because in admitting patients he did not distinguish between the races—white, black, or red—making this one of the nation's first hospitals operating without segregation or discrimination.

In November 1918 Oklahomans approved the prohibition amendment banning the manufacture and sale of alcoholic beverages, and, by a narrow margin, the state granted women's suffrage. Governor James B. Robertson, taking office in January of 1919, attempted to ease the state's postwar depression by asking voters to approve a fifty-million-dollar bond issue for highway construction. This failed, but Robertson did get funding to build 1,300 miles of paved roads. This was not enough to ease the economic woes of the state, which had enjoyed high prices for its agricultural and petroleum output during the war years. Farmers had gone into debt to plant "fence row to fence row" and to open new acres to cultivation. Labor unions called massive strikes in the coalfields that led to 9,000 miners staying away from their jobs. Governor Robertson declared martial law and sent the National Guard to Henryetta,

This black law firm set up offices under canvas following the disastrous fire of the Tulsa Race Riot of 1921. Courtesy, Tulsa County Historical Society

Coalgate, and McAlester. Foreclosure sales of farms also led to near violence in many counties. When a sheriff came to conduct an auction sale, sympathetic neighbors would often gather and threaten anyone who bid except the bankrupt farmer himself, who thereby was able to buy back his acres at a ridiculously low price.

The strain of this economic distress led to the collapse of Oklahoma's bank deposit guaranty system in 1920, and several banks failed, causing great anguish to depositors (and to bank directors, who were then faced with personal as well as business liability). In Tulsa the situation was especially critical, for bankers there had advanced capital to oil men who, with prices plummeting, could not repay their debts. Early in 1920 the American National Bank closed its doors, causing anxious depositors to mill about in the street and to begin to talk in ugly tones. Across the street at the Exchange National Bank, which had been conservative in its loans and thus was totally solvent, Robert M. McFarlin, a director, saw the mob in front of the American National Bank waving their passbooks and demanding their money. He quickly took action to prevent disaster, for he realized that the failure of one bank would strain the resources of other banks in the city and region. Emerging from the Exchange National Bank, he shouted until the mob quieted. He then calmly told the seething crowd that they could bring their passbooks into the Exchange National Bank and be paid the full amount of savings they had in the collapsing American National Bank. This was a desperate gamble, for if all depositors in the American National accepted his offer it would have bankrupted the Exchange National Bank. After a few minutes of discussion, however, only a few in the mob accepted McFarlin's offer; the others went home, and the banking crisis was over in Tulsa.

Yet violence was not long in coming to that city. During the economic hard times, with jobs scarce and blacks competing with whites for employment, racial hatreds seethed into open conflict on May 31, 1921. Dick Roland, a black, was arrested on charges of assaulting a white girl, and a white mob gathered at dusk at the courthouse where Roland was being held. From the Greenwood section of Tulsa, sometimes called "the Black Wall Street of America" because of its many successful businesses, a large crowd of blacks came by cars intent on preventing what they feared would become a lynching. When a policeman tried to disarm a black and he resisted, the policeman shot him—and a riot of tragic proportions followed. Blacks and whites broke into hardware stores to arm themselves, and shooting became general. Fires then broke out in the Greenwood section, but the melee prevented firemen from fighting the blaze. The result was two miles of burned-out businesses, leaving thousands homeless. The next morning Governor Robertson declared martial law and sent in the National Guard, but it was late afternoon before shooting could be halted and order restored.

Official estimates of the casualties counted seventy black and nine white deaths, but unofficial estimates of the death toll ran as high as 600. In the investigation that followed, the Democratic sheriff blamed the Republican police department, while the Republicans blamed the Democrats—and the citizens blamed their city officials. Blacks were interned at baseball fields and other makeshift centers for several days before being allowed to return to homes and businesses that had been destroyed. The Greenwood section of Tulsa would never regain its former economic status, and several hundred blacks left the city to never return.

The race riot in Tulsa was but one product of what many Oklahomans saw as a lawless era of vice and crime, widespread immorality, and a turning away from traditional Christian virtues. Nationally the decade of the 1920s was a time of marathon dances, flagpole sitting, bathtub gin, flapper dresses, "kissproof" lipstick, cigarette smoking, and bobbed hair. Dresses suddenly seemed too short and too tight, women were smoking and drinking in public, and dances and movies attracted many into the cities. F. Scott Fitzgerald called these years "the gaudiest spree in history" with some truth, but to conservative, Protestant Oklahomans they seemed spawned by the devil to lure young people into sin. If law officers could not enforce prohibition or halt lawlessness, then some Oklahomans were willing to take the law into their own hands.

The organization that took advantage of this feeling was the Ku Klux Klan. Reborn in the South in 1915, the modern Klan was anti-Catholic, anti-Jewish, and anti-black, but as it spread from Texas into Oklahoma just after World War I its stated goals were a return to the old-time virtues and an end to crime. Reportedly the head of the Klan in Oklahoma when it organized was Dr. Edwin DeBarr, a vice-president at the University of Oklahoma. He was succeeded in 1923 by N.C. "Clay" Jewett of Oklahoma City. So great was the attraction of the Klan in those early days that some of its meetings drew huge crowds. At Muskogee in 1922, for example, one rally was attended by 5,000 people. Klan membership at a point reportedly reached 100,000, mostly from the middle and upper classes.

Special efforts were made by Klan leaders to attract church members and ministers into the ranks of the organization. This often was done by having Klan members appear during a church service in full regalia

The Ku Klux Klan was a potent political force in Oklahoma in the early 1920s. Courtesy, Western History Collections, University of Oklahoma Library

of robe and hood to make a speech about the organization's goal of enrolling "one hundred percent Americans who believe in law and order." The Klansmen would then make a donation to the church and leave. For example, the pastor of the Baptist Church at Eufaula was given twenty-five dollars one Sunday evening by six masked Klansmen who spoke to the congregation about their group's desire to halt bootlegging, drug selling, crime, and immorality. By 1923 an estimated 60 to 95 percent of all Protestant ministers in the state reportedly were members of the Klan.

Although Oklahoma's Catholic population was small—some 3 percent of the total population—the Klan's bitter denunciation of "Papists" fitted into the tenor of that era. Robert O'Brien, a Catholic oil field worker, later recalled that he was so fearful of Klan violence against his family that whenever anyone knocked on the door of his home after dark his wife would wait to answer the front door until her husband had time to slip out the back door with a shotgun, circle around the house, and set his sights on whoever was at the front of the house. Some teachers were fired when school boards discovered they were Catholic. In addition, women speakers posing as ex-nuns were allowed to use municipal convention halls to "expose" the evils they said existed in Catholic convents—and large crowds came to hear such messages. This was an era of intolerance and bigotry, not only in Oklahoma but across much of America as well.

Robed and masked Klansmen marched in city parades and made other public appearances, and in many towns and cities they had a Klan meeting hall much like other fraternal organizations. Some politicians running for office in 1922 openly sought the endorsement of the Klan. By 1923, however, the brutal nature of the organization was becoming evident, and the better element of Oklahoma society began to withdraw from membership. Some victims of its night-riding efforts, whipped or tarred and feathered and ordered to leave the state, were known lawbreakers, but others were selected on the basis of hearsay evidence and judged guilty of moral violations.

In June 1923 Governor Jack Walton declared martial law in Okmulgee County because of numerous Klan beatings there, quickly followed by martial law in Tulsa for the same reason. Walton, in fact, suspended the writ of habeas corpus in Tulsa, and when a grand jury convened in Oklahoma City to investigate this violation of the state constitution, Walton placed the entire state under martial law, saying this was necessary because of "the deadly Invisible Empire [the Klan]." When the legislature began impeachment proceedings against Walton, he responded by citing evidence of Klan wrongdoing uncovered by military courts where martial law had been declared. The governor asserted, "some of these cases present outrages and heartrending cruelty in the extreme, in the form of mutilation such as cutting off the ear of one man and an attempt made to force him to eat it; burning a woman with acid . . . ; burning houses, striking women with six shooters . . . ." He concluded by offering to resign if the legislature would pass an anti-Klan law. Instead the legislators impeached Walton.

When an Anti-Ku Klux Klan organized in the fall of 1923 and held a statewide convention in Oklahoma City in December, the legislature began a serious investigation of the Invisible Empire. The result was passage of a public anti-mask law on January 14, 1924. Without the right to parade in secret regalia, the Klan gradually lost influence—and membership. As late as the election of 1926, however, the Klan tried to organize political support for some candidates, but by then no politician wanted this public endorsement. By the end of the 1920s the Klan had ceased to exercise an influence, and its membership had shrunk to almost zero.

By that time Oklahomans had other things to worry about, particularly the Great Depression then settling on the land. Factories closed because there was no market for their products, and the price of oil plummeted, as did prices for agricultural commodities (Elma Kilgore of Muskogee later recalled paying only ten dollars for a bale of cotton—two cents a pound—in 1930). Soon soup kitchens were feeding the hungry in Oklahoma City, Tulsa, and other towns, and some city dwellers returned to farms to live with rural kinfolk who had food from their gardens. Organized criminal gangs, such as those of Charles A. "Pretty Boy" Floyd and Matt Kimes, engaged in bank-robbing sprees and seemed to operate with the approval of bank-hating neighbors who helped protect them.

To fight the Depression, in 1932 Oklaho-

his remarks with a common sense that the public recognized and appreciated. He was always proud of his Indian heritage and his Oklahoma roots, and he never lost an opportunity to speak on behalf of both. Moreover, he was a philosopher poking fun at the pompous and prosperous. When the Depression hit, he gave benefit performances to raise funds for distressed Oklahomans and other Americans. When Rogers died in an airplane crash at Point Barrow, Alaska, with famed aviator—and fellow Oklahoman—Wiley Post, the state was thrown into mourning. Thousands of people donated to build the Will Rogers Memorial at Claremore, and some five decades later tens of thousands of tourists annually visit this testament to the state's favorite son.

Only the outbreak of World War II in 1939, and the end of the Dust Bowl, brought a return of prosperity. Once again Oklahoma's farm commodities commanded high prices, as did its oil, lead, zinc, and coal. During the war, Oklahoma, because of its mild climate, became the site of many major air training bases, among them Oklahoma City's Tinker Field, named for Major General Clarence L. Tinker, an Osage Indian killed on a bombing raid in the Pacific; and Will Rogers Field at Oklahoma City, named for the Oklahoma philosopher-humorist. British and Canadian pilots trained at air bases at Tulsa, Miami, and Ponca City. The Army had twenty-eight installations and the Navy had thirteen bases in the state, including the Technical Training Center at Norman through which passed some 15,000 aviators. In addition, Oklahoma's colleges and universities became training centers for Army and Navy personnel. Many prisoner-of-war camps were located in Oklahoma, including those at Fort Sill, Fort Reno, Camp Gruber, Tonkawa, Chickasha, Alva, Tipton, and Okmulgee. Prisoners were allowed to work on nearby farms and ranches, earning some money for themselves while helping farmers and ranchers, who were desperately short of manpower.

President Roosevelt's call for volunteers for the armed forces met an enthusiastic response in Oklahoma: more than 212,000 people joined the Army, the Navy, and the Marine Corps. Notable sons of the Sooner State in the war included J.J. "Jocko" Clark, a Cherokee who thereby became the highest ranking person of Indian descent in American military history. Casualties from

mans joined other Americans in electing President Franklin D. Roosevelt, and participated in a variety of New Deal programs. For young men there were Civilian Conservation Corps (CCC) camps, while unemployed adults took jobs with the Works Progress Administration (WPA) raking leaves, laying sidewalks, painting murals on post office walls, and a host of other makework employment. For businessmen there was the National Recovery Administration (NRA) with its blue eagle symbol displayed in store windows. Yet the New Deal did not end the Depression, for in 1935 there were 150,000 Oklahomans unemployed and 700,000 on relief. The state was steadily losing population, and "Okie" was becoming an ugly word.

Countering this image at both the state and national level was Oklahoma's best-known native son, Will Rogers. Born at Claremore, Indian Territory, in 1879, he was the son of Clem V. Rogers, a mixed-blood Cherokee who ranched near Chelsea and who served with distinction in the Oklahoma Constitutional Convention. Although Will later liked to pose as uneducated, he had more schooling than was average for his day. After working as a cowboy, he began entertaining in Colonel Zach Mulhall's Wild West Show, then traveled in several foreign countries, and finally landed a prominent part in Ziegfeld's Follies in New York City. He later became a movie star and newspaper columnist.

Known as a rural humorist, Rogers laced

Oklahoma included 6,500 killed and 11,000 wounded.

Home-bound Oklahomans faced wartime rationing of gasoline, meat, sugar, coffee, shoes, automobile parts, tires, and many other items. They participated in scrap-metal drives, grew "victory gardens" to conserve food, and took part in war bond drives. Yet at the same time they prospered. The price of wheat, corn, oil, lead, and coal soared, and for the first time large industries came to the state. The Douglas Aircraft Company manufactured bombers in Tulsa and operated a smaller plant in Okla-

homa City. Tinker Field in Oklahoma City employed thousands to repair and rebuild B-24 and B-29 bombers. At Pryor the federal government had a plant manufacturing smokeless powder, while the Navy maintained a large ammunition depot at McAlester. Because such facilities were erected almost overnight, housing was in desperately short supply in most Oklahoma cities during the war.

The end of World War II brought wild celebrations in the Sooner State, along with a host of new problems. Veterans returning to begin or continue their college educations swelled enrollments at state institutions of higher learning, causing rapid growth and the need for larger appropriations. The construction industry struggled to keep pace with the demand for new housing, while farmers prospered from continued high prices for their agricultural goods. The number of Oklahomans employed in industry rose to 55,000 by 1949, with total wages amounting to more than $143 million. The principal industries were refineries (at Bartlesville, Ponca City, Enid, Cushing, Wynnewood, and smaller locations), aircraft manufacturing in Tulsa and in the vicinity of Oklahoma City, flour milling, meatpacking, zinc smelting, and lumber processing plants. By 1953 the state's largest single employer was Tinker Field with 23,650 on its payroll.

By the early 1950s almost every major city and town in the state had created an Industrial Development Board to purchase land and attract industry. Governor Roy Turner (1946 to 1950) pushed the legislature to reduce corporate income taxes by

Oklahoma's famous son, Will Rogers, was an entertainer and writer of world fame. His witty comments on the events of the day brought a ray of hope into the lives of many destitute people. OHS

Bottom, left
Major General Clarence Tinker died during the Battle of Midway in 1942. An airfield, Tinker Field, in Oklahoma City was subsequently named in his memory. Tinker Air Force Base is one of Oklahoma's leading employers. OHS

Below
Raymond S. McLain became the highest ranking Oklahoman during World War II. He commanded the XIX Corps during the final drive into Germany. OHS

manufacturers at several towns, a major meatpacking concern in Oklahoma City, and several petroleum-related industries at many sites in the state, particularly in Tulsa. Between 1950 and 1960 the number of Oklahomans engaged in agriculture dropped from 155,000 to 74,000, while the number in non-agricultural employment jumped from 599,000 to 713,000. By the 1980s agriculture would still be the largest producer of income in the state, industry second, and tourism and recreation third.

The outbreak of the Korean War in 1950 did not slow this new growth and prosperity. The draft returned to take many of Oklahoma's young men to fight, while Marine reserve units in Tulsa and Oklahoma were called to active duty to take part. Almost two decades later these veterans would see their sons drafted to fight in Vietnam, as Oklahomans continued their proud tradition of defending the country whenever called upon by their president.

Despite the growth and prosperity of the state, caused by a prolonged drought in the 1950s, the population declined slightly from 2,333,351 in 1950 to 2,328,284 in 1960. This drop was principally caused by a re-

Above
Wheat elevators, jokingly called "prairie skyscrapers," are often filled to capacity during the bumper harvests enjoyed by farmers in Oklahoma. Photo by Jim Argo

Right
Oklahomans have always enjoyed a good show. When Margaret Mitchell's classic Gone With The Wind *was re-released in the late 1950s, Tulsans waited in 112-degree heat to see Scarlett O'Hara and Rhett Butler. Courtesy, Tulsa County Historical Society*

one-third, and he restructured the Planning and Resources Board, which advertised Oklahoma's industrial potential. Gradually this paid dividends as several major firms moved to the state: Western Electric at Oklahoma City, tire manufacturing concerns at Ardmore and Lawton, a bicycle manufacturer at Enid, clothing and carpet

duction in farm population. Many sons and daughters of farmers went off to college and then sought challenges outside the state. Another cause was farm consolidation. When farmers reached retirement age and sold out to enjoy sunny weather in Texas or Florida, their land was purchased by other farmers and consolidated into larger holdings which, owing to improved farm machinery, employed fewer workers. The decade of the 1960s saw the downward trend in population reversed, however, as increased industrialization attracted thousands of new residents and kept more young people at home. By 1970 the population had reached 2,559,253—surpassing the census of 1930 for the first time.

By the late 1960s certain new trends were evident in the Sooner State. Because of a change in national consciousness about the plight of Indians, many Oklahomans were no longer ashamed to admit that their ancestry included some Indian blood. Moreover, as the federal government stressed the hiring of minorities, many people with no Indian blood whatsoever began claiming to be part Native American (leading some Indians laughingly to call these people "Sycamores"). Thanks to federal legislation in the late 1960s, many Oklahoma tribes began reorganizing tribal governments, acquiring property, and fighting for tribal rights.

In the 1960s and 1970s Oklahoma's young people joined in the national protests against the war in Vietnam, for an end to the draft, and for the right of eighteen-year-olds to vote. There were no major riots on Oklahoma campuses, but there were demonstrations and protest rallies for many causes, including gay liberation. The young began dressing in clothes of any style: overalls, blue jeans, work shirts, Indian headbands, castoff pieces of military uniforms, sandals, and work boots—or no shoes at all—while young men let their hair grow long and their beards sprout. A few enterprising promoters tried to cash in on the popularity of rock music by staging rock festivals, but these generally failed. Illicit drug usage saw a startling increase and became so profitable that many knowledgeable observers estimated that Oklahoma's largest cash crop was marijuana, grown on small plots and harvested to be sold in the cities. Most of Oklahoma's young people retained their basic good sense through this difficult

During the height of the oil boom in the Tulsa area, a popular style of architecture was Art Deco. One of the most beautiful examples of this very ornate style is the Boston Avenue Methodist Church in Tulsa. Designed by Oklahoma architect Bruce Goff, this landmark stands as one of the Oil Capital's finest contributions to the state's architectural heritage. Courtesy, Don Sibley, Metropolitan Tulsa Chamber of Commerce

time, however, working to secure an education, enter the job market, begin families, and worship in the churches of their forefathers.

The OPEC oil embargo brought soaring prices for gasoline and natural gas, while the cost of electricity doubled and then doubled again. Teachers and professors were demanding higher and higher wages, and many Oklahomans believed that government should provide welfare services for everyone, while those who worked and paid the astronomically high taxes saw inflation robbing them of any hope of bettering themselves and their families.

Oklahoma's penal system consumed far more tax dollars than in past years. The prison population soared and prisoners at McAlester rioted in 1973, destroying a significant portion of the facility. Judge Luther Bohanon of Oklahoma City assumed jurisdiction of the system and ran it for some ten years. Despite a second riot at Hominy in 1983, the federal court returned jurisdiction to Oklahoma officials early in 1984. Another source of difficulty was the Department of Human Services, which in the early 1980s was charged by federal officials with abuse of minors in its care. The public was growing restless at the spiraling costs of the social services performed by this agency, an area of concern not yet fully addressed by legislators.

During this period another boom came to Oklahoma; this one—like many in the past—was the result of soaring oil prices caused by petroleum industry deregulation in 1979. The rush to the Sooner State by unemployed people from the Northeast, the northern Midwest, and even from California seemed to match the influx of Boomers in

1889, and by 1980 Oklahoma's population had increased to almost three million. Tax collections soared, thanks to levies on the petroleum industry, and state legislators increased salaries of state employees and boosted the benefits of welfare recipients. By 1982 independent producers had pumped such a volume that the price of oil dropped from a high of forty-two dollars and more to twenty-nine dollars a barrel. Tax revenues dropped proportionately and Oklahoma was in a financial crisis, its revenues no longer able to sustain appropriations made by the legislature. This, in turn, led to another round of tax increases in 1984—but not to any meaningful reform of the tax code that might attract more industry to the state. Nor has there been real reform of other facets of state tax collection, such as automobile license fees. For years this system has been operated on the basis of state senatorial patronage that enriches the favored few while depriving local school districts of revenues intended for educational purposes. Despite obvious and flagrant abuses, the only result has been removal of the tag agents in Tulsa, Oklahoma, and Cleveland counties from senatorial patronage.

By the early 1980s the vast majority of Oklahoma's work force was employed in industry and related businesses and services. In 1981 the state numbered one-and-a-half-million workers, 193,000 of them in industry, but only 50,000 in agriculture. In fact, industry at this time was employing more people than were involved in agriculture and the petroleum industry combined. Then in the economic downturn that began in 1982, the state lost 35,000 jobs in manufacturing that have not been regained. Still the political leaders of the state have not made the legal reforms needed to attract more industry— with concomitant jobs and payroll—to the Sooner State.

In addition, in 1981 Attorney General Jan Eric Cartwright hurt efforts by various cities to attract industry by declaring unconstitutional the tax breaks given to such giant corporations as General Motors. Because surrounding states offer a wide range of subsidies and tax breaks to gain a source of employment for their citizens, the Oklahoma legislature in 1985 proposed and the voters approved giving new industries a five-year tax moritorium. This began paying dividends quickly.

Still more changes need to be made to improve the business climate in Oklahoma, for too much of its agricultural output continues to be shipped elsewhere for processing, its oil and natural gas sent outside the state to be refined into petrochemicals, and its lead and zinc transported to Arkansas and Missouri for smelting. There also have been dramatic changes in agriculture and the petroleum industry, the two areas that Oklahoma relies upon to keep its citizens working.

No longer did there seem to be great potential for any meaningful increase in the number of people employed in oil and agriculture. The petroleum industry experienced numerous cycles of boom and bust, and there were periods of high unemployment—but not like in years past, for the world of the mid-1980s faced an oil glut. Similarly, the state's farmers were plagued with overproduction, while cattlemen faced increasing costs of production and decreasing prices for their beef. In 1981 agriculture employed just 4 percent of the state's work force, and there seemed little likelihood that this number would increase significantly. The degree of mechanization in farming and the increasing size of farms meant that even if agriculture entered a boom period in the future, there would be few new jobs created.

Compounding the economic confusion in the early 1980s had been state (and federal) legislation allowing limited chain banking in the Sooner State, merging of some banks into giant financial organizations, and allowing savings and loan institutions to perform many bank functions. Fears of a few giant financial institutions controlling state banking spread, but consolidation nevertheless moved forward—at a time when decreasing prices for petroleum brought an increasing number of bank failures.

This economic dislocation and change has been matched by a dramatic change in social attitudes in what once was described as "the buckle on the Bible Belt." In a 1983 special election, Oklahomans permitted pari-mutuel betting on horse racing, and the following year, in a hotly contested election, authorized liquor-by-the-drink by county-option (ending decades of the illegal sale of mixed drinks so prevalent that many said Oklahoma had "liquor by the wink").

Yet through the turmoil of recent years, as well as the problems associated with out-of-control state and national spending, the people of the Sooner State have remained positive, vibrant, and dynamic. They have remembered the state motto, *Labor Omnia Vincit*—"Labor Conquers All Things"—and they have acted on this premise despite their hardships.

Just before statehood Robert M. McFarlin and James A. Chapman mortgaged their ranch near Holdenville to take a lease in the Glen Pool Oil Field. They subsequently went into the Cushing and Healdton fields with their McMan Oil Company, and through their labor they became titans of independent oil production. In the 1930s three merchants in western Oklahoma— R.E. Tomlinson, E.L. Gosselin, and R.A. Young—joined together to form T G & Y, a merchandising giant now headquartered in Oklahoma City, but stretching across the nation and employing some 30,000 people. In the 1950s O.W. Coburn of Muskogee developed and marketed machinery that revolutionized the optical industry in the United States and around the world. Oklahomans have seen rewarded the inventive genius of Sylvan Goldman of Oklahoma City, who built and patented the grocery store shopping cart, and Virgil Browne of Oklahoma City, who developed the formula for a nationally manufactured soft drink and who devised the "six-pack" as a marketing tool for soft drinks. These are but a few of the Oklahomans who have helped build a state with the highest quality of life in the entire republic and whose deeds inspire today's young men and women to take chances in the marketplace with their ideas in spite of the state's tax structure.

The 89er statue in Oklahoma City honors the pioneers who made the first and later land runs into the state. Photo by Jim Argo

Two of Oklahoma's economic mainstays, oil and agriculture, when both were booming in the 1980s. Courtesy, Terry Zinn

CHAPTER XVII

It Was Just One Thing After Another

Oklahoma in the late 1970s continued to experience a prosperous and robust economy. The two mainstays, oil and agriculture, were leading the boom that produced record revenues for the state. The 1973 Arab-Israeli War, and production cuts by members of the Organization of Petroleum Exporting Countries (OPEC), created a shortage of oil in the United States. As America's dependency on foreign oil has increased, the volatility of events around the world has had a direct impact on Oklahoma's economy.

This impact produced a surge in activity in the oil patch to seek new fields and re-tap old well sites to take advantage of higher prices at the pump. The price of crude skyrocketed from $12 to $35 per barrel. In 1978 oil and natural gas wells were operating in seventy-one of the state's seventy-seven counties.

Coupled with the boom in oil and gas was the surge in cattle prices due to a meat shortage. Moreover, crop failures around the world spurred sales of various commodities such as wheat, corn, and other staples that allowed for farmers and ranchers to expand operations. As the state's largest industry there were some 73,000 farms and ranches throughout Oklahoma, with a total coverage of 35 million acres. In 1979 alone, farmers and ranchers received over $3 billion for their crops and livestock.

The banking industry was experiencing a very competitive, market driven boom as well. As oil and gas companies required the necessary capital to explore and drill new sites, commercial lending on prospective results and returns was creating a very fast-paced environment. This, in turn, led to investment lending by many banking institutions in real estate and construction projects.

It was this vibrant climate of prosperity that greeted newly elected Governor George Nigh

Official portrait of Governor George Nigh. Nigh has served more terms as governor than any other person and was the first to be able to succeed himself in office. Courtesy, OHS, © 1979

when he took office January 8, 1979. Nigh seemed born into politics in Oklahoma. Having served in the legislature, he was elected as the youngest lieutenant governor in the state's history in 1958. He was elected to that position again in 1966, 1970, and 1974.

George Patterson Nigh was born in McAlester, Oklahoma on June 9, 1927 to Wilbur R. and Irene Crockett Nigh. He attended schools in McAlester and served in the United States Navy from June, 1945 to September, 1946. He graduated from East Central State College at Ada, with a degree in 1950. From 1952 to 1958 he taught at McAlester High School with an emphasis in Oklahoma history.

George Nigh, as author Bob Burke wrote in his biography, *Good Guys Wear White Hats, The Life of George Nigh* came to the governor's office with definite ideas and plans for Oklahoma's future. That future in 1979 was very bright indeed. With state revenues filling the treasury at an impressive rate, Burke continued to state that "George [was] in the enviable position of not having to worry about asking the legislature for a tax increase to finance the growing state government."

Oklahoma's economy, like other states, has weathered boom and bust cycles. When the economy is doing well, Oklahomans share in the prosperity. However, when there is a downturn, it is more pronounced than in most states. This is largely due to the fact that for many years there have been only two major industries supporting the economic growth in the state—oil and agriculture. The need to diversify the state's economy to soften the blow during a bust cycle began to take a more aggressive mode in the late 1970s.

State officials along with leaders from Oklahoma City began to campaign to actively recruit General Motors when that company was searching for a location in the United States for a new automobile assembly plant. Oklahoma subsequently was chosen because of the excellent vocational-technical school system, work ethic of the people, central location in the country, and other incentives provided by the city and state leaders. The first of the new cars began rolling off the assembly line in 1980.

Another sign of the booming economy was the number of financial institutions providing personal, commercial, and real estate loans through 490 banks with total assets of over $17 billion. That trend continued in 1980 as assets grew to nearly $23 billion dollars. Also, manufacturing employed some 191,500 persons in industries that included food products, fabricated metals, electrical products, machinery, printing, publishing, and petroleum refining. Income from this sector grew by 18.3 percent from 1979 amounting to more than $3 billion.

In July 1980 Bob Burke wrote in his biography of George Nigh, "...the pulses of oil and gas wells were throbbing with growing rhythm across the state of Oklahoma." As Governor Nigh was quoted as saying while meeting with state officials, "...the state of the state is great!" His enthusiasm brimmed with pride as there was a $100 million surplus in the state treasury. Wisely, Nigh suggested that not all of the money be used to fund government services. The excess not appropriated would be set aside as a "rainy day fund" to be used in special emergencies.

On a lighter note, Oklahoma received national attention in 1981 when Elk City native Susan Powell was crowned Miss America. Miss Powell, whose operatic voice has charmed many on and off Broadway, became the third Oklahoman to receive that distinction. Norma Smallwood of Tulsa was the first from Oklahoma to be chosen as Miss America in 1926 and later Jane Anne Jayroe of Laverne was crowned in 1967.

Unfortunately, by the end of 1981, a scandal that led to 230 convictions—with 110 against county commissioners alone—demonstrated that the illegal practice of bribing county officials occurred in sixty of the seventy-seven counties. The scandal at the time was the largest in terms of people indicted and/or convicted in state history.

The diamond jubilee commission was formed in late 1981 in preparation for Oklahoma's seventy-fifth anniversary as a state. Governor Nigh appointed fifty-three people to the commission along with three staff members to coordinate the promotion of Oklahoma and its history through a variety of public events across the state. Nigh selected Ada native and Oklahoma City banker Jack Conn to serve as the chairman of the commission. In 1982 plans to celebrate Oklahoma's milestone anniversary began to emerge. Some 1,500 projects were approved, culminating the yearlong series of activities in Guthrie—the first state capitol. In 1982 Governor Nigh also marked a first in state history by appointing a woman to the state supreme court. As Bob Burke noted, this was one of "George's most personally satisfying appointments."

Judge Alma Wilson, a native of Pauls Valley, was sworn in February 17, 1982. Justice Wilson was eventually chosen to be chief justice of the supreme court. She died at age 82 in July 1999.

Justice Alma Wilson, a native of Pauls Valley, became the first woman appointed to the state Supreme Court in 1982. Courtesy, OHS

The year also brought continued surplus revenues largely fueled by the gross production taxes from natural gas and petroleum. However, there were signs on the horizon that the economic boom was beginning to lose steam. By mid-year a more ominous event occurred that impacted Oklahoma's economy for the rest of the decade.

In a front page article dated July 3, 1982 in the *Oklahoman & Times*, the chairman of Penn Square Bank, Bill P. Jennings was quoted as stating that he "denied reports that his financial institution is [was] in serious trouble...". He was further quoted as saying, "We are open for business." Though reports circulated by the *Washington Post* indicted that federal officials were trying to arrange the bank's reorganization. The *Oklahoman & Times* article continued to report that bank president Eldon L. Beller was quoted as saying that, "he could not speculate on the *Post* story because it was speculation itself." Beller was further quoted as stating that, "to my knowledge, there is no plan, program, or commitment on anyone's part to close the bank next week."

Monday July 5th was a federal holiday. Tuesday's edition of the *Oklahoman & Times* in a bold front-page headline stated PENN SQUARE BANK DECLARED INSOLVENT. The closing of Penn Square Bank was just the tip the iceberg. As banker John Marshall observed, "the banking industry was permeated on the lending side with the 'more bang for your buck' philosophy of making commercial loans, larger in nature, than installment loans. Collateral or asset-based lending was popular, however, more unsecured or thinly secured commercial loans were taking place." Marshall further commented that, "collateral like drilling rigs were being evaluated as if value declines were unlikely."

The fall of Penn Square set in motion a domino effect that rippled through Oklahoma's economy. It affected the oil and gas industry, agribusiness, real estate, and small business development. The demise also contributed to a negative image about the state that took years to reverse.

As late as two years after the collapse of Penn Square Bank, warnings by state and federal officials cited the possibility of other banking institutions being closed. In his report to Governor George Nigh dated June 30, 1984, Robert Empie, state bank commissioner, wrote: "The complex influence of economics and deregulation among Oklahoma's financial institutions, together with the competitive fervor among them, all of which challenges the banking department, has no way decreased. Painful effects continue to surface as revealed through the bank examination process." Empie continued by stating that, "the banking department is closely monitoring twenty-one banks, where potential failure exists, unless prompt action is taken to correct the weaknesses, and an additional five banks and trust companies, where the probability of failure is high."

By the mid-1980s consolidation, mergers, and hostile takeovers by corporate America were sweeping the nation. Some Oklahoma companies were ripe for the picking. One such native company was Phillips Petroleum of Bartlesville, Oklahoma. Founded in 1917, Phillips had grown to be the eighth largest petroleum company in the United States by 1984. Its payroll of $339.7 million in 1983 was second only to Tinker Air Force Base with $548 million. The company employed over 8,600 people throughout the state, some 7,700 in

Bartlesville alone. Phillips has led the petroleum industry in the number of research and technological patents, claiming some 5,480 in the United States and 1,642 foreign patents as of 1984.

Bartlesville was the epitome of a company town and Phillips was the consummate benefactor for the community. Rick Moore, field representative for then Congressman Mickey Edwards, was just becoming acclimated to his new position in Bartlesville when a hostile takeover attempt by former Phillips employee, and now chairman of Mesa Petroleum, T. Boone Pickens occurred. Moore, a native of Del City, had worked on Edward's successful campaign for the fifth district congressman. Appointed after the November 1984 election to direct the field office in Bartlesville, Moore was thrust into a turbulent situation less than one month on the job.

Pickens, a native from Holdenville, was born in the late 1920s. He spent his early years in the Hughes County community where his father, Thomas Boone, Sr., was an independent petroleum landman and as T. Boone described him, "he would ferret out landowners willing to lease their mineral rights and then 'turn'sell the leases to an oil company."

As the shock began to set in regarding Pickens bid to take over Phillips, Moore and others were appointed to a crisis task force. As Moore stated, "the community was scared." Phillips officials and community leaders held a forum to rally the people into action. As Moore recalled, "T. Boone was burned in effigy."

The crisis task force met weekly, keeping the worried community apprised of what was happening. With Christmas approaching, merchants felt an immediate impact as no one in town was buying gifts. Since Bartlesville did not have a diverse economic base, what happened to Phillips would directly impact everyone in town.

Congressman Mickey Edwards, whose district included Oklahoma City, Ponca City, and Bartlesville, had the distinction of having three home-grown oil companies in his district—Phillips, Conoco in Ponca City, and Kerr-McGee in Oklahoma City. Edwards' position was not against free enterprise, but was against the efforts of individuals or companies whose purpose in taking over companies in a hostile fashion was to then dissolve them for the tax breaks. Edwards wanted to develop tax incentives that would lessen the attempts of this type of takeover and still allow the "overtaken" company to survive.

A deal was reached on Christmas Eve, 1984. As word spread around Bartlesville, a collective sigh of relief was felt as if a millstone had been lifted from everyone's neck. Ironically, it would be another oil company with origins in Oklahoma that would acquire Phillips.

In 2001 Conoco, formerly known as Marland Petroleum out of Ponca City and later Houston, Texas, merged with Phillips—creating ConocoPhillips. In 1984 Phillips had 7,700 employees at its headquarters in Bartlesville— by 2001, only 2,400 remained. Though efforts by then Governor Frank Keating to keep the last major publicly-held integrated oil company in Oklahoma, the last ditch maneuvering failed. Since then, T. Boone Pickens has contributed over $70 million to his college alma mater, Oklahoma State University.

In 1980 manufacturing employment exceeded 191,500 people. By 1985 that figure had dropped to just under 170,000, or just over an 11 percent decrease in jobs. Coupled with the loss of 2,000 farms and ranches during the same period, Oklahoma's economy was faltering.

Governor George Nigh began his first administration with high expectations and the revenues to achieve some of the priorities he set. However, by the middle of his first term, the running spigot of tax monies began to slow to a trickle.

The Ogallala aquifer can be found in seven states from northwest Texas to southern South Dakota. All but a small portion in the extreme northwest corner of the panhandle of Oklahoma is included. Use of the aquifer has become more important recently, from its use in farm-related activities to those population centers within its domain. Even industry taps into the precious resource. Nigh's concern stemmed from studies that predicted that the aquifer "would be depleted by more than 50 percent in forty years, leaving 330,000 acres in the crop-heavy panhandle too dry to cultivate."

Geography and climate have always played a major role in land and water usage. Rainfall in the panhandle is as light as fifteen inches per year. The growing season in this semi-arid portion of the state is around 180 days. As with any area pertaining to agriculture and related businesses, weather dictates whether you have a good year or bad. Supporting this fact is the study published by John Opie in 1993 titled, *OGALLALA Water for a Dry Land*. Opie cites the usage, especially by major oil companies, as being one of the main culprits depleting the water to extreme levels. He also takes the Oklahoma Water Resources Board (OWRB) to task for its indifference of this limited resource in favor of corporations over the needs of the people and fragile ecosystem.

At one time, in order for a person to irrigate land, one would need the permission and signatures of neighbors before going to the OWRB for a permit. All that has changed, and not to the liking of the farmers and ranchers who have tried to be good stewards of the limited supply and essentially non-renewable resource of the aquifer.

The drought that plagued the panhandle region from 2001 to 2004 is over. The rain came, but some still say the region has a drought every year—it's just a question of what months. The spring of 2004 saw elevated levels of rain, all of which was beneficial.

In eastern Oklahoma two different water issues have made headlines. One revolved around chicken waste that was introduced into the rivers and streams that bordered along the Oklahoma-Arkansas state line. The other, that is more complicated, has its origins in the first years of the twentieth century.

Tar Creek is located in Ottawa County in the extreme northeastern corner of Oklahoma. In 1983 the Environmental Protection Agency (EPA) added Tar Creek to its list of "superfund sites" as a national priority. The site covered some forty square miles and included the communities of Picher, Cardin, Quapaw, North Miami, and Commerce.

The story of how Tar Creek became an environmental hazard began in the early 1900s, and to some extent continued until the late 1970s. This area was known for its zinc and lead ore. As mining occurred, mine tailings were disposed of by collecting in piles. These piles, known as chat, contained elevated levels of lead and other heavy metals.

According to a report prepared by the Oklahoma Department of Environmental Quality, the EPA and various state agencies had "determined that the mining and milling of lead and zinc ore left miles of underground tunnels, open mines shafts, and drill holes." The EPA began work in 1984, and continued through 1986, in an effort to "build dikes, plug abandoned wells, and divert surface water around abandoned mines and collapsed mine shafts."

Various projects to work the affected area have taken place, including the remediation of properties—mostly residential, schools, parks, and business—at a cost of $100 million. Yet, after twenty years of work, tests, and millions of dollars spent, no settlement is in sight. Tar Creek is arguably the most contaminated area of the state, and no solution is forthcoming.

Wheat harvesting near Enid
in the 1980s. Courtesy, OHS

The other water related problem is the discharge of chicken waste from poultry farms into rivers and streams in western Arkansas and eastern Oklahoma. This growing problem is still being discussed among representatives of both states. It's too early to know what results will be reached in order to resolve this issue.

In 1983 oil prices dropped like a lead balloon. Oil and gas drilling peaked at 900 rigs then fell to around 200. With oil prices per barrel plummeting, thousands of oil related jobs were lost. Manufacturing declined as well as construction across the state. A national recession hit the state hard. For the first time in several years, tax increases were proposed to stave off a $90 million shortfall in state government services.

Now well into his second term as governor, George Nigh had experienced record surpluses—only to see them evaporate. It also demonstrated rather acutely how Oklahoma's economy was being tied so closely to petroleum and agriculture. In 1996 Guymon in Texas County, in the center of the Oklahoma panhandle, gained a significant new industry—hog processing.

When Seaboard Farms was looking for a new location for a hog processing facility, Guymon actively courted the company. After the town was ultimately selected in the early 1990s, it immediately began to feel the effects of a growing population that was coupled with an acute housing shortage.

Seaboard built a 500,000-square-foot facility northeast of town. The first full production began in 1996. Overnight, Seaboard became Guymon's largest employer. It hired 2,300 people, with an annual payroll plus benefits exceeding $100 million.

Today, the plant produces over 800 million pounds of pork yearly. Some 4.5 million hogs are processed per year, or some 16,000 head per day during a six day week. Seaboard Farms is the largest manufacturing company west of Oklahoma City, paying some $1.2 million per year in property taxes.

Much has been written regarding the migration of individuals from rural to urban centers of the state. From 1991 to 2001 the five largest population centers in the state were Oklahoma City, Tulsa, Norman, Lawton, and El Reno/Yukon. No surprise that the five smallest in terms of population were all located in the western portion of the state.

To offset dwindling population and core businesses in smaller communities around the state, the department of commerce along with community leaders created the Oklahoma Main

Street program in 1986. The intent was to assist in reviving historic downtown areas across Oklahoma.

Duncan, located in south central Oklahoma, was the first to apply to the program. With heritage tourism becoming more economically important, the revitalizing of historically rich business districts in towns across the state has been an unqualified success. More than $371 million in public and private investment has reinvigorated communities that were on the verge of decline.

Politics in Oklahoma has always been interesting. As political advisor Martin Hauan once said, "politics ain't for sissies." In 1986 former United States Senator Henry Bellmon was encouraged to run once again for the office of governor. First elected to that post in 1962, Bellmon made political history by being the first Republican to be elected since 1907—but made the history books again by winning the office in 1986.

At his inauguration in January 1987, Bellmon was assuming the reins of a state government in serious financial straits. One issue, besides the budget crisis, that would demand attention was education. Of major concern was the loss of the best and brightest young men and women who left the state after graduating from college. This "brain drain" as it has come to be called has had a definite ripple effect throughout the state.

The average beginning salary in Oklahoma was slightly over $15,000. It was evident that in order to keep quality educators in the classrooms, something had to be done. Bellmon proposed a special session of the legislature to concentrate on education. In the meantime, a special committee dubbed "Task Force 2000" had been authorized by a legislative act in 1989. House Bill 1017 emerged from that effort, which involved a major tax increase.

Meanwhile Governor Bellmon traveled to Michigan to meet with representatives of Ford and General Motors. Each had considerable assembly facilities in the state. When Bellmon asked Ford officials what could the state do to "improve the economic climate for the company factory in Tulsa, without a moment's hesitation the reply came: "Improve your schools."

In the intervening years, Oklahoma ranked nationally between forty-sixth or forty-eighth in funding. According to Dr. Don Wentroth, a principal at Putnam City High School in northwest Oklahoma City, with over 25 years as an educator, House Bill 1017 achieved its purpose. However, the flight of quality teachers to other states, Texas in particular, has created or will soon create a critical shortage of qualified educators in the classroom.

Texas recruits actively in Oklahoma. According to Wentroth, if a teacher signs a contract to teach in the Lone Star State, the person receives a $5,000 signing bonus. To counteract this siphoning off of potential educators, Oklahoma has developed a certification for teachers. If an educator earns that certification, he or she receives a $5,000 bonus each year for the next ten years—providing they remain in the profession and stay in the state. According to Governor Bellmon, the passage of House Bill 1017 was "one of the happiest days of his political career."

Another event that occurred during the Bellmon administration was the centennial celebration of the Land Run of 1889. Though only affecting the central region of the state, many celebrations took place to mark the occasion. However, this and similar events that would take place in 1991, 1992, 1993, and 1995 would not be welcomed by the Native American community across the state. Those events from 100 years earlier signaled the loss of land. To many tribal members their sovereign rights, as per treaty agreements, concluded between the various tribes and the United States, were lost.

Politically, Oklahoma is considered a conservative state. Its roots were populist in nature, which resulted in a profound distrust of big government. Oklahoma has also been considered the belt buckle of the "Bible Belt." So in the mid to late 1980s, the legislature was pondering whether to pass pari-mutuel betting to allow horse racing in the state. The battle was often bitter, pitting horse owners against religious leaders. Ultimately, the horse racing industry won.

In 1987 Remington Park in northeast Oklahoma City began construction. Owned by the DeBartolo Corporation, Remington opened with much fanfare in 1988. In its first two years of operation the average daily attendance was 9,800 people, with a daily handle of $1.1 million.

Since Remington's debut, Blue Ribbon Downs opened in Sallisaw and, later, Will Rogers Downs in Claremore was added to the mix. Blue Ribbon Downs has since gone bankrupt and was recently purchased by the Choctaw Nation of Oklahoma—even though the racetrack is located in what is generally recognized as Cherokee Indian country.

Bellmon's successor was an articulate, young, aggressive individual who had run for the office in 1986 only to lose to the veteran governor. In 1990 David L. Walters, a native of Canute, became the first governor elected from western Oklahoma. Born in 1951, he became one of the youngest to hold the office. Graduating from Canute High School, Walters attended the University of Oklahoma and graduated in 1973 with a degree in industrial engineering. He obtained his master's of business administration from Harvard University.

When Walters took office in January 1991, the state's economy was slowing beginning the climb from the abyss. If any lessons were learned from the 1980s, it was that Oklahoma needed to diversify its economy. For example, in 1989 manufacturing related jobs numbered around 165,200 people. By 1991 that figure rose to 168,500. Banking was leaner by the end of the decade.

In 1980 there had been 480 banks; by 1991 there were only 411 lending institutions. The oil industry was showing signs of recovery, however, but not at the level that was seen at the beginning of the '80s.

Early in Walters' administration he was chairman-elect of the Interstate Oil and Gas Compact Commission. Walters issued a position paper on the state of natural gas and its impact on the national economy. Walters stated, "I believe that we must encourage the development and use of domestic natural gas while curbing our dangerous dependence on foreign oil."

Walters advocated the use of natural gas as a clean burning fuel which was domestically abundant, thus decreasing the need to import foreign oil. Walters was so committed to using natural gas for automobiles that he had his own vehicle converted to compressed natural gas (CNG).

The new governor was not your typical politician. Coming from a background rooted in the private sector as a businessman, Walters was not a person who was going to endorse a "business as usual" attitude in running state government. It was this belief that sparked the public interest in his election.

The governor hit the ground running. State spending was slashed to meet requirements stipulated from House Bill 1017, which was enacted in 1990. A new innovation to provide incentives for companies to expand or relocate to Oklahoma was created through the Quality Jobs Act. This generated new jobs through tax breaks, which ultimately enhanced the state economy.

Persistent rumors about campaign irregularities dogged the governor during his years in office. In June 1992, by order of the Supreme Court of Oklahoma, a multi-county

grand jury was convened to look into allegations of wrong-doing by the Walters campaign. After a sixteen-month investigation, the grand jury issued a nine-count indictment against Governor Walters. One count was a misdemeanor and the other eight were felonies for various campaign violations.

On October 21, 1993 Walters entered a plea of guilty to the one misdemeanor count, in exchange for the dismissal of the eight felony indictments. In late 1993 the grand jury recommended that the Oklahoma State Legislature undertake impeachment proceedings.

The legislature did draft a resolution to create a special investigation committee. With the possibility of impeachment, Walters' effectiveness lessened his chances of running for reelection in 1994. As a lame duck governor, he still was able to overhaul the juvenile justice system and workers compensation reform. Walters often quoted former Governor William H. Murray saying, "it was just one damn thing after another."

Also elected in the fall of 1990 was J.C. Watts of Eufaula, Oklahoma. Watts was elected to the corporation commission. History was made because Watts was the first African American elected to a statewide office since statehood. Moreover, Watts was elected as a Republican—only the third person from that political party to achieve that distinction. Watts later ran successfully for Congress from the fourth district and became the first Black to be elected from a southern state in 120 years.

In September 1993 communities across northern Oklahoma, from Perry to Woodward, celebrated the centennial of the largest of the five land runs to open Oklahoma for settlement. Known as the Cherokee Outlet, this area borders from Osage County to the east, Kansas to the north, the panhandle to the west, and Highways 51 and 60 to the south. More than 100,000 persons made the run in 1893. Communities such as Alva, Cherokee, Enid, Ponca City, Blackwell, and several others held celebrations to mark the event.

With the fall election of 1994, the Republican party captured the governor's office once again. Frank Keating of Tulsa received his bachelor of arts in history from Georgetown University and earned his degree in law from the University of Oklahoma in 1969. Keating had a stint with the Federal Bureau of Investigation and then later became an assistant district attorney for Tulsa County. In 1972 he was elected to the Oklahoma House of Representatives and two years later to the State Senate. In 1981 Keating was appointed as U.S. attorney for the northern district of Oklahoma by President Ronald Reagan.

In January 1995 during his inauguration speech, Governor Keating was upbeat about Oklahoma. In less than three months, the governor and the people of Oklahoma would be thrust onto the world stage by a senseless cowardly act of terrorism.

Wednesday morning April 19th was cool, with overcast skies. Rick Moore, assistant to Mayor Ron Norick, was walking from his office on Couch Drive in Oklahoma City to attend the mayor's prayer breakfast being held at the Myriad. Moore, who was associated with Congressman Mickey Edwards, joined Norick's staff in 1988.

He had just returned to his office around 9:00 a.m. when he heard a boom. At first Moore thought that an airplane had crashed, since just south of downtown is a small airport. Going outside to see what had happened, he saw "debris falling from the sky."

Making his way toward the federal building, the full impact of what happened was overpowering. Moore saw individuals struggling to get out of what was the Alfred P. Murrah Federal Building. The buff brown and glass front facing Fifth Street had collapsed. Moore began to assist people out of the rubble.

By this time, all the city television and radio stations were broadcasting round the clock about this unfolding tragedy. Soon, live broadcast feeds were being sent to CNN and national broadcast news organizations.

All police and available fire department personnel had been dispatched to the Murrah site. Governor Frank Keating was informed and

Congressman J.C. Watts of Eufaula, Oklahoma was the first African American to be elected to state or national office since 1908. Courtesy, Chester Cowen, OHS, © 1994

*Governor Frank Keating
(center, wearing trench coat)
takes questions from the news
media regarding the bombing
of the Alfred P. Murrah
federal building. Photo by Joe
Todd, OHS*

*An aerial view of the Murrah
federal building after the
April 19th bombing. The
building was razed on May
23, 1995. Courtesy,
Oklahoma City National
Memorial*

immediately declared Martial Law. As survivors were being extracted from the devastated remains of the federal building, the Federal Emergency Management Agency (FEMA) was dispatched from around the country to assist with rescue.

By nightfall, a cold drizzle was falling. A woman, whose leg was wedged under concrete, was the last person to be rescued alive. It soon became evident that rescue operations would cease and recovery efforts would begin.

Remarkably, crime in the metropolitan area came to a halt. Though the National Guard was patrolling the streets while the police were downtown at the site, no reports of any looting, petty or major crime took place.

Near Perry, Oklahoma Highway Patrolman Charlie Hanger pulled a car over on Interstate 35 for speeding and an expired license tag. A check of the vehicle revealed that it had been stolen. Hanger arrested the driver and impounded the car.

By the morning of April 20th some 900 survivors had been accounted for. Tragically, 168 men, women, and children died the day before in the worst act of domestic terrorism since the World Trade Center bombing two years earlier.

Surveillance cameras and eyewitness accounts were being compiled so a description of the assailant could be circulated around the country. By the time the composite drawing hit the airwaves, the folks in Perry, county seat of Noble County, noticed a resemblance to the man brought in by Officer Hanger.

Federal authorities were notified, and soon a positive match was made. Timothy McVeigh was charged with the bombing and subsequent

murders of 168 innocent people at the Murrah Federal Building.

Thus, Oklahoma was thrust onto the world stage by a horrific tragedy. Almost immediately after the bombing occurred, thousands of people around the country—and the world— wanted to help in some way. Children wrote letters or made drawings to help ease the pain of those who survived or witnessed that terrible crime against humanity.

The cards, letters, donations, and drawings all found their way to a city in shock. A makeshift fence was erected around the Murrah site to keep out onlookers while FEMA and other authorities continued to sift through the rubble. The fence soon became a memorial where flowers; toys, mostly teddy bears; cards; and other mementos were placed for those who died.

In the years following the tragedy of April 19th, Timothy McVeigh was tried and convicted in federal court in Denver, Colorado and later executed for his crime. A state trial for co-conspirator Terry Nichols concluded in July 2004.

Nichols, who was convicted on eight murder counts during his federal trial, is serving a life term in a federal prison with no hope of parole. His trial by the state for 160 murders was held in McAlester in the southeastern area of Oklahoma in March 2004.

Prior to April 19, 1995 Oklahoma City was not known as a place where people would likely stop and visit. In fact, most individuals from outside the state had a generally negative image about Oklahoma, going back to John Steinbeck's book *The Grapes of Wrath*. The image of dust storms, cowboys, Indians, and rednecks dominated people's perception of what one thought about the state.

After April 19th all that changed. The world, via television, saw the compassion of the Oklahoma people as never before. No longer considered the dust bowl Joad's, the Murrah bombing and now the memorial to that tragedy has created a new image. Instead of being a "pass through community" it is now a community that people want to visit. Tourists want to see for themselves the area that endured— and survived—that terrible April spring day.

As many are quick to say, Oklahoma's weather can change in an instant. From droughts to tornadoes, flash floods to hail the size of softballs, extreme cold to searing heat— living in the state can be difficult to say the least.

In May 1999, Oklahoma achieved a new record. Each year from late April to mid-June the Midwest,from the Texas panhandle to the

Stephen Jones, an attorney from Enid, Oklahoma, was the court-appointed counsel for bombing suspect Timothy McVeigh. Courtesy, OHS, © 1997

251

An aerial view of the destruction caused by a tornado that struck Stroud on May 3, 1999. Photo by Ben Frizell, © 1999, Courtesy, OHS

Canadian Border, endures a tornado season. On May 3, 1999 an outbreak of tornadoes occurred. They spawned near Cyril in southwest Oklahoma, struck portions of Chickasha, hit Bridge Creek, then stayed on the ground for more than an hour—striking Moore and leveling everything in its path.

The storms continued to the northeasterly path toward Stroud, located in Lincoln County.

By the end of the day, thousands of homes and businesses were destroyed and forty-four people died. The tornado that struck Moore was classified as an F-5 with wind speeds clocked at 315 miles an hour—a new record.

Some 3,000 buildings were destroyed with another 5,000 damaged. The estimated loss was over $950 million. Moore and Stroud were two communities hardest hit. Stroud lost its main

The path of the May 3, 1999 tornado that destroyed businesses and homes in Moore, Oklahoma. Photo by Ben Frizell, © 1999, Courtesy, OHS

revenue source, Tanger Outlet Mall, that was located northeast of downtown on the east side of Interstate 44.

For Stroud, the recovery has been slow. Besides the destruction of the outlet mall, the town suffered the loss of its hospital. Yet, in 2004, signs of economic recovery were on the horizon. A medical center is in the planning stage and will likely be built on the former mall site.

For many communities though, the loss of medical services has been difficult. Since 1985, according to the Oklahoma Hospital Association, thirty-four hospitals have either closed or been acquired by other facilities. Wetumka in Hughes County was closed in July 2003 and Boise City in the panhandle passed a sales tax to keep their facility open. However, despite struggles, tremendous advances in medical research have taken place in the state. The Oklahoma Medical Research Foundation, along with Presbyterian Health Foundation in Oklahoma City and St. Johns Hospital in Tulsa, has made breakthrough discoveries in finding cures for a number of life threatening diseases.

With any city large or small, the transport of goods and services is important. Whether by rail, air freight, or trucking, it provides an economic lifeline to that community.

Oklahoma has 112,533 miles of roads, of which 606 will ultimately be toll roads. There are twenty-three railroads that operate within the state, using nearly 2,900 miles of track. In the 1990s Interstate 35 was designated a major route for the North American Free Trade Agreement with Mexico. With ever increasing usage of that route, traffic has become extremely heavy. The Port-to-Plains route from Laredo, Texas to Denver, Colorado was proposed to ease that congestion. Depending which way the route would take would determine the economic futures for several communities in New Mexico and Oklahoma.

Ultimately, the Cimarron County Chamber of Commerce at Boise City was determined to win the new route along Highway 287. Locked in a fierce battle with New Mexico, the route would bring a much needed infusion of money and jobs to an area that needed both. Though several years away, the prospect of new business and the creation of jobs will aid this sector of the state.

Whether it be "firsts" in the past or "firsts" in the future, Oklahoma continues to be a leader. From Wiley Post to Gordon Cooper, from General Tom Stafford to Dr. Shannon Lucid, Oklahoma has a rich aviation history. It has contributed greatly to the development and

growth of air travel. In fact, when it comes to space travel, Oklahoma has had more astronauts than any other state—most recently John Herrington.

Realizing the importance air and space travel may have on the economy led to the creation of the Oklahoma Space Industrial Development Authority (OSIDA) in late 1999. The authority envisions the redevelopment of the Clinton-Sherman Air Force Base which has been closed for several years.

Located near Burns Flat in the western portion of the state, the OSIDA mission is "to create in this decade a commercial spaceport that will expand and economically develop the Oklahoma Space Frontier with advanced spacecraft operating facilities." The authority

Above:
The Honorable Susan Savage, current secretary of state for Oklahoma. As the former mayor of Tulsa (1992-2002), she shepherded over $1 billion of improvements into Tulsa's infrastructure during her tenure. Courtesy, William D. Welge.

Below:
General Jay T. Edwards (retired), former director of the Oklahoma Space Port Authority, points to a possible aircraft mock-up that may be used in sub-orbital space flight from Burns Flat, Oklahoma, circa 2004. Courtesy, William D. Welge

Businessman Quang-Nguyen owns Ben's Cleaners and Alterations. Nguyen came to the United States in January 1993 from Vietnam. He is among a growing Asian population in Oklahoma. After arriving in the United States, he worked many long hours at minimum wage jobs saving his money so he could own his own business one day. He recently added the cleaners next door to his alterations shop. Courtesy, William D. Welge

A young Latino girl enjoys a ride on the merry-go-round as part of the annual Primavera Fest in south Oklahoma City. Courtesy, William D. Welge

has generated interest and has aviation companies looking to locate at the base.

The retail industry in Oklahoma reached a turning point in the 1980s. Several home-grown retail institutions such as C. R. Anthony's established in Cushing, Oklahoma Tire and Supply Company (OTASCO), and John A. Brown Company in central Oklahoma were sold or closed due to high-volume, low price retailers. This trend continues in the first decade of the twenty-first century.

Oklahoma is also a place that has many qualities that that make it unique among states. It is second in the number of Native Americans with over 390,000 persons claiming tribal status.

The population of the state has changed in the last quarter century. The diversity of ethnicity adds to richness of cultures that includes many Asian and Hispanic groups. This mix of European, African, and Native American adds to the flavor that enhances that richness.

On a more traditional front, Oklahoma has a wellspring of talent in the sports and entertainment industries. Whether it is high school, collegiate, or professional sports, Oklahomans can always be found lending their special talents.

Since the mid-1980s the University of Oklahoma has had several national champion teams in football, most recently in 2000. Oklahoma State University has earned national recognition in basketball, baseball, and wrestling. Oklahoma City University has excelled in both basketball and baseball and the University of Tulsa is always in contention for league conference play.

In the entertainment world, whether in theatre, film, or music, Oklahomans have left their mark. Talents such as country singers Garth Brooks, Reba McEntire, Vince Gill, Toby

University of Oklahoma women's Big-Twelve championship basketball team. Seen at right is head basketball coach Sherri Coale. Courtesy, OU Sports Media Department, © 2002

Keith, and many others have received awards and recognition for their craft.

Susan Powell, former Miss America, and actress Kristen Chenoweth have performed in theatre. Former Oklahoman Ron Howard has gone from actor in television and film roles to becoming one of Hollywood's most distinguished motion picture directors. James Garner, most-widely known for his work on *The Rockford Files*, has also had a career in television and film. The list could go on, but suffice it to say Oklahomans have added much to the fabric of entertainment and sports in this country.

As Oklahoma and its people enter into its second century as a state, all its residents may look back with pride. For they have overcome many obstacles and feel a great sense of accomplishment, yet they will always look forward to a bright future. The future is here, and Oklahoma will continue to meet it head on.

The University of Oklahoma 2003 national championship gymnastics team. Courtesy, OU Sports Media Department, © 2002

Chronicles
of
Leadership

From the prehistoric era to the twentieth century, the economy of the region that is now Oklahoma has been based on the bounty of the land. Native peoples relied on game—especially the buffalo—and some crops indigenous to the area. When members of the Five Civilized Tribes began arriving in Indian Territory in the 1830s, they brought with them the agricultural traditions they had developed in their original homelands. Most established small subsistence farms, although a few wealthy individuals created large plantations. Later, the area was home for the range cattle industry, as members of the Five Civilized Tribes raised cattle and leased vast areas of their lands to non-Indian cattlemen. The Indians also established a forest industry in southeastern Oklahoma that continues to thrive more than a century later.

Oklahoma's agricultural economy grew to become the state's single most important industry. At first, cotton dominated Oklahoma's agricultural economy; however, it gradually was replaced first by corn and finally by wheat, which contributed millions annually into Oklahoma's economy. Cattle-ranching and feedlot operations also were important sectors in the state's economy, as were crops such as peanuts and pecans. The bountiful natural resources beneath the land have played a major role. Coal mining was important in Indian Territory before and after statehood, bringing immigrants of Italian, Polish, Slavic, and Russian heritage into the area. Moreover, Oklahoma has been a giant among the oil and gas-producing states. Indeed, the region's energy industry began as early as 1859, when Lewis Ross completed Oklahoma's first oil well; however, it was not until the Nellie Johnston was brought in near Bartlesville in 1897 that the state's modern oil boom began. During the first three decades of the twentieth century, Oklahoma's oil wells would yield more dollars than the combined wealth of the California Gold Rush and Colorado's silver mines. More than 3,906,012,375 barrels of crude were pulled from the earth during these years. Some of the discoveries were astounding. The Cushing Field, for example, produced 17 percent of the nation's total output of crude in 1917, and the Greater Seminole Field contained five of America's greatest discoveries: Little River, Seminole City, Earlsboro, Bowlegs, and St. Louis. Such a tremendous outpouring of crude made Oklahoma a mecca for oil men and gave birth to several international energy companies. Oil production remains an important factor in the state's economy, with Osage County ranking second among counties in the nation in the number of producing oil wells.

Oklahoma's natural gas industry began with statehood in 1907 with the discovery of the Hogshooter Field, which became the principal supplier of natural gas for the region. In the

following decades the industry grew into a billion-dollar-a-year business. Moreover, the vast Anadarko Basin in western Oklahoma is recognized as one of the largest gas fields in the world.

Manufacturing centers and large metropolitan areas were well established in other regions of the United States by the time Oklahoma began to emerge from the frontier. Thus, with the tremendous agricultural and mineral bounty of the land, agriculture and energy remained the dominant forces in the state's economy at the turn of the twentieth century. It was these sectors that furnished the capital during the early years of the twentieth century to develop the state's strong financial basis and bring in thousands of new citizens.

Yet Oklahomans endeavored to diversify the state's economy as early as the turn of the twentieth century. The effort has intensified in recent years as state leaders have attempted to capitalize on the state's resources, interstate highway network, and outstanding aviation facilities to bring new types of economic opportunities to the state. The capital generated by oil, gas, and agriculture made the effort possible, and Oklahoma has made significant progress toward becoming a major Sunbelt manufacturing center. In addition, oil, gas, and agriculture provided

many of the necessary raw products for an active manufacturing economy to be established.

Along with various manufacturing operations, tourism has been developed as a major factor in the state's economy. Oklahoma also has developed a national reputation for its outstanding medical centers, which have the potential of spawning a major biotechnological industry in the state. With both the energy and agricultural sectors of the economy in a recession in the mid-1980s, the push for increased diversification of Oklahoma's economy became even more intense. Yet the traditionally optimistic spirit of the Sooner State remained strong, with its citizens determined to continue the steady improvement in Oklahoma's economy and quality of life that had begun decades earlier.

The organizations whose stories are detailed on the following pages have chosen to support this important literary and civic project. They illustrate the variety of ways in which individuals and their businesses have contributed to the state's growth and development. The civic involvement of Oklahoma's businesses, institutions of learning, and local government, in cooperation with its citizens, has made the state an excellent place to live and work.

ALBRIGHT STEEL AND WIRE COMPANY

Albright Steel and Wire Company is a wholesale distributor of steel products supplying lumberyards, hardware stores, sheet metal shops and individual customers throughout Oklahoma. The company's home office is located in Oklahoma City and has two full-service warehouses, one in Lawton and the other in Enid. Products supplied by the company are used for residential and small construction projects, as well as industrial fabrication and agricultural industries. The founder, Clyde Albright, began the company in 1952 with one concern in mind—his customers. His loyalty to them is a trait passed down and carried on through his descendants. This allegiance is why the company has continued its success for more than half a century.

Clyde Albright graduated from the Draughon School of Business in Oklahoma City in 1937. He began working in the steel business with a company called

Clyde Albright standing behind a roll of welded wire.

Central States Steel. He had a dynamic and outgoing personality which lent itself perfectly to sales. In a short period of time, he had cultivated a vast number of customers throughout Oklahoma. When the time came, Albright served in the Pacific with the United States Army during World War II. While overseas, Albright sent letters back home and remained in contact with customers who had, by then, become friends.

When Albright returned from the war, he resumed working for Central States

President and CEO, Leah Beale.

Steel. Shortly thereafter, the company became a victim of the country's economic downturn of the early 1950s. It was forced to abruptly close operations. Albright, in fact, was still on the road meeting with customers. He returned with a handful of orders that he had promised would be delivered within days. When he knew he wouldn't be able to fill those orders through the now fallen company, he had to find a way to keep his promise. He decided to start a company of his own.

He quickly went to his bank and asked to borrow the money needed to purchase inventory from the closing company. Because of his good banking practices and impeccable reputation, the bank

agreed. Not only was he able to fulfill his outstanding orders, other orders came in and so did new customers. All his clients were impressed by his loyalty and tenacity to turn bad luck into good fortune—not only for himself, but for his faithful clientele.

The Albright Steel and Wire Company began in 1952 and incorporated as a family-held corporation. The new company had three employees. Albright was the president, chief executive officer, and salesman. His wife, Virginia, managed the office and credit department and Albright hired a truck driver to make the deliveries.

Believing in a strong America, Clyde Albright focused on domestically produced steel and wire products. He refused to compromise on quality believing that his business would grow from content customers. "He lived by the Golden Rule," proudly says Leah Beale, president of the company. "Treat everyone as you would like to be treated given the same circumstances. Show them the dignity and respect they deserve as human beings."

Albright was known for his strong handshake and affable personality. He often provided extended credit which encouraged new accounts. The self-made businessman knew that when a client succeeded, Albright Wire and Steel acquired another loyal customer.

Leah Albright Beale has been integrating her father's philosophy for more than twenty years. Since 1985 Beale has been

Delivery trucks and warehouse at the home office in Oklahoma City.

at the helm of the Albright Steel and Wire Company. However, she has worked for the company periodically since high school. "As soon as we (Beale and her two sisters) were old enough to drive, we would go there to work," Beale says. Customer loyalty was not the only good trait taught by her father. Leah Beale also learned to have a strong sense of family loyalty.

Beale's first love was medicine. She set her sights on becoming a doctor, but at the age of eighteen she thought it was too much to be in school for ten more years. "When I realized I was going to be in school until I was twenty-eight, that seemed like an eternity," Beale confesses. She opted for nursing school, instead.

Beale headed off to school at the University of Oklahoma. However, in 1971 her beloved father passed away. Shortly thereafter, Beale left nursing school and returned home to the family business. She was fifteen hours short of reaching her nursing degree. "It was not something I had to do, it was something I wanted to do," says Beale, who has been with the company ever since.

Beale began working in the payroll department and gradually became familiar with every area of operations. She watched and learned as managers made decisions. As her tasks expanded, she became aware of areas of need. She took it upon herself to help wherever she was needed. This gave her a growing sense of owner-ship and responsibility. After her mother's death in 1987, Beale purchased all of her sisters' stock and became sole owner of the company.

Today, twenty-two employees operate out of the corporation's three locations in Oklahoma City, Lawton, and Enid. The company's combined warehouse space is more than 95,000 square feet. The business carries flat sheets, structural steel, light aluminum, concrete reinforc-ing materials, roofing, siding, flashing and construction accessories, and a supply of wire and fencing.

In some ways operations have remained the same as when the company began in 1952, but in many ways they are differ-ent. The most distinguishable difference is the company's increase in walk-in clients, which make up about 35 percent

Pictured at the Oklahoma City sales office, members of the second and third generation look forward to the next fifty years.

of the overall 1,750 active customers. For this reason, sales display areas are located in the main office in Oklahoma City and in both warehouses in Lawton and Enid.

A third generation is being groomed for the future of the Albright Steele and Wire Corporation. With twelve years of experience in the steel industry, Trey Lewis, Beale's nephew, travels down from Tulsa, Oklahoma two days a week to learn the company's operations. Lewis,

now thirty-five, was only four years old when his grandfather passed away. He is now learning about the founder of the company through a tradition of loyalty and bits of memorabilia. Having a strong sense of family and sentiment, Lewis is responsible for creating the "Albright Museum"—a collection of old promo-tional items which would, otherwise, be thrown away. Beale proudly introduces Lewis to her customers by saying, "I am the past and the present, but he's your future."

The Oklahoma City administration and sales office.

AMERICAN FIDELITY ASSURANCE COMPANY

Founded on the principles of fairness and financial security more than forty years ago, American Fidelity Assurance Company has achieved unparalleled success. It is the top life insurance firm in Oklahoma and the second-largest private, family-owned life and health insurance company in the nation.

The Oklahoma City-based company serves over 1 million customers in forty-nine states and twenty countries. In 2004 American Fidelity (AF) was ranked thirty-first among *Fortune* magazine's 100 best companies to work for in the United States, and was the highest ranking insurance company on the list. Since 1982 AF has consistently been rated "A+" by A. M. Best Company, one of the leading insurance rating services in America.

C.W. Cameron was a pioneer in voluntary payroll deduction insurance, known today as worksite marketing.

At the heart of this company's achievements are the three generations of the Cameron family, men whose resilience and steadfast vision enabled them to triumph over professional setbacks and personal tragedy. "This is a family business and I like the feeling that I am adding on to the foundation that my grandfather and father built," says company chairman and CEO Bill Cameron. "I am proud of the products and services we sell and the difference we make in people's lives. Reputation means everything."

C.W. and C.B. Cameron founded American Fidelity in 1960. It has grown to become the second-largest private, family-owned life and health insurance company in the nation.

Bill's grandfather, C. W. Cameron, and his father, C. B. Cameron, started AF in 1960 as an outgrowth of an insurance agency C. W. had operated since 1930. The elder Cameron's humble beginnings make the present-day success of the company all the more remarkable.

The oldest of seven children, C. W. was raised on a small tenant farm near Mangum, Oklahoma. When his father became disabled, C. W. dropped out of school at age fourteen to help take care of the family and run the farm. He later worked odd jobs as a carpenter, cotton picker, and part-time bank clerk. Life was uncertain and financial struggles persisted. "I think a lot of what my grandfather went through in his childhood left an impression on him and was the genesis for him going into the insurance business," says Cameron.

C. W. worked his way up to assistant cashier at the First National Bank of Altus, earning $135 a month. He noticed that insurance salesmen seemed to bring in larger paychecks, so he decided to try that line of work. He partnered with a farmer in starting the Boise and Cameron agency in 1930. The business prospered until the Great Depression took its toll, forcing Boise to leave the agency in 1932.

Using his savings, C. W. bought one-third of an agency in Davidson and sold fire and casualty and disability insurance. He also sold insurance for other firms, but his big break came when he started selling insurance for North American Accident and Health Insurance Company of Chicago in 1933. C. W. sold his interest in the Davidson agency and became the local agent for North American. Two years later he moved to Oklahoma City to become North American's general agent for the state of Oklahoma. In a short time C. W. distinguished himself as the top-selling agent, managing the most profitable North American branch in the nation. By the mid-1940s, he was the general agent for four states.

Much of Cameron's success was the result of pioneering efforts to make insurance available to the working class. He was an early leader in voluntary payroll deduction insurance, known today as worksite marketing. Cameron sold group accident and health insurance to state agency employees and to trade associations. His agency was also one of the first of its kind to offer insurance to schoolteachers. Building on that beginning, AF is now the largest provider of voluntary disability insurance to teachers across the United States.

As the agency prospered, the need arose for more office space. Cameron constructed his own office building on

Classen Boulevard in 1954, one of the first suburban office buildings in Oklahoma City. In 1959 C.W. and Gene McCrory started the affiliated North American Insurance Agency to focus on property and casualty insurance.

The North American Company in Chicago experienced changes in ownership in the 1950s and was eventually acquired by the CIT Group. Since CIT wanted to focus on selling individual insurance, Cameron proposed that he take on all of the accident and health business previously handled by the Cameron Agency for North American. His son, C.B., had recently returned home from the Air Force, and the pair decided to start their own insurance underwriter. In 1960 American Fidelity was born.

Their new company grew very rapidly until, at the height of their personal and professional success, the Cameron family's world literally crashed in when a Thanksgiving plane flight turned deadly in 1977. Returning from a Colorado ski trip, the plane slammed into a mountainside and two days went by before rescue teams found the passengers. C. B. died in the

American Fidelity's headquarters in Oklahoma City have expanded to hold nearly 1,000 of its 1,400-plus employees. The company has twenty-six locations across the United States.

accident and the rest of his family, their friends, and the pilot were severely injured.

After the death of his son, C.W. promoted William E. Durrett to president of AF. Following C.W.'s death in 1991, Durrett became chairman of the board, a position held until 1998 when he moved to senior chairman and Bill Cameron became the chairman of the board. During the tenure of Durrett and his CFO (and later president) John Rex, the company built a strong financial base and grew rapidly.

C. B.'s son, Bill, joined AF following a two-year period at Liberty Bank where

Bill Cameron serves as chairman and CEO of American Fidelity Assurance Company. Courtesy, The Oklahoma Publishing Company, © 2001.

he began work after graduating from Dartmouth in 1982. In 1987 Bill led the recapitalization efforts for Commercial Bank that has subsequently become First Fidelity Bank, and which is affiliated with AF through the Cameron family's ownership.

In the twenty-first century AF has continued to grow rapidly with strong internal growth plus the acquisitions of Mid-Continent Life and American Public Life in 2000. It has also planted the seeds for future expansion through the establishment of the Latin American Life Division that sells insurance in seventeen countries in Latin America; the Pacific World Group, which brokers property and casualty insurance in Malaysia, Singapore, and Hong Kong; and Asset Services/InvesTrust which provides investment management consulting and independent trust services.

Despite AFA's impressive national and international success, Bill Cameron is proud that the company his grandfather and father started is still operated like a family business. "We are committed to keeping the company private and independent," he says. "I'm building on their foundation, and I want to pass these opportunities on to my kids and to future generations."

BECK DESIGN

The architects at Beck Design create a marriage between use and design, consistently melding the need for presence and the desire for inclusiveness. The result is quite often an elegant and subtle use of the surrounding environment, while gracefully and unobtrusively opening up the interior of a structure to the outside world.

Formed as Beck Associates in 1982, this award-winning architecture and design firm changed its name to Beck Design in 2004 to more accurately represent the scope and nature of the company's work. Specializing in higher education facilities, libraries, historic preservation, museums, research campuses, and athletic and wellness centers, the company has built an impressive track record. Their success is based upon a distinct philosophy: to create spaces that are not only functional, but that also enhance the quality of life for those who visit and work there.

To the company's credit is the architectural creation of more than 300 major public and private buildings including several structures at the University of Oklahoma, Oklahoma State University, and Oklahoma City University. The firm has also designed more than seventy libraries across the U.S., including the Ronald J. Norick Public Library in Oklahoma City which opened in 2004.

Beck Design has also renovated many structures, such as the Carnegie Library in Guthrie, Oklahoma and "Bricktown" in Oklahoma City. Many of its renovations are listed on the National Register of Historic Places. The firm's most recent projects include the massive Oklahoma History Center, the Oklahoma Jazz Hall of Fame, the Wanda Bass Music Center, and the National Weather Center at the University of Oklahoma.

The principal of the firm is Donald Beck, who was born in Iowa and grew up on a farm in Iowa. For him, being an architect is the fulfillment of a dream that started back in his youth. He attended the University of Oklahoma at Norman where he received his degree in architecture. Later, Beck also deepened his knowledge of architecture by doing graduate work at Harvard University.

However, Beck's architectural designs began winning awards even before he

The three-story atrium frames the solid cherry inlay at the height of the 80-foot space in the Meinders School of Business at Oklahoma City University.

graduated from college. His first citation was an honorable mention he was awarded by the National Institute of Architectural Education, for a street fair design competition in 1976. That was quickly followed by another honorable mention in 1977, for his design of a performing arts center, which he earned in a design competition sponsored by the Society of American Registered Architects. The next year, in 1978, Beck won first place in the R.S. Reynolds Aluminum design competition.

One of Beck's earliest award-winning projects led him to set up his firm early in his career. Helping out a friend who was also one of his first clients, Beck designed the Classen Glen Condominiums in Oklahoma City. The project

garnered him an "Award of Commendation for New Construction" from the American Institute of Architects (AIA) in 1985. He also received the "Solomon Andrew Layton Award" presented by the Oklahoma Masonry Institute for excellence in masonry construction for his condominium design. The demand for Beck's talents grew almost overnight and it was evident that his best plan would be to establish his own architectural firm.

Don Beck believes there are a number of important factors to be considered when designing any structure, some of which the average person may not even think about as part of the design process. One of the greatest challenges is devising unique and creative solutions to tight budget constraints, which often means finding ways to use existing and prefabricated materials in inventive ways. Another item on the Beck Design checklist is functionality. This takes into account how the space relates to the existing environment and the impact on the day-to-day operation of the facility and its employees. The quality of the interior environment, such as the scale of the space, lighting type and levels, and the comfort of the interior, is another area of importance that Beck routinely addresses.

The design of libraries is only one area in which Beck's firm has gained national prominence. Most recently it received wide attention for the stunning and modernistic architecture of the new Ronald J. Norick Public Library, part of the Oklahoma City Metropolitan Library System. The long and narrow site, a challenging location for a library, relates to its physical surroundings in some unique ways. Through the use of large panes of glass, passersby are visually invited into the space, breaking barriers that were typical of older libraries. For library patrons, being able to view the outside world creates a fluidity that melds both the exterior and interior

The Gothic-influenced architecture of Oklahoma City University's campus is portrayed in the Meinders School of Business and its 150-foot clock tower.

environment in more natural ways.

In creating the Norick Library, Beck Design used a strategy that illustrated its goal of functionality by incorporating the needs of the facility's visitors and workers. An example of this is the children's library.

To determine how best to create the space, the firm invited approximately 100 local children to participate in a design brainstorming session. Each child was supplied with pencils, crayons, and paper and asked to sketch out what they would consider to be the ideal kids' library space. Many of the ideas and

The 220-seat interactive lecture symposium at the Meinders Global School of Business is used to conduct video teleconferencing with Oklahoma City University's China campus.

concepts were then incorporated into the final design of the children's library. Beck has also successfully used this strategy with adults and employees, resulting in more user-friendly spaces and work environments that complement the staff.

Donald Beck's expertise and innovation in library design has set a new standard for the profession. A text he co-authored, *Your Library's Future Size,* is part of the architecture curriculum at Harvard University.

In some cases the need for superior user-friendly work environments is a matter of major concern. Such is the case with the new 260,000-square-foot National Weather Center (NWC) facility under construction on the campus of the University of Oklahoma at Norman. The project is a joint venture between the university's meteorology school and the National Oceanic and Atmospheric Administration (NOAA). The NWC's National Weather Service (NWS) is the primary source of weather data for the entire United States and issues critical warnings during life-threatening weather situations. Because of the extreme stress these scientists endure, Beck Design is collaborating with Stanford Research Institute (SRI).

The goal is to create an environment that addresses the biorhythms of the workers, helping them to cope better when sleep is at a minimum and stress levels have peaked. The team is using breakthrough technologies such as a novel "circadian lighting" system which simulates natural daylight. The system will be able to sense when light, temperature, and humidity levels within the work-spaces should be adjusted to maintain optimal working conditions for the scientists. Because the center is located in what is called "Tornado Alley," the structure is being designed to withstand an F5 tornado—the most severe level on the Fujitsu Scale. This also means that windows will be at a minimum on the exterior of the building. To address this problem, Beck is creating interior atriums that will give employees the ability to safely experience natural daylight.

Natural light, or "daylighting" as Beck refers to it, is central to almost all of the firm's design projects. This is particularly true of the new 250,000-square-foot Oklahoma History Center with its glass "Main Street," which creates the illusion

The 200,000-square-foot Oklahoma History Center, located in Oklahoma City, symbolizes the state's past and future.

of two buildings that symbolize Oklahoma's past and future. Beck Design teamed up with the St. Louis firm of Helmuth, Obata, and Kassabaum to create the museum section of the complex, which had to meet stringent codes and requirements set up by the Smithsonian. For the actual structure, Beck utilized materials native to Oklahoma such as red sandstone, and designed the surrounding landscape to spotlight native grasses, trees, and shrubs. Part of the exterior design includes a fountain with freeform outcroppings of red sandstone from which the water flows.

Donald Beck did not want the architecture to be so bold that museum visitors were more focused on the building design rather than the artifacts. He

The National Weather Center on the University of Oklahoma campus was designed to withstand an F5 tornado—the most severe on the Fujitsu Scale.

believes that if his firm does its job well, when people leave the building they will first talk about the wonderful artifacts and then about the beauty of the structure—which for him is a perfect marriage of the two elements.

Historical preservation is another area in which the firm excels. They have recently been selected to create the new Oklahoma Jazz Hall of Fame which will be housed in the old Tulsa Union Train Station, built in about 1931. The 40,000-square-foot art deco building, which still contains many of its original fixtures and elements such as chandeliers, limestone, and marble floors, will be completely restored by Beck.

Beck Design also supports the development of young architects by participating in the preceptorship program at the University of Oklahoma. Through the program, Beck has brought architectural students into the firm to acquire hands-on experience in a professional architectural setting. For several years running Beck has supervised students who intern after school hours and on weekends. They assist in several areas honing their skills, such as drafting on actual projects.

A number of Beck's senior architects, including Don Beck himself, have participated on a myriad of committees and design competitions at several state universities. Don Beck also serves on the

The Ronald J Norick Library/Learning Consortium, centered in the heart of downtown Oklahoma City, provides higher education for numerous colleges in the area.

Beck Design has won numerous prestigious awards from organizations including the American Institute of Architects, the American Society of Interior Designers, the State Historic Preservation Office, the State of Oklahoma, the Department of Commerce/ Main Street Program, and the National Institute of Architectural Education.

Since the firm began in 1982, Donald Beck has designed more than 600 buildings, but points out that good design does not occur in a vacuum. He believes that each employee plays a vital role in the success of the company and that new employees bring in fresh ideas and can provide the company with wide-ranging ideas. Beck has established his firm on an organic approach where there are no set solutions, no single style, nor any dominant signature. It's an approach that can clearly be measured by the company's continuing rise to the top.

The four-story atrium of the Ronald J Norick Downtown Library infuses the space with natural light that flows throughout the building.

board of visitors at the University of Oklahoma and has on occasion taught design to architectural students. Today, Beck Design employs about twenty-five people, including architects, architectural designers, interior designers, graphic designers, three-D modelers, and others. The firm's main office is located in Oklahoma City, with a branch office in Tulsa. In addition to architectural design, interior design and historic preservation, the firm's services include master planning, restoration and renovation, landscape architecture, engineering coordination, construction bidding and negotiation, construction observation, project management, capital campaign support, grant application assistance, image development, signage and environmental graphic design, lighting design, furniture design and selection, communication technology, ADA code compliance, and National Register nomination.

DEACONESS HOSPITAL

Deaconess Hospital's reputation as a friendly and warm place where quality care and Christian compassion go hand in hand is so prevalent, many people don't realize that Deaconess is on the cutting edge of twenty-first century medicine and technology. Deaconess treats patients from all parts of Oklahoma and beyond in inpatient, outpatient, and emergency settings. Services are also provided in physician offices, clinics, and healthcare settings thoughout Oklahoma City and Bethany. Nearly every major medical, surgical, obstetrical, gynecological, and psychiatric service is offered. However, while the hospital has grown into a major healthcare provider, many people still associate it with its very humble beginnings.

The year was 1900 when a group of Free Methodist women evangelists came to the aid of unwed pregnant women and girls with the Oklahoma Rescue Home—the first of its kind in the state. The organization went by different names over the

Paul Dougherty, FACHE, president and CEO of Deaconess Hospital, celebrated as J.D. Power and Associates and HealthGrades honored the facility as the "2003 and 2004 Distinguished Hospital," the first hospital in Oklahoma to be so recognized. The award focused on Deaconess' service and clinical excellence.

years: Holmes Home of Redeeming Love, the Home of Redeeming Love, and Deaconess Home. The ministry moved from Guthrie to the current location of Deaconess Hospital in Oklahoma City in 1910.

Without any government or institutional support, the venture faced severe financial struggles. The ladies and their staff sacrificed unstintingly, often without pay, and personally solicited gifts to sustain their work. They farmed their 40 acres and lived off the farm products. They even attempted to sell spring water to sustain their ministry.

Despite their financial troubles, the organization expanded to include a training program, nurses' training, and a residence for elderly, needy women. The focus, however, remained on the unwed mothers. A freestanding hospital to provide pregnancy care and meet other medical needs of the patients was a natural outgrowth of the home's mission. In 1931 the first medical facility in northwest Oklahoma City, consisting of 22 beds, was constructed and later expanded to 45 beds. With modest facilities and limited finances, in 1944 the medical facility became Deaconess Hospital.

Over the years, the not-for-profit hospital has been a forerunner in the field of medicine and counts several important advances to its credit. Some innovations include being the first Oklahoma hospital specifically dedicated to family practice medicine, the first intensive care unit in Oklahoma, the first outpatient surgery center in Oklahoma, the first to have remote monitoring of EKGs, the first senior diagnostic psychiatric facility, the first lithotripsy facility in western Oklahoma, the first to offer heart catheterization with a high-speed X-ray tube, and the first Oklahoma City hospital to open a single birthing room unit.

Deaconess Hospital is now firmly entrenched in the twenty-first century with excellent facilities in both Oklahoma City and Bethany. After approximately $50 million in remodeling and expansion, the two campuses boast 313 licensed beds and cover approximately 1 million square feet. The main hospital in Oklahoma City is home to units for surgery, cardiology, obstetrics, rehabilitation, and critical care; the birth center; fourteen

Radiologists and technologists use the EXCITE MRI to give physicians clearer, faster images.

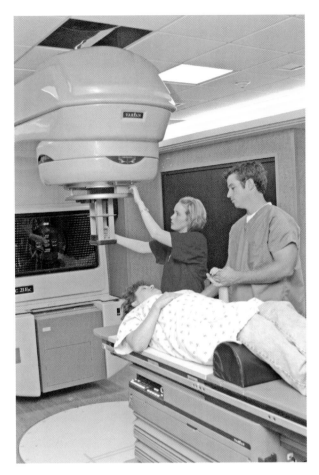

A new linear accelerator was recently added at the Deaconess Cancer Center radiation oncology department. It delivers intensity modulated radiation therapy, enabling oncologists to precisely target and attack cancerous tumors with higher doses of radiation, while surrounding tissue is protected.

emergency treatment rooms; decontainment facilities; and two medical office buildings. The Bethany location consists of about 100,000 square feet and houses home health, the wound care center, the sleep diagnostic center, behavioral medicine, and outreach radiology and lab services.

The expansive facilities are a far cry from the original Witteman Building, which the Oklahoma Rescue Home used in the early twentieth century. That building housed little more than twenty beds and cribs. On some occasions, they actually ran out of cribs for the newborns and had to lay the babies in the grass until a crib became available.

Now with its sprawling, modern buildings, Deaconess has reached the status of a major healthcare provider. The hos-

pital employs approximately 1,500 staff members and more than 700 physicians are on the medical staff at its two campuses. In 2003 Deaconess admitted 14,571 patients, had 34,000 ER visits, and administered to thousands more on an outpatient basis.

As Deaconess' size, services, and reputation has grown, it has become known within the state and even nationally for certain specialties. The hospital's wound care center in Bethany has been recognized on a national level for its excellent care. Other specialties include radiation therapy, nursing care, its overall quality of care, and its birthing center.

The birthing center is steeped in heritage and harkens back to the earliest days of the institution. Unlike the stark rooms found in the original Witteman Building, today's center offers eighteen elegantly appointed single room maternity suites, allowing mothers to share the birth experience with family in a beautiful, home-like atmosphere. New mothers stay in the same room for labor, delivery,

recovery and postpartum care. In addition, prenatal education classes are offered, including early pregnancy, childbirth preparation, breastfeeding class, and sibling class.

Under the direction of its current president and CEO, Paul Dougherty, quality care and customer service continues to be the focal point. Every day, the healthcare professionals at Deaconess go the extra mile to help patients feel more comfortable, to ease their pain, and bring healing. The time-honored tradition of offering compassionate, Christian care has become known as "Distinctively Deaconess." That moniker has been used internally for some time but has recently been used to let others know what sets the organization apart.

The emphasis on customer service has paid off with national citations. Deaconess has been recognized for both service and clinical excellence under the Distinguished Hospital Program, a collaborative effort by J.D. Power and Associates and HealthGrades. The institution earned the highest score in Oklahoma from HealthGrades and ranked in the top 3 to 4 percent of the

Physicians representing a wide variety of medical disciplines provide patients at Deaconess Hospital with comprehensive medical care. Pictured from left to right: Matthew A. McBride, M.D.; Louis H. Cox, M.D.; William P. Truels, M.D.; and John R. Taylor, M.D.

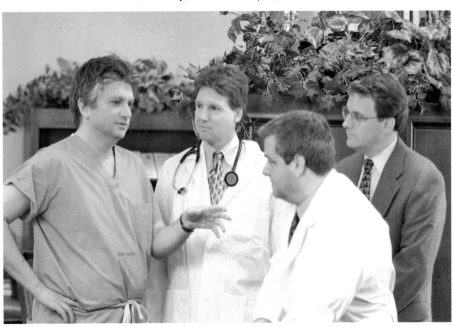

nation in terms of quality care. *Money Magazine* also included Deaconess in its 2003 listing of "Best Hospitals."

In addition to taking care of patients, Dougherty is determined to take great care of what he sees as Deaconess' most valuable asset: its employees. The hospital boasts a philosophy dedicated to retaining employees, growing them, and promoting from within. To help employees further their skills, the organization funds tuition reimbursement and grants for workshops, and offers courses such as "Managing Change" and "Leadership" in-house. On top of that, employees set aside money each year for an educational fund that helps other employees with continuing education.

At a time when the nation is struggling with a shortage of nurses, Deaconess is taking measures to attract and keep nurses on staff. In an effort to decrease turnover and increase morale, Deaconess has instituted a policy of shared governance. That means the nurses are involved in the

Deaconess Wound Care Center physicians use the latest technology including hyperbaric oxygen therapy to treat patients with chronic, non-healing wounds. The 93 percent cure rate speaks for itself.

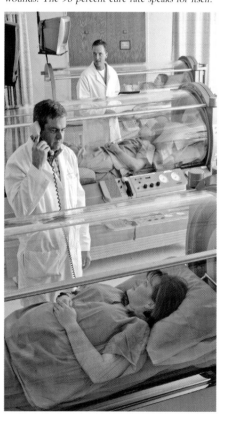

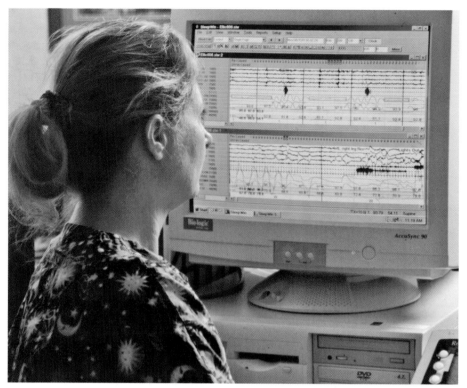

Deaconess Sleep Diagnostic Services offers diagnosis and treatment for sleep disorders such as snoring, sleep apnea, and other conditions. While the patient sleeps, the staff monitors and records patterns for the physician's diagnosis.

decision-making process at the hospital, thereby giving them a sense of ownership.

Just as Deaconess has taken great strides to take care of its employees and its patients, it also strives to be a good corporate citizen. Its ministries include health screenings at local schools, the Open Arms Free Clinic, and Deaconess Home Pregnancy and Adoption Services.

Since 1900 Deaconess Home Pregnancy and Adoption Services has helped thousands of women in unplanned pregnancies and successfully placed nearly 5,000 children in permanent homes. By focusing on the relationships it is helping to create, Deaconess Home strives to meet its mission of strengthening families through unconditional acceptance to women in crisis, improving homes for children, and assisting adoptive parents in the creation of their family.

The Open Arms Free Clinic is a collaborative effort of the MacArthur Free Methodist Church, the Oklahoma County Medical Society, and Deaconess Hospital. It serves and ministers to the medically uninsured and disadvantaged residents of Oklahoma County by offering free clinic healthcare, education, and spiritual encouragement.

There's no doubt that Deaconess has evolved into a major force within the

community. However, its status as the only independent hospital in Oklahoma City has presented several challenges. These days, with skyrocketing health costs and shrinking reimbursements from health insurance companies, most hospitals have opted to partner with larger entities. As an independent, Deaconess is constantly challenged to come up with the financing to stay competitive and keep up with technology.

Dougherty admits that with the existing climate in healthcare, Deaconess may eventually choose to go that route and partner with another entity. However, he insists that even if Deaconess does join forces with a larger organization, it will never lose touch with its heritage or its reputation for compassionate care. And as Deaconess continues to prepare for the future with exciting new technology and additional services, Dougherty remains resolute that Deaconess will never stray from what makes it "Distinctively Deaconess."

*Pictured here are patches of
azaleas in Muskogee, where
the Azalea Festival is held
each April. Courtesy, William
D. Welge*

DOLESE BROS. CO.

John Dolese, 1868-1941.

Henry D. Dolese, "H.D.," 1870-1944.

Peter Dolese, 1872-1930.

Roger Dolese, a prototypical Westerner with an integrity that defines the region itself, served as president of Dolese Bros. Co. for over sixty years, until his death in 2002. The Oklahoma firm, older than the state of Oklahoma, first began operations in the Midwest. The four Dolese brothers, William, John, Henry, and Peter, established their contracting business in Chicago during the late nineteenth century. They constructed streets, sewer facilities, and other public projects throughout the city.

William Dolese soon left the firm, leaving the company in the sole ownership of his three younger brothers. John, Henry, and Peter Dolese grew impatient with city construction and responded to the lure of the West, as so many did in the early days of the century. They moved their operation to the railroad-owned ballast plants located along the main railroad lines in Kansas, Oklahoma, and New Mexico, contracting to operate the plants for the railroads.

The thousands of miles of railroad track that were being laid at that time required "ballast," the stones that lined the track on which the iron rails and wooden ties were laid. The three Dolese brothers, recognizing opportunity, began to buy the quarries from the railroads and

soon established themselves in Oklahoma. On January 1, 1907 they began operating the Richards Spur quarry, located north of Lawton in Comanche County, quarrying the stone that would be used to line railroad beds. Stone from that quarry is still delivered by rail and by truck, as it was in the early days.

Before Oklahoma territory became a state in November 1907, the brothers owned and operated quarries serving numerous railroads, including the Rock Island; Chicago Rock Island and Pacific; and the Gulf, Colorado, and Santa Fe Railroad at Buffalo, Iowa where crushed stone was shipped by barge on the Mississippi River. The Buffalo quarry closed when seepage from the Mississippi made quarrying there no longer economically feasible. Dolese operated two quarries, Crusher and Big Canyon, from the same hill south of Dougherty in Murray County, Oklahoma along the Washita River. The poetically named quarries furnished ballast for the Santa Fe Railroad, lining the steep grades that ran through the rugged Arbuckle Mountains.

By 1913 the brothers had branched out again, warehousing various construction materials in Oklahoma City, and even serving for a time as retailers of

coal. The company moved with the times, entering the ready-mixed concrete business in 1927, primarily as a way of providing a larger market for the crushed stone from its quarries. Dolese Bros. Co. quickly established ready-mixed concrete batch plants in several Oklahoma towns. In later years, Dolese entered the ready-mixed concrete market in Wichita, Kansas and Baton Rouge, Louisiana.

When highways began to compete with the railroads, the Dolese brothers stepped into that market as well. They furnished a large volume of stone and sand for construction of the first Oklahoma highway system, particularly U.S. routes 66, 81, and 77. During this period the brothers acquired and established sand plants to meet the new industry's demand for sand.

World War II and increased U.S. military involvement brought new challenges for the Oklahoma firm. During the 1940s the company furnished hundreds of thousands of tons of stone to U.S. military installations at Fort Sill, Tinker Air Force Base, and Vance Air Force Base in Oklahoma; Sheppard Field, near Wichita Falls, Texas; and Perrin Air Force Base, near Pottsboro, Texas. In 1944 Roger Dolese followed his father, Peter, into the business. He became the firm's leader in 1946 after his Uncle Henry's death.

Today, the company operates from its general offices at 20 N.W. 13th Street in Oklahoma City. Its employees number over 1,000. In Oklahoma thirty-seven concrete plants and 240 trucks supply ready-mixed concrete to customers on a daily basis. Eleven quarries and stone yards produce and market stone for the construction industry. Four sand plants provide washed sand products within the Oklahoma City area.

Current company president Tony Basolo, who has been with the firm over thirty years, speaks with great warmth of Roger Dolese. He especially notes Dolese's integrity, leadership, and under-stated style that so endeared him to his

This bronze bear was chosen by Roger M. Dolese to symbolize his affection and respect for all God's creatures. It stands as a memorial to him in the general offices of Dolese Bros. Co. on a sculptured base containing his ashes.

employees. A commanding photo of the former company president shows the weathered face of an outdoorsman, partly from time spent at his Colorado ranch, near Pagosa Springs. Basolo also recounts that Dolese, who studied engineering at the University of Michigan, could exhibit almost total memory recall. The trait served him well in the quarrying business. After a 1949 fire in the firm's Richards Spur quarry, Dolese reconstructed the quarry. The reconstruction, completed in 1951, still serves as a "state-of-the-art" model within the industry. Many quarry owners have traveled to the site to view Dolese's design there.

Roger Dolese's work within the quarries, which encompassed many phases of the operations, also endeared him to his employees. They have

Roger M. Dolese, 1916-2002.

demonstrated an exceptional loyalty to his company over the years. One long-time worker at Dolese's largest quarry has been with the firm for over fifty-six years.

Current employees continue to embrace Dolese's exceptional manage-ment style. In a firm newsletter published in spring 2004, department heads encouraged everyone to get out and notice the redbud and Bradford pear trees in bloom. Births and deaths are noted in addition to recent firm acquisi-tions. One "note of appreciation" from an out-of-town caller expresses thanks to two Dolese mixer truck drivers, who had the good grace to stop their trucks during a funeral procession.

This Oklahoma firm, founded over 100 years ago "on the sound principles of customer service and quality at a fair price," in the words of Roger Dolese, continues to enhance Oklahoma's cor-porate culture with nineteenth century principles and twenty-first century technology. Its continued excellence honors his legacy of hard work, dedica-tion, and service.

FAMILY MEDICAL CARE OF TULSA

At Family Medical Care of Tulsa, the name says it all. The doctors specialize in family medicine which treats the whole person and the whole family, for their whole lives. From birth to post-retirement, a patient can see the same doctor for a lifetime. But for the doctors at Family Medical Care, treating the whole person means more than just providing medical treatment. It's the care that really sets them apart from other medical practices. In fact, the group's slogan is "Caring… It's What We Do Best." To fulfill that claim, the doctors provide far more than what medical science can offer. Convinced that spiritual issues have a lot to do with the healing process, the Christian doctors also offer prayer and counseling to their patients.

Family Medical Care was founded in 1987 by six original shareholders who were faculty at the Oral Roberts University School of Medicine. One of the original shareholders and current president and CEO, Dr. Pat Bolding, explains their philosophy, saying, "We believe that true health is defined as wholeness in spirit, mind, and body. We are all composed of a body, mind, and spirit, intricately integrated. Together, they comprise the

A resident physician with In His Image does door to door community health outreach in the blind section of a squatter camp in Jos, Nigeria.

City of Faith Medical and Research Center, birthplace of Family Medical Care of Tulsa.

whole person, which cannot be separated. Modern medicine attempts to dissect the "whole" person into independent parts addressing primarily the body, to a lesser degree the mind, and essentially not at all, the spirit. Numerous studies indicate that the majority of people would like

their physician to at least acknowledge their spiritual beliefs. Interestingly, we have found that our patients rarely object to an offer of prayer, even if they are not a Christian." Family Medical Care's unique philosophy of integrating ministry and medicine extends far beyond the Tulsa area. In addition to their medical practice, which is one of the largest family practice groups in Oklahoma, the doctors at Family Medical Care partner with In His Image (IMAGE: International Medicine And Graduate Education). The ministry has been offering a unique Christian-based residency program since 1989.

That was the year Oral Roberts University made the surprise announcement that it was going to close its School of Medicine and the City of Faith Medical and Research Center. Along with those closures, it was going to terminate its longstanding Christian-based family medicine residency program.

The physicians of Family Medical Care felt there was a tremendous need for a program that provided training for Christian doctors who wanted to offer patients more than just medical science. With the residency's future uncertain, the physicians gathered together and held a prayer session. Through prayer, they believed that God wanted them to find a way to continue the program.

Together, the physicians set out to preserve and retain the residency program. The doctors approached several local hospitals in an effort to find a backer for the project, which emphasized the marriage of ministry and medicine. Thanks to determination, persistence, and a lot of prayer, the group found a supporter. In October 1989, just one month after Oral Roberts University had delivered the stunning news, Family Medical Care formed an affiliation with Hillcrest Medical Center. To administer the residency program, the doctors created In His Image in 1990.

Since then, more than 100 residents have graduated from the program that integrates faith in Jesus Christ into every part of the program. Medical students are recruited from around the nation and even from foreign countries to attend the fully accredited and well-respected program. The strong academic curriculum includes all the basic rotations and training in procedures, computers in medicine, and international health. The residents receive hands-on education at several local medical facilities, including Hillcrest Medical Center, University Village Retirement Center, Claremore Comprehensive Indian Health Facility, Tulsa City/County Health Department, and the Family Medical Care offices.

Upon graduation, the physicians venture off to start practices of their own in a wide variety of settings—especially among the medically underserved. Many graduates eventually land in domestic missions, whether it's in a clinical setting or serving in a church in a rural area. Others head for foreign medical missions. Many have stayed on to become staff physicians at the facility.

All of the physicians at Family Medical Care are board-certified specialists in family medicine. Becoming a family practice physician requires years of training. After graduating from medical school, doctors must complete a comprehensive three-year family practice residency program and are required to pass an extensive written examination. To maintain board certification, family practice physicians are required to take the examination again every seven years. Because of that, Family Medical Care's physicians must stay on top of new

Praying Hands, *at the entrance of Oral Roberts University, was originally located at the City of Faith and symbolizes the joining of prayer and medicine.*

methodology, new treatments, and new technology. An ongoing education program helps the doctors keep pace with the latest advances in medical care.

Because Family Medical Care treats everyone from newborns to seniors, they offer a vast array of services. The list includes pediatrics, adolescent and adult medicine, obstetrics and gynecology, mammography, preventive healthcare and immunizations, laser services, biofeedback, bone density testing, and minor surgeries. In addition to traditional medical services, psychological counseling is also available for patients of all

ages. Whether a patient is a child, a teen, or an octogenarian, they can participate in individual, family, marital, or group psychotherapy sessions.

In addition to providing a wide scope of services for people of all ages, Dr. Bolding and the other doctors are determined to provide comfort and convenience for patients. To make it as easy as possible for patients to receive medical treatment, the facility provides many of its services onsite. The group also offers extended hours to accommodate patients' schedules.

A full-service onsite laboratory for tests and blood work eliminates inconvenient and time-consuming additional visits to other facilities. With a doctor's order for tests, patients can come to the lab at their own convenience any day of the week from Monday through Friday. They don't even need an appointment. Other on-site services include mammography and x-ray services, which are available on weekdays. The clinic is also equipped to perform minor surgeries and to provide emergency treatment for lacerations and fractures.

Sign at South Lewis location, showcasing the company logo and motto.

The 7600 South Lewis facility includes 28,295 square feet.

The doctors at Family Medical Care know that in order to treat the whole person, they need to have the whole story. That's why they implemented an innovative medical records system that's fully computerized. With the new system, each patient's complete medical history is instantly available to the physician via computer. This assures that the physician can have the total picture at any time for medical evaluation to determine the best course of treatment for a patient. Doctors can access the information at the clinic or at the hospital, and of course, patient privacy is protected.

Just as the services offered by Family Medical Care have expanded since its debut in 1987, so have the facilities, the number of locations, and the personnel. From its original six partners, the staff has grown to twenty-eight staff physicians, two nurse practitioners, and over 150 support staff. Those dedicated professionals now cater to patients in four locations: the Lewis office, Broken Arrow, Harvard Parke, and SouthCrest. In addition to these facilities, there is also a doctor and nurse available at the University Village Retirement Center.

The group moved into its current spacious building at 7600 South Lewis on September 5, 1994. At 28,295 square feet, the facility is twice the size of Family Medical Care's original building which was located just down the street. At the time, Dr. Bolding said,

"The new, larger facility will enable us to better serve our patients, operate more efficiently, and allow for room to grow." Although Hillcrest put up the funds for construction and owns the building, it allowed the staff of Family Medical Care to design the new structure so it would meet its needs. The doctors and staff designed the single-story facility with convenience and quality care in mind. The building houses an in-house lab, x-ray department, minor surgery facilities, and many other services.

For years, Family Medical Care was known as "the best-kept secret in South Tulsa." Eventually, the doctors wanted to take their unique brand of caring beyond Tulsa's city limits. On January 2, 1996 they opened a clinic in Broken Arrow. The group bought an existing practice from a doctor who had previously been within the Family Medical Care fold but had left to branch out on his own. With this purchase, that doctor once again became part of the family. Today, he is joined by a nurse practitioner in providing care to local residents.

In November 1999 the group continued its expansion with the purchase of another existing practice at Harvard Parke, which currently has two doctors on staff. In May 2000 Family Medical Care opened a new office in the South-Crest Hospital medical office building with two physicians, which rapidly grew to six. The SouthCrest location offers a gastrointestinal clinic, an on-site laboratory, and medical spa services in addition to routine office visits.

With each new location, each new service it offers, and each new graduate of the In His Image residency program, Family Medical Care spreads its philosophy of Christian-based medicine. No matter how large the group grows, their faith in their mission never falters. They remain focused on their corporate scripture of Jeremiah 29:11. "For I know the plans I have for you declares the Lord, plans to prosper you and not to harm you, plans to give you hope and a future." And in spite of the many challenges facing healthcare providers today, they do everything in their power to remain dedicated to that mission.

Their Christian love and compassion also compels these special doctors to provide medical care for those who can't afford it. From In His Image and Family Medical Care came the development of Good Samaritan Health Services, which provides a mobile medical van offering free medical care to those in need. Doctors and nurses from the two groups and the medical community at-large volunteer their time in the van to minister to patients throughout the community. The mobile medical van goes out into the community at least once a week to provide care.

After more than 15 years in business, Dr. Bolding feels like Family Medical Care is an extended family itself. It has always been very important to him to create a working environment where doctors, nurses, residents, and administrative staff care about each other as much as they care about the patients. When

Left: Family Medical Care at Broken Arrow.

Below: Family Medical Care at University Village.

Left: Family Medical Care at SouthCrest.

Below: Family Medical Care at Harvard Parke.

new staff members comment on how wonderful the atmosphere is at Family Medical Care, Dr. Bolding can't help but feel a sense of pride and accomplishment.

With multiple locations, a faith-based residency program, and a commitment to the community, there's a lot for the doctors and staff to be proud of. However, the thing that makes Dr. Bolding most pleased is what he hears from the people they help. "Receiving feedback from our patients about how they truly feel that we care about them," he says. "It validates our slogan "Caring…It's What We Do Best."

FEED THE CHILDREN

In 1979 on a dusty side street in Port Au Prince, Haiti, a small, thin boy approached Larry Jones with a request. "Lorry," he said, mispronouncing Larry's name, "Can you spare a nickel?" Larry asked what it was for and the boy answered, "So I can go to that store over there and buy me a roll. I haven't eaten all day." When Larry reached in his pocket for the coin, the boy asked, "Do you have three pennies? For that they'll cut the roll in half and put butter on both sides." Larry gave the boy the money and said, "You'll need something to wash it down with. How much is a Coke?" "Twelve cents," replied the boy, Jerry. A mere twenty cents bought everything that little boy would eat for a day. Not a nutritious meal, but a meal nevertheless.

Larry Jones had just read an article about surplus grains being dumped by American farmers, and soon after returning home from Haiti, he raised enough money to pay for a shipment of surplus wheat to Haiti to feed hungry children such as Jerry. The result? Feed The Children was born.

Larry and his wife, Frances Jones, then appeared on several television shows, telling the story of the little boy and what they had experienced in Haiti. Their question was simple: Why should children be starving to death while we have surplus wheat in America?

Larry and Frances Jones, co-founders of FTC, stand among a group of children in a feeding center in Angola, Africa. Circa, 2000.

Larry Jones, president and founder of Feed The Children, helps in a camp for displaced persons in Ethiopia. Circa, 1984.

Larry knew there was a way to ship the grain and aid American farmers, save U.S. taxpayers the expense of storage, and guarantee bread for hungry boys and girls overseas. He was determined to find a solution that would benefit everyone. Since that initial small relief project, Larry and Frances' work has evolved into the tenth largest charity in the United States in terms of private support and the sixteenth largest charity overall. Feed The Children's (FTC) mission to deliver food, medicine, clothing, and other necessities to needy families around the globe has made the agency a worldwide name.

In the United States, FTC operates programs targeting food and childcare and disaster relief. The organization also enhances learning opportunities for underprivileged children by distributing books and other educational materials to impoverished rural and urban communities. Overseas, the organization operates programs in more than a dozen foreign countries through Feed The Children International. The agency has more than twelve field offices in Eastern Europe, Africa, Asia, and Central America, which receive and distribute in-kind gifts. In December 2001 Larry Jones personally led the first private, non-UN, humanitarian mission to the displaced persons camp near Herat in western Afghanistan—the largest such camp in the world.

FTC shipped a total of 230 tons of rice, shoes, socks, and clothing to the area.

On the homefront, Feed The Children's efforts have also been crucial during two of the worst times in United States history. Just miles from FTC's Oklahoma City headquarters, the Alfred P. Murrah Federal Office Building was torn apart in a terrorist explosion in 1995. Literally within minutes, Feed The Children had brought together more than 400 volunteers to prepare sandwiches and hot food for rescue workers, while bottled water and other emergency supplies were loaded on to a large truck and taken to the disaster site. In the weeks that followed, FTC provided more than 130,000 meals and other assistance to rescue workers and displaced people of the Oklahoma City disaster.

FTC responded again immediately after the tragedies of September 11, 2001. The organization sent truckloads of bottled water, blankets, flashlights, shovels, hammers, dust masks, food, and other items to the World Trade Center and other areas that were hit by the disaster. With a dedicated fleet of 55 semi-tractor trailer trucks, operated by its wholly-owned subsidiary FTC Transportation, Inc.,

Feed The Children is often the first relief agency to reach the scene during a disaster

The humanitarian work of Feed The Children is well known. So is the humanitarian spirit of Larry Jones. Over the years he has received national and international recognition for his service to others including the "Humanitarian Award" from the National Conference of Christians and Jews in 1995, "Oklahoman of the Year" in 1994, the "National Caring Award" in 1993, *ABC News* "Person of the Week" in 1990, plus humanitarian commendations from Armenia, El Salvador, Guatemala, Iran, and Lebanon. Additionally, Larry Jones is the author of numerous books including *Life's Interpretations, God's Opportunities; How to Bend without Breaking; How to Make It to Friday; The 15-Second Secret*; and the soon to be released novel, *The Black Box.*

From the organization's inception, Frances Jones took on a full-time role in the ministry, establishing and managing the child sponsorship department and the Frances Jones Abandoned Baby Center in Kenya. Over the years she has also helped women in economically distressed countries start their own small-scale enterprises.

Recognized as a leading humanitarian, Frances Jones has received numerous awards in recognition of her compassion and service to others. She was named "Woman of the Year" in 1992 by the American Biographical Institute of International Research and was honored as one of the "Ladies in the News" in 1992 by the Oklahoma Hospitality Club. In 1995 she also received the "Byliner Award for International Relief" from Women in Communications. In 2000 both Frances and Larry Jones received the "H. J. Heimlich Humanitarian Award" for relief efforts throughout the world.

Most recently, in 2002, Frances Jones was named as one of the The Leading Women Entrepreneurs of the World™. She was among thirty-eight individuals chosen for the award for that particular year and the first woman ever selected from the philanthropic community. Additionally, Frances is the author of four books including *Sweetheart, I'm*

Larry and Frances Jones, co-founders of Feed The Children, survey damage outside the Alfred P. Murrah Building after the bombing in 1995.

with Jesus (about the death of her father); *A Circle of Love: The Oklahoma City Bombing Through the Eyes of Our Children; Christmas Moments, Cherished Memories;* and *The Legend of The Empty Bowl.*

Since 1980 Feed The Children has shipped supplies to individuals in a total of 109 countries. Particular care is given to children who are disabled, homeless, or living in the streets. In August 2001 FTC opened its first Abandoned Baby Center (ABC), which provides a safe

home and family-like environment for abandoned babies and toddlers. The ABC center is located near Nairobi, Kenya, and serves childhood victims of the AIDS pandemic.

The FTC Medical Team travels four times a year to developing countries to provide assistance to people who cannot afford, or who do not have access to, regular medical care. Top priority goes to poor countries that have suffered natural or manmade disasters. In 2004 the medical team completed its 100th mission trip. Each year the team treats more than 45,000 medical, vision, and dental patients.

In addition to providing emergency and long-term humanitarian assistance, FTC's other international objective is to develop sustainable, long-term improvements in the quality of life for people. For example, Feed The Children has helped construct fish hatcheries, protect fish breeding grounds, build model farms and agricultural training centers, establish micro-loan programs, and develop water sanitation projects.

Whether here in America or across the world, Feed The Children is dedicated to offering spiritual, educational, vocational, technical, and psychological support to those in need. It is a mission the organization takes seriously and one that will always be near and dear to hearts of Larry and Frances Jones.

Larry Jones talks with police officers at "Ground Zero" in the aftermath of the World Trade Center attacks on September 11, 2001.

HYDROHOIST INTERNATIONAL, INC.

Located in Claremore, Oklahoma, HydroHoist International Inc. is the world's premier manufacturer of floating-in-the-water dry docks. Capable of lifting 900 to 130,000 pounds of all types of watercraft, HydroHoist has been the industry leader for nearly 40 years. It has grown to serve a worldwide marketplace in all aspects of pleasure craft, service boats, Personal Water Craft (PWC), and other floating vessels. The company is also known for being the creator and manufacturer of the innovative medical intervention lift that was used in the release process for Keiko, the whale of *Free Willy* movie fame.

Founded in 1966 by Henry Rutter, who owned a marina on Grand Lake in Oklahoma, the idea for a boatlift grew from a need to dry dock boats on water, since land space near bodies of water was quickly reaching a premium. It was also evident that there were other advantages to creating a hydro pneumatic boatlift system. For example, it was more convenient to dock and return the boat to the water with a minimal amount of energy and time.

Rutter's boatlift system was an immediate success and by 1971 he sold his marina. He then, along with his brothers Harold and Neal, moved the company

A dealer meeting during the early years of the company, with Henry Rutter at the far right.

into an old World War II munitions plant in Claremore, where part of the business still exists today.

In 1976 a controlling interest in the firm was bought by Ron Liebl, a former project engineer at North American Rockwell. Rutter stayed on as a consultant and project developer and continued working for the business until he retired in 1984. He did, however, hold on to his boatlift patents.

The business continued selling boatlifts throughout the next decade, but did little regarding research and development

during that time. In 1990 Liebl began looking for a prospective buyer of HydroHoist, and Joe Cox stepped up to the table. Cox bought half of Liebl's shares as well as Rutter's patents, trademarks, and copyrights in January 1991. Cox had worked for many years with Borg-Warner and had recently retired from Hughes Tool. It was there that he was responsible for creating CL Lift, an offshoot of Hughes, which manufactured for the oil industry.

Cox immediately began a reassessment of the company's manufacturing, distribution, and marketing strategies. The first thing he did was set up a research and development department. He hired top level engineers in the field to create new products, and redesign and improve on the company's existing product line. Cox also took a hard look at the distribution system and quickly realized that it was in need of a major overhaul. Of the 200 distributors HydroHoist had on their books in 1991 only 15 percent were kept on with the company. Some proved to not be distributors at all, while others had distributorships in low sales markets or were not good sales people. With this knowledge in hand, Cox seized the opportunity to build exclusive dealerships and distribution sites. A building was

Keiko is placed in his pen in Iceland.

leased in Bernice, Oklahoma not far from the company's Claremore location, and within the first year the firm had doubled its sales volume under Cox's new structure. Today, that same location in Bernice sells nine to ten times the volume it did when it opened fourteen years ago.

In October of that year HydroHoist bought the Charles Industries Marine Group, a manufacturer of marine power pedestals which are still widely used at marinas and recreational vehicle parks. Cox believed these power pedestals would be a good complement to their line of products, and would create a marketing synergy. In the end, Cox had the Charles marine power pedestal completely redesigned, and it took the company into a new direction.

Building on its experience and knowledge, Cox took the HydroHoist line of boatlifting products and built the company up to be number one in its industry. Today, the company offers the latest in lift technology as well as proven boatlift products that have endured for years. HydroHoist continuously upgrades and enhances existing products while developing new models to serve the expanding marketplace and better satisfy today's boater.

J.L. Cox, president and CEO of HydroHoist.

The company prides itself on the fact that its products are designed by employees who actually use them. HydroHoist employees also recognize that product details and new technology can make all the difference between an adequate boatlift and a top-rated one. Constant efforts are made by a full-time engineering staff to create these new products by listening to HydroHoist customers, dealers, and employees on ways to better serve the boatlift market. Input from all Hydro-

Hoist divisions also assures constant attention to detail and provides quality control that reaches beyond the norm.

HydroHoist makes several lift products for a myriad of boats and watercraft including high performance and powerboats, cruisers, sail boats, houseboats, seaplanes, yachts, and small submarines. The lifts can also accommodate boats and personal water craft (PWC) that weigh from 900 to 130,000 pounds.

Designed for boats up to 8,800 pounds, the Ultra Lift "UL" model contains polyethylene tanks which are designed and manufactured by HydroHoist. They are also highly resistant to impact and low-water damage because they flex when they're stressed, and thereby return to their original shape completely unharmed. All of Ultra Lift's steel parts are above the water, a new concept in the boatlifting industry that helps to resist rust and corrosion.

Created for boats up to 8,000 pounds and up to 28 feet in length, the Level Lift "L" Series is made of ultra tough, marine fiberglass tanks and hot-dip, zinc galvanized structural steel. The lift is offered with a number of options including custom hull pads, side-of-boat walk-

Henry Rutter at his dry storage facility where he developed the HydroHoist Boat Lift.

Aerial view of the company's current manufacturing facilities in Claremore, Oklahoma.

ways for wide slip applications, custom configurations for sailboats, and centering guides for positioning.

The Level Lift "Mega L" Series has been designed for watercraft weighing from 10,000 to 40,000 pounds and are 28 feet to 42 feet in overall length. This lift comes with drive-in or back-in installations and can be used in floating docks and U-shaped slips.

The "Side-Tie B" Series, with capacities up to 30,000 pounds, is designed to provide single-side mooring in any type of dock including floating or stationary docks for both power and sailboats. Floating walkways on each side of the lift act as a guide when the boat is down, a step out of the boat when moored, and a step into the boat when the boat and the lift are fully raised.

The Cruiser Lift "C" Series, known as the "The BIG BOAT Boat Lift" offers level-lifting. Utilizing high-strength stainless steel cable to keep the hoist level as the fiberglass tanks lift the boat from the water, the "C" model is ideal for cruisers, fixed keel sailboats, and large runabouts. It is easily decked for full access to boat hull and out-drives.

The Front Mount "FM" Series is designed for lifting boats measuring up to 26 feet in length and weighing up to 6,600 pounds in wide boat slips. The FM attaches to the boat dock or pier at the front of the hoist and at one back corner. The HydroHoist Front Mount Hoist is perfect for double-sized slips and "L" shaped moorings.

The Personal Watercraft Lift Series can hold watercraft weighing up to 900 pounds and jet boats up to 1,800 pounds and are available in either front-mounted or side-mounted models. The front mount unit hinges from the dock at the front of the hoist; the rear of the unit lowers to accept the PWC, then rises to dry dock it.

The side mount unit is attached to the dock from the side of the hoist, lowers vertically to accept the watercraft, then rises to dry dock it.

In 2004 the HydroPort PWC Docking Platform became one of HydroHoist's newest innovations. It offers the best in protection for PWCs up to 1,500 pounds, while still allowing fast and convenient access to the water. Watercraft can easily be driven on to the platform to load and rolled off to launch. The HydroPort is made of an ultra tough polyethylene construction and is available with front or side-mount mooring hardware, an anti-skid walk area, molded-in tie down loops, replaceable keel guide, and a bow bumper. It can be used in fixed, floating, or pier mooring situations.

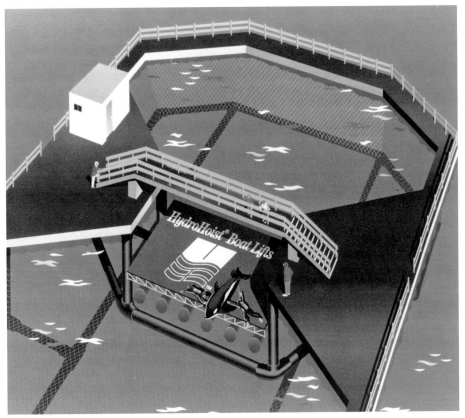

The artist's rendition of Keiko's pen and the HydroHoist Lift.

As a result of a continuously growing demand from the European market, Cox took the company global. In 2000 Hydro-Hoist opened a manufacturing plant and distributorship in Worms, Germany. The business also created product that is specifically designed for the European boater.

The EuroLift is the result of Hydro-Hoist's forty-plus years of experience and innovation. It has been designed to meet the needs of the international boating community and allows owners to store their boats while utilizing a minimum amount of space. Using high-density polyethylene for its tank construction, the lift has been designed to have only a minimum of its heavy-duty, steel galvanized frame exposed to the water. The design is both rugged and robust and is recommended for boats up to 15 metric tons, 16 meters in length, and moored in floating or fixed docks.

HyPower, a division of HydroHoist, is responsible for creating a new generation of power pedestal technology which can be used in marinas and RV campgrounds.

The PowerPort is the result of years of research and technological advancements gained by the company's team of engineers. Unlike old-fashioned power pedestals that are hardwired, the Power-Port has modular snap-in panels. The receptacles, breakers, phone, and television outlets are all located in lockable panels. The unit has a 400-amp capacity and is expandable.

One of the company's high points came from an attempt to save a neglected killer whale who lived in a Mexican aquarium. Keiko's plight had drawn the attention of the entire world after he was featured in the motion picture, *Free Willy*. It was around that time that HydroHoist was approached by the Free Willy/Keiko Foundation, a private, non-profit organization whose goal was to return Keiko back to the ocean. The plan was to place the whale into a floating bay release pen, which would contain a treatment and observation platform. The platform would need to be a lift, so Keiko could swim above it easily and be safely raised.

HydroHoist accepted the task of creating the lift, donating 50 percent of its costs for parts and labor. This became the firm's greatest challenge, but with the genius of one of the company's engineers, Todd Elson, the task was successfully completed. Joe Cox marks the day he saw Keiko use the platform in Iceland as one of his proudest moments—one that could not be easily topped.

Cox is very aware that none of the company's successes or innovations would be possible without his staff. He believes that all employees should be treated with dignity and in turn they should treat their co-workers with the same respect, regardless of rank or placement in the company business.

Under the leadership of Joe Cox, HydroHoist has grown from twenty-three to ninety-five employees since 1991. It now has six major company-owned HydroHoist distribution centers in the United States and Germany, as well as dealers in more than twenty countries across the globe.

HyPower division, HydroHoist International.

IMPERIAL COLLEGE OF EDMOND

For the first three decades of his life, Herbert W. Armstrong did not consider himself a religious man. With a successful career in advertising, religion had no real appeal in his life until his wife of nine years, Loma, challenged him into an almost night-and-day intensive study of the Bible.

He came to feel that most of mainstream Christianity does not get its beliefs from the Bible—and that the gospel that Jesus Christ had proclaimed nearly 1,900 years earlier was taught virtually nowhere.

Armstrong's commission became to preach this gospel "in all the world for a witness unto all nations" (Matthew 24:14). By the end of his life, he had achieved that commission. In January 1934, *The World Tomorrow* radio program began airing. One month later, the *Plain Truth* began in humble form with just a few hundred copies. In 1939, the *Good News* was established mainly for members and co-workers.

In the fall of 1947, Ambassador College was founded in Pasadena, California. Later, colleges were started in Bricket Wood, England, and Big Sandy, Texas.

Herbert W. Armstrong led a full life of ninety-three years—his legacy includes founding the Worldwide Church of God, the World Tomorrow *television program, the* Plain Truth *magazine, three campuses of a liberal arts college and the Ambassador International Cultural Foundation.*

During the 1950s and 1960s, the church's media began growing in impact. *The World Tomorrow* began airing in Europe on Radio Luxembourg and then on television. The *Plain Truth* was made available in several languages.

Armstrong spent much of the 1970s traveling worldwide, meeting heads of state, including Romania's Nicolae Ceausescu, Japan's Eisaku Sato, Ethiopia's Haile Selassie, Egypt's Anwar Sadat and Hosni Mubarak, and Jordan's King Hussein, to name just a few. By the time of his death on January 16, 1986, church income had grown to $200 million, *The World Tomorrow* was on 400 stations worldwide, and *Plain Truth* circulation had topped over 8 million.

Though his successor pledged to follow in Armstrong's footsteps, it wasn't long before the new administration began dismantling the core doctrines that Armstrong had restored to the church. The Worldwide Church of God (WCG) began to speak of Armstrong with embarrassment, and wanted nothing to do with the legacies he left behind.

Then came Gerald R. Flurry, a WCG minister who had been serving in central Oklahoma. Early in 1989, three years after some subtle but vital changes in the direction of the WCG, Flurry was disturbed by the church's direction. He began to compile a manuscript that he intended to show to WCG leadership to correct the problems. When others caught wind of the manuscript, Flurry was fired. Thus began what would soon be another globe-girdling work—the Philadelphia Church of God—intending to "prophesy again" the truth that Armstrong had declared for over fifty years.

Since Armstrong died, all three Ambassador College campuses have closed. In establishing the school, Armstrong pioneered the way for students to learn about abundant living and peace. Imperial College of Edmond embodies Herbert W. Armstrong's educational philosophy.

The awesome amount of knowledge mankind has produced, especially in the last century, makes the head spin. But rather than solve the world's pressing problems, troubles have only increased. This is the great paradox of modern education. "All of this knowledge," Herbert W. Armstrong once wrote, "yet virtually no happiness—just accelerating troubles, problems, evils. It's like being stranded on a raft in mid-ocean. Water everywhere, but not a drop to drink." He believed that modern educational institutions do not teach the knowledge

Since 1974 Ambassador Auditorium, the crown jewel of the Ambassador College campus, stood as the epitome of the cultural legacy Herbert Armstrong left behind—a legacy which the Philadelphia Foundation aims to revive today in central Oklahoma.

most essential to life—knowledge that leads to real abundant living and peace.

Imperial College (IC) of Edmond aims to fill that void. Though founded in 2001 by the Philadelphia Church of God (PCG), IC is not a "Bible college"— rather a coeducational, liberal arts institution. Its objective is to teach its students how to live and the different ways to earn a living. IC focuses on teaching skills, concepts, and values that lead to success in life, not just the work place. The IC education helps prepare young men and women for worthwhile service to God and humanity. A major part of the training is focused on personality development and building leadership qualities. Its curriculum includes theology, history, classic literature, language, social sciences, natural sciences, mathematics, physical education, and music.

IC is located just a few miles north of downtown Edmond, just outside Oklahoma City, and has all the advantages of big city life. Yet, because of the spacious 165-acre campus, it also offers many of the advantages of rural American life. Two large ponds on the property, one of which is spring-fed with crystal-clear water, provide opportunities for swimming, boating, and fishing. The rest of the campus is best described as rolling meadows of natural grass, shrubs, and trees. Its serene beauty offers ample space for walking, jogging, outdoor study, and contemplation.

The John Amos Field House is the hub of campus life. This 27,000-square-foot multipurpose center is where students attend class, services, concerts, eat meals, play sports, dance—and more. Outside the field house there is a soccer field and a softball diamond. In addition to the wide open spaces and the natural beauty of central Oklahoma, the well-equipped athletic and educational facilities help support the college's educational aims.

The work of the PCG is by no means limited to Imperial College. The church also takes advantage of developments in information technology to spread its message of hope.

Information is the most powerful and lucrative commodity in the world. The

Gerald R. Flurry is founder of the Philadelphia Church of God, presenter for the Key of David *television program, editor-in-chief of the* Philadelphia Trumpet *magazine, and chancellor of Imperial College of Edmond and the Philadelphia Foundation.*

average American consumes a huge amount every day. The challenge is to find a source that can provide answers to life's most basic questions. A source that delivers the plain truth.

In today's news media, journalists either report briefly on an event, offering no real depth, or—for those who try to tackle the issues more intensively—don't get to the real meaning behind the issues,

but rather pose more *unanswered* questions. The Philadelphia Church of God (PCG), through two powerful forms of media, aims to provide what it believes is the missing dimension in news reporting today. *The Key of David* television program and the *Philadelphia Trumpet* magazine—the two most visible aspects of the PCG's work—aim to give the real meaning behind events in today's world.

The Key of David is firmly established in many markets worldwide, with access to nearly 300 million people in the U.S., Canada, Latin America, the Caribbean, Australasia, South Africa, parts of Europe, the Middle East, and Asia. For most of its lifetime, *The Key of David* has remained in the top ten of weekly devotional programs, according to Nielsen Media Research. In the spring of 2004 it moved up to fourth. The program has also received various awards in recognition of broadcast excellence.

The success of the program can be greatly attributed to its similarity in format and message to Herbert W. Armstrong and the *World Tomorrow* television

As part of his cultural efforts, Herbert W. Armstrong arranged the U.S. tour of a group of Chinese prodigies in music and dance—"The Little Ambassadors of Shanghai"—in May 1984. The tour culminated with a performance for First Lady Nancy Reagan.

program—with its clear, understandable declaration of the plain truth of world events. Each week, presenter Gerald Flurry delivers powerful messages on issues facing our perilous world—tackling global news about rising superpowers, violence in the Middle East, and the nuclear dangers facing our world. He looks deep into the meaning of the news and provides a frank, outspoken presentation of the truth he sees. Flurry also addresses a variety of social issues—pornography, religion, family, and education.The program is not motivated by greed or shackled by political correctness. Because it is not funded by advertising dollars and has nothing to sell, organizers feel they are free to present the truth as they see it.

This unique perspective is also contained in print within the church's flagship periodical, the *Trumpet* magazine. It started in February 1990 with the humblest of beginnings, like the *Plain Truth* which it is modeled after. It is now a full-color, 40-page monthly newsmagazine with over a million readers. Like *The Key of David,* the *Trumpet* is a

Gerald Flurry sits at the desk of the new Key of David *studio, completed and fully operational as of May 2004.*

source for real news and understanding behind the news. It endeavors to give solid, understandable analysis and the meaning behind significant social trends.

What gives these two instruments such fresh perspective? Their content is based on the Holy Bible. The PCG believes that the Bible is not merely a record of history, but that it actually *foretells* events before they occur. Bible prophecy shows which, out of all the profusion of events, are most important

to watch. And it tells where those events are headed. This perspective, overlooked in mainstream journalism, is what they believe gives *The Key of David* and the *Trumpet* their edge.

The *Trumpet* is also an invaluable tool for everyday living. Each issue has several pages devoted to family, health, religion, and a plethora of other subjects that make abundant living practical, even in this ever-changing world.

Another arm of the Philadelphia Church of God—the chiefly humanitarian side—is the Philadelphia Foundation. This aspect of its work, like the college, traces its roots back to the founder of the Worldwide Church of God—Herbert W. Armstrong and the unparalleled humanitarian organization he began, known as the Ambassador International Cultural Foundation (AICF).

Although the AICF conducted humanitarian activities worldwide—its most prominent achievement was undoubtedly its concert series, held in the incomparable Ambassador Auditorium in Pasadena. This series brought excellence in the performing arts to the Los Angeles area by showcasing the greatest performers from all over the world during the 1970s and 1980s, such as the Vienna Philhar-

The Philadelphia Trumpet *is a free, forty-page, full-color magazine that is printed ten times a year.*

monic, Luciano Pavarotti, Joan Sutherland, Vladimir Horowitz, and Mel Tormé.

In January 1995—less than a year after Armstrong's death—WCG officials said they no longer had the money to subsidize the arts. Ambassador Auditorium, which was sold, sits empty today. AICF projects around the world were stopped as well.

In the mid-1990s the PCG began a humanitarian department, the Philadelphia Foundation. The two-pronged concept to all of the foundation's activities and goals are the same as the AICF's: 1) That man is a unique being,

Imperial College's intramural sports program is one of the highlights of extracurricular activities. In addition to basketball, the college also offers flag football, volleyball and softball.

possessing vast mental, physical, and spiritual potentials—the development of which should be aided and encouraged; and 2) that it is the responsibility of all men to attend to and care for the needs of their fellow men.

In August 1996, for its first venture, the foundation took over a project that, ironically, the defunct AICF had left behind in Amman, Jordan. In 1998 a small concert series began—in hopes that it would one day grow to be a grand series in Armstrong's tradition—supporting the

arts by giving monumental cultural experiences to the area. Now called the Philadelphia Foundation Concert Series, it is providing cultural excellence in central Oklahoma. In November 2000 and November 2002, the foundation brought the world-famous Vienna Choir Boys to Edmond. The 2002–2003 season also featured the internationally acclaimed Russian pianist Valery Kuleshov and German cellist Tess Remy-Schumacher. The 2003–2004 season launched with the Edmond debut of the world's most famous and beloved brass

In May 2004, the second graduating class, numbering 13 students, received their diplomas for finishing Imperial College's two-year program—with most of these continuing on to finish the four-year program.

Internationally acclaimed artists, like cellist Tess Remy-Schumacher and pianist Valery Kuleshov, have graced the stage of Imperial College as part of the Philadelphia Foundation Concert Series.

ensemble, the Canadian Brass, which had also performed for the AICF series.

In July 2004 the PCG even obtained some of the treasures from Ambassador Auditorium: a nine-foot Hamburg Steinway concert piano and two candelabra which were commissioned by the Shah of Iran to celebrate the 2,500th anniversary of the Persian Empire in 1971. To house these artifacts, the PCG has begun planning for a new auditorium—a beautiful concert hall modeled after Ambassador Auditorium to adorn the Imperial College campus.

INTEGRATED MEDICAL DELIVERY

It began with a simple concept to improve the delivery of patient care through an integrated medical delivery system. Over the past decade, one man's idea has evolved into an innovative company that boldly challenges the established norms and embraces progressive change for improved healthcare for patients. Its name, Integrated Medical Delivery, defines its purpose.

John T. Perri is founder & president of Integrated Medical Delivery (IMD), a diversified healthcare management company based in Oklahoma City. IMD provides healthcare facilities, physicians, and insurance companies with the resources to make sound business decisions for the effective and efficient delivery of patient care. The company's business model encourages all participants to actively take part in the delivery of quality patient care in settings that are comfortable and conducive to prompt recovery and patient wellness.

From developing a concept that many did not think could ever work, to building a highly successful company, Perri has been called a pioneer, a visionary, and a forward thinker. "I saw a need for a better system of healthcare delivery that was more patient-focused and efficient," Perri says. "To create a successful delivery system, providers should be held accountable so that the best providers are free to focus on patient care."

ODI was Oklahoma's first multiple location imaging company. ODI's four locations average more than 15,000 procedures per year.

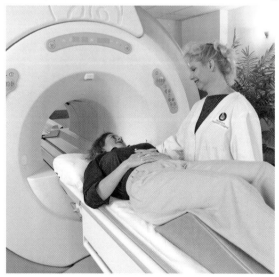

John T. Perri, IMD founder and president, with Dan Simmons, CompCHOICE president.

Perri came from a financial background. "I did not have any healthcare experience, but I understood customer service," says Perri. "So when we developed this model, we were not burdened by preconceived ideas of how things 'should' be done. IMD's business philosophy is based on the simple belief that a successful client relationship is based on trust and communication."

Timing was a significant factor in IMD's rapid evolution as a company. Technology and managed care were driving changes in healthcare. Technology was allowing surgeons to perform procedures on an outpatient or short-term stay basis, requiring the industry to respond with specialized facilities focused on efficiency.

Managed care was requiring providers to focus on cost. Perri's goal was to develop an integrated system that managed a patient from the time of the initial physician visit, through the insurance company's payment for the service. This model had been tried by insurance companies and large hospital networks, but never succeeded because of the inherent distrust among the physicians, facilities, and insurance companies. As an independent company, IMD sold services to all participants, but was beholden to none. The goal was to develop an organization that could provide the infrastructure to smaller surgical and diagnostic facilities and provide managed care focused on reduced costs.

In May 1992 IMD contracted with its first client, Oklahoma Diagnostic Imaging (ODI). ODI was a well-established Oklahoma City outpatient imaging center that offered MRI. IMD presented a strategic business plan, and with only a handful of employees, began the transformation of the company.

Intrinsic to the proposed business model were the concepts of consolidating overhead and outsourcing administrative services. IMD suggested using all the facility space for clinical services. This allowed ODI to provide new services and allowed the staff to focus on patient care. IMD provided the information system upon which the business operations were built. Integrating all the information into one multi-layered system enabled IMD staff to more efficiently complete patient scheduling, insurance pre-certification, transcription, coding, patient account services, provider relations, and accounting and payroll services.

The time was also right for expansion. Diagnostic imaging was becoming a widely accepted tool, and market demand increased. The vision was to create Oklahoma's first imaging company with multiple locations, offering high-field and open MRI, computed tomography (CT), and x-ray.

In November 1993 ODI acquired a center in Midwest City and opened a third imaging center in southwest Oklahoma City in July 1997. Soon thereafter, IMD developed Northern Oklahoma Diagnostic Imaging to serve patients in the northwest region of the state. It opened in June 1998.

Each center was designed for maximum clinical efficiency, and all non-clinical services were centralized in IMD's Oklahoma City office. This model proved effective. Combined, the two companies averaged more than 15,000 procedures per year, with gross charges exceeding $18 million.

With an established infrastructure, IMD was poised to meet its next challenge—developing surgical facilities, including hospitals and ambulatory surgery centers.

As with all aspects of its business, IMD recommended a focused approach to patient care. Facilities developed their scope of service primarily around neurosurgery and orthopedic surgery. Multi-specialty facilities offered additional services, including general surgery, plastic surgery, ophthalmology, and urology.

Technology opened up this door of opportunity, as the outpatient and short-stay surgical industry boomed. IMD was eager for the prospect and accepted two surgery center clients. Applying the same model as they had to ODI, the urban surgery center became the largest and highest-producing center in the state. The rural surgery center outperformed everyone's expectations and was quickly pursued by a large national company.

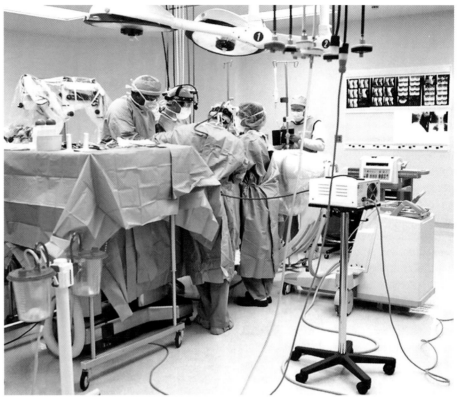

Surgical facilities are designed for ease of workflow and efficiency.

One of IMD's most significant milestones was opening the first specialty spine hospital in the U.S. in November 1999, located in Oklahoma City. This progressive endeavor offered patients the first hospital dedicated to providing

CompCHOICE provides evaluation and treatment of workplace injuries. PhysiciansCHOICE is a network of providers specializing in the treatment of workplace injuries.

advanced medical and surgical treatment for patients suffering from diseases of the spine and chronic pain, through quality health services intended to restore, maintain, and improve patient wellness.

Each hospital thereafter applied the patient-focused concepts that set the

spine hospital apart. The hospitals raised the overall standard of care, to make their facilities exemplary. All patient rooms were private. For more personalized care, nurse-to-patient ratios far exceeded industry standards. Family reception and waiting areas were comfortable and spacious. The total patient experience was measured through patient satisfaction tools. Well received by patients, the facilities consistently achieved over 98 percent satisfaction ratings.

IMD provides services to five hospitals in four states. Combined, all facilities perform an average of 40,000 surgical procedures per year and generate more than $300 million in gross charges. IMD has overseen a total of more than $125 million in facility development and capital improvement.

Brett Gosney, CEO of Animas Surgical Hospital, states that IMD allows his hospital's physicians and staff to focus on patient care. "With the help of IMD, we are able to dedicate our resources to providing proper care, while leaving the administrative details to them," Gosney says. "They focus on the business operations of our hospital."

Parallel to the healthcare facility outsourcing venture, IMD was continuing on its singular path of developing a fully integrated medical delivery system. The development of the managed care company was well underway.

Perri knew that developing a managed care product was a critical component in this integrated delivery system. However, the service line development would require an unsullied approach so that it did not resemble the failed system with which so many people were dissatisfied. To accomplish this goal, he set out to find a leader who could build a new service line from the ground up, and apply the fundamental philosophy of allowing the best providers to focus on patient care. Perri chose Dan Simmons for this demanding task.

"Dan was perfect for this undertaking because he understood all sides of the system," Perri says. "He had been a practicing doctor of chiropractic medicine for seventeen years, so he understood what it meant to be a provider, from both a patient care and business

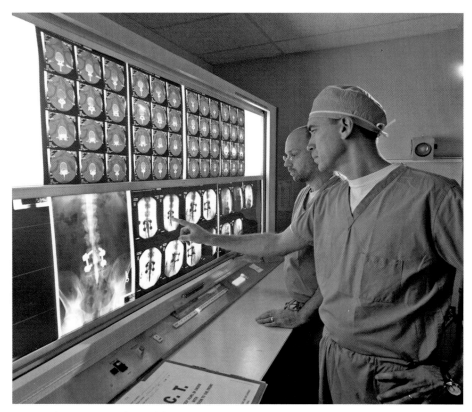

IMD opened the first specialty spine hospital in the United States, in Oklahoma City, Oklahoma in November 1999.

perspective. He was also a risk manager for a fourteen-state national retail chain, so he understood the employer's need to reduce costs."

With Simmons' skill set and Perri's business acumen, they formed CompCHOICE and PhysiciansCHOICE. CompCHOICE is a managed care product providing evaluation and management of workplace injuries, and PhysiciansCHOICE is a network of providers specializing in the treatment of workplace injuries. The underlying strategy was to establish a partnership among employers, their payers (risk bearers) and medical providers, thereby avoiding the adversarial atmosphere frequently associated with workers' compensation.

CompCHOICE focuses on the timely, appropriate and effective treatment of the injured worker through its network of contracted providers. Most patients they encounter have back, musculoskeletal, or soft tissue injuries. To more effectively treat these injuries, CompCHOICE, in conjunction with a full array of practicing surgeons, developed comprehensive post-surgical return-to-work guidelines commonly used for work-related injuries. When evaluation, treatment, communica-

tion, and resources are timely, appropriate, and both medically and cost effective, employees and employers are well served.

CompCHOICE provides services to more than 300,000 covered lives. They have twenty large insurance company clients, with many listing up to 100 companies under each corporate umbrella. Since 2002 CompCHOICE has processed more than 22,000 workers' compensation cases.

CompCHOICE is effective because of its inherent efficiencies and attention to detail. Early access to proven providers, timely treatment, and closely monitored case management results in better outcomes. This translates into cost-savings. In fact, objective cost savings reports indicate an annual savings of almost $12 million.

"This system is very innovative in the industry. It is win-win for everyone," says Dan Simmons, CompCHOICE president. "Our clients have been so pleased with every aspect of this system that they requested that we establish service in other states where they do business. That is a tremendous compliment and vote of confidence in our capabilities." To meet client needs, CompCHOICE expanded into three more states.

As CompCHOICE and PhysiciansCHOICE succeeded in the workers' compensation market place, the decision was made to further expand the PhysiciansCHOICE network to include group health. In July 2000 IMD acquired PPO Oklahoma and merged it with PhysiciansCHOICE. The network offered Oklahomans access to more than 6,000 providers, 126 facilities, and served more than 240,000 lives for group health services. Together, PPO Oklahoma and PhysiciansCHOICE offered the strongest network for workers' compensation.

The fortitude of IMD's company leadership and commitment of quality staff, continued in a straight path of growth. In 2001 the perseverance paid off when the Greater Oklahoma City Chamber of Commerce ranked IMD as the city's fastest growing independent business—with more than 600 percent growth and revenue exceeding $11 million. The year following, IMD ranked number three and continues to list each year as one of Oklahoma's prominent, growing companies.

In 2003 IMD's PPO Oklahoma achieved the status of being the largest independent PPO provider in the state. PPO Oklahoma had more than 350,000 members and processed nearly $1 billion in claims. This was the defining moment for IMD; the goal that had been set in 1992 had been achieved. IMD had developed an integrated system that managed a patient from the time of the first visit to the physician's office through the time of the insurance company's payment of the claim. This was the first such system in the U.S.

Healthcare had traditionally been a "top down" industry, with insurance companies directing providers, and providers directing patients. Perri and Simmons developed a new paradigm, a "bottom-up" philosophy that when you stay focused on patients, provide access to quality providers, and reduce cost, you can be effective and successful. IMD's reputation and focus stood for itself.

Doctors, hospitals, insurance companies, and industry professionals began seeking out IMD to enlist their expertise.

IMD has strategically implemented and successfully brought this philosophy full circle by creating an integrated system that has the ability to take a patient through the continuum of care, from point of entry through maximum recovery. Each step of the way, IMD stopped and assessed itself. Through leadership meetings, survey tools, and interviews, IMD asked, "How are we doing?" IMD asked patients, doctors, nurses, technologists, employers and insurance companies, "What do you want from your healthcare delivery team?" The answers were attentive medical care; access to quality doctors; convenience; a positive work environment; access to quality and technologically advanced equipment; and reduced cost and risk.

From their responses, IMD continues to refine a system that addresses their issues, desires, and concerns, and also takes it a step further with a quality improvement plan to continually enhance services.

To what does Perri attribute IMD's success? "Our ability to listen to client needs and respond, and great employees," he says. "If we remain focused on those two things we will continue to succeed. The healthcare industry is very dynamic, and this will position us to change and adapt with it."

IMD is now a company nearly 200 employees strong, conducting business in Oklahoma, Texas, Louisiana, Arkansas, and Colorado. It has a proven reputation for developing healthcare facilities, offering cost-effective daily operations support services for client success, and providing insurance companies with a comprehensive managed care system for treatment of work-related injuries.

"Looking back, it has been very exciting," Perri says. "We accomplished our initial goal." Most importantly, Perri defines IMD's true success as being measured by the relationships it has with clients, providers, and patients.

An integral element of IMD's focus has also been an unwavering commitment to the community that made all this possible. Oklahoma is known for its deep-seated pioneer tradition. IMD's staff, who contributed the resources and tireless energy to start a company and evolve with it as it flexed and grew, embodies that spirit.

IMD enjoys the opportunity to contribute to Oklahoma's future through its support of medical research, the arts, and education. IMD is also committed to the state's economic growth, by continuing to expand its workforce and create job opportunities for Oklahomans.

IMD focuses on the business operations of the facility, allowing the doctors and clinical staff to focus on patient care.

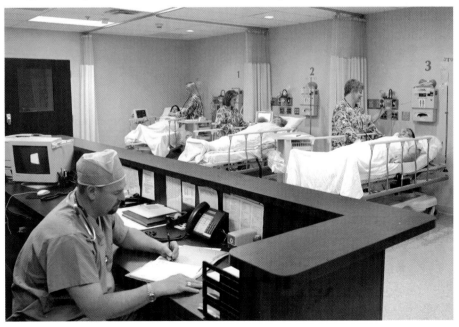

KERR-MCGEE CORPORATION

The United States was plunging into the depths of the Great Depression in 1929, a time when opportunity and success were as difficult to come by as a regular paycheck. However, for two visionaries in Ada, Oklahoma who had just $50,000 in assets, it turned out to be the perfect time to launch what today has become a multi-billion-dollar energy and chemical company.

Kerr-McGee Corporation began as Anderson and Kerr Drilling Company, back when James L. Anderson and Robert S. Kerr purchased two steam drilling rigs from Bill and Bert Dixon. Eight years later, the company began looking for a skilled geologist to aid in the search for oil and gas. Dean A. McGee was hired and within a year he made the company's first major oil discovery—the Barnett Number 1 in the large Magnolia field in Columbia County, Arkansas.

In 1943, a year after McGee was named executive vice president and operating head of what had become Kerlyn Oil Company, exploratory efforts led to the discovery of oil northwest of Oklahoma City, a find which set off the West Edmond boom. Three years later

Robert S. Kerr Sr. (right), who co-founded Kerr-McGee in 1929, stands with Dean A. McGee, who guided the company's operations for more than forty years.

Kerlyn Oil Company became Kerr-McGee Oil Industries, Inc. Soon, in 1947, the company forever altered the future of the oil industry with the world's first commercially productive oil well—out of sight of land in the Gulf of Mexico.

The success of Kermac Rig 16 in the Gulf also led the company to increase its lease holdings in the region, especially in Breton Sound, where Kerr-McGee found oil using the first rig built for offshore work. Several years later, Kerr-McGee achieved another industry first when it pioneered the use of a semi-submersible barge for offshore drilling.

During the 1940s Kerr-McGee expanded its focus from simply finding oil to refining it, by purchasing a refinery in Wynnewood. The purchase came at a time when oil supplies sometimes exceeded demand, and it moved Kerr-McGee into the downstream segment of the oil business.

McGee officially became Kerr-McGee's first president and chief executive officer in 1954. Two years later, the company's common and preferred stock was listed for the first time on the New York Stock Exchange under the ticker symbol KMG.

In 1963, upon the death of Robert S. Kerr, McGee became only the second chairman of the board in Kerr-McGee's history. Later that decade, the company branched out in a new direction with the acquisition of American Potash & Chemical Corporation and its pigment facility in Hamilton, Mississippi. The achievement marked Kerr-McGee's entry into the titanium dioxide pigment business, which would eventually become one of its two core businesses.

In 1973 the company moved into the thirty-story Kerr-McGee Tower in downtown Oklahoma City. The site remains the firm's corporate headquarters for all its worldwide activities.

In 1983, after 46 years of leadership, Dean A. McGee stepped down as chairman. A new era began soon after with the election of Frank A. McPherson as the company's third chairman and chief executive officer. Shortly thereafter, Kerr-McGee invested a then record $87 million in federal leases in the Gulf of Mexico. Today, the company is one of the largest U.S.-based independent producers in the gulf.

Kerr-McGee Chemical entered into a joint venture to build an integrated

In 1947 Kerr-McGee made history and launched the offshore industry when it drilled the first commercial oil well out of sight of land in the Gulf of Mexico.

The sun sets over a Kerr-McGee drilling rig in the Greater Natural Buttes area in Utah's Uinta basin, another core area for Kerr-McGee.

titanium dioxide project in Western Australia, and in 1991, production began. The effort established Kerr-McGee as a global producer and marketer of titanium dioxide pigment, which brightens and whitens hundreds of the consumer products used every day, including: coatings, paint, plastics, paper, printing ink, food, pharmaceutical products, and cosmetics.

In 1997 McPherson retired. Luke R. Corbett was elected chairman and chief executive officer, becoming the fourth person to hold that title in Kerr-McGee's history. Under Corbett's leadership, the company has grown nearly five-fold, expanding its global presence in the oil and gas and chemical industries.

Corbett streamlined the company, focusing on the growth of two core businesses—oil and gas exploration and production, and the production and marketing of titanium dioxide pigment. With Corbett at the helm, the spirit of innovation remains evident. Deepwater projects like Neptune, the world's first production spar; Nansen, the world's first

In 2002 Kerr-McGee again led the industry in the use of innovative technology, when the company developed the Nansen field with the world's first truss spar floating production facility. The field is located in 3,675 feet of water, in east breaks blocks 602 and 646, in the Gulf of Mexico.

The thirty-story Kerr-McGee building, completed in 1973, is a landmark in downtown Oklahoma City and is the corporate headquarters for the company's worldwide operations.

truss spar; and Red Hawk, the world's first cell spar set the company apart from others. All three were industry milestones that established Kerr-McGee as a leader in deepwater exploration and production.

Kerr-McGee's production is located in the Gulf of Mexico, the U.S. onshore, the U.K. sector of the North Sea, and China's Bohai Bay. In addition, Kerr-McGee explores high-potential trends offshore Alaska, Australia, the Bahamas, Benin, Brazil, Canada, Morocco, and Trinidad and Tobago.

Under Corbett's leadership, Kerr-McGee has profitably grown through a series of strategic acquisitions and mergers. Since 1998, the company has merged with Oryx Energy, HS Resources, and Westport Resources. The three transactions greatly increased Kerr-McGee's oil and gas assets and provided additional value and balance to the company.

Corbett also led the company to become the world's third-largest marketer and producer of titanium dioxide

pigment. The company operates pigment facilities in Botlek, Netherlands; Hamilton, Mississippi; Kwinana, western Australia; Savannah, Georgia, and Uerdingen, Germany.

A commitment to corporate responsibility underpins Kerr-McGee's business strategies and operating policies. The company places high priority on safety, care for the environment, and community support at all of its operations worldwide. From deepwater marine ecology to wildlife preservation, Kerr-McGee strives to improve quality in every aspect of its operations and uses technology and innovation to enhance the efficiency of our natural resources.

Kerr and McGee laid the foundation for the company. Their vision and integrity are still ingrained in the firm's corporate fiber today. Because of this basis, current leadership, and direction, Kerr-McGee has not only survived—but thrived—in the ever-changing global energy and chemical marketplace. Today, the company continues to call Oklahoma home and after seventy-five years of successful operations, Kerr-McGee looks forward to continued growth in the oil and gas and titanium dioxide industries.

Kerr-McGee's titanium dioxide pigment is used in numerous everyday products including paint and coatings, plastics, and hundreds of other consumer items.

L.A. BOILER WORKS, INC.

Originally located in California, the Los Angeles Boiler Works Inc. was founded as a boiler manufacturing business. Now based in Blackwell, Oklahoma and under the leadership of Paul E. Clark, this once small company has grown into a multi-million dollar concern. No longer a boiler manufacturer, the company is now known for delivering top quality American made parts for the petroleum, chemical, water treatment, boiler, pressure vessel, steam generation, and heat exchanger industries. The company is also known for holding an inventory of specialized products and has earned a reputation for flexibility and quick response time with special fabrications and customized parts.

L.A. Boiler Works got its start on June 12, 1892 when Wilbur Hankey set up shop at 105 Roundout Street in down-town Los Angeles. It was in the heart of the city's industrial district, an area then full of foundries and mills. Hankey became known for producing a quality product and excellent repair work. As his reputation grew, so did his business. By 1900 Hankey brought his son Fred into the business. Industry in the region was

Paul E. Clark, president of L.A. Boiler Works.

growing at a rapid pace and with it the demand for steam boilers, the main source of energy for the manufacturing plants that were sprouting up like weeds.

In 1912 the company moved from its original location to 134 Elmyra Street. It resided there for seventy years until its move to Oklahoma. Tragedy struck the business in 1918 when Wilbur Hankey

became a victim of the Influenza Pandemic, leaving his son Fred to run the business. Unfortunately the company began to fail and Fred sold it to Bill Fickett and Ed Pine, men who were experienced boilermakers and who had been employees at L.A. Boiler Works for ten years.

Years later, in 1931, Ludwig S. "Andy" Andersen bought the company outright for half a million dollars. Andersen hired on two dish and flange men, who had come up with a better way to make the tank heads, which moved the company into a new and prosperous direction. It was this new path that kept the company alive through the lean years of the Depression.

Andersen sold the business in January 1940 to Guy H. Brooks and M.J. "Bill" May. Brooks had worked for American-Standard Plumbing for several years and had built up an impressive list of contacts in the trade. May was an expert in pipes and tanks and also possessed a great skill for solving difficult fabrication problems. Together the men made a very successful team.

The company obtained its first American Society of Mechanical Engineers (A.S.M.E.) certifications for "U" and "S" pressure vessels in the late 1930s. It soon became a certified manufacturer for the U.S. Coast Guard, U.S. Navy, American Bureau of Shipping, Lloyds Registry of Shipping, and Underwriters Laboratories. These certifications opened the door to a large amount of military work in World War II. May also designed lift rafts for the U.S. Coast Guard victory ships, and the company built parts for military bombers. The firm's tank head business continued to grow, and during the war it introduced the pressure-type manhole and handhole assemblies for tanks

L.A. Boiler Works, Inc. in the 1950s.

and boilers—products that would become mainstays of the business.

After the war, L.A. Boiler Works took on Van Ferry as a new partner. In 1951 the company expanded again with the purchase of Pioneer Blacksmith, a manufacturer of small tractor implements. In 1952 Pioneer's facility was used to create the Airlite Patio Door Company, a division of L.A. Boiler Works, which manufactured the first sliding glass doors. By 1954 Bill May took over the patio door business, leaving Brooks as the sole owner of the Boiler Works.

L.A. Boiler Works officially incorporated in 1964 and set up a profit sharing plan. Long-term employees were offered the option to buy stock in the new corporation. In July 1967 Paul E. Clark was brought in as a temporary employee to cover for a secretary who was on leave. Clark had received extensive training as a draftsman at Fluor Corporation in Los Angeles, California, which was a great asset to the company. His skills would lead to a career at L.A. Boiler Works that Clark could have never imagined.

In the early 1970s a new product was introduced, the flanged and flued expansion joints. Van Ferry developed the process of manufacturing the product over a twenty-year period. This new procedure allowed the shop to make any odd-sized joints that the exchanger or duct fabricator might require.

One-third of L.A. Boiler Works was sold to Paul Clark in 1974 for $20,000. Clark paid for the purchase by taking on a night job at a gas station and acquiring a bank loan. By 1979 Clark was in a strong enough position to buy the shares of the remaining two partners for nearly half a million dollars, through bank financing.

Clark's rise to his ownership position is somewhat remarkable, considering his humble beginnings. Son of a low-paid Colorado ranch hand and deputy sheriff, Clark came to California with $46 in his pocket and only a high school diploma to his credit. However, he also possessed a strong entrepreneurial spirit.

Once the company was under Clark's control he made significant changes to the operations. Most importantly, he

Employee dishing large tank head.

created a marketing strategy that until then was non-existent. He established a catalogue of parts and a list of all potential customers throughout the U.S. He then spent the next ten months on the road selling the company product. Within one year, company sales had doubled to $1 million dollars. By 1983, however, sales had soared to $4 million under Clark's leadership and marketing ingenuity.

Employee flanging large tank head.

L.A. Boiler Works was quickly outgrowing its physical space. So, in 1983 Clark moved the business to Blackwell, Oklahoma, a rural town of roughly 6,500 people that was known as one of the early settlements of the Oklahoma Land Rush of 1889. Clark bought eleven acres of land in Blackwell for $30,000, where he built a 20,000-square-foot building with 2,400 square feet of office space.

Even though the company has been located in Oklahoma for more than 21 years, it still kept its original name. The business continued to expand during those two decades, with 56,000 square feet of manufacturing space and forty employees by 2004. It continues to be a leader in the manufacture of tank heads, manholes, handholes, weld caps, and hinged closures. The company counts among its direct and indirect clientele nearly all major industries throughout the United States, Canada, and Mexico. The company also has clients in England, Australia, Brazil, and the Middle East.

Clark has also built on his entrepreneurial talents by building a Comfort Inn hotel, a Subway sandwich shop, and a restaurant along Oklahoma's Interstate 35. He sees it as a way to revive business in the Blackwell community, which is located less than three miles from the interstate. Clark is also currently working on constructing a second hotel and his community development efforts have helped attract at least a dozen other businesses into the area.

Clark has also given back to the people of Blackwell through philanthropic gifts such as a $25,000 donation to create a birthing room at the Integris Blackwell Hospital. He has also been a major supporter and fundraiser for the

Elliptical manholes.

Maude Bryant Scholarship Fund, a vocal scholarship offered through Blackwell High School.

Paul Clark believes that his religious faith as a member of the Church of Jesus Christ of Latter Day Saints is the source of his strength and success. Clark became a Mormon just before he was offered the opportunity to buy his first shares in L.A. Boiler Works. He began to tithe to the church and met a number of highly skilled professional people who have continued to give him expert advice and moral support to this day. Clark feels none of his accomplishments would have been possible without these people and his strong beliefs in the Mormon faith. Clark remains an active leader in the church, and was on the High Stake Council in Oklahoma for twelve years.

The qualities Clark ascribes to his faith are also what clearly make him a compassionate employer and a good businessman. Clark treats his customers with great respect and gives their needs top priority. He has been known to personally drive more than 1,000 miles to deliver a part to a client who needs it in an emergency. What may surprise some is that Clark treats his vendors with the same amount of value and respect as he does his customers and employees. He also believes in treating his staff members like partners and makes a point of letting them know how vital they are to the health of the company. The company set up a profit sharing plan in 1964 and the current employees share in the more than $3 million fund, based on their length of employment. In Clark's own words, "Your workers are the number one part of your industry. If you treat your employees well they will do good by you. After all, you reap what you sow."

Hot forming flanged and flued head.

Local businesses and civic organizations host the
Bethany Balloon Festival each summer. Courtesy,
Oklahoma Historical Society (OHS)

LANGSTON UNIVERSITY

Dr. Ernest Holloway has a long history with Langston University. His association with the historically black college began in the 1950s when he was a student in the vocational agriculture department. The young scholar had no idea at the time that in 1963, more than a decade after he graduated, he would return to Langston as an educator. Throughout the last several decades, Holloway has served as assistant professor of biology, assistant registrar, registrar, dean for student affairs, professor of education, vice president for administration, acting president, and interim president. Eventually, on October 10, 1979 he took his place as the institution's fourteenth president—a position he has held for twenty-five years.

Holloway's rich history with Langston reflects the university's own powerful history. The school is a land-grant college that was founded through the Morrill Act of 1890, which attempted to make education accessible to blacks. Under the act, seventeen southern states established schools specifically for this purpose. Oklahoma was one of those states. But it wasn't until March 12, 1897

Dr. Ernest L. Holloway, Langston University's fourteenth president.

James A. Wallace, assessment/career placement director, assists a student with a scholarship application.

that Langston opened its doors as the Agriculture and Normal Colored School.

The man responsible for founding the school was a gentleman named Edward P. McCabe. Back in those days, the town of Langston was known as Freedom, Oklahoma, and McCabe thought it was the perfect site for an institution of learning. After the Morrill Act had passed, McCabe put out a call to black men and

women to come forth to Freedom and be educated. People traveled from all across the country with the hopes of an education.

However, there was a major roadblock that threatened to prevent these potential students from achieving their dreams. The territorial act stipulated that the settlers must purchase the forty acres of land on which the school would be built. In spite of the fact that they had no money and no jobs, the settlers persevered. While still living in tents, these determined individuals did whatever they could to raise money, including selling pies and cakes, cooking, cleaning, auctioning off their belongings and soliciting donations. Thanks to their tireless efforts, it took only one year for the group to earn enough money to purchase the land. When the school first opened its doors in

The E'kika La Garza Institute leads the nation in goat research.

1897, it offered classes at the high school level and even at the grade school level. Only later did it add college level courses.

Today, Langston University is home to more than 3,000 students, and it offers associate, baccalaureate, master's, and doctoral degrees in dozens of academic programs. Much of the university's current success is thanks to Dr. Holloway who embodies the determination and hope of those first settlers. Like many of those people, he came from very humble beginnings. He was born on a farm in

Oklahoma where he was the oldest of five children. His parents were determined that their children would get a college education. When the time came, Holloway made the journey to Langston University to fulfill that dream just like those early settlers had done so many years earlier.

The late 1940s and early 1950s, when Holloway attended Langston, were a tumultuous time in America's history and on the nation's college campuses. Many veterans from World War II were finally returning home after their tours of duty and were taking their places as students on America's campuses. The debate over Brown vs. Board of Education was raging, and college students everywhere joined in on the discussion. The emerging civil rights movement sparked heated protests and debates on campuses around the country, especially at the nation's historically black colleges like Langston.

At Langston, students were passionate about a number of social issues. Holloway remembers the climate on campus as a particularly exciting one, teeming with intellectual discussions and interest in social causes. These days, he looks back on his college years fondly and speaks freely of his love for the institution that

The Langston University Lions rush to the goal line for another touchdown.

provided him such a great opportunity to learn and develop.

Coming from a family of farmers, Holloway majored in vocational agriculture education at Langston, which had approximately 800–900 students at the time. As part of that major, he was required to take several science classes and found them fascinating. Ironically, Holloway never actually worked in the field of vocational agriculture, but he insists that it prepared him in many ways

for his future career as an educator. On the other hand, the science courses he took paid off when he landed his first job in education as a science teacher.

While he was still in college, Holloway held decidedly less lofty jobs to help pay for his tuition at Langston. During his freshman and sophomore years he spent hours washing dishes in the student cafeteria. As a junior and a senior, he worked in the campus post office as a student postal clerk. Little did he know at the time, but less than twenty years later that campus dishwasher/postal clerk would be president of that very same university.

After graduating from Langston in 1952 Holloway took his first job as a science teacher at Boley High School, where he was later promoted to the post of principal. However, working full-time never prevented Holloway from continuing his education. The hard-working scholar earned a master's degree in science education from Oklahoma State University in 1955. He followed that with a doctoral degree in higher education administration from the University of Oklahoma in 1970. Truly a man who

Student researchers have access to over ten computer labs on campus, plus internet access, inter-library loans, and "okshare" cards.

loves to learn, Holloway has also taken courses at the University of California, Berkeley and at Ohio State University.

Stocked with excellent credentials, Holloway first returned to Langston in 1963 as an assistant professor of biology and assistant registrar. In 1964 he was promoted to registrar and still taught classes whenever he had the time. For the longtime educator, teaching has always been his first love. "I think that it's in the classroom that you gain a true perspective about who students are," he says.

When Holloway took his place as the university's fourteenth president in 1979, the learning institution was faced with numerous challenges. The previous decade had been one of instability with four or five presidents during that time period. On top of that, the college had recently been charged with a new mission—an urban mission—in addition to its original mission as a land-grant college. The new urban mission called for Langston to provide educational opportunities for city residents and to train and fully educate citizens for living, working, and coping with the realities of urban life. It was up to Holloway to implement this new mission.

Langston University offers a wide variety of technological degrees, ranging from drafting design to computer information science.

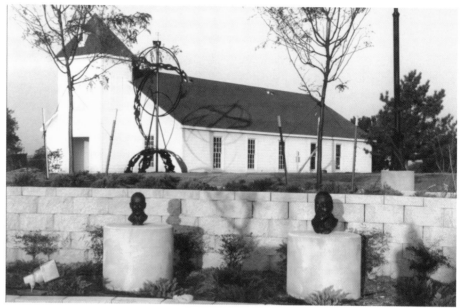

Centennial Plaza, dedicated in 1977, features the bust figures of the first fourteen presidents of Langston University.

To meet this challenge, Langston branched out with two satellite campuses in urban areas—one in Tulsa and another in Oklahoma City. They both provide career counseling, placement, testing, community service, and more, to urban dwellers. Offering only upper division courses, these campuses cater to nontraditional students, mostly those who work full-time. The urban centers and metropolitan areas also serve as resources for direct dialogue and interaction, urban planning and research, internships, systematic identification and analysis of urban problems, urban ecology studies, and related urban dynamics and phenomena.

The urban mission was only one of many challenges Holloway faced when he took his place as president. In the late 1970s government officials were calling for the desegregation of historically black colleges around the nation—including Langston. In an effort to achieve this goal, Holloway turned to one of its urban centers. The Tulsa facility actively encourages non-black students to enroll in classes, and that number has risen dramatically. To further desegregation efforts on the Langston campus, the university offers scholarships to non-blacks. Today, Langston boasts a student body that is multi-culturally diverse while at the same time maintaining the heritage and history of African Americans for which the institution was founded.

Another obstacle Holloway encountered as the new leader of Langston was

an inadequate infrastructure. In the early days of the college, income came from two main sources—the state of Oklahoma and student tuition. However, as the college grew over the years, its avenues of income expanded to several sources. For a relatively brief time, the university simply didn't have a satisfactory system of accounting and accountability to deal with the additional revenue streams. This was one of the first things Holloway would have to tackle in his new position. Today, he is proud to say that the university has achieved full accountability with advanced accounting systems and financials that are fully auditable.

Just as the university's infrastructure wasn't sound, the school's actual physical structures were also in desperate need of repair. In the early 1980s Holloway embarked on a multi-million-dollar renovation project in which nearly every building on campus received some sort of upgrade. The widespread project included adding square footage, landscaping, replacing the air conditioning system, installing new lighting and fully renovating several buildings. Following the completion of these initial projects, Holloway dedicated another $3 million to additional renovations, including $1 million set aside for new equipment and technology.

Holloway's overhaul of Langston didn't stop there. Under his supervision, the institution's academic programs underwent a review process that resulted in some being dropped and several new ones being added. Now, students at Langston can choose from nearly forty academic programs within the schools of arts and sciences, education and behavioral sciences, agriculture and applied sciences, nursing and health professions, business, and physical therapy. For years, Langston had only offered a baccalaureate degree in these disciplines. Holloway changed that too, adding associate, master's, and most recently, doctoral degrees.

The school made history in 2002 when approval was granted to offer the doctor of physical therapy degree. The program was previously offered as a baccalaureate degree, but standards have changed and a doctoral degree is now required in order to become a physical therapist. Since the field has always been a popular major at Langston, Holloway wanted to continue offering the degree to students. It has been actions like these that have earned him a reputation as a leader in education.

However, one of Dr. Holloway's greatest achievements at Langston came

The Langston University Marching Pride band is 150-plus members strong and plays various pop, R&B, and classic arrangements, entertaining audiences locally and abroad.

almost two decades earlier. In 1983 the longtime educator developed a groundbreaking program that would transform Langston from a small Midwest college into a world-renowned research institution. The program that put Langston on the map was goat research.

Students and professors began conducting intensive research on every aspect of the goat, including nutrition, meat, byproducts, and fiber (angora and cashmere come from goats). The research proved to be so impressive and important to Langston that it created the American Institute for Goat Research in 1986. Holloway is particularly proud of the university's contributions to the world with this research. "Nowhere else in America or in the world is goat

research being conducted at this level," he boasts. "Scientists come from around the world to visit our facilities." Not only that, but Holloway also travels around the world spreading the word about their findings on the goat.

By 1997, the university's 100-year anniversary, Holloway and Langston had had many successes. To celebrate, the school hosted a centennial celebration with events taking place throughout the academic year. The homecoming celebration and football game drew the largest crowd ever to assemble on campus. It included alumni who had come from across the country and around the world for the once-in-a-lifetime event. All but one of the living past presidents of the university also came to the festivities.

Capping off the year-long celebration was the 1997 commencement ceremony, which represented the highest number of graduating students ever. Also invited to the graduation ceremony were alumni from each year ending in a "7." Alumni from the graduating classes of 1987, 1977, 1967, 1957, 1947, 1937 and one member from the class of 1927 participated.

In honor of the centennial year, Holloway instituted a widespread fundraising campaign called the "Century of Excellence." This fund drive afforded alumni, friends, and supporters an opportunity to give back financially to the university.

The world wide web opens up many methods of study for student research.

The money donated was earmarked for scholarships for future students. Within one year of launching the fundraising campaign, the university had already reached 60 percent of its goal.

Providing young people with the means to attend college is only part of Holloway's personal mission. The inspired leader is determined to make each student's college experience invaluable, and that means offering more than just quality academic programs. That's why Langston also provides opportunities for students to participate in athletics and campus organizations. To provide further enhancement, Langston has a long history of playing host to distinguished speakers. In the 1995–1996 academic year, students had the opportunity to hear guest speakers Rosa Parks—the mother of the civil rights movement—and Dr. Maya Angelou— internationally renowned poet, novelist, screenwriter, actress, and educator.

Determined to turn out students who are prepared to become leaders in the nation and the world, Holloway launched a summer study abroad program during the 1998–1999 academic year. Students spend six weeks in one of a number of foreign countries, including Senegal, Gambia, the Dominican Republic, and Belize. Because they live with families overseas, students generally see a marked improvement in their foreign language skills and an increased awareness and appreciation for other cultures. "Students are never the same when they return," remarks Holloway. "They have a new outlook."

A student takes time out to peruse his textbook on the steps of Sanford Hall.

Vince Orza, former television anchor and Garfield restaurant owner, interviews Dr. Holloway during the university's years of hardship.

During the 2002–2003 academic year, the study abroad program tried something new. Instead of traveling to another country, students took a journey into the past. They visited the southern areas of the U.S. that were associated with civil rights struggles, such as Arkansas, Tennessee, Georgia, Alabama, South Carolina, and the St. Helena Islands.

That same year marked the opening of Langston Commons, a distinctive residence facility that provides quality housing for students who have children. Holloway explains the genesis of Langston Commons saying that it evolved from a trend that was taking place in the late 1990s. According to the longtime educator, he had noticed that a growing number of high school students were graduating with a child. "In my day, if you had a child in high school out of wedlock you would be expelled, but not today," he says. "These young mothers and fathers were enrolling in college. In light of this fact, we changed our living environment."

Langston began moving away from traditional dormitories and residence halls. Today, there is only one such dormitory left. Instead, the university now offers what Holloway calls "venues" or "villages." One of these living areas is set aside exclusively for students who have children. Other living quarters are reserved for scholars who maintain a certain grade point average.

Holloway's dedication to providing the best opportunities for Langston's students doesn't come without a price. He expects his students to work hard for those opportunities and for them to give back to the community that has given them so much. In the future, Holloway hopes to see Langston students act as mentors to local high school students and encourage them to go to college.

Students benefit from various grants and scholarships within its biology department.

In keeping with the school's original land grant mission, Holloway feels the university has a responsibility to rural America. That's why he would like to see Langston students reach out to minorities and encourage them to join youth organizations like the 4-H Club. He explains that many minorities don't participate in these kinds of organizations in high school and he's determined to change that. Holloway also hopes to step up volunteer efforts by working with the public schools in Tulsa to offer after-school programs.

Holloway's overall philosophy could best be described as one of tough love. "Throughout my professional career, I have always had high expectations for students," he says. "I have always emphasized that good is not enough, only the best will be enough for a successful career. As president, my message to students is to seek excellence without excuses."

Langston's president is a shining example of someone who pursues excellence without excuses. Obstacles and challenges only make him work harder to achieve his goals—and his many successes haven't gone unnoticed. He is the recipient of more than 200 awards and citations and holds memberships in professional and civic organiza-

Graduation is the highlight for Langston students.

Students stroll to and from class on LU's campus which dates back to the 1800s.

tions on the local, state, national, and international levels. Among his many awards, Holloway was inducted into the Oklahoma Afro-American Hall of Fame in 1987 and the Oklahoma Educators Hall of Fame in 1996. He earned a place in the Oklahoma Higher Education Hall of Fame in 1999 and the Oklahoma State University Alumni Association Hall of Fame in 2001. One of the most prestigious awards presented to Holloway was the "Thurgood Marshall Scholarship Fund Education Leadership" award, the highest honor ever bestowed upon a sitting

president of a public, historically black college or university. In 2002 Holloway's appointment to President George W. Bush's advisory board on historically black colleges and universities helped Langston gain national exposure.

There's no doubt Holloway takes great pride in the accolades. "I'm most proud of our students and where they go from here," he says. "Everywhere I go around the world, I run into a Langston graduate. They're making a difference in our world. They're making an impact. That's our reward."

For Dr. Holloway, there have been so many rewards associated with Langston. His own education provided him with a wealth of opportunities. Two of his three children graduated from the university and thousands of other students have graduated under his watch. But with his advancing age, the longtime president knows that retirement is on the horizon. Holloway hasn't made any official plans to step down, but when he does, it will be a sad day for Langston. However, with all of his accomplishments there's no question that Holloway's legacy at Langston will live on forever.

MERIDIAN TECHNOLOGY CENTER

For more than thirty years Meridian Technology Center in Stillwater has provided local men and women the opportunity to learn valuable skills to achieve career success. By offering training in a wide range of technical and professional disciplines, the organization helps students reach their potential while developing a qualified workforce for local business and industry. This, combined with the school's commitment to excellence and service, continues to ensure the region's prosperity and vitality.

The center was founded on July 1, 1973 as Indian Meridian Area Vocational-Technical School, inspired by the passage of the National Vocational Education Act of 1963. This legislation provided federal funds to states for creating their own "career tech," originally called vocational-technical systems. Established in 1966, Oklahoma's version of career tech has become uniquely successful due to the state's creation of a new legal entity. The technology center district consolidates existing tax bases and makes it feasible to offer these high-cost programs to high school students.

Meridian's classes commenced in August 1975 in a 92,000-square-foot facility located on seventy acres. At the time there were thirteen daytime programs

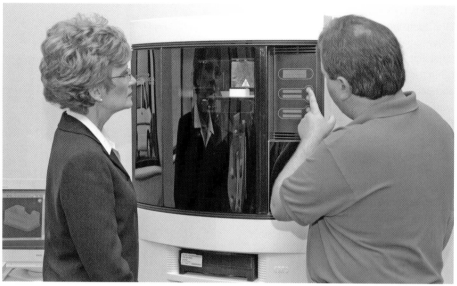

and approximately thirty staff. The school served 1,635 students in its first year.

Renamed Meridian Technology Center in 1994, today the school encompasses more than 200,000 square feet. It has grown to thirty-four, full-time programs, with approximately 900 students attending in this capacity. The school employs over 100 full-time staff members, and an additional 150 instructors on a short-term basis. Total enrollment, which includes short-term adult courses, business and industry training, daytime instruction, full-time adult programs, and customized training, averages over 11,000 students per year. With the majority of funding coming from local sources, tuition is waived for in-district secondary students.

As one of twenty-nine technology centers spread over fifty-four campuses statewide, Meridian Technology Center serves parts of five counties and ten school districts within an area of more than 900 square miles—including Agra, Carney, Guthrie, Perkins-Tryon, Mulhall-Orlando, Stillwater, Glencoe, Morrison, Perry, and Pawnee. Full-time programs are one or two years long and are based on career clusters that include architecture and construction, business management and administration, finance, health science, hospitality/tourism, information technology, and manufacturing. Short-term courses range from computer certification, medical training, and transportation technology to child care careers, online education, and security guard training.

Dr. Andrea Kelly, Meridian superintendent, observes a 3D printer demonstration by CAD instructor Russell Frick. The device is used by business and industry to do rapid prototyping for manufacturing, and students in the Meridian CAD program receive training on this advanced equipment.

Local employers keep graduates in demand from the more than thirty disciplines, and this symbiotic relationship encourages business to relocate to the area or expand services. The center enjoys partnerships with some of the region's largest employers such as MerCruiser, which trains staff for the company's Stillwater facility. Similar

Participation in student organizations helps Meridian students develop employment and leadership skills that are in demand by businesses.

A popular program at Meridian Technology Center is culinary arts. In addition to classroom instruction, students receive hands-on training in a commercial kitchen, full-service restaurant, and snack bar.

relationships exist with such companies as Armstrong World Industries, Charles Machine Works, National Standard, and Quebecor World.

Meridian Technology Center has enjoyed a boom in enrollment in recent years, regularly reaching or exceeding its capacity of 832 enrollment spaces for full-time programs. It consistently strives to keep up with its enrollment demand, as well as advances in technology and work-force challenges. The center continues to grow, adding new programs and teaching methods and improving existing programs and practices. Among these advances are boosting business technology training in computer software and word processing, and offering a variety of online courses. The center also employs an open-entry enrollment system that allows students to get started in various programs more quickly and lets them move at their own pace. In this way, the center is more flexible and adaptable than it has ever been.

The renovation and expansion of the center's West Wing is a result of increased demand for training in medical and health-related fields. This structure will house medical programs including practical nursing, radiological technology, certified massage therapy, and health careers. It will also house culinary arts and cosmetology programs. These are among the school's programs that are always at capacity, along with welding and automotive technology.

The success of Meridian Technology Center may be credited in part to Dr. Fred A. Shultz, who served as superintendent for thirty-one years. He took on the role in 1973, and retired in 2004, with the longest tenure of any staff member in the statewide Career Tech system. One of Shultz's most significant endeavors began in 1998 when he led an effort to establish the Meridian Technology Center for Business Development.

The Center for Business Development creates a high-tech entrepreneurial support system for start-up companies based on technology platforms. Its mission is to provide an environment conducive to applied research and development activities, while offering business development assistance during the early

stages of the entrepreneurial process. Start-ups are given a pro-active, supportive environment that enables them to focus on core product development and market potential. The facility's staff and resources provide assistance with a wide variety of business services and operational needs including secretarial, janitorial, and technological support.

Meridian Technology Center does not provide any direct investment to client companies or require any equity from them. However, it does provide access to business resources and channels for staged financing. Companies may spend an average of two to three years housed there before they relocate to independent headquarters. With a waiting list for access, Meridian is considering expanding the facility.

Located on the main campus, the Center for Business Development boasts

A technician in the FoodProTech laboratory prepares samples for testing. FoodProTech is one of 16 companies housed in Meridian's Center for Business Development, an incubator that provides early stage assistance for start-up companies.

Many international delegations, like this one from Bangladesh, visit Meridian Technology Center to observe career and technology training programs that are emulated worldwide.

more than twenty successful alumni companies. Since its founding, the division has secured nearly $25 million in research grants and investment capital.

In July 2004 Dr. Andrea Kelly took on the role of Meridian Technology Center's superintendent and CEO. She has served as deputy superintendent since 1997 and has been with the organization since 1982. Dr. Kelly and Meridian Technology Center plan to forge ahead with the goal of nurturing the citizens of tomorrow through educational options and opportunities, as well as helping district patrons improve their quality of life.

"Just as those who founded Meridian Technology Center more than thirty years ago could not have imagined the technological advances to come," Dr. Kelly says, "we begin our fourth decade of educational excellence, curious about what the future holds, but confident that our traditions, philosophies, and commitment will make Meridian even stronger."

Through staying responsive to the changing needs of the area's workers and employers, she and the staff cultivate economic development through workforce training. This, they believe, will continue to allow companies to stay in Stillwater and surrounding communities, thereby creating jobs and contributing to the area's sustained economic success.

THE SAMUEL ROBERTS NOBLE FOUNDATION, INC.

The Samuel Roberts Noble Foundation, Inc. headquartered in Ardmore, Oklahoma is a nonprofit organization that conducts agricultural, forage improvement, and plant biology research; provides grants to nonprofit charitable, education, and health organizations; and assists farmers and ranchers through educational and consultative agricural programs. The foundation employs more than 300 men and women in agriculture, plant biology, forage improvement, and administration. Since its founding by Lloyd Noble in 1945, it has spent more than $500 million on charitable projects.

Born on November 30, 1896, Noble was a well-respected oil and businessman and a passionate philanthropist who was

Foundation founder Lloyd Noble, 1896 to 1950.

A young Lloyd Noble and his father, Sam.

also committed to preserving agricultrure and traditional rural values. His father, Samuel Roberts Noble, moved from New York to Ardmore, Chickasaw Nation, in 1893. There, he and his brother started their own wholesale grocery business. However, it was destroyed in a fire that devastated Ardmore in 1895. The following year the enterprising pair founded Noble Brothers Hardware.

By the early part of the twentieth century, Ardmore had become a regional commercial hub, rich in agriculture, especially cotton. For a time, the town was known as the largest inland cotton ginning center in the world. Oil was beginning to take its place as a dominant component of the local economy. Indeed, one of the country's largest oil fields— Healdton—was established fifteen miles west of Ardmore in 1913.

It was clear that oil could be a key to financial and professional success; the gears in young Lloyd Noble's mind began turning. He was, however, unsure of his career plans.

In 1914 he enrolled at Southeastern State Teacher's College in Durant where he earned his teaching certificate. Briefly he taught in the Ardmore area; then he entered the University of Oklahoma as a pre-law student in 1916. Lloyd Noble left school after his father's death in 1917 and enlisted in the U.S. Navy, serving during World War I from 1918 to 1919. He reenrolled at the university in 1919 and two years later he decided it was time to take his shot in the oil business. Before long it was clear that his legal career would never come to pass.

That year, he convinced his mother, Hattie Edith Skinner Noble, to co-sign a loan for $20,000 to buy a drilling rig. Working in partnership with Art Olsen, he drilled well after well, forming the Noble Drilling Corporation. He quickly became a prominent local businessman and was elected secretary of the Republican state committee in 1921. Soon, he was operating wells from Canada to the Gulf of Mexico and expanded his business to include several production companies. He married Vivian Bilby on May 24, 1924, and they had three children. His partnership with Olson would dissolve a few years later in 1930, but the businesses continued to thrive.

Noble was one of the earliest executives to use a corporate aircraft, which enabled him to travel among his companies' various worksites quickly and easily. It was during his many flights

The Samuel Roberts Noble Foundation in 1960.

that he noticed dramatic erosion in the land covering southern Oklahoma and northern Texas. Weather conditions that had contributed to the Dust Bowl, combined with a growing population and wasteful farming practices, had left the land he once knew as lush and rich almost completely drained of agricultural potential.

Noble's concern grew into worry due, in part, to the many people who counted on agriculture for their income and livelihood. Many of his employees had come from a farming background, and he appreciated their work ethic and values. He knew he had to do something about the land before it was too late.

For several years, he concentrated on his family, his businesses, and other pursuits. This included his active service, which began in 1934, on the board of regents of the University of Oklahoma. Having become well-connected politically, there were rumors that he might consider running for state office.

Instead, in the early 1940s, he committed himself to matters he had come to consider of greater importance—caring for and preserving the land from which he had been able to derive his livelihood. On September 19, 1945 Noble founded the Samuel Roberts Noble Foundation, naming it in memory of his father and his charitable and compassionate character. Its first offices were at Main and C streets in Ardmore, and early efforts focused on agriculture. The organization held soil and produce contests, awarded prizes, hosted events such as pasture demonstrations, and offered free soil and forage analysis. These initiatives would evolve to form the foundation's agricultural division.

During its first year, the Noble Foundation also began its practice of awarding grants and scholarships. It donated a $14,000 electron microscope to the University of Oklahoma and established fellowships for a variety of research projects. By 1948 the foundation had a staff of twenty-five and was growing quickly. Noble was pleased and excited by the foundation's progress.

Tragically, Lloyd Noble passed away suddenly in Houston on Feb. 14, 1950, at the age of 53. Upon his death the bulk of

From left to right: Foundation President Michael A. Cawley, with Ann Noble Brown and E.E. Noble, Lloyd Noble's two surviving children.

his estate, including ownership of Noble Drilling Corporation and Samedan Oil Corporation, an oil and gas production company named for his three children—Sam, Ed, and Ann— was transferred to the Noble Foundation. The 1969 Tax Reform Act prohibited a nonprofit foundation from owning 100 percent of a commercial company, thus Noble Affiliates was established as a holding company for both entities. Subsequently, a public stock offering was made of Noble Affiliates and earnings from the sale were added to the foundation's endowment.

In 1952 the foundation moved just east of Ardmore, to a new location at Headquarters Farm, where it

The Samuel Roberts Noble Foundation in 2002

remains today. Currently, the foundation has three operating divisions: plant biology, forage improvement, and agriculture.

Another division, biomedical, was established in 1952 and helped pioneer many treatments that are now being utilized in the battle against cancer. This division, inspired by Noble's desire to understand the relationship of soil nutrition to human nutrition, was transferred in 1993 to the Oklahoma Medical Research Foundation in Oklahoma City. In the 1950s and 1960s it was responsible for numerous important discoveries related to cancer treatment. Researchers discovered L-Asparaginase as a treatment for certain types of leukemia; the division was also credited with development of the protein building blocks leading to the discovery of Interleukin I as an anti-cancer drug with therapeutic impact. It was also well regarded for its body of nutritional research.

The agricultural division evolved from the original set of directives that were established at the foundation's inception. In the early 1950s its emphasis was on erosion control, soil improvements, and water conservation. This shifted over time, and today the division concentrates on its consultation program.

Livestock specialist Clay Wright addresses agricultural producers at the foundation's "Red River Demonstration and Research Farm's Public Field Day."

Presently, the division consults with more then 1,000 farmers and ranchers called "cooperators." It also offers a wide variety of educational programs, seminars and has a telephone call-in center, the Ag Helpline.

The agricultural division's primary mission is to help its cooperators meet their production, financial, and quality-of-life goals. To meet the challenge, consultation services are offered free of charge. Special projects include the division's retained ownership program, which allows producers to send calves to be evaluated for performance and carcass information; and the AgVenture program,

a summer camp for high schoolers that educates them about agricultural careers. The agricultural division is involved in cross-divisional research projects with the plant biology and forage improvement divisions and also works on collaborative research with universities such as Oklahoma State, Texas A&M, Mississippi State, Colorado State, and the University of Arkansas.

The foundation established its plant biology division in 1988. Its mission is to perform both fundamental and applied research on plant-microbe interactions and to genetically modify plants for improved disease resistance and production potential. Collaborative efforts with the agricultural division provide a unique opportunity to see the results of cutting-edge molecular research reach the nation's farmers and ranchers.

Basic biochemical, genetic, and genomic research is conducted to create forage improvements, improved animal and human health, and production of novel products in crops. One of these projects, for example, was to design a more digestible, bloat-safe alfalfa. That

Dr. Richard A. Dixon, right, director of the plant biology division, explains an aspect of the Medicago Genomics program to Michael Salisbury (left), a non-resident fellow of the agricultural division.

could contribute to improved animal performance and result in environmental benefits such as reduced methane emissions, nitrogen excretion, and manure waste. A state-of-the-art greenhouse boasts modules equipped with computer-controlled lighting, moisture, and air movement. In addition, in 1999, the Center for Medicago Genomics Research was created within the plant biology division to study the molecular biology, biochemistry, and genetics of legumes. There, scientists conduct studies designed to make significant contributions to molecular biology, biochemistry, and genetics research.

The forage improvement division was established in 1997 to develop better forage varieties that farmers and ranchers could use to decrease livestock production costs. The goal is to create cool-season perennial forages to help area livestock producers. The unit's four main program areas are breeding and genetics of grasses, breeding and genetics of legumes, applications of molecular markers/genomics to

Dr. Malay Saha reviews a polyacrylamide gel image of a tall fescue mapping population. He is looking for the molecular markers present or absent in different genotypes.

Hands-on events like the "Grazing School" allow agricultural producers to learn by doing.

identify useful genes, and tissue culture/transformation technologies to incorporate value-added traits. In 2003 the division co-hosted the International Conference on Molecular Breeding of Forage and Turf in which nineteen countries participated. Its growth has led to the construction of a new 85,000-square-foot research and support facility in 2004.

In addition to its three operating divisions, the foundation has an administrative division that handles grant-making, which continues to be an important aspect of the organization's charitable mission. Recent grants include $2 million to assist in the purchase of an MRI unit at the Mercy Memorial Hospital; $3 million for aiding in the construction of the Noble Research Center at Oklahoma State University; and $7.5 million for the Sam Noble Oklahoma Museum of Natural History at the University of

Oklahoma, the largest university-affiliated museum in the world, named for Lloyd Noble's eldest son.

The foundation also funds many technology and agricultural scholarship programs at various state-supported colleges and universities through annual grants and endowment programs. It also supports two internal scholarship programs: The Noble Educational Fund (for the children of Noble employees) and The Sam Noble Scholarship in Agriculture and Technology. This program, established by the late Sam Noble, is designed to support outstanding students interested in studying agriculture or vocational technology.

Today, the Noble Foundation is directed by a board of trustees, which includes several members of the Noble family. Since 1992 President Michael A. Cawley has directed day-to-day operations. The foundation continues to add innovative programs and events, which are designed to help accomplish its overall mission. One such example is the eCattlelog, a free, online listing service for cattle producers which launched in 2000 with seven categories. It also runs the Junior Beef Excellence program, recognizing the carcass merit of steers exhibited at the junior livestock shows by 4-H and FFA members in nine south central Oklahoma counties. Cash awards are given to the exhibitors of the top ten steers.

Since its inception, the Noble Foundation has grown to become one of the most respected institutions of its kind. According to President Cawley, the Noble Foundation is unique in the private foundation world because of its board of trustees' focus on the continual pursuit of the vision of its founder, Lloyd Noble, who said, "On the farms will be found our greatest bulwark against dictatorship." In 2001 Noble was named to the Oklahoma Hall of Fame—the first ever inductee to be honored posthumously.

NORTHEASTERN STATE UNIVERSITY

Northeastern State University (NSU) is the second oldest institution of higher learning west of the Mississippi River. It is deeply rooted in the traditions and culture that were brought to the Tahlequah area by Cherokees who crossed the Trail of Tears in the 1830s.

The story of NSU begins in 1846 with the founding of the Cherokee National Female Seminary in nearby Park Hill. When fire destroyed the building on Easter Sunday in 1887, the Cherokee Council chose to rebuild on a 40-acre site north of tribal headquarters in Tahlequah. Two years later, dedication ceremonies for the new Cherokee Female Seminary signaled fresh beginnings for the institution, and the edifice would one day become the centerpiece of Oklahoma's premier regional university.

Throughout the U.S., the capitol of the Cherokee Nation enjoyed a reputation as a center of culture and education in northeastern Oklahoma. From 1889 until 1909,

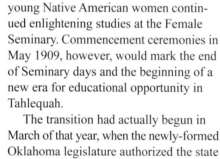

Below: NSU class of 1900.

Bottom: The Cherokee National Female Seminary, circa 1890.

young Native American women continued enlightening studies at the Female Seminary. Commencement ceremonies in May 1909, however, would mark the end of Seminary days and the beginning of a new era for educational opportunity in Tahlequah.

The transition had actually begun in March of that year, when the newly-formed Oklahoma legislature authorized the state to purchase the seminary building from the Cherokee tribal government. When classes convened in September 1909 at the new Northeastern State Normal School, 180 students passed through the halls. By the end of the semester that number had grown to 405, launching a trend toward enrollment increases that continues to distinguish Northeastern into the twenty-first century.

Classes officially opened at NSU's Broken Arrow campus in 2001.

To keep pace with a changing society, the institution underwent several name changes that reflected the expansion of course offerings and student services. In 1919 Northeastern State Teacher's College began offering a four-year curriculum leading to the bachelor's degree. Twenty years later, the state legislature authorized changing the name to Northeastern State College. After World War II, returning servicemen swelled enrollment numbers, and in the 1950s, Northeastern emerged as a comprehensive state college, adding liberal arts and master's degree programs to the curriculum lineup.

During the 1970s, following another growth surge fueled by an influx of Vietnam War veterans, Northeastern's degree programs broadened to include business and service areas. By 1974 the institution evolved to become Northeastern Oklahoma State University, and in 1985 the legislature changed the name to Northeastern State University. Five years later, the NSU College of Optometry opened, and the university's first doctoral degrees were awarded during spring commencement of 1983. NSUCO remains the only college of optometry in the state of Oklahoma, holding exclusive rights among colleges of optometry nationwide to perform laser surgery.

Continued expansion directed the university's focus northeastward in 1981.

It joined with Oklahoma State University, the University of Oklahoma, and Langston University to form a consortium that provided upper division and graduate education classes in Tulsa. Meanwhile, the university moved forward with plans to construct a branch campus in Muskogee, officially dedicated in spring 1993.

Four years later, NSU launched a new era when Dr. Larry Williams was named the university's fifteenth president. The following spring, the state legislature allowed restructuring of educational institutions in the Tulsa area and granted NSU the opportunity to pursue another branch campus. In December 1998 Broken Arrow voters approved a one-half cent sales tax to fund construction of an NSU campus on a 246-acre site in southeast Broken Arrow. Ground breaking ceremonies were held in spring 2000.

As a new clock tower graced the Broken Arrow skyline, growth continued in Tahlequah and Muskogee. Soon after the new wing adjacent to the College of Optometry was dedicated, dirt was turned to construct the new Mike Synar Center at Muskogee (named for the late Oklahoma congressman). Voters in Tahlequah approved a one cent sales tax to improve athletic facilities at NSU, and shortly thereafter construction began on the university's first apartment-style housing unit on the Tahlequah campus.

While university officials studied blueprints for a new science center on the north side of Seminary Hall and an indoor athletic practice facility at Doc Wadley Stadium, voters in Tulsa County approved the progressive "Vision 2025" sales tax. An October 2004 groundbreaking would launch Phase II of a master plan to expand the NSU Broken Arrow campus to accommodate an anticipated 4,000 more students by 2006.

As the saying goes, necessity is often the mother of invention, and this was the case as university officials dealt with a steady drop in student enrollment that had started in the early 1990s. By streamlining the enrollment process and accelerating recruitment efforts, retention took an upward turn by the year 2000. In addition, each successive freshmen class has exceeded enrollment of the previous fall.

NSU officials join President Larry Williams, center, to break ground for the Broken Arrow campus in May 2000.

Like many colleges and universities across the nation, Northeastern dealt with a fiscal crisis following the events of September 11, 2001. University officials were forced to reduce operating expenses, while responding to the challenge of growing enrollment. In early 2004 NSU underwent a dramatic academic and organizational restructuring that resulted in the consolidation of programs and colleges campuswide. The number of full-time faculty increased, and today Northeastern offers nearly 100 under-

Columns from the original Cherokee National Female Seminary in Park Hill grace the lawn in front of Seminary Hall, which was completed in 1889.

graduate and graduate degree programs, plus the doctorate of optometry, in five academic colleges on three campuses.

For many area residents and alumni, attending NSU special events is a life-long pastime. NSU's athletic programs provide exciting sports events during the school year, with notable wins that include the 1994 NAIA football championship and the 2003 NCAA Division II men's basketball title. A wide range of cultural activities fill the academic calendar, including the acclaimed summer repertory shows that run from June through August.

Capital improvements and rising enrollment position Northeastern State University to move toward the 2009 Centennial Celebration with a solid foundation for continued growth. With financial assets exceeding $10 million, the NSU Foundation continues to pursue an annual fund campaign that will provide opportunities for individuals and corporations to partner with the university. Together with this thriving institution, friends of NSU will drive the university's mission into its second century by continuing a legacy of outstanding educational opportunities and service to the communities of northeast Oklahoma.

NORTHERN OKLAHOMA COLLEGE

For more than a century Northern Oklahoma College has provided opportunities for higher education to those seeking a life rich in cultural, social, and economic achievement. The college offers more than sixty-five associate degrees in arts, science, and applied science. With a variety of exceptional educational programs available, it strives to be a model teaching and learning community that is guided by its mission and goals.

The state-supported college, founded in 1901 by the Oklahoma territorial legislature, is one of the oldest two-year college in the state. Its original 120-acre campus is situated in Tonkawa, Oklahoma, a rural community of 3,500 residents approximately twelve miles west of Ponca City. Enid, home of the college's second campus, is a city of more than 45,000, located eighty miles north of Oklahoma City. A third campus is situated in the city of Stillwater, which has a population of 40,000. Total enrollment at the college is more than 4,000, with over 1,000 students at both the Stillwater and Enid campuses and approximately 2,000 students at Tonkawa. With more than 100 full-time and adjunct faculty, the school offers a student/faculty ratio of just twenty-nine to one.

Northern's stated mission is to provide higher educational opportunities to students seeking the associate degree, cultural enrichment, and economic achievement. Its goals include providing programs in basic fields of academic

Central Hall, the school's original building.

Dr. Joe Kinzer, NOC president.

study for students to transfer to senior colleges for the bachelor's degree, as well as providing comprehensive professional and technical programs for career-oriented students. Northern also aims to enhance student success by providing a counseling program, developmental education for individuals who need assistance, enriched options for academically advanced students, and assistance with academic financial obligations. The school strives to provide students opportunities that will inspire civic, cultural, and social responsibility.

Dr. Joe Kinzer, president of Northern Oklahoma College since 1990, has spent over twenty years in higher education as a faculty member and has the same length of experience as an academic administrator. During his tenure at Northern, Dr. Kinzer has focused on implementing a variety of advanced technological and instructional resources. The school's devoted leadership also includes Roger Stacy, Ed.D., vice president for academic affairs, who came to Northern Oklahoma College in 1998. Both Dr. Kinzer and Dr. Stacy champion the school's commitment to enriching offerings through continuous development of ambitious new programs—each designed to give Northern graduates a professional advantage.

Northern Oklahoma College boasts some of the most advanced programs in the state in a wide range of disciplines, including medical training, astronomy, and digital media. In the fall of 2004, the school's multimedia digital and communications program was renamed the Digital Media Institute (DMI). The DMI is designed to equip students with the knowledge and skills necessary to communicate their ideas through the art of advanced computer graphics. All DMI students learn web and broadcast design, 2D and 3D animation, and DVD and video production. Programs also teach 3D modeling and animation, graphic design for print or broadcast, visual effects, and web technologies.

Students of the DMI can earn an associate of applied science degree in digital media animation and design with two semesters of general education and core competency courses, followed by an intensive, specialized summer session. Through a cooperative agreement between Northern and Cameron University in Lawton, graduates can transfer their AAS degree to complete a bachelor's degree at Cameron in just two more years. DMI students also have access to excellent internship opportunities with local companies and organizations.

Established in 2002, Northern's astronomy program gives students the opportunity to gain hands-on experience in a research observatory, while they participate in one of the most advanced astronomical observatories in Oklahoma. The school's state-of-the-art facility at the Enid campus has a fourteen-inch research grade telescope, capable of remote operation through the Internet and equipped with modern instruments and sun filters. Twelve other telescopes are mounted outside the observatory building.

Students can work on research projects with other students in colleges that are members of the Selman Living Laboratory Consortium, including Northern, the University of Central Oklahoma, Northwestern Oklahoma State University, Western Kentucky University, Santa Clara University, the University of California at Berkeley and Leeward Community College in Hawaii. The consortium works to develop programs for education and research that can lead to grants. Members of the public can also use the facility for approved research projects.

Through Northern's two-year "process tech" program founded in 1999, students learn basic skills in a unique program that prepares them for careers as safe, efficient, environmentally responsible process technologists. Studying such subjects as safety, health and work practices, principles of quality, industrial instrumentation, and process trouble-shooting en route to an AAS degree in engineering technology/process technology, students use computer, instrumentation and process labs with state-of-the art equipment. Some of this equipment is donated by such companies as Conoco-Phillips and British Petroleum, who employ many process tech graduates.

Northern also boasts one of the highest pass rates in the state for its nursing program, part of the college's impressive roster of medical training curricula. Nursing students can take courses on any of the school's three campuses, which are linked together via an instructional

television system. The program helps to fill a growing demand for medical professionals and healthcare specialists in the state and surrounding areas.

In addition to its degree programs, Northern Oklahoma College is also a partner in what is known as the NOC/OSU "Gateway Program" with Oklahoma State University. This initiative, called a "Partnership for Oklahoma," launched in 2003 to provide greater access to higher education for Oklahoma's college-bound students—and a better chance for success in the classroom. Developmental courses in math, English, reading, and science are offered at Northern's Stillwater facility, as well as to students at OSU who have deficiencies in these areas. Services such as financial aid, tutoring, and testing are also available.

Northern is also proud of its participation in an ambitious project known as Oklahoma's EDGE, or Economic Development Generating Excellence, kicked off by the state in 2003. The goal of EDGE is to bring more wealth to the state and increase the competitiveness of local business and industry,

The opening ceremonies for the NOC/OSU Gateway Program in Stillwater.

while providing greater employment opportunities and assisting in economic development efforts within the state. Northern's contribution via its Oklahoma Partners for Industry and Education program involves developing degree programs based on the labor needs of several core industries and companies, including ConocoPhillips, Mercruiser, Oklahoma Gas and Electric, and Ditchwitch. The goal is to educate students for careers with these corporations so they raise the academic level of the average incoming worker and help them become better decision makers. The hope is that the plan will provide an "edge" to sell the state to business and industry in the U.S. and abroad.

With these initiatives and others, Northern Oklahoma College strives to raise the bar for professional education for the people of Oklahoma while holding true to its commitment to excellence, innovation, and access. Throughout its history, the college has evolved to meet changing needs in the workforce and to teach the skill-sets career-minded individuals need to become successful. As such, its graduates can be proud of their achievements, as well as have the opportunity to contribute to a thriving statewide culture and economy.

The Marshall Building in Enid.

OKLAHOMA RURAL WATER ASSOCIATION

Every time a person living in the Oklahoma countryside gets a drink of cool, clean water from their tap, they can thank the Oklahoma Rural Water Association for helping to provide it. The agency has been offering training, technical assistance, and other services to rural water districts since the 1970s. Today, it is very proud to be in its fourth decade of service to rural areas.

Prior to 1963 people living in rural areas in Oklahoma had to forage for drinking water from wells, ponds, and other dubious sources. Unfortunately, that water was often unsafe to drink and posed a host of health risks. Without a remedy for the problem, many people would have been forced out of the countryside and into bigger cities and towns where potable water was readily available.

In an effort to provide safe water to country dwellers, a network of rural water districts was created in Oklahoma and throughout the nation in 1963. The "Sooner State's" first rural water district began operating the following year in 1964. Others soon sprang up in the state's seventy-seven counties.

The newly created water districts did more than just provide clean water to residents, however. They also indirectly contributed to the economic development of rural areas. With safe drinking water readily available, rural areas became more attractive to outside businesses. That in turn led to an improved quality of life for residents as additional service providers and retailers set up shop in the countryside. There's no question that the systems had a positive impact on the overall health and well-being of rural dwellers.

However, the network of water systems ran into its share of stumbling blocks. The main problem was that each new system required at least one certified operator, but there simply weren't enough to go around.

That predicament prompted the districts to join forces and create the Oklahoma Rural Water Association (ORWA) in 1970. In those early days, the ORWA focused solely on providing training for operators who needed certification. By 1976 the association had added on-site

The ORWA offices in Oklahoma City.

technical assistance to its services. Oklahoma's comprehensive training and assistance program proved so successful that the National Rural Water Association used it as a model for its own nationwide program.

Since its debut in the 1960s, the number of rural water districts in Oklahoma has continued to rise. Today, there are approximately 400 districts throughout the state ranging in size from twenty to 6,000 customers each. Together they boast a total of 600,000 customers who use an average of 5,500 to 6,000 gallons of water per month. That amounts to millions and millions of gallons of water every month.

The ORWA has expanded in conjunction with the increase in districts. From its originally lean staff of only three employees in the early 1970s, it has grown to twenty-one full-time staffers who now handle drinking water, wastewater systems, ground water, and source water protection. To meet the changing needs of its expanding membership, the association has introduced several new services. However, state-approved classroom training, field training, and on-site technical assistance are still mainstays of the non-profit association. Last year the ORWA provided approximately 2,000 hours of training and made more than 4,000 on-site technical assistance visits.

Aside from training, the ORWA has taken an advocacy role to promote rural water system development and to enhance the image of water and sewage systems in Oklahoma. The association promotes cooperation among water districts and acts as a clearinghouse for information to its members. It also works to protect systems from excessive and discriminatory taxes, fees, and assessments. According to Gene Whatley, the agency's executive director who has been on staff at the ORWA since 1978, that is one of the services it offers that customers appreciate most.

"Probably the most important issue facing water systems today is the increasing number of federal regulations," Whatley says. "The additional requirements often come with a cost that makes affordability a problem for smaller systems. It's a big concern for us. We all favor safe drinking water, but if regulations are imposed that have minimal health impacts, it can prove quite costly."

To prevent regulations that could be prohibitively expensive for its members, the association actively promotes legislation that is beneficial to its smaller districts. Over the years the ORWA's legislative actions have saved its

"Quality on Tap! Our Commitment, Our Profession" is proudly displayed on a standpipe in rural Oklahoma.

members hundreds of thousands of dollars. Among its many victories is legislation that now requires the Oklahoma Department of Transportation to pay utility relocation costs associated with state and turnpike highway construction. Previously, the systems were forced to pay for these costs. Another success story involving the Farmers Home Administration allowed many water systems to save an average of 35 percent on repayment of outstanding loans.

The ORWA has found other ways to put money back into the pockets of its members. During the mid-1980s insurance costs skyrocketed more than 300 percent, making it virtually impossible for rural water systems to afford. In some instances coverage wasn't even available at any price. This crisis drove the ORWA into action, seeking out alternative sources for reasonably priced insurance.

After much debate and a tremendous amount of effort, the Oklahoma Rural Water Association Assurance Group was formed in 1988. The self-insurance program offers comprehensive liability

protection with rates significantly lower than those charged by most commercial insurance companies. The association has also teamed up with major insurance carriers to offer discounted rates for workers compensation, group health, and even a retirement program.

In addition to tackling financial issues, the association is dedicated to providing information on issues that concern water systems. To keep members up-to-date, the organization uses its website and

publications, the *Advocate* and the *Update*. These periodicals address an array of issues including water conservation, management issues, leak detection, smoke detection, water audits, billing, bookkeeping, and emergency response plans. Those plans were put into action a few years ago when the town of New Cordell was hit by a tornado. The association dispatched 25 percent of its staff to the town for several days following the disaster.

It's that kind of dedication that members have come to expect from the ORWA over the past four decades. Furthermore, it's that kind of commitment that will continue in the decades to come. As the needs of rural water districts continue to change, the ORWA is certain to adapt to meet those requirements. Small towns can rest assured that they have a big supporter in the ORWA.

Another view of ORWA's offices.

OKLAHOMA STATE UNIVERSITY

To look at an early photo of the Oklahoma State University (OSU) campus is to understand the true meaning of optimism and courage. Seeing Old Central, OSU's first permanent academic building, sitting bravely alone on a desolate, treeless prairie makes one appreciate the sacrifices, hard work, and ingenuity that changed this unpromising landscape into one of the nation's best and most beautiful universities.

The story of Oklahoma State University officially began on Christmas Eve 1890 in the McKennon Opera House, at Oklahoma's territorial capital of Guthrie. Territorial Governor George W. Steele signed legislation establishing an Oklahoma Agricultural and Mechanical College in Payne County. That was the easy part. Actually getting the college off the ground would take several months, as civic leaders in the county bickered over where it would be located.

A college was a dream come true for Stillwater's officials, but others in Payne County—primarily those in Perkins, a few miles south of Stillwater—had their own ideas. Perkins was the logical choice. It had better soils and was closer to the territorial capital. In the end, it

Old Central was the first academic and administrative building at Oklahoma Agricultural & Mechanical College. A boardwalk connected the building to the western limits of Stillwater.

came down to who could throw a bigger party. By the time Stillwater boosters wined and dined the site commissioners, Perkins was left in the Oklahoma dust.

The first students assembled for class on December 14, 1891 even though there were no buildings, books, or curriculum. Students attended classes in the Stillwater Congregational Church. The original campus consisted of 200 acres that were donated by four local homesteaders. After the college received title to the property, volunteers burned off the tall grass and used teams of mules and horses to plow the virgin land. Temporary buildings were soon springing up on

OSU is Oklahoma's only university with a statewide presence. The OSU system is comprised of five campuses: OSU-Stillwater, OSU-Okmulgee, OSU-Oklahoma City, OSU-Tulsa, and the OSU Center for Health Sciences in Tulsa, which includes the OSU College of Osteopathic Medicine. System-wide enrollment is about 32,700.

campus, but the school needed a permanent facility. It was becoming inconvenient to hold classes in makeshift locations around Stillwater.

Supporters were eager to start building, but they faced obstacles. The town of Stillwater had voted to issue $10,000 in bonds for a building, but the town did not have the required taxable property to support the bonds, nor sufficient population to incorporate. Stillwater residents hired a "special" assessor to reevaluate the town's property, and a town leader conducted a "special" census, which determined that numerous residents had not been counted the first time around. After the bond issue was passed, Stillwater citizens and college faculty bought interest-bearing notes of $33 apiece, but no one had enough money to purchase the ten, $1,000 bonds. Finally, a Guthrie banker bought a $10,000 bond at a discounted price, and the Central Building (now called Old Central) was built at a cost of $14,998. The territorial legislature made up the difference.

By 1894 the Central Building was completed, and 144 students were using the facility. In 1896, the school held its

first commencement, with six male graduates. By 1918, it had sixteen brick buildings. A new science building, gymnasium-armory, home economics building, and animal husbandry facility would soon be added. Residence halls for students also were available.

Though often referred to as the "agricultural" college, the school—also known as Oklahoma A&M, always strived to develop a well rounded curriculum. In the beginning, it offered only a major in agriculture, but specialization in engineering and other areas was in the works. By the 1910s, graduates were no longer limiting their careers to farming and business, but were seeking professions as attorneys and medical doctors. Several organized schools of study existed. These included engineering, commerce and marketing, education, science and literature, agriculture, home economics, and veterinary medicine. There was still no graduate college, but students could continue their college careers by taking courses at the master's level.

Because of its land-grant heritage, Oklahoma A&M also stressed military training. Even women were required to train in the military arts. Not until 1965 would then Oklahoma State University do away with compulsory military instruction.

Growth came to the college during the 1920s, with several new buildings springing up and numbers of faculty increasing 45 percent from 1923 to 1926. Many faculty now held advanced degrees. However, the end of the decade would bring a retrenchment due to the Great Depression of 1929. Positions and salaries were cut. Thirty-five faculty and athletic staff were let go. In Oklahoma, the grim economic hardships were made even worse by the terrible drought that would become known as the Dust Bowl and last throughout the so-called "dirty thirties."

On the positive side, enrollment actually increased during the Depression years. By 1938 the school had 5,500 students. To help them with expenses, the college began a number of self-help industries that included the college farm, a cafeteria, the ceramics factory, a hooked rug operation, a duplicating service, a

Dr. Henry G. Bennett, president of Oklahoma Agricultural and Mechanical College from 1928–1951, shown here announcing the university's twenty-five-year plan. Bennett was known as "the great builder" for his vision and leadership. The plan that he revealed early in his administration is still followed today.

cabinet making shop, and a broom factory. New Deal programs, such as the National Youth Administration and the Federal Emergency Relief Administration helped many students remain in school.

The college's great building period began under the administration of one of its most famous presidents. Henry G. Bennett served as president from 1928–1951. One of his greatest achievements was to develop and propose a twenty-five-year campus master plan that called for uniform architecture, replacement of antiquated buildings, better landscaping, and additional improvements that included streets, sidewalks, and other infrastructure. His plan would result in some of the university's most famous structures, including the Edmon Low Library and the OSU Student Union—the largest student union in the world. The architectural style proposed in the plan was generally known as Williamsburg Georgian. Planners hoped to turn the Stillwater campus into the "Williamsburg of the West." The architecture remains to this day and is now referred to as "modified Georgian."

This grand building plan would eventually become a reality, but everyone's dreams came to a halt on Dec. 7, 1941 when the Japanese attacked Pearl Harbor. The next day America entered World War II. Enrollment dropped drastically as both students and faculty left for the military or to work in defense

plants. The administration geared the college toward the defense effort. Courses to prepare students for defense work were added to the curriculum. By March 1942 the first of thousands of military servicemen and servicewomen were on campus for training. During World War II, Oklahoma A&M trained twice as many soldiers as all other schools in the state combined. It also had more service personnel on its campus than any other college in the nation.

Following the war, the school experienced a big enrollment surge. It purchased surplus housing, and soon a growing student town called "Veteran's Village" was thriving on the northwest edge of campus. By 1949 Veteran's Village boasted a population of 5,000 and had actually incorporated into a municipality.

Residents had their own laundry facilities, post office, grocery store, fire station, recreation center, nursery, and maintenance shop. Soon, the little town was teeming with children and family pets. To announce the birth of his new son, one mayor of the town flew a bright, red monoplane over the area and dropped boxes of cigars and gum on the joyful

After a multi-million dollar renovation, OSU's historic Gallagher-Iba Arena has a capacity of more than 13,000 and was named the nation's top collegiate basketball venue by CBS Sportsline.

residents. The Veteran's Village era was one of the happiest times in the college's history.

The mid-1940s also were a golden era for athletics at Oklahoma A&M. In a 90-day period in early 1945, the school's teams won the Cotton Bowl, the NCAA championship in wrestling, and the NCAA championship in basketball. The next year, the wrestling and basketball teams repeated as national champions, and the football team won the Sugar Bowl.

Players and coaches during that era are now sports legends. Coach Henry Iba set a national standard in basketball, Edward Gallagher took the college's wrestling teams to international prominence, and Bob Kurland became famous as the first of the "big men" in college basketball. This preeminence in athletics continues to the present day.

The college, now known as Oklahoma State University (OSU), is a member of the prestigious Big Twelve athletic conference. It offers sixteen varsity sports and is the home of forty-five national championships. Only USC, UCLA, and

Stanford have claimed more team titles. Modern OSU sports legends include Hall of Famer Barry Sanders, football great Thurman Thomas, wrestling coach John Smith, golfers Scott Verplank and Bob Tway, baseball player Robin Ventura, and many others.

From the 1890s the college's sports teams had been referred to as the "Agriculturists," "Aggies," the "Farmers," and officially, but not popularly, the "Tigers." At the time, Oklahoma A&M envisioned itself as the "Princeton of the Prairie" and had adopted the school's orange and black colors and mascot. But by 1924 Charles Saulsberry, sports editor

of the *Oklahoma City Times*, and other writers who regularly covered college events, began to refer to Stillwater's teams as the "A&M Cowboys." The Athletic Council authorized Athletic Director Edward C. Gallagher to have 2,000 balloons printed with, "Oklahoma Aggies—Ride 'Em Cowboy" for sale at football games in 1926.

The nickname was quickly adopted, yielding an identity that had long been missing on campus and the community. Around 1923 Frank B. "Pistol Pete" Eaton, a former U.S. deputy marshal, headed Stillwater's armistice day parade. At the parade's end, the search for a replacement for the Tiger mascot was over.

The spirited image of a tough, proud, self-reliant cowboy became a cartoon drawing, and the new mascot was easily woven into campus life. For thirty-five years, the crusty old marshal was a living symbol of the college, representing the area's colorful past. He would attend athletic events and building dedications to sign autographs, pose for photographs and reminisce about the Old West with anyone who would listen.

In 1950, the college began building a legacy of international involvement when President Henry G. Bennett was named director of the U.S. Technical Coopera-

Oklahoma State University scientists conduct research in almost every area of science. The university has a group of scientists studying biological agents that could be used by terrorists. OSU scientists are leading multi-million dollar research projects to produce chemical, biological, and other sensors for use in the fight against terrorism.

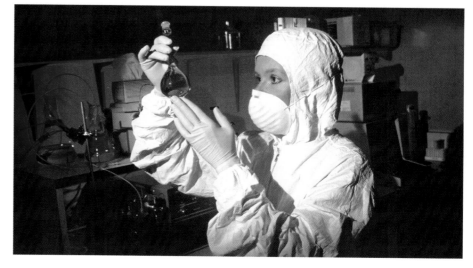

tion Administration, which administered President Harry S. Truman's famous "Point Four" program of assistance to underdeveloped nations. Bennett became an international celebrity, but his assignment ended tragically. He and his wife, Vera, were killed when their plane crashed in Iran while on a mission for the program.

Bennett was succeeded by Dr. Oliver Willham, who served as president until 1966. The college's involvement in the Point Four program would lead to contracts for several international technical assistance programs, most notably in Ethiopia. In addition, hundreds of the college's faculty and staff served overseas in places such as Brazil, Pakistan, and Thailand.

By the mid-1950s, the school community was ready for the "next level." The little college hungered for university status. Suggested names for the "new" institution were Great Plains University, International University, and Atomic University. However, in 1957 the institution was renamed the Oklahoma State University for Agriculture and Applied Science. During the next three decades, the school would build academic programs to match its new status. Enrollment more than doubled from 10,385 in 1957 to more than 23,000 in the 1980s. It also would become a statewide university as it added technical branches in Okmulgee in 1946 and Oklahoma City in 1961. The school merged with the Oklahoma College of Osteopathic Medicine in 1988, and OSU-Tulsa was born in 1999. Of course, OSU has always had a presence in all Oklahoma counties because of its agricultural experiment station and cooperative extension programs.

In 1966 Dr. Robert B. Kamm assumed the presidency. Dr. Kamm's people-oriented leadership style helped the school get through the turbulent 1960s without some of the problems that plagued other universities in the nation. This also was a time of great building at OSU. The campus mushroomed in size with new buildings for business administration, life sciences, agriculture, veterinary medicine, and mathematical sciences. The Colvin Recreational Center was built and additions were made to the

Dr. Robert B. Kamm became OSU's thirteenth president in 1966. The Kamm years at OSU are remembered as a time of growth and prosperity. Many of the university's modern labs, residence halls and other facilities were built during this time. The president and his wife, Maxine, were loved by students, staff, and faculty.

library and student union. The Seretean Center for the Performing Arts was completed and formally dedicated in 1971. Meanwhile, the university's first academic building, Old Central, was placed on the National Register of Historic Places.

Dr. Lawrence Boger succeeded Dr. Kamm in 1977 and served as president for more than a decade. Dr. Boger's administration was characterized by strong, solid growth and accomplishment. He was a firm believer in the power of technology to transform the institution. During his tenure, the university constructed a state-of-the art telecommunications center, which beamed academic courses and conferences by satellite throughout the world. OSU became headquarters for the National University Teleconference Network and was a pioneer in offering courses to underserved Oklahoma high schools, via satellite.

Dr. Boger also launched the "Centennial Decade" program, in preparation for the university's 100th birthday in 1990. His idea was to use the decade prior to the centennial as a public relations tool to capitalize on opportunities and make improvements beyond those that would normally occur. Several history books were written, and the university observed its birthday in style with numerous events and celebrations.

OSU Graduate Ed Roberts is the acknowledged "Father of the Personal Computer." After graduation in 1968, Roberts served with the U.S. Air Force, then started his own company called Micro Instrumentation Telemetry Systems. MITS produced the first desktop calculators and introduced the Altair 8800, the first inexpensive general-purpose microcomputer.

David J. Schmidly, Oklahoma State University president and system CEO, is shown with some of OSU's Truman and Goldwater Scholars. OSU is a Truman Honor Institution and has gained a national reputation for it success in preparing students for prestigious national scholarships.

During this time, OSU graduate F.M. "Pete" Bartlett and his wife Helen "Pat" Bartlett contributed $1 million toward the renovation of Gardiner Hall. The old residence hall, which was built in 1911, was completely gutted and renovated to provide 40,000 square feet of space for classrooms, offices, a large auditorium, studios, an art gallery, and a modern home for the art department.

Dr. Boger also launched OSU's first major capital building drive to raise $15 million for the Noble Research Center for Agriculture and Renewable Natural Resources. In a first-of-a-kind partnership, the money would be matched by the Oklahoma legislature to build one of the state's finest research facilities. Boger also led the drive to modernize OSU's athletic facilities, including an expansion of historic Gallagher Hall which is now called Gallagher-Iba Arena.

Dr. John Campbell took the reins as OSU's president in 1989. He and his wife, Eunice, traveled throughout the state, strengthening ties to alumni and friends. Dr. Campbell pushed for OSU to achieve excellence in all its programs.

Dr. James Halligan assumed the presidency in 1994 and reversed twelve years of declining enrollments with student-centered programs and facilities. The university began a program to groom students for national scholarship competitions and produced fifteen national scholars in nine years, including a Rhodes Scholar. OSU was named a Truman Honor Institution for its success in producing Truman scholars.

During this time, numerous classrooms and OSU's Classroom Building underwent extensive renovation and modernization. Willard Hall was renovated as a new home for the College of Education. An addition to the Student Union brought offices that served students under one roof. More than $150 million in new student housing was constructed.

During the Halligan years, OSU launched a record capital campaign that raised more than $260 million. Gallagher-Iba Arena was expanded to nearly double its capacity, and it was later named the nation's top collegiate basketball venue by *CBS Sportsline*.

Among the $380 million in new facilities brought online during the Halligan years were the Advanced Technology Research Center, designed to host joint industry-university research, and the Food & Agricultural Products Research & Technology Center, which offers pilot plant space to Oklahoma entrepreneurs. He also opened the first

university technology transfer office. The university soon joined the city of Stillwater and Meridian Technology Center in winning two federal grants to build the Oklahoma Technology and Research Park, just west of Stillwater.

Dr. Halligan and his wife, Ann, also helped OSU get through one of its worst tragedies. Ten people associated with the school's basketball program perished in an airplane crash in Colorado on the evening of January 27, 2001. The president and his wife took a leading role in helping the university deal with the ordeal and the aftermath of the crash.

After serving as president of Texas Tech University, Dr. David J. Schmidly became CEO of the OSU system and seventeenth president of Oklahoma State University on Nov. 25, 2002. His title reflected the growth and complexity of what had become a genuine university "system," instead of only one campus in Stillwater.

A Levelland, Texas native, Dr. Schmidly came to OSU with impressive credentials as both a leader and scholar. A noted scientific author and researcher, his book, *Texas Natural History—A Century of Change*, describes what has happened to Texas' natural environment during the past century. Dr. Schmidly is a member of the Texas Hall of Fame for Science, Mathematics and Technology, which recognizes Texans who have played major roles in significant scien-

Dr. Lawrence L. Boger served as OSU president from June 15, 1977 until June 30, 1988. Under his leadership, OSU was the first university in the nation to have an uplink satellite capability. He also spearheaded the university's first major capital fund drive, which resulted in the Noble Research Center for Agriculture and Renewable Natural Resources.

tific accomplishments. Inductees include Nobel laureates and former astronauts.

It was this combination of executive leadership experience and scholarly credentials that made Dr. Schmidly the ideal candidate to lead OSU into the new century. Throughout his career, he has been recognized as a leader who emphasizes strategic planning, communications, and accountability. Soon after taking on the role, Dr. Schmidly began an unprecedented strategic planning initiative designed to elevate OSU to a position of prominence among the nation's top seventy-five research and academic universities. An initiative such as this had never been attempted at any university in Oklahoma.

The result has been 278 integrated strategic plans representing all of the campuses, areas, and units within the OSU system. Each plan focuses on strategic themes such as academic instruction, research, outreach, educational partnerships, image enhancement, quality of life, diversity, and service to Oklahomans.

Dr. Schmidly believes that national prominence is attainable; however, he knows that achieving that will not happen unless resources at all system campuses are focused on strategic goals that have broad support. For this reason, the strategic plan has been developed by the entire OSU system community, including faculty, staff, administrators, students, regents, alumni, friends, and the citizens of Oklahoma.

President Schmidly also has stressed the need for more ambitious fund-raising, and OSU received the largest personal gift and the largest corporate contribution in the institution's history during his first year in office. Dr. Schmidly also launched a drive to raise $50 million for student scholarships.

The president believes strongly in educational partnerships that provide access and success for Oklahoma's students. Under his leadership, the university established a "gateway" partnership with Northern Oklahoma College (NOC) that allows students to take developmental courses at NOC-Stillwater and strengthen their academic credentials prior to enrolling at OSU.

Dr. Schmidly also began a campus health initiative to encourage healthy lifestyles among students, faculty, and staff. OSU was chosen to receive Oklahoma's first "Certified Healthy

David J. Schmidly, Oklahoma State University's president and system CEO, and his wife Janet are OSU's "first couple." The Schmidlys love students and are hosts at many campus events.

Business Certificate of Merit" for its physical fitness and wellness educational programs.

He and his wife, Janet, also began OSU's first parent's association, which is designed to provide improved programs and services to students and their families. The association received national publicity.

Dr. Schmidly has worked diligently to improve retirement and other benefit programs that will make OSU more competitive in recruiting and retaining the nation's top faculty and staff. Under his leadership, the OSU retirement program was revamped to provide more portability choices for faculty and staff. Dr. Schmidly is also a strong proponent of economic development initiatives and has proposed the formation of an Oklahoma land grant triangle that will establish a rural/urban technology enterprise region in the area bounded by OSU's campuses.

"Now is the time to build on OSU's legacy and develop even higher aspirations," Dr. Schmidly says. "As we enter a new century in our institution's history, OSU will aspire to a national standard of performance and recognition in scholarship, research, instruction, and engagement. The university will become one of the leading land-grant institutions in the U.S., the educational system of choice for Oklahoma's high school and community college students, as well as adult learners, and widely recognized as a best educational buy and premier learning center. Now is our time to achieve greatness."

From six graduates in 1894 to more than 220,000 by 2004, and a record OSU system enrollment of 32,700 students, Oklahoma State University has grown and prospered far beyond the wildest dreams of its founders. Alumni are now spread around the globe, and the university's teaching and research programs have gained international recognition. Throughout its history, OSU has shown a resilience and an ability to adapt to and capitalize on constantly changing opportunities and conditions. With a strong new leadership team assembled by president Schmidly, the future looks brighter than ever.

PHIL-GOOD PRODUCTS, INC.

For as long as she can remember, Phil-Good Products, Inc. has been a part of Peggy Phillips' life. Childhood memories hearken back to summer afternoons playing with her brother and two sisters in the treehouse across the road from the family business. Like the company, she has experienced much growth and change in her own life. Now she has come full circle. Today, Phillips is proud to serve as the president of the company her grandfather and father started over four decades ago.

Based in Oklahoma City, Phil-Good Products, Inc. is a plastics manufacturer that specializes in the design and production of injection molded materials. From sump pump parts to window latches to binder tape reels used in copier machines, the company has distinguished itself as a full-service custom molder that can mass-produce thousands of parts for a single customer. Most of its customer base is centered in Oklahoma and Texas.

Phillips' grandfather, Harry Goodman, was a plumber, die caster, and master inventor with more than 25 patents to his credit. He and a life-long friend, Doc Wolfe, developed the Vaporizer—the world's first submersible electric motor-

Peggy and Walt Phillips look at a binder tape reel.

Walt Phillips and Harry Goodman work at a drafting table in 1963.

driven pump. This invention led Goodman and Wolfe to establish the Little Giant Pump Company in the 1940s.

His son-in-law, Walt Phillips, worked as an engineer and salesman at Little Giant Pump Company. For extra income, Phillips opened a machine shop for metal-cutting and metal fabrication in Goodman's two-car garage. By this time Goodman had sold his interest in Little Giant Pump, and he became excited about this new venture. The two decided to go into partnership together and in 1957 Phillips-Goodman Engineering Company was born. Even Goodman's wife, Velma, became immersed in the family enterprise. She became the secretary and turned a corner of her kitchen into an office.

Initially the business focused on production of metal parts for aviation and other industries. However, the two blossoming entrepreneurs quickly recognized the potential in plastics manufacturing. They purchased an injection molding machine and eventually eliminated their metalworking services altogether.

Incorporated as Phil-Good Products in 1959, the business grew rapidly and necessitated a larger facility. A 7,000-square-foot building was constructed on Reno Avenue in 1961 on a lot that was surrounded by farmland. The company has remained at the same location ever since, expanding twice in the 1960s and adding a 10,000-square-foot warehouse in the mid-1990s. In the early days, there were lots of places for Peggy and her siblings to explore while their parents and grandparents worked in the plant. The cottonwood trees across the parking lot were particularly enticing.

"My brother built a treehouse in one of the cottonwoods. He and my sisters and I would hang out there drinking Cokes and eating candy, and we would play until it was time for Daddy to go home," recalls Phillips.

After high school, Phillips attended the University of Oklahoma and studied history. She helped out as a molding machine operator at the family business during her summer breaks, but had no plans to stay permanently. Instead, Phillips got a job in a doctor's office. She found that she enjoyed the working environment, and was the office manager there for ten years. She then returned to school and earned an associate's degree in paralegal studies.

During this time Walt Phillips continued to guide the company through downturns and prosperity. Harry Goodman, who had served as vice president and manager, died in 1971. His wife, Velma, continued to work at the company until age 87, although their daughter gradually assumed the responsibilities of secretary/receptionist.

"At one point Mom and Dad looked at selling the company and decided that was not what they wanted to do. They asked me if I was ready to come to work at the company," says Phillips. "I had experience as a receptionist. I joined the company in 1990, and after a few years, they told me it was their intentions to someday turn the company over to me."

Phillips received the shock of her life one morning six years later. "My dad walked by my desk and told me, 'I'm turning over the presidency to you tomorrow.' I went from being the receptionist to the president overnight."

The three of them managed the company together until Phillips' mother was diagnosed with lung cancer in February 2000. She died several months later and Walt lost interest in the company after that. The loss of her father in December 2003 left a great void in Phillips' life, but she was determined to build on his legacy and make the family business stronger than ever.

She was tested immediately. A stagnant economy coupled with competition from overseas markets forced Phillips to make some tough decisions. "We had to take a hard look at ourselves. We had become complacent," says Phillips. "Now we're going back to our roots. We have found that to survive today, we must be a full-service molder."

In the past year, Phil-Good has undergone a transformation. Tim Cassil, an eighteen-year veteran of the company, is the new vice-president. Phillips' nephew, Michael Glass, joined the company as marketing director in March 2004. He works in New Jersey, where he is trying to establish an East Coast presence for Phil-Good. Glass is the fourth generation to be involved in the family business.

"It's a new day for us. There has been a new sense of excitement with the management team and our recent ISO certification," Phillips says. "All of the team has plans for the future growth of the company and that vision hasn't been here for a long time."

What has not changed about Phil-Good is the family atmosphere. Most of the employees have worked at the company for at least ten years, and several have stayed there for twenty-five to thirty-five years. "When you say a family company, that's what we are—family," says Phillips. "The people here like their jobs and they care about each other. They are what makes this company what it is. They are a part of my family." And that's just the way her grandfather and father would want it.

Velma Goodman, who worked until age eighty-seven, sits behind her desk at Phil-Good.

PIONEER TELEPHONE COOPERATIVE, INCORPORATED

Located in the beautiful historic town of Kingfisher, Oklahoma, Pioneer Telephone Cooperative, Incorporated is the third largest telephone cooperative in the United States. Having celebrated its fifty-year anniversary in 2003, it is also among the oldest. It is very fitting, then, that its executive offices are housed in a landmark Victorian-style building renovated to its original beauty by Pioneer itself. A half of a century of history and strong heritage is built upon the persistence and true pioneering spirit of one man, Senator Roy C. Boecher.

From 1953 to 1975, Boecher served as general manager of the Pioneer Cooperative. He not only broke new ground by pushing through legislation, an act that allowed the formation of telephone cooperatives; he also responded to the desire and practical need of individuals living in Oklahoma's rural communities—the need for communication.

Before helping create Pioneer, Boecher was general manager of another cooperative, Cimarron Electric. While at Cimarron, he experienced first-hand the positive effects of the Rural Electrification Act which allowed for cooperatives to extend electrical service to farms and ranches across the U.S. Once he was elected to the Oklahoma Senate in 1948, he could do something about it. The Telephone Cooperative Act passed in 1952 and the right to create telephone cooperatives became legal.

Pioneer Telephone Cooperative, Inc. coverage area map.

In 1953 Pioneer Telephone was formed as a cooperative telephone company with an initial investment of $50,000, four exchanges, and only four part-time employees. Led by Boecher, the experienced board of trustees of the Cimarron Cooperative lent a helping hand to the newly created co-op and served a dual role as the board for Pioneer Telephone. There were nine original board members.

Pioneer now has thirteen members on its board of trustees. This governing body is elected by fellow cooperative members from thirteen different districts. The board members are individuals who are well-respected leaders in their communities and professions and each represents the members in their respective districts. The board is responsible for

The Pioneer Telephone management team, standing from left to right: Jim Eaton, assistant general manager; Loyd Benson, president and principal executive officer; Richard Ruhl, general manager; and Leslie "Pete" Peterman, assistant general manager. Seated from left to right: Harold Logsdon, general counsel; and Jeff Martin, assistant general manager.

the economic viability of the co-op. Trustees determine company policy and evaluate significant expenditures, acquisitions, and new areas of expansion for the telephone company. Cooperative members take this into consideration when choosing their representative.

Initial members of Pioneer were few and paid approximately $10 to gain membership status. Now there are over 50,000 membership families living in thirty Oklahoma counties. There are seventy-six exchanges extending over 10,900 square miles of coverage. The Pioneer family of employees includes 560 people serving 140,000 customers across the state.

The company has experienced substantial growth over the past two decades for one main reason—diversification. In addition to landline telephone service, the company now provides cellular service, business solutions, long distance service, I.E.T.V., pagers, and has branched into Internet/DSL service, security systems and digital television. "Find out the needs of your customers and then

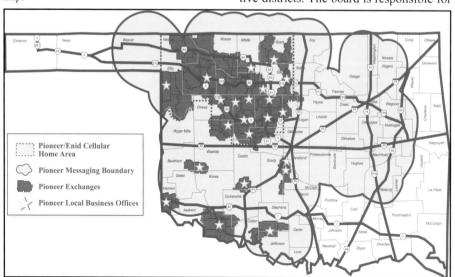

Pioneer/Enid Cellular Home Area

Pioneer Messaging Boundary

Pioneer Exchanges

Pioneer Local Business Offices

start giving them what they want," says Johnnie Ruhl, former CEO of Pioneer and one of the four original employees. "We call it being service driven. We see what the demand is and then provide it." This willingness to take risks, expand into new areas of telecommunications products and services to meet the needs of subscribers, not only strengthened the company, but it benefited the individual co-op members.

Cooperatives such as Pioneer seek to provide their patrons with the highest quality service at the most affordable rate; however, it is not always possible to establish rates that ensure the money collected exactly equals the money spent. At the end of each fiscal year, the cooperative allocates all of its margins to the patrons on a prorated basis, in proportion to their patronage. These allocations to patrons are known as capital credits. Upon approval by the board of trustees, a portion of these credits are refunded to the members on a yearly basis if the financial condition of the cooperative permits. With an actual stake in the co-op's business operations, members participate actively and share in its success.

The Pioneer Telephone Cooperative, Inc. headquarters, illuminated by the street lights of downtown Kingfisher. The memorial plaza and bronze bust of Senator Roy Boecher can be seen at the left corner of the building.

In the mid-1980s the board of trustees determined it was time to give back to the members. Since 1984 the cooperative has given back over $25 million to its members. The cooperative now generates revenues of approximately $95 million annually, with consolidated assets of $230 million; therefore, the overall patronage received by members is quite considerable," proudly says Richard Ruhl, general manager of Pioneer. "The Pioneer Telephone Cooperative family of companies...are dedicated to our customers and employ-

ees, while being partners in progress with our communities."

Members aren't the only ones who have profited by Pioneer's success. Public school systems within Pioneer's service area have benefited by participating in the "Be A Partner" program—created and facilitated by Pioneer. One cent of every minute of usage on long distance calls goes to participating schools in Pioneer service communities. The program, which began in February of 2003, has already given $97,000 to 130 Oklahoma school programs as of August 2004. In addition, Pioneer has a college scholarship program where qualified applicants may receive tuition for up to four semesters at any state-supported institution. Each scholarship covers up to eighteen credit hours per semester and up to $300 for books.

The company has also done its part in enhancing the esthetic of the quaint town of Kingfisher. In 1991 Pioneer took on the huge undertaking of renovating the historic Anheuser-Busch building which was built in 1899. Pioneer successfully restored the building to its former Victorian beauty. In recognition of this accomplishment, Keep Oklahoma Beautiful, Incorporated presented the "Beautification and Landscaping Award" to Pioneer Telephone at the statewide Environmental Excellence Awards banquet in August 1998.

The board of trustees decided to honor the cooperative's visionary Roy Boecher in 2004, during the closing ceremonies of the year-long fiftieth anniversary celebration by dedicating a bronze bust which now rests in a place of honor in front of Pioneer's headquarters building on Main Street, in Kingfisher, Oklahoma. "We are all very proud of the heritage of Pioneer Telephone," says Loyd Benson, president and principal executive officer of the corporation. "We look forward to continuing this legacy of Pioneer leadership for the next fifty years in western Oklahoma."

The Pioneer Telephone board of trustees, standing from left to right: Leroy Lage, Dr. Gary Green, Greg Heath, Dave Krittenbrink, Dennis Mueggenborg, David Shepard, Mike Dobrinski, and Ralph J. Choate. Seated: Mary Petty, D. W. Leathers, Loyd Benson, Linda Dich Randall, and Gail Parker.

PRECISION MACHINE & MANUFACTURING INC.

Tommy Caudill, the founder of Precision Machine & Manufacturing Inc. (PMM) in Grove, Oklahoma, is living proof that the "American dream" is alive and well.

The president of this award-winning, multi-million-dollar manufacturer of aerospace and general aviation parts wasn't born with a silver spoon in his mouth. In fact, Caudill grew up in rural Oklahoma with no electricity, no running water, and only a wood-burning stove for cooking. Although the young man was extremely bright, his school days ended in the eighth grade when he felt the need to support himself.

Caudill's rise to business success can be credited to honest and hard work, ingenuity, and a dream that refused to die. Married in 1952 at age sixteen to his fifteen-year-old sweetheart, Anita, he

Top: Tommy and Anita celebrate their fiftieth wedding anniversary wth their children.

Above, left and right: Tommy and Anita on their anniversary and their wedding day.

Below: In front of the first building for Precision Machine & Manufacturing Company (PMM) sits the truck that Tommy used to haul his first machine. Bottom: The PMM offices today.

soon found himself having to provide for a quickly growing household. By 1959 when he took a job at a Tulsa machine shop that paid $1.10 an hour, he and Anita had four children and were living in a one-bedroom house.

Some people in his shoes might have felt as if their prospects were bleak, but not Tommy Caudill. He truly believed that if he developed his God-given talent, worked hard, and treated his employer right, he'd have an opportunity to advance. The determined young man committed himself to producing the highest quality products and keeping an upbeat attitude at work—and his efforts paid off. When he got his first paycheck he discovered that his employer had voluntarily bumped him up to $1.25 per hour because of his work ethic.

Even though Caudill had landed a secure job, he still wanted more. The ambitious young man had always dreamed of owning his own business. The only thing holding him back was a lack of capital. He finally found a solution to that problem in 1964 when he sold the tiny one-bedroom house and made a profit of $500. He took that sum and invested in his first piece of equipment, a lathe.

Caudill was so proud of his purchase that he took his nine-year-old son, Tony, with him to pick it up. The lathe was loaded onto the truck with a forklift, but the pair neglected to tie it down. As soon as Caudill pulled out onto the street, the machine toppled off the truck and broke into numerous pieces. To this day, Tony Caudill remembers chasing tiny parts of the lathe out into the street. Together, they wrangled up all the broken pieces, got it back on the truck, and took it to Tommy Caudill's brother's garage. Signifying the debut of a true family endeavor, the Caudill men spent the next few weeks putting all those pieces back together and rendering the machine fit for use.

With his equipment in working order, Tommy Caudill rented out about 600 square feet in a local shop in Tulsa for $15 a month. Some of his first jobs included making small parts for aircraft and the aerospace industry. He quickly earned a reputation for quality work and competitive pricing, and his workload increased rapidly. The owner of the small shop started adding on space to accommodate the increase in Caudill's business

Tommy Caudill receives the U.S. Department of the Navy's "Admiral's Flag for Total Quality Management."

and, eventually, PMM occupied 2,500 square feet and had six employees. The business was doing very well in the Tulsa location, but Caudill had a deep desire to bring industry to the small town where he was raised.

In 1969 he moved the shop and his family—which now included a fifth child—back to Grove and built a 5,000-square-foot facility. The new location seemed vast at the time, but it barely compares to the firm's current 81,350 square feet. The company thrived in the small town and in 1994 Caudill branched out, opening up a subsidiary with forty square feet in Owasso, Oklahoma, called Precision Components. Over the next six years, PMM's growth sustained a breakneck pace, going from about $3.5 million in sales in 1994 to about $30 million by the year 2000.

It looked as if nothing could stop PMM's rapid expansion, which also included adding a sales and support office in Fort Worth, Texas. But then the unthinkable happened on 9/11/2001. Following the devastation of the terrorist attack on America, the airline and aerospace industries were hit hard. The trickle-down effect meant fewer jobs for PMM, and the company was forced to retrench. Only now, with about 200 employees at its three locations, is the firm once again hitting its stride with sales numbers equal to what they were pre-9/11.

PMM's recovery is a testament to Caudill's irreproachable work ethic. His commitment to excellence is also what has earned the company numerous industry awards throughout its history. One of the most prestigious accolades came in 1994 when PMM earned the "Admiral's Flag Award for Top Quality Management" for its work on the Tomahawk cruise missile. In 2001 PMM was named "United Space Alliance's Supplier of the Year" for its contributions to the space shuttle. In 2004 the department of defense awarded PMM the "Nunn-Perry Mentor-Protégé Award."

Although Caudill is very proud of the awards, he feels more satisfaction that he has helped provide a good living for so many employees and family members. Ever since he took Tony with him to pick up that first piece of equipment, PMM has been a family business. With the exception of one brother, Wayne, who was afflicted with cerebral palsy; Caudill's other brothers and sister worked and made significant contributions to the machine shop, along with some of his own children, his nieces and nephews, and eventually his grandchildren. Although Wayne was unable to work at PMM, it is Tommy's belief that

he also made a major contribution by holding him, the employees, and the company up in prayer.

Young Tony Caudill pitched in from day one, starting with janitorial duties. Following his high school graduation, he went to work full-time at PMM and has held many different titles over the years, including drill press operator, mill operator, shop foreman, manufacturing manager, and currently vice president of operations and general manager.

Two of Tommy Caudill's daughters— Cathy Hutchison and Delaine Sanders— eventually joined their brother at the firm. Cathy, the firm's vice president of administration, started working at PMM as a receptionist in 1977 when she was twenty-four years old. In addition to working in the quality department and the contracts division, she supervised all the administrative tasks associated with getting the Owasso facility up and running. Delaine joined the company in 1991 at the age of thirty-three, working in the accounts payable/receivable department before taking on her current role as director of human resources.

Today, there are also several third-generation family members involved in the business. Delaine's daughter works in the finance department and her son serves as a machine operator at the Owasso facility. Tony's son is currently training to become the master production scheduler. Cathy's son works in the Owasso facility as the quality manager. Like the second-generation family members, the third-generation group is gaining experience in several areas of the company so they have a strong under-standing of all aspects of the business as they move into key leadership roles.

To this day Tommy Caudill holds the title of president, but he is slowly relinquishing power to Cathy, Delaine, and Tony—who will eventually take over as president. As he becomes less active in the day-to-day dealings of the business, he continues to provide leadership for the company's overall direction. Under his watchful eye, the firm is prepared to tackle the challenges of the twenty-first century. And if the past is any indication, PMM will continue to thrive for decades to come. Now that's the American dream.

PRE-PAID LEGAL SERVICES INC.

Can one man really make a difference in life? Harland Stonecipher believes so. The Oklahoma native has made it his mission to offer inexpensive, high-quality, legal services plans to millions of Americans who normally couldn't afford to hire a top lawyer. To achieve this goal, he launched Pre-Paid Legal Services Inc. in 1972. Ask Stonecipher how the company got its start, and he freely admits it was by accident, literally.

It was an early June morning in 1969. Stonecipher, an insurance man by trade, was driving on a desolate road on his way to a business meeting. In the blink of an eye, a car came out of nowhere and turned left right in front of him. Stonecipher tried to avoid the crash but it was no use. The two cars smashed into each other with such force that Stonecipher's car flipped over. To this day he remembers almost nothing about the crash.

When he came to in the hospital, he learned that rescuers had pulled him out of the backseat of his overturned vehicle. Miraculously, that was the only part of the car that wasn't crushed. Doctors assured him that although his injuries were serious, he'd make a full recovery. That was the good news. The bad news was the legal nightmare that followed.

Harland C. Stonecipher and his wife, Shirley, have always believed in their dream to make "Equal Justice Under the Law" a reality for all.

Founder, chairman, and CEO Harland C. Stonecipher with Wilburn Smith, national marketing director.

Even though the accident wasn't his fault, the other driver sued, and Stonecipher ended up forking over thousands of dollars in legal fees. "I was astounded that in America you could live your whole life as a hard-working, law-abiding citizen and still wind up as a defendant in a court or the target of a legal shakedown that could destroy your finances overnight and even jeopardize your personal freedom," Stonecipher wrote in *The Pre-Paid Legal Story*, a book he published in 2000.

As an insurance man, Stonecipher had always been confident that he was adequately covered. But this experience proved that something very important was missing: legal protection. When he tried to add it to his plan, he discovered that it didn't exist anywhere in the United States. That's when he decided to do something about it.

"Equal Justice Under Law"—these words are engraved in marble on the west wall of the United States Supreme Court, and they form the very foundation upon which our great nation is built. The notion that any American, regardless of age, gender, or race can have access to the legal system is a noble one. However, Stonecipher discovered that it is also seriously flawed. In America, approximately 10 percent of the population already has or can afford legal coverage and another 10 percent have access to legal aid or a

public defender, leaving 80 percent without legal coverage.

Stonecipher made it his mission to provide legal protection for the 80 percent. In 1972 he started a company that would eventually become Pre-Paid Legal. The endeavor was a leap of faith for the entrepreneur. Here was a man with a family to support, his finances drained, and no real executive track record. Nonetheless, he was determined that he was going to start a new industry, spread it across the nation, and change the legal system.

Right off the bat, families and consumers loved the idea. Unfortunately, law firms, bankers, and regulators were much harder to convince. Bankers didn't see how the firm would make money. Regulators couldn't figure out how to define it—was it an insurance company, an auto club, or a law firm? Lawyers thought the concept would taint their industry and it wouldn't be easy to change their minds.

That was more than three decades ago. And in what Stonecipher jokingly calls "a 30-year overnight success story," Pre-Paid Legal has since evolved into a company that was recently ranked twelfth on *Forbes'* list of the "Top 200 Small Businesses in the U.S." The company has also been featured in *Fortune* magazine as one of America's fastest-growing companies, and in 1998 was rated by *Money* magazine as the thirteenth hottest company in America, ahead of businesses like Microsoft. In 2003 Harland Stonecipher earned Ernst & Young's "Southwest Region Master Entrepreneur of the Year" award.

The accolades are well-deserved. Just look at the numbers. In 2003 the firm boasted revenues of $360 million and 1.4 million member families. Total new memberships that year alone rang in at 671,857. Providing services to these members are some of the best law firms in each of the fifty states. In 2003 alone, provider law firms fielded more than 5 million calls and more than 2 million requests for services.

Selling memberships and keeping customers happy are 300,000 associates who are part of a nationwide network-marketing team. For Stonecipher, opting for this distribution method wasn't his first choice. In fact, he admits he had to be drawn into it kicking and screaming. But Pre-Paid Legal's numbers prove that the method works. These days the company founder is extremely proud of the fact that he provides a business opportunity that offers the potential for hard-

Pre-Paid Legal's corporate management team has over 220 years of combined experience with the company.

Corporate officers (left to right): Kathy Pinson, vice president; Randy Harp, COO; Harland C. Stonecipher, CEO and president; and Steve Williamson, CFO.

working Americans to become millionaires. The firm's leader augments those sales with other marketing methods, including group sales and alliances with some of biggest insurance sales networks.

Over the years the company has continuously upgraded its product. Today, Pre-Paid Legal offers product for the middle-income family, small business owners, teachers, law enforcement officers, and commercial drivers, along with other specialty plans. Most recently, the company unveiled the new "Identity Theft Shield"—aimed at addressing the fastest growing white collar crime in the country.

In spite of the company's success, Stonecipher has chosen to keep it headquartered in Ada, Oklahoma where it first

began. Other counties are constantly inviting the company to move, offering all kinds of incentives. One even sent a check for $3 million. But Stonecipher has no intention of moving. He believes he can find the highest-quality employees with the best work ethic right in Ada.

In December 2003 the firm moved into a new six-story, 180,000-square-foot building in Ada. The tallest building in town, the "skyscraper" as they like to call it, offers outside lighting, ample parking, a cafeteria, and a gym. With facilities like these, it's no wonder that among the seven hundred employees who work in the company's headquarters, the average number of years on the job is fourteen.

In the more than thirty years he's been in business, Stonecipher has made great strides with his revolutionary concept. Yet he has no intention of slowing down. With only 2 percent market penetration thus far, the company is poised for massive expansion. In fact, he envisions a day when Pre-Paid Legal will offer legal services plans to five, ten, even twenty million Americans.

In his book, he writes, "I'm filled with plans and dreams and great hopes for the future. Every day we're pushing this wonderful country a little bit closer to the time when equal justice under law will be a promise fulfilled." With his accomplishments, Stonecipher is proof positive that one man really can make a difference.

SAINT FRANCIS HEALTH SYSTEM

For over forty years, patients in Tulsa, Oklahoma; western Arkansas; southern Kansas; southwestern Missouri; and most of eastern Oklahoma have benefited from Saint Francis Health System's compassionate care.

William K. Warren, a native of Tennessee, moved to Oklahoma at the age of nineteen. He first worked for a railroad company, then as an accountant for Gypsy Oil. Shortly after his marriage to Natalie Overall, he founded Warren Petroleum Company in 1922 with $300 of his own savings. His firm rapidly grew into the multi-million dollar concern that became Warren Petroleum Corporation.

On October 1, 1960 Warren and Natalie broke ground for Saint Francis Hospital's first site in Tulsa. Before its doors opened, Natalie recruited a small group of volunteers for the first Saint Francis Hospital Auxiliary group, giving them $1,500 in seed money. The funds went to open the volunteers' gift shop, a familiar site today in the Saint Francis lobby. The auxiliary's volunteer services have proved to be an invaluable part of the hospital's tradition of service.

At a cost of $16 million, the facility was to serve as both a hospital and a research center, When the 275-bed hospital operated at a loss its first year, however, Warren stepped in to pay the employees' salaries. He believed that the success of the hospital depended greatly on the quality of doctors who practiced there.

In 1969 the Congregation of Sisters of Charity of the Incarnate Word took

The Broken Arrow Medical Center, adjacent to Saint Francis Hospital, opened in 2002 and houses a variety of primary and specialty physicians.

Above: The Saint Francis Hospital campus, once con-sidered on the outskirts of Tulsa, now sits in the thriving south Tulsa corridor. With 918 licensed beds, the hospital serves as a regional referral center.

Below: Warren Clinic, established in 1988, employs over 150 physicians in clinics across northeastern Oklahoma.

operational responsibility for Saint Francis Hospital. Their commitment to the sick and suffering, and the scripture which inspired them, became a part of Saint Francis Health System's legacy. On December 3, 1975 the hospital celebrated its fifteenth anniversary with the opening of the Natalie Warren Bryant Cancer Center—one of the country's first centers to group all medical and support services together for better patient care. In 1979 the hospital opened a skilled nursing facility and fetal maternal medicine unit. That year it also established Tulsa Life Flight, the hospital's helicopter service, which became the first of its kind in the city. Today, St. Francis' emergency services support over 70,000 area patients annually.

The 1980s represented a period of significant growth for the facility. In 1986 Saint Francis Hospital at Broken Arrow became affiliated with Saint Francis Hospital. Broken Arrow, founded in 1942 as a 25-bed hospital by father and son doctors Orris and Sam Franklin, was renamed Franklin Hospital in 1969 to honor its founders. In 1985, to better reflect its location and ties within the community, Franklin Hospital became Broken Arrow Medical Center. The facility became officially affiliated with Saint Francis Health System in 1998, and in 1999 was again renamed as Saint Francis Hospital at Broken Arrow. Today, it faithfully serves the community there through its rehabilitation center; clinical pharmacy; and diagnostic imaging, cardiac, and surgical units.

In January 1988 the system established the Warren Clinic in Stillwater, Oklahoma. Starting with three internal medicine specialists, the clinic system has grown to include practices in ten northeastern Oklahoma cities—including almost thirty practice locations in Tulsa.

Every Warren Clinic facility offers a wide spectrum of patient care services, from disease prevention to the treatment of chronic conditions. The clinics, developed to meet the state's burgeoning need for primary care doctors, now offer support services to more than 165 physicians.

In as early as 1945, Warren had recognized the need for a foundation to support Tulsa's medical and research concerns. That same year, he established

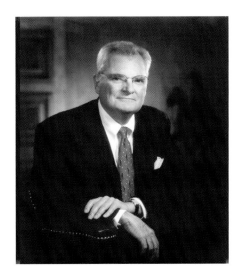

William K. Warren, Jr. (far right) and John Kelly Warren (right). For three generations the Warren family has illustrated their dedication to the community. William K. Warren, Sr. founded Saint Francis Hospital in 1960.

Above: Saint Francis Heart Hospital offers all-digital imaging and electronic medical records, as well as a wide range of patient and family amenities.

Above right: Saint Francis at Broken Arrow offers private rooms, twenty-four hour emergency care, and diagnostic and medical/surgical services.

the William K. Warren Foundation. Nearly forty-five years later, in 1989, the foundation established the Laureate Psychiatric Clinic and Hospital. The facility offers a comprehensive range of treatments for children, adolescents, and adults. The Laureate Clinic's eating disorder program is nationally recognized for its outstanding care for those with bulimia and anorexia.

In 1993 Saint Francis opened its Heart Center, and Tulsa saw its first heart transplant performed. In 2000, the year of Saint Francis' fortieth anniversary, the Religious Sisters of Mercy joined the health system. As religious leaders and professionals, the sisters consider it their mission to provide care and apostolic works to those in need.

The Children's Hospital at Saint Francis, a "hospital within a hospital,"

offers care to area children. It also leads the region in treatment of critically ill children through an intensive care unit and specialty services such as pediatric cardiology and cardiac surgery. Young patients with cancer and blood disorders are treated through the system's Pediatric Ontology/Hematology Clinic.

Jake Henry, Jr. joined Saint Francis in July 2002 as the system's new president and chief executive officer. His leadership has established consistency and predictability throughout the organization. Its mission which is "To extend the presence and healing ministry of Christ in all we do" and the core values of excellence, dignity, justice, integrity, and stewardship serve to guide the future of Saint Francis Health System. Henry also led the development and opening, in early 2004, of the Saint Francis Heart Hospital the state's only freestanding hospital of its kind

William K. Warren Jr., who serves as trustee to the Saint Francis Health System, remains dedicated to preserving his parents commitment to the community. Warren Jr.'s son, John-Kelly Warren, who

Laureate Psychiatric Clinic and Hospital, a premier inpatient and outpatient behavior health facility, was completed in 1989 and is actively involved in behavioral health research to find new methods for treating mental health illnesses.

serves as the president of the William K. Warren Foundation, represents the family's third generation of leadership.

Over 1,000 physicians, all dedicated to superior patient care and clinical research, now serve on the staff of Saint Francis Health System. All personnel, from doctors to nurses from staff to volunteers, remain dedicated to the system's proud tradition of Catholic healthcare and dedicated, compassionate service.

SCHEFFE PRESCRIPTION SHOPS

Oklahoma's pharmaceutical history, like much of the state's early history, can be traced back to the homesteaders who "opened" Oklahoma on April 22, 1889. The tent cities of those early settlers included pioneer pharmacists who set up shop with their horse-drawn wagons filled with drugs. The Oklahoma Territorial Pharmaceutical Association was formed in 1890, and in 1891 legislation was enacted to restrict the pharmacy practice to qualified practitioners.

A shortage of qualified pharmacists led to the founding of the School of Pharmacy at the University of Oklahoma in 1893. The first degree awarded from the territorial school at Norman in 1896 was called pharmaceutical chemist.

Walter P. Scheffe, founder and president of Scheffe Prescription Shops in Enid, might not trace his roots back quite as far as those early pharmacists. But he has been a leading figure in both the pharmaceutical industry and his community in northwestern Oklahoma for almost sixty years.

Born in Kansas, Scheffe moved to Enid at an early age. He began his pharmacy career while still in high school. Delivering prescriptions for a drug store during the Depression piqued the teenager's curiosity about the pharmaceutical profession. "It intrigued me—what those pharmacists were doing in their stores," he says.

Scheffe Medical Arts Prescription Shop with Ray Downs, pharmacist.

Walter P. Scheffe, pharmacist and president of Scheffe Prescription Shops, Inc.

The young Scheffe took preparatory courses in high school, and entered the University of Oklahoma at Norman. He graduated from the College of Pharmacy in 1939. After working for a pharmacy in Enid for a year, Scheffe was called to military service as a second lieutenant. In his second year of service, he was transferred to the U.S. Army Air Corps, which became the U.S. Army Air Forces in 1941. After training in Texas, he earned his wings and flew overseas for two years.

The young war veteran returned to Enid, where he opened his first pharmacy on East Randolph Street in downtown Enid in March 1946. At that time, Scheffe recalled that the average cost of a

prescription was $4. Revenues for the first month were $3,500, with approximately 10,000 prescriptions filled. Now Scheffe estimates the average prescription costs $45. Revenue increases have been enjoyed annually for fifty-eight years.

Ten years after opening in downtown Enid, Scheffe opened his second store. A smaller pharmacy was added to the Medical Arts building at 302 South Fifth Street. Several years later, Scheffe opened his third pharmacy at Parkview Medical at 330 South Fifth Street. The satellite pharmacies are staffed by two employees at each location. The remaining twenty-seven employees work at the large downtown shop.

When the first Scheffe shop opened, penicillin had become readily available as the first effective treatment for bacterial infections. "Things were very different in those early days," he says. "We didn't have the sophisticated medicines that we have now. Now we're furnishing medications for conditions and diseases never treated before."

Scheffe led a volunteer effort to combat the deadly childhood disease of polio in the early 1960s. Thanks to Scheffe, a national pioneer in inoculation efforts, more than 40,000 of Garfield

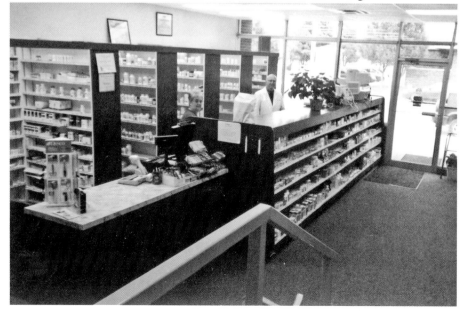

County's 50,000 residents were inoculated in 1962.

In 1996 Scheffe Prescription Shops celebrated fifty years in business. During that period, the community pharmacy served over 300,000 patients, filled over 7 million prescriptions, and delivered more than 1 million orders. With a personal touch, it continues to thrive despite competition from large chain stores, insurance changes, and the ever-rising costs of prescriptions.

"We've remained in business thanks to the services we provide," Scheffe says. "We service people, have a good number of charge accounts, make 125 deliveries a day, and offer mail order. We know our people, we know the prices, and we know the physicians."

The 4,300-square-foot downtown store is divided into departments with pharmacists trained in specialty areas, including: diabetics, prescription drugs (Scheffe's offers one of the largest stock of drugs in Oklahoma), ostomy supplies, and over-the counter products for customer convenience. The shop on Randolph Street also features a durable medical equipment center with products such as wheel chairs, battery operated chairs and scooters, walking aids, lift chairs, and oxygen equipment.

The Scheffe commitment to service extends far beyond the walls of the three Scheffe Prescription Shops. Founder Walter Scheffe has exemplified community service through a lifetime of extensive volunteer contributions to many organizations. Ranging from the donation of funds for the Walter P. Scheffe Service Center for the Cimarron Council of the Boy Scouts to the creation of the Walter P. Scheffe Endowment for Pharmaceutical Education at the University of Oklahoma, which provides an annual continuing education program for pharmacists throughout the state, Scheffe proves his commitment to the community again and again.

His additional contributions to continuing education at the University of Oklahoma College of Pharmacy include serving as chair of the dean's advisory council, the building development committee, the pharmacy visiting committee; member of the University of

The Scheffe Prescription Shop in downtown Enid.

Oklahoma board of visitors; and president of the College of Pharmacy Alumni Association. He also serves on the national advisory board of the college and was awarded the "Distinguished Alumni" award from the University of Oklahoma.

Scheffe joined the Phillips University board of trustees in 1986 and served as chair of the development committee for the Enid institution.

His extensive professional participation includes past presidencies of the American College of Apothecaries and the Oklahoma Pharmaceutical Association. He was recognized by the National Community Pharmacists Association as

The licensed pharmacists at the downtown location, from left to right: Walter Scheffe, Pat Whitmer, Scott Holle, Leland Freeze, and Rick Hill.

"Independent Pharmacist of the Year" and also received the "Ralph D. Bienfang Outstanding Practitioner" award.

Scheffe employees are also very active in their communities as well as in their professions, and once again Walter Scheffe leads by example. He was chairman of the Enid Community Chest Campaign, director of the YMCA, president of the Enid Kiwanis Club, and president of St. Mary's Hospital advisory board, among other community positions. In a fitting tribute to a man who has given so much to his community in northwestern Oklahoma, Walter Scheffe received the "Outstanding Citizen of the Year" award in 1998 from the Enid Chamber of Commerce.

SPARKS

Driving through Tulsa, visitors might not see the name of Gary Sparks on any billboard. However, the evidence of his influence can be seen on hundreds of buildings and spaces including schools, churches, banks, sports complexes, hospitals, and parks throughout Tulsa and the surrounding region. From company headquarters at 1717 South Boulder in the Mapco Plaza, architect Gary Sparks and his team provide full-service architectural, engineering, and interior design services to a wide variety of clients. With a focus on architecture and interior design, SPARKS also offers services in mechanical, electrical, structural, and plumbing engineering to provide comprehensive facility services.

Creating spaces that enhance the minds, bodies, and spirits of the people who use them is the principle that has guided the architect since he founded SPARKS (formerly The Gary Sparks Companies) in 1986. "We don't come in with a preconceived image of what a building should look like," says Sparks. "We find out what the client's needs and goals are. Then we develop a design that functionally and aesthetically creates what they want. We make an effort to bring out the best for the client."

The results of such a collaborative approach show in the visually stunning buildings and interior spaces created by the architects, engineers and interior

Left to right: Jerri Sparks, Gary Sparks, Caroline Knutson, Pete Knutson, Julie Knutson, Will Knutson, Ben Knutson, Paxton Sparks, Beth Sparks, and Jill Sparks. Photo by Chris Claussen Photography.

designers at SPARKS. A long list of award-winning projects includes the Stillwater National Bank in Tulsa (for corporate design), the St. Paul United Methodist Church in Muskogee (for masonry work), the Daily Family YMCA in Bixby (for energy conservation), the Union Multipurpose Activity Center in Tulsa (for architectural design), and the Pediatrics/Peds Intensive Care Unit at the Hillcrest Medical Center in Tulsa (for product, furniture, and interior design detail).

Another award-winner is one of the largest projects ever undertaken by the SPARKS team. The high-profile Athletic Center at Oklahoma State University (OSU) gained an even higher profile with renovations to the Gallagher-Iba Arena, which were designed and directed by SPARKS and completed in 2001.

In April of that year, *CBS Sportsline* named the Gallagher-Iba Arena college basketball's best arena. "The ultimate combination of history, uniqueness, location, and excitement, Gallagher-Iba has even survived a recent expansion to remain the nation's best facility to catch a game," said writer Dan Wetzel at the time. The finished project, which took twenty-nine months and cost $42 million to complete, received awards from the Recreation Management First Annual Innovative Architecture & Design Awards, the American School and University Educational Interiors Showcase, and the Associated Builders and Contractors.

The Union Multipurpose Activity Center in Tulsa. Photo by Jon B. Petersen Photography, Inc.

But to Gary Sparks, even though the Gallagher-Iba Arena holds special meaning for the OSU alumnus, that project was not more important than the hundreds of other design and building tasks completed by his team. Anytime we do a project, and people can appreciate it and enjoy it, I feel like we've hit a home run," Sparks says. "We've designed a lot of buildings that people enjoy using. The satisfaction we get from that success is like the applause you get when you're an actor."

Among the hundreds of projects, the numerous awards, and the many clients that Gary Sparks can name, there are two projects that hold special meaning for him. National tragedy struck the OSU community on January 27, 2001 when a plane, carrying eight men associated with the OSU basketball program and two pilots, crashed in Colorado. Following the initial shock, plans were made for two memorials—one at the crash site and one at Gallagher-Iba Arena. The OSU community turned to alumnus Gary Sparks, whose team was working on the renovations for the athletic complex, to design the memorials.

"It was a very devastating event for all of us," Sparks comments. "But it was an honor to design a memorial for those ten men and their families." The memorial in the Colorado pasture near Boulder, consisting of contrasting bands of granite and marble with pictures of the men and words chosen by their families, was dedicated on August 25, 2001. A similar monument, with a kneeling cowboy added, was dedicated at the Gallagher-Iba Arena on February 23, 2002.

The history of one of Tulsa's leading architectural, engineering, and interior design firms is the measure of one man's success overcoming some early obstacles. The son and grandson of heavy equipment operators, Gary Sparks had an early fascination for earth-moving machines and construction. Born in North Carolina, Gary spent his childhood in homes throughout most states east of the Mississippi River, moving frequently when his father decided it was time to head to another job.

"Dad didn't think anything of getting up in the morning, packing us in the

station wagon, and moving to another town," Sparks says. He lost track of the total number of schools he and his brother attended in their nomadic childhood. "It's hard for some people to comprehend, but it was normal for me to go to three or four different schools each year."

One thing that remained constant was the Alabama home of his grandparents, where Gary and his brother spent several summers. One of his grandfathers operated a road grader, and he and his

Top and above: Asbury United Methodist Church in Tulsa. Photos by Jon B. Petersen Photography, Inc.

brother learned the family skills of operating heavy equipment on highway and dam construction projects.

In 1960, after high school, Gary traveled from Jasper, Alabama to Sand Springs, Oklahoma to work on the Keystone Dam. College plans were not in his

The Gallagher-Iba Arena (top) and the Oklahoma State University Athletic Center (above) in Still-water, Oklahoma. Photos by Reyndell Stockman.

For the first three years Gary and Jerri operated the business from their home. Jerri also ran a daycare center at the house as she helped with the financial affairs of the young firm—which grossed revenues of $70,000 in its first year. "For the first few years our game plan was just survival," recalls Gary. "We had a lot of help from people like my in-laws, and good staff and management."

Part of that management was another OSU alumnus named Ivan Griffith, now senior vice president of SPARKS. He mentored Gary in the early years and has been "a real rock to the company." Gary also credits his strong religious faith with helping him through some challenging times. A member of the First United Methodist congregation, Gary names his belief in "a God that loves me uncondi-tionally" as an essential part of his story and success. "I could not have done all this without my faith," he says.

By 1992, economic conditions were improving and The Gary Sparks Compa-nies grew as the architect took the firm beyond survival mode to become a sought-after architectural firm. In 1997 the marketing division was created, headed by Daryl Whitmer. By 1998 the firm enjoyed a good reputation with twenty to twenty-five employees and revenues of $2 to $3 million. Sparks also credits his success and that of his team with the ability to take a good look at the company and the willingness to make needed changes. According to Sparks, "Every three or four years we stop, take a good look at what we've done and where we're going next."

In 2001 it was time to reevaluate once again. With an eye toward national ex-pansion, Sparks hired the local marketing firm IdeaStudio to analyze the company and develop new marketing strategies and tools. After in-depth research, staff and client interviews, facilities tours, and industry reviews, the company was reborn as SPARKS.

The company that Gary Sparks founded in 1986 celebrated its fifteenth anniversary in December 2001 with a name change, new look, new website, new location, and internal reorganization. The firm now known as SPARKS created four specialty divisions focusing on

future, until he began talking to a young man who was taking architecture classes at OSU. "Something about it clicked," he says. "Even though you might say I was academically challenged from my childhood education, I was determined." He enrolled at OSU and began his training.

In 1964, as a financially struggling student, Gary made arrangements to take a blind date to a basketball game in the Gallagher-Iba Arena. It was the first date with his future wife, an elementary education major from Bartlesville, Oklahoma. Gary and Jerri were married in 1966, and six months later Gary was sent to Germany for his two years of military service. Returning to Tulsa in 1968, he worked for various architectural firms before founding The Gary Sparks Companies in 1986.

Oklahoma State University's Boone Pickens Stadium in Stillwater. Photo by SPARKS Sports.

health, education, spiritual facilities, and sports. With its sixty-five employees, SPARKS earned revenues between $6 and $7 million in 2003.

Along with creating buildings that move people's passions, Gary Sparks has also created an atmosphere that fosters creativity among his architects, engineers, and designers. "I like to give our staff a lot of freedom to create whatever they have the potential to achieve," Sparks says. "I don't like to put people in a box." More than twenty of the SPARKS employees own stock in the privately-held company.

The development of technology has played a huge part in advances in architecture and building design services during the last fifteen years. "For years and years, there was very little change in the architectural process," Sparks says. Then fifteen years ago technology really took off, and it's been accelerating at the speed of light."

Keeping up with the technological advances and tools available to the team of architects, engineers, and designers is a constant, if welcome, challenge. "Staying ahead of the curve can be tough, but you have to do that to grow and expand," according to Sparks. "What we're doing with computers now is really incredible."

SPARKS designers can create an animation of an imaginary building—inside and out—to present a realistic view of what the finished result will be. "With blueprints, people had to use their imagination. Now we can walk them through the entire building, down to the furniture placement, before we ever put a shovel in the dirt," Sparks exclaims.

As more emphasis is placed on creating buildings and building systems that are kinder to the environment, Gary expects the "green" movement in architecture to expand. "That's the next big movement in architecture," he says. Cost considerations in building and operating a facility can make it harder to create alternative energy solutions. But Gary predicts that future technological and environmental advances will make costs more in line with what's affordable as well as better for the environment.

As SPARKS embraces green advances in architecture and strives to stay ahead of the technology curve, the firm has set its sites beyond Oklahoma. With projects in Arkansas, Missouri, and Hawaii, the company plans to expand into surrounding states and the Northwest. In 2003 SPARKS opened a second office in Bricktown at 114 East Sheridan Street in Oklahoma City.

As the firm grows, the family connection remains. Jerri Sparks, who worked in finance and human resources for many years, retired in June 2004. The Sparks' have three daughters, Julie, Jill, and Beth, and nearly half a dozen grandchildren. Their daughter, Jill, works as an interior designer for SPARKS. And Gary can see the makings of another builder-architect in his three-year-old grandson who can't get enough of those noisy earth-moving machines. "He's fascinated by diggers, dozers and graders," Sparks remarks. "It's in his blood."

Stillwater National Bank in Tulsa. Photo by Reyndell Stockman.

TULSA REGIONAL MEDICAL CENTER

Caring for the citizens of rural eastern Oklahoma, Tulsa Regional Medical Center (TRMC) has grown to become one of the nation's largest acute-care, osteopathic healthcare centers. It is also considered to be one of the premiere osteopathic teaching hospitals. Under the watchful eye of Dr. Dan Fieker, who has been CEO of the medical center since 1999, this 415-licensed bed facility with a medical staff of 424 is nationally recognized for exemplary services, including emergency, cardiovascular, obstetrical/gynecology, pediatrics inpatient and outpatient surgery, and behavioral health services. The Medical Center also offers specialized services including vascular care, an expansive telemedicine program, comprehensive wound care, a sleep center, and oncology care.

Back in 1944 when TRMC was known as Oklahoma Osteopathic Hospital, one of the first actions of the hospital's founders was to create graduate training programs for the nation's future doctors. Today, TRMC boasts the largest osteopathic graduate education program in the nation. The Medical Center hosts residents and interns who are graduates of the nation's twenty-two colleges of Osteopathic Medicine. Over eighty of these physicians graduated from Oklahoma State University College of Osteopathic Medicine, which has been named by *U.S. News & World Report* for three years running (2002–2004) as one of the best medical schools in the nation

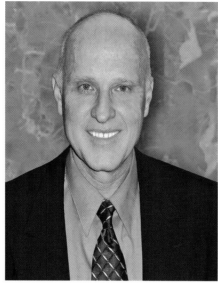

Dan Fieker, D.O., is chief executive officer of Tulsa Regional Medical Center.

for educating and training primary care physicians.

All potential applicants are carefully reviewed in terms of academic qualifications, prior experience, and interest in the profession. TRMC offers postgraduate students more than fifty internship opportunities in areas such as family medicine, anesthesiology, diagnostic radiology, emergency medicine, general surgery, internal medicine, obstetrics and gynecology, otolaryngology, facial plastic surgery, pediatrics, and ophthalmology. These specialties are also offered through TRMC's residency program, as well as cardiology, orthopedic surgery, nephrology, and interventional radiology. Since the beginning of the residency program TRMC has trained more than 1,700 doctors. Only thirty of the approxi-

mately 130 applicants are accepted into this much sought after program each year. The Medical Center's educational program also includes the clinical training of nurses, therapists, and other medical professionals.

Because the Medical Center treats a vast array of high acuity cases, the administration sees the training program as a critical priority. The postgraduates who are part of the TRMC/OSU program are given the potential to work along with more than 300 staff physicians, 90 percent of whom are board certified or eligible. Fieker, who has played a very hands-on role in the teaching program, believes that his success comes from the fact that he is not only an administrator, but a physician as well. Earlier in his career, he also completed a fellowship in the area of infectious diseases and supervised the microbiology laboratory at TRMC.

TRMC is also considered to be on the cutting edge of technology with its telemedicine program, which reaches out to the rural medical community. "Telemedicine" is defined by TRMC as the use of telecommunications to provide medical information and services to widely dispersed facilities. The Medical Center uses the technology in the areas of teleradiology and teleechocardiology, and for use in telemedicine specialty clinics and for telehealth education. It is also actively used in the area of mental health.

The telemedicine program currently includes thirty regional hospitals and clinics, making it one of the largest such programs in the state. TRMC partners with Diagnostic Imaging Associates (DIA) and Oklahoma State University College of Osteopathic Medicine to provide these technologically advanced services. TRMC's teleradiology service was installed in late fall 1999 and currently serves more than twenty-five communities, with more regional facilities requesting services. Radiologists based at TRMC read more than 600 exams a day including CT, MRI, and general radiology. In cardiology the technology is applied to diagnostic exam interpretation, emergency room, triage, and for communication with specialist clinics.

Tulsa Regional Medical Center's family practice and internal medicine residents spend time caring for children in the hospital's pediatric unit.

Tulsa Regional Medical Center's strong partnership with Oklahoma State University's College of Osteopathic Medicine has allowed for the formation of the Tulsa Regional–Oklahoma State University Academic Health Science Center.

In a rural setting such as eastern Oklahoma, telehealth education has proven to be an excellent way of keeping the community informed on medical advances, programs, and happenings in other parts of the state and country. To that extent, the technology is used for meetings, patient education, community education, and medical training.

Another use of the technology is that it gives doctors and patients in rural areas the ability to consult with specialists, who are hundreds of miles away, through the use of two-way interactive television (IATV). For patients who are not able to travel such distance, real-time, face-to-face consulting technology can be a lifesaver, as well as cutting what could otherwise potentially be high medical costs. An example of this is the new tele-cardiology program, which was created through a federal grant for residents of the communities of Wagoner, Henryetta, and Sigler, where no cardiologist currently practices.

TRMC provides a comprehensive cardiology program that incorporates diagnostic, interventional, and preventive care. TRMC recently expanded its cardiology services to include two new catheterization labs. The hospital also hosts a cardiology fellowship.

TRMC's full range of diagnostic and therapeutic radiology modalities includes mammography, diagnostic radiology, nuclear medicine, ultrasound, CT, MRI, and a comprehensive radiation therapy department. In addition, interventional radiology services include venous access

establishment and maintenance; vascular diagnostic; intravascular infusion therapy; occlusion therapy; percutaneous trans-luminal angioplasty and vascular stents; non-vascular imaging studies; balloon dilation/stenting of soft tissue; and percutaneous ostomies.

The surgical department at TRMC offers a safe and comfortable environment for patients and personnel alike and provides optimum assistance to surgeons in meeting the preventative and restorative health needs of its patients. The department contains surgery suites in the main hospital, an ambulatory surgery center, and prescreening and post-anesthesia care units to support both areas. Services are provided for operative and other invasive procedures. Immediate post-operative care is given on a 24-hour basis for both inpatients and outpatients.

Maternal–Child Health Services, located at TRMC, addresses many patients' medical and reproductive concerns. TRMC offers special services for new mothers and their babies, which include obstetrical services and an inpatient unit for childhood injuries. Staff members have been trained to emphasize family involvement and offer educational programs, which address the special health concerns of both mother and child.

Regional's telemedicine program services nearly 20,000 patients every year and is available at more than thirty sites and twenty-five communities throughout eastern Oklahoma.

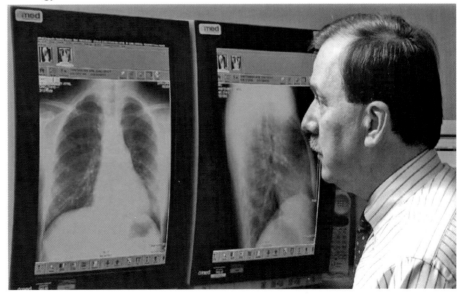

There is also a Level II special care nursery with a staff of neonatologists that provide individualized care for newborns and infants with special needs. In 1999 services for premature newborns were expanded through the establishment of a neonatal transport team. This specialized group works in conjunction with Hillcrest AirEvac to provide closely monitored transport.

Children's Medical Center (CMC) Behavioral Health Services provides inpatient psychiatric care for children and adolescents on the TRMC campus. Comprehensive behavioral health services are incorporated into four specialized units including adolescent acute and residential, and children's and early adolescent units. CMC is the only psychiatric facility in eastern Oklahoma to offer an early adolescent unit, providing specialized care for children ages ten to thirteen.

TRMC also offers a complete and modern program for the diagnosis and treatment of patients with cancer. Oncology services include radiation therapy, chemotherapy, immunotherapy, and advanced oncology surgical techniques.

The Center for Diabetic Education addresses the needs and concerns of both newly diagnosed patients and those having difficulty maintaining appropriate blood sugar levels. The team includes a diabetes program coordinator who works with a trained dietitian and the Wound Care Clinic, one of the most unique services offered in the region. The TRMC Wound Care Clinic brings together a team of wound care specialists including physicians, nurses, therapists and other medical professionals.

The TRMC Sleep Lab provides assistance to physicians and restorative health needs for patients in a safe and comfortable environment. Services at the lab include treatment for patients with obstructive sleep apnea, central sleep apnea, narcolepsy, restless leg syndrome, periodic limb movement disorders, and other sleep disorder associated illnesses.

The emergency department at TRMC provides Level 3 trauma services capable of treating advanced trauma patients from Tulsa and the surrounding region. A full-time staff of five board-certified emergency medicine physicians offers the

A dedication to research and education keeps Tulsa Regional physicians abreast on the latest medical techniques and procedures.

core medical direction for the eighteen-bed unit. A specialized four-bed Chest Pain Evaluation Unit (CPEU) enables staff to fully evaluate patients with complaints of chest pain and respond quickly and efficiently to cardiac emergencies. In addition, the department provides a five-bed Urgent Care Fast Track area, which reduces wait time for those non-emergency cases. Specialists from ten different areas including internal medicine, orthopedics, ENT, pediatrics, surgery, ophthalmology, GI, cardiology, interventional radiology, and OB/Gyn are on call twenty-four hours a day to provide consultation with the emergency department physicians.

The TRMC nursing staff is considered one of the most highly skilled groups in Tulsa, with a large percentage of staff members possessing advanced certification in emergency care. The TRMC emergency department is one of two dedicated facilities that serve as receiving stations for the AirEvac Life Team air ambulance service. The helicopter and mobile intensive care ground units provide critical care transport services throughout eastern Oklahoma.

TRMC also hosts the Hillcrest Specialty Hospital, which includes a satellite location at HMC. This long-term acute care hospital provides specialized care for medically complex patients who are critically ill and require aggressive and continuous acute care services. Patients have an average stay of twenty-five days. The hospital provides cost-effective, high-quality care that focuses on returning patients to their optimal level of wellness.

CEO Fieker is especially proud of the fact that TRMC has always welcomed and cared for patients regardless of their ability to pay. For him, TRMC is not only a medical facility. Through innovations such as its telemedicine program, Tulsa Regional has its feet planted firmly in the technology of the future, and yet has still managed to hold onto those old-fashioned, core human values that address the needs of the surrounding community. In addition, the center's residency program is clearly meeting the educational demands of twenty-first century medicine. This combination has proven to be a strategy for success that would not have been possible without the insight and leadership of Dr. Dan Fieker.

*A colorful penguin adorns the Tulsa campus of the
University of Oklahoma's Schusterman Center.
Penguin art can be found all over the Tulsa area,
helping to promote the Tulsa Zoo. Courtesy,
William D. Welge.*

TULSA SPINE HOSPITAL

In keeping with the strong, optimistic spirit of the Sooner State and Oklahoma's national reputation for prominent medical centers, twelve Tulsa physicians opened a hospital where they could be leaders and innovators within their specialty. The two-year hospital construction project is the culmination of a long-held dream belonging to the local physicians—all board-certified or board-eligible neurosurgeons, pain management specialists, and radiologists—who have dedicated themselves to providing their patients with the most up-to-date spinal surgical and pain management care in a comfortable and attentive environment.

Tulsa Spine Hospital (TSH) opened in December 2002 and is dedicated to delivering the best in spinal surgery, pain management, and diagnostic imaging services. With a nurse-to-patient ratio of one-to-four, TSH is both high-tech and high-touch. This level of attention is unparalleled in the Tulsa area. Designed as a 76,000-square-foot state-of-the-art medical center, the Tulsa Spine Hospital anchors the newly developed 54-acre Olympia Medical Park complex which is situated on the north side of Seventy-First Street between U.S. Highway 75 and the Arkansas River.

Tulsa Spine Hospital houses twenty-one private inpatient rooms within easy

From left to right: Frank Tomecek, MD; Steve Gaede, MD; Bruce Hudkins, MD; Andrew Revelis, MD; Scott Anthony, DO; and Terry Woodbeck, CEO.

access of a surgical suite of four operating rooms. All patient areas are designed to provide the ultimate in post-operative care. Using a team approach, the hospital employs over 100 full-time personnel—bringing together the talents of medical specialists, sub-specialists, nurses, and support staff to provide compassionate and professional care—while placing attention on the individual and unique needs of each patient.

The facility's design was driven by the physicians' desire to provide their patients with excellent treatment, comfort, and the very best in personalized services. That "VIP" attention begins from the moment the patient enters the building, purposely designed on one level with close access to parking lots from all areas of the facility, including three patient drop-off sites at the facility's front door.

First-class amenities, such as terry-cloth bathrobes and toiletry gift items, spacious and beautifully decorated private rooms—rich and warm with faux wood floors and furniture, each with its own personal bath—allow the Tulsa Spine Hospital to emanate gracious hospitality with quality care.

Tulsa Spine Hospital offers patients a full range of spinal care services, including a state-of-the-art pain management center, spacious surgical facilities and the most advanced MRI, CT and myelography technology, as well as competent and caring nurses.

At Tulsa Spine Hospital, pain management specialists use the latest advances in non-surgical treatment technologies. They work with the specific goal in mind to reduce pain and increase function in both acute and chronic spinal conditions, including bulging discs, arthritis, and other pain disorders.

When surgery is necessary, Tulsa Spine Hospital neurosurgeons and orthopedic surgeons offer patients a wide range of specialized nerve and spine procedures and services, ranging from simple to complex. The primary advantages of the facility include the lower nurse-to-patient care ratio and medical personnel who are trained to support one type of surgical patient. This level of attention and specialization directly impacts quality of care and improves recovery outcomes.

The Tulsa Spine Hospital also offers state-of-the-art MRI scans, CT scans, and myelography equipment for fast and convenient outpatient testing of spinal

Tulsa Spine Hospital radiologist, Dr. Matthew Powers.

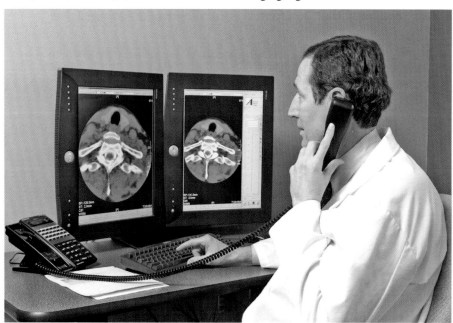

and cranial disorders. The facility's MRI equipment offers the latest in technological capabilities and is the quietest and least confining of all closed scanners, providing full comfort for the patient.

Since the Tulsa Spine Hospital opened its doors, the physicians have recognize that their ability to provide the best possible patient care is improved by direct involvement in quality assurance, resource management, and cost control issues. All of this attention to detail did not happen by accident. "When you have physicians who have been involved since the beginning of the design process, you get a facility that works for everyone," says chief executive officer Terry Woodbeck. "There are no elevators, no parking garages, people don't have to sit and wait around for outpatient procedures, and every detail of your patient care experience has been thought through to make this a unique medical facility."

"It's our goal to reduce pain and increase function," adds Dr. Steve Gaede. Pain management specialists use the latest diagnostic and therapeutic techniques for relief of a number of acute and chronic problems including bulging discs and spinal arthritis. When surgery is necessary, neurosurgeons and/or orthopedic surgeons offer procedures and services from the simple to the most complex.

"The quality of medicine in this city is quite good," says Dr. Gaede. "We think, however, we can do it better at TSH with our unique approach to providing quality specialized care to patients with certain spinal and neurological disorders. Specialty hospitals such as Tulsa Spine Hospital are changing the way medical facilities do business and TSH is setting the standard in spine care. "It's time for change in the medical system and our vision involves doing business a different way."

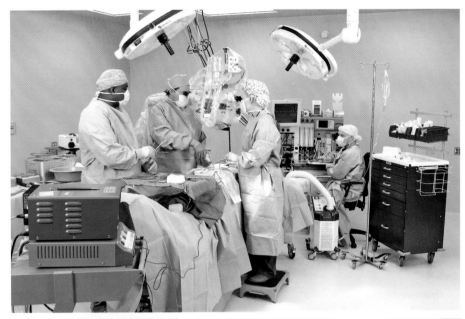

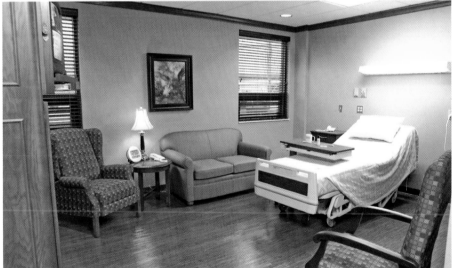

Top: Tulsa Spine Hospital includes a state-of-the-art surgical suite that houses operating rooms within easy access of inpatient rooms. The department supports specialized nerve and spine procedures from simple to complex.

Middle: One of the facility's inpatient rooms.

Bottom: The spacious lobby is decorated and arranged for the peace and comfort of patients and family members.

UNIVERSITY OF OKLAHOMA

From humble beginnings, the continued quest for excellence by University of Oklahoma leaders, faculty, staff, and students has created one of the nation's premier learning institutions. Accepting the challenge of the territorial legislature in 1890 to secure the university in Norman, the Cleveland County community donated forty acres of land for the campus and voted to approve $10,000 in bonds. When legislative wrangling resulted in the need for $10,000 in cash, the funds were raised by the community—in part through subscription bonds sold to Norman businessmen.

Classes began at the University of Oklahoma (OU) in 1892 with three rented rooms in downtown Norman, 119 students, and four teachers—including the university's first president David Ross Boyd. One year later, having overcome difficulties with deficits, contractors, suppliers, and workers, classes moved to the first building on the permanent campus, Science Hall.

Today, OU's pursuit of excellence has led to an expansion that encompasses campuses in three cities, about 4,000 acres, and more than 30,000 students. In addition, OU has a major impact on the economy of the state, employing more than 11,000 faculty and staff, including more than 370 endowed faculty.

Many of the traditions OU students and alumni proudly claim as their own

came into being in the early days of the university: colors (crimson and cream) were selected in 1895; the alumni association was founded in 1898; the first pep band, which became the Pride of Oklahoma in 1904, was organized in 1901; and the fight song "Boomer Sooner" was written in 1905.

The first courses at OU were largely preparatory classes. Students came from homestead families who were willing to sacrifice to give their children an education and a better future. In its second year, the university only had one college ranked student, Nahum E. Butcher; many of the state's college-bound students were sent "back east." That same year, the School of Pharmacy was founded, and in the spring of 1896 the first degrees in pharmaceutical chemistry were issued to students who had completed two years of high school and two years of college study.

A class of two, C. Ross Hume and Roy P. Stoops, received the first bachelor's degrees granted by the University of Oklahoma in 1898; Hume was awarded the institution's first master's degree in 1900. Around 1901, Mrs. J.F. Paxton received the first degree granted to a woman by the university. The first doctoral degree was awarded to Mary Jane Brown in 1929.

In the university's first decade, the "Seed Sower" became the university

Gaylord Hall, new home of the Gaylord College of Journalism and Mass Communication, is a state-of-the-art media education facility. It is designed to incorporate the latest in technology for teaching print and broadcast journalists and accommodating future technological developments.

seal; the university motto, "For the Citizens and For the State," was adopted; and plans for the Commons, centered on an oval rather than a square, were finalized. The first women's residence hall was established, as well as two women's basketball teams. During the same period, the first literary society, debating societies, musical club, and geological club were established, and the first yearbook was published.

However, there were obstacles to overcome. In January 1903 the original building, which held all of the university classrooms, the library, and administration offices, burned to the ground. Most of the institution's valuable papers, many books, and a significant amount of equipment were saved thanks to the quick thinking and bravery of those who battled the blaze. Eager to fend off those who wanted to relocate the university to their own cities, classes resumed in the original rock building downtown, and construction quickly began on new facilities. Fires in 1907 and 1929 would seriously challenge the rapidly growing university and require the addition of more new facilities.

The modern campus and the Norman community are different than what President Boyd saw when he stepped off the train from Kansas in 1892. Finding an endless prairie with no trees in sight, Boyd used his own funds to purchase and plant thousands of trees, tending them through drought, transplanting them around campus, and offering them to members of the community at no cost—as long as recipients kept the trees alive. The large elm tree in front of Evans Hall is one of the first that was planted by Boyd.

Today, the grounds of the university offer a vibrant landscape of trees and flowerbeds, fountains and statuary. This is thanks to a significant tree planting initiative in the late 1970s and early 1980s under President Banowsky; a major improvements plan implemented by David L. Boren, OU's thirteenth president; and a $3 million endowment for flowers and landscaping initiated by the university's current first lady Molly Shi Boren. The university also works closely with the city of Norman on beautification and environmental projects that benefit the entire Norman community.

One of the earliest "donations" by students to the institution was the 1906 Class Rock, located in the North Oval. An unfinished gravestone, the marker was found and hauled to campus by a team of young men and inscribed with their class year. Students of other classes have continued to beautify the campus with donations of gifts that include the arches at the entrance to the North and South Ovals; an endowment for Reunion Garden and the OU reflecting pool; a new plaza between Carnegie and Monnet Halls; a bronze OU seal located in the Memorial Union; fountains at different locations on campus; and a replica of "The Guardian," a statue by Senator Enoch Kelly Haney which sits atop the dome of the state capitol.

In 1894 a sophomore college student became the first university librarian with a salary of $10 per month and a budget of $500 per year, mostly for books requested by the professors. The library consisted mainly of donated texts, many of them religious in nature because they

were donated by area ministers. By 1897, having been designated a government repository, the library boasted 1,800 volumes. Unfortunately, the library was destroyed in the 1901 fire.

In 1925 the university's new president, William Bizzell, embraced his pet project—the construction of a new library, which he considered to be vitally important to the life of the university. He asked the legislature for $500,000 to construct the first unit of a library designed to hold 1 million volumes and refused to negotiate for less. He later asked for an additional $60,000 for stacks. The opening of Bizzell Memorial Library in 1930 marked what Bizzell considered the most important achievement of his career, and still remains as an outstanding symbol of his administration.

Today, the University of Oklahoma Libraries have an annual budget of $15 million, contain 4.5 million volumes, and rank in the top two in the "Big Twelve" in the number of volumes held. The library system, which has been the recip-

The W.R. Howell Pleistocene Plaza offers the most dramatic view of the Sam Noble Oklahoma Museum of Natural History.

ient of several significant endowments in recent years, is the largest in Oklahoma.

OU Libraries maintain one of the three most important collections of early manuscripts in the history of science in the U.S. It contains Galileo's own copy of his work, which first used the telescope to prove the Copernican theory, with corrections in his own handwriting. The Bizzell Bible collection of 665 books includes a hand-painted manuscript prayer book on vellum from the fifteenth century, while the Bob Burke Bible Collection, made up of more than 2,000 bibles and related works dating back to 1492, includes rare editions and foreign language translations.

The John and Mary Nichols Rare Books and Special Collections, created to promote scholarship in the field of English literature, includes an 1843 copy of Charles Dickens' *A Christmas Carol;*

the Bass Business History Collection contains almost 2,000 rare books, including a 1670 copy of Roger Cokes' *A Discourse of Trade*; and the Walter Stanley Campbell Collection of authors' copy books includes many of Campbell's own books with signatures and notes.

The university boasts many other fine collections of historical documentation: the Julian P. Kanter Political Commercial Archive houses the world's largest collection of political commercials, dating back to 1936 for radio and 1952 for television; the Carl Albert Congressional Research and Studies Center, the nation's leading research center for congressional studies, holds the papers of more than fifty current and former members of Congress; and the Western History Collections is one of the largest collections in the world of documents and photographs relating to the American West.

By 1895 the university was growing rapidly, adding instructors, including the first woman, and taking baby steps in athletics. The first OU football team, whose members had never seen a football before that fall, took to the field in December for one game coached by John A. Harts. Later in the year, Harts also helped coach members of the university's first baseball team in their one game, where they defeated their opponents 20–7.

Harvard graduate Vernon L. Parrington, who received a Pulitzer Prize in 1928 for his scholarly writings in American intellectual history, nurtured the football program through its infancy. He coached, managed, officiated, and transplanted the Eastern atmosphere to campus.

A short time later, the university acquired the "Sooner" team name and Coach Bennie Owen, for whom Owen Field was named, began what has become a winning athletic tradition. In the 1950s "Bud" Wilkinson and Gomer Jones presided over one of the most outstanding periods in college football anywhere, compiling a record of 139–27–4, winning three national championships and toppling rushing, passing, and defensive records. The teams still hold the record for the longest consecutive winning streak in college football, forty-seven straight games.

Known as one of the most beautiful rooms in Oklahoma, Bizzell Memorial Library's Peggy V. Helmerich Great Reading Room is an architectural masterpiece and a favorite study place for students.

In the 1970s Coach Barry Switzer took the Sooners into another golden era. An outstanding recruiter, Switzer brought athletes to campus who helped him achieve a 90 percent win record, and three national championships in all, including back-to-back championships in 1974 and 1975. Coach Bob Stoops came to OU in 1999, and in his second year as head coach he led the Sooners to another national championship in football.

In addition, basketball, baseball, track, gymnastics, volleyball, tennis, and golf continued the winning tradition and helped produce such legendary athletes as Olympian Bart Conner. For the four years from 2001 to 2004, OU's men's gymnastics team ranked first or second in the nation, including winning back-to-back national championships in 2002 and 2003.

When the baseball season ended in the spring of 2004, OU held twenty-three national championships in men's and women's sports. In addition, the university was ranked among the top twenty in the U.S. Sports Academy Cup in the years 2000 to 2004, achieving its highest ranking ever (fifteenth) in the 2003–2004 academic year. This award ranks the overall excellence of an athletic and academic program based on points accumulated through performance. In 2003 OU led the Big Twelve with the highest graduation rates of its student athletes.

OU's athletics program is also one of a small number of Division I-A universities to receive the CHAMPS award. Based on academic and athletic excellence, personal and career development, and community service, the CHAMPS award recognizes programs that excel at preparing student athletes for life.

Soon after the athletic program was organized, the music program and student publications were introduced. Sixteen-year-old Grace King joined the faculty as head of the music school, founding the glee club and providing music for the first campus dances; Parrington, head of the university's first English department, founded the first official student publication, *The Umpire*. The director of OU's college of fine arts, Fredrik Holmberg, founded the state's first symphony orchestra at OU.

Today, the A. Max Weitzenhoffer Musical Theater Program is one of the few university programs in the nation that allows students the opportunity to be cast with professional Broadway actors in new productions. The School of Music is on the leading edge of technology and includes internationally recognized instruction and research programs.

The OU Press, established by President Bizzell in 1928 and considered one of his important contributions to the university's national recognition, is the oldest in the Great Plains and is a leading publisher of books about Native Americans and the American West. The highly acclaimed journal of international literature, *World Literature Today*, is published at OU, and the university is home to the Neustadt International Prize for Literature, considered to be second in prestige only to the Nobel Prize and often referred to as the "American Nobel." OU's student newspaper, *The Oklahoma Daily,* and the *Sooner* yearbook are consistently ranked among the best in the country.

From 1905 to 1920 the university grew by leaps and bounds. Fraternities came to campus, and the student government was established. The university expanded to include, among others, colleges of medicine, engineering, fine arts, law, and journalism. The permanent Cherokee gothic architectural design of the institution began to take shape with the construction of University and Monnet Halls, a new Science Hall, the Carnegie Library, residence houses, and a gymnasium.

By 1940 extensive expansion had occurred: DeBarr Hall, a new library, a

OU President David Boren, a former U.S. senator and governor of Oklahoma, teaches an introductory course in political science each semester, and keeps in close touch with students.

student union, a field house, and a football stadium were among the construction projects that had been completed on campus. A school of religion and the University Medical Center had been established, and most of the Sooner traditions were firmly in place: the Ruf Neks were an organized pep group and the OU chant had been written.

In 1949 the university again experienced disaster when it was ravaged by both a fire and a tornado. However, there

The Harold G. Powell Garden at the entrance of historic Parrington Oval spells out Oklahoma U. in chrysanthemums. The garden was endowed in honor of the fiftieth anniversary of Harold's Stores Inc., the national chain of clothing stores that the OU alumnus began on Campus Corner in 1948. In the background is the 11-foot bronze sculpture "May We Have Peace" by the renowned Native American artist Allan Houser.

have been other obstacles to overcome in the school's history. Faculty compensation and funding for construction have been priorities, requiring attention since the university was founded. Political unrest in the state and the nation occasionally interrupted the campus community.

The institution became a battleground in the fight for full integration when Ada Lois Sipuel sued the board of regents for admission to the law school, where she had been denied entrance based on her race. The leadership skills of President George Lynn Cross allowed the University of Oklahoma to negotiate a peaceful path to desegregation. Sipuel eventually earned both a law degree and a master's of history from OU, later serving on the university faculty and as an OU regent.

During the late 1960s and early 1970s the Medical Center faced financial problems and threatened closure. The legislature also was cutting higher-education budgets.

The University of Oklahoma has grown and continues to prosper because of the commitment of the university community, administrative leaders, and loyal faculty and staff. Primarily, the vision and perseverance of university leaders and their ability to plan for the long term and navigate through stormy political waters is the hallmark of the university's growth. From President Boyd, who found an empty prairie and left behind a growing and respected university, to President Brooks, who was responsible for bringing the university to national standing and acquiring significant amounts of property for future expansion, to President Brandt, who was responsible for establishing the University College and the Research Institute and working to create a more participatory and democratic administration, the presidents of the University of Oklahoma have served to make the institution what it is today.

Especially significant to the institution was President George Lynn Cross, who led OU for a quarter of a century, longer than any other president in the university's history. Cross was responsible for steering the school through its unprecedented growth after World War II; he increased faculty input into administration and campaigned for the creation of research professorships. With Cross leading OU, graduate and doctoral programs and enrollment increased and the value of the university's holdings more than doubled—hundreds of acres were acquired for future expansion and thirty-seven buildings were constructed or expanded during his tenure.

Since 1994 OU has been led by President David L. Boren, Oklahoma's former governor and U.S. senator. While fund-raising from private sources has always enhanced the university's development, with Boren's leadership more than $1 billion in private funding has been secured in the past ten years. The OU fundraising base has increased from 18,000 to 82,000 in a decade. During

Oklahoma Memorial Stadium: A $75 million expansion and renovation of OU's football stadium transformed a towering concrete structure into a beautiful facility featuring brick and cast stone that characterizes OU's historic buildings. The stadium is named in honor of the Edward L. Gaylord family of Oklahoma City for the family's extraordinary gift to the project.

that time OU joined the ranks of the top 25 public universities in the nation in private endowments.

In addition, OU ranks first among the Big Twelve in the growth of federal research funding. According to the National Science Foundation, OU's research and training programs have grown twice as fast as the national average in the past ten years. The university ranks in the top seven in total revenues received from intellectual properties developed in proportion to total research revenues generated.

OU's Norman campus has been expanded and transformed by $700 million in construction projects since 1995. Improvements include a $74 million stadium project; the renovation and expansion of Holmberg Hall, home of the university's music and dance programs

and a historic performance venue; renovation of the student union; the construction of a $67 million National Weather Research Center; a $19 million addition to the Michael F. Price College of Business; and the construction of Gaylord Hall for journalism and mass communication and the Stephenson Research and Technology Center, projects that cost $17 million and $27 million, respectively.

Today, OU ranks number one among comprehensive public universities in the per capita number of freshman National Merit Scholars and is in the top five in the nation in the graduation of Rhodes Scholars among all comprehensive public universities. According to ACT and SAT scores, OU currently has the highest academically ranked student body of any public university in state history.

Students come from more than 100 countries in pursuit of degrees from nineteen colleges, choosing from 150 possible majors at the baccalaureate level, 142 majors at the master's level, 76 majors at the doctoral level, 30 majors at the first professional level, and 5 graduate certificates.

The university has been ranked in the top 10 percent of all American universities by *Fiske Guide to Colleges* and among the best college buys in America by an independent higher education research and consulting organization. Many of OU's schools and colleges are rated among the top in the nation, including the colleges of business and law and the schools of petroleum and geological engineering and dance.

OU is now home to one of the two largest natural history museums in the world which are associated with a university. The Sam Noble Oklahoma Museum of Natural History has more than 5 million artifacts, and includes the largest Apatosaurus on display in the world and the oldest work of art ever found in North America.

The Fred Jones Jr. Museum of Art soon will open the Mary and Howard Lester wing, designed to house the Weitzenhoffer Collection of French Impressionism, including works by Van Gogh, Monet, Renoir, Gauguin, and Pissaro. The collection is the single most important gift of art made to a public university in U.S. history. OU's total art collection of more than 7,000 pieces also includes the Fleischaker and Thams collections of southwestern art, with works by members of the Taos colony, the former U.S. state department embassy art collection, and the Dorothy Dunn collection of Native American art.

With the leadership of President Boren, the university has continued to grow and prosper. In addition to construction and financial growth, he has put a tremendous emphasis on academic programs. He began the faculty in residence program, which puts faculty members in apartments in every student residence hall and the program which returns retired professors to the classroom to teach their beginning classes.

He also elevated the honors program to college status, providing intensive classes of twenty-two or fewer students for those who desire accelerated pro-

The $67 million National Weather Center will be the largest of its kind in the nation. It will house OU's world-famous and highly regarded School of Meteorology as well as top weather research specialists of the National Oceanic and Atmospheric Administration.

grams—including President Boren's new freshman writing program—and making available a wide variety of continuing education programs.

President Boren also has focused on globalization. OU hosts a strong and ethnically diverse student body and curricula. The university leads all other American institutions in exchange agreements with universities around the world making it possible for students to choose study options at 143 universities in fifty-one nations.

Innovative new friendship programs improve the lives of students and the international community. The OU Cousins program started by President and Mrs. Boren pairs international and American students on campus.

The university also hosts national and international scholars and policy makers during conferences and symposia. Speakers such as former President George Bush; Secretary of State Colin

Powell and former Secretaries of State Henry Kissinger, James Baker, and Madeline Albright; former Soviet President Mikhail Gorbachev; Supreme Court Justice Sandra Day O'Connor; former British Prime Minister Margaret Thatcher, Nobel Peace Prize winner Archbishop Desmond Tutu; and Jordan's Queen Noor have all been guests at the international affairs conferences.

President Boren came to OU with the belief that the nation will be restored from the roots up and not the top down; that no state can be great without a great university; and that nothing is more important than providing a good education to the next generation of leaders. His vision is to further the development and emergence of the University of Oklahoma as a pacesetter institution in American public higher education.

By leading the university to secure gifts and funding, providing for new construction, establishing new and innovative programs, working to ensure that OU retains more students each year, and meeting the financial needs of students, President Boren is leading the University of Oklahoma into a new century of growth and prosperity ensuring that every Oklahoman can proudly sing, "Live On, University!"

VIP SALES COMPANY, INC.

In 1950 Guy Lewis was diligently attending Drury College in Springfield, Missouri. However, the young man never ended up completing his studies. Lewis had just recently gotten married and was looking for a way to provide a better life for his new wife. It wasn't long before he got an offer he couldn't refuse—a full-time job in the food business. He jumped at the chance to earn a decent wage and dropped out of college. The move proved to be one that would pay off handsomely in the future.

After learning the ins and outs of the food business as an employee, Lewis felt that he was ready to branch out on his own. In 1954 he opened a company called Arctic Foods that specialized in frozen food. In spite of all his hard work, the endeavor didn't pan out. The business

VIP founder Guy Lewis with a handful of his innovative smoothie products.

An article on VIP that appeared in Tulsa World *on May 28, 1967.*

National marketer Guy W. Lewis

National Market Rights Obtained

Guy W. Lewis, formerly manager of the frozen foods division of Fadler Produce Co. here, has formed Guy W. Lewis, Inc., to become national marketer of the VIP frozen food products line.

Fadler, a big wholesaler of produce and frozen foods in Oklahoma, Arkansas, Kansas and Missouri, introduced the VIP label in this territory in 1965.

Consumer acceptance was so "dramatic," according to Lewis, that he negotiated with VIP Foods, Inc., Seattle, for national marketing rights.

He resigned from Fadler to set up his own business and now is actively seeking distributors and large chain operations

throughout the U.S. to serve marketing areas on an exclusive basis.

The VIP line includes vegetables, fruits, juice concentrates, potatoes and specialties.

Lewis said an opaque white polyethylene bag used to package 1¼ and 1½-pound sizes in the VIP lines established the label's early U.S. success. He said this type of packaging originated in Canada, where the process is patented, and gave the label impetus in the United States when it was introduced here.

Technically, Lewis said, the material protects contents from light dissection and virtually eliminates condensation and frost formation.

went belly up just a year later in 1955. Lewis was disheartened by the failure, but not defeated. The experience had taught him a great deal, and he vowed to open his own business again someday.

In the meantime, he went to work for a frozen food/produce distributor where he stayed for more than a decade. With each passing year, he gained more knowledge about what it took to make it in the frozen food industry. He also made sure to tuck away some money to help fund the business he planned to start one day.

Finally, in 1966, Lewis took the plunge and ventured out on his own again. This time he launched VIP Foods, Inc., again specializing in frozen food products. A few years later he added two other food-related companies to his repertoire. In 1969 he created VIP Sales Company Inc., which acted as the exclusive sales and marketing arm for VIP Foods. That same year marked the debut of a food broker that he named Guy W. Lewis, Inc.

With this new foray into the frozen food market, Lewis was determined to make a splash. At first, the company offered five frozen vegetable products: corn, peas, mixed vegetables, green beans, and baby lima beans. Although there

wasn't anything particularly exciting about these vegetables, Lewis found an innovative way to make them stand out.

The entrepreneur opted to package his frozen food products in full-color, printed, opaque polybags, a ground-breaking move at the time. During the late 1960s, frozen foods were normally packaged in clear bags, which posed several problems. Exposure to light would turn peas and other green vegetables a whitish color and caused them to lose chlorophyll. The vegetables would also appear frosted, making them less attractive to buyers. The new opaque bags allowed vegetables to maintain their natural colors and prevented discoloring.

Although Lewis couldn't patent the opaque packaging, he certainly capitalized on it. In fact, he credits the innovative packaging with giving VIP Foods a foothold in the industry. After witnessing the superiority of opaque packaging, other companies began using it too. The innovation proved so successful that it has become the standard in the frozen food industry today.

The breakthrough with opaque packaging was only the first of many changes to come. To this day, VIP continues to be an industry leader in packaging, and Lewis still makes it a priority. The firm has earned a reputation for creating distinctive packages for each of its product lines. As proof of that, VIP has won awards from both the packaging and frozen food industries.

Long before the company ever won any awards, however, VIP began as a one-man operation. Lewis ran the upstart business from a dingy second-floor office located in a Tulsa strip mall. The cramped quarters had no windows so Lewis always kept a flashlight handy in case the lights went out. Soon enough, the tasks of running a business on his own caught up with him and he decided to hire an employee. When that person quit, his wife filled in on a temporary basis until he could find a replacement. The replacement never arrived, and her "temporary" job ended up lasting more than twenty years before she retired in the 1990s.

Lewis' wife, Shirley, isn't the only family member to join the business. In fact, VIP has evolved into a real family affair. All three of Lewis' children are currently VIP employees. His eldest child, Vicki Barnett, acts as receptionist and assistant to the CEO. Middle child, Rick, heads up VIP's I.T. department. The youngest, Michael, handles sales for industrial and food service clients.

One of these bright second-generation employees could eventually take the helm at VIP. Of course, that would require Lewis, who is in his mid-70s, to retire. Although he admits he thinks about retiring, he still loves coming in to work every day so much that he has yet to come up with a succession plan.

The corporation Lewis will eventually retire from bears little resemblance to the struggling firm he launched so many years ago. With $70 million in annual revenues, the company currently employs as many as 100 people during the busy seasons of fall and winter. Unlike Lewis' tiny original second-floor office, VIP's Tulsa headquarters now take up a sprawling 10,873 square feet across two floors in two buildings. The Tulsa offices handle all the sales and accounting efforts for the company, while a state-of-the-art

Above: Veggie combos were introduced in 1980 and trademarked in 1983.

Below: VIP Gourmet, in microwavable cartons, was introduced in 1984.

processing facility in Fort Worth, Texas produces many of the products.

The 26,269-square-foot Fort Worth plant is zoned for twenty-four hour operation and runs two ten-hour shifts. Thirty-four full-time employees handle the first shift and fifteen others handle the second shift. The company uses a staffing service to provide up to forty more contract workers as needed. All processing and packing at the plant takes place in a dual climate-controlled room to ensure optimum product quality. Blending and packaging occur at twenty-eight degrees and boxing and palletization happen at thirty-four degrees. Products stay in that area for no more than fifteen minutes before being transferred to cold storage at minus ten degrees. The plant also uses automated hoppers to ensure that the weight and number of pieces of each package are accurate.

After more than thirty years in business, VIP has emerged as one of the most established and respected companies in the frozen foods industry. It is presently engaged in the sale, marketing, and distribution of branded and private label frozen foods to grocery retailers, food processors, and food service distributors.

The VIP product line has grown into one of the most comprehensive Grade A frozen food programs available. The firm currently offers more than 150 products, including frozen vegetables, vegetable blends, stir-fry vegetables, fruit, pie shells, French fries, tater tots, hash browns, Asian entrées, soup mixes, seasonings, pasta dishes, and smoothies. These products make their way to many of the nation's leading retailers, including Albertson's, Kroger, Publix, Meijers, and Wal-Mart Super Centers. VIP also counts military commissaries worldwide among its buyers. Grocers Supply in Houston, Texas was one of VIP's first big customers, and remain so today.

Landing such top-flight customers, and keeping them, has proven to be one of the biggest ongoing challenges for Lewis. To ensure that VIP retains its best clients, he has made customer satisfaction a top priority. In fact, Lewis credits his long-term success to taking care of the customer.

Seeing to customers' needs is something Lewis can control. Unfortunately, the frozen food provider learned quickly that in a produce-based business, there are other factors that are beyond his power. Lewis explains that Mother Nature can play a pivotal role in this industry. "If there's any kind of weather disaster, such as a freeze or a drought, it can create big problems with supply," according to Lewis.

When the company first started out, all of its produce came from the Pacific Northwest. That meant that a weather problem in that area could mean disaster for VIP. To offset potential shortages in supply, Lewis branched out and secured produce sources in the Midwest and Northeast as a safeguard. These now long-standing relationships in various regions provide protection from growing conditions that may adversely affect supply. Additionally, VIP searches out alternative suppliers to avoid problems caused by labor disputes, production issue, or other factors.

Although VIP has grown considerably since its early days, Lewis still thinks of the firm as a "small guy in a land of giants." Being a modest operator has certainly posed its share of challenges for Lewis, but it has also proven to be beneficial. The entrepreneur thinks that the company's lean size has actually helped VIP in many ways. Without all the layers of management that come with huge conglomerates, VIP is able to respond to changes in the marketplace rapidly. It can embrace and act on new trends much faster than its larger competitors. For example, VIP was one of the first firms to offer frozen stir-fry vegetables. The wildly popular product helped VIP gain distribution throughout the nation and introduced them to many new customers.

Another major innovation arrived in 2002. That's the year Lewis introduced an entirely new category to the marketplace: smoothie mixes. Several years earlier, Lewis was vacationing in Hawaii where he sampled a fruit smoothie. He fell in love with the cool, refreshing drink

VIP's first stir-fry vegetables were introduced in 1987.

and when he returned back home to Tulsa, he started making them for himself everyday for lunch. The only problem was that he had to keep five or six bags of various frozen fruits in the freezer. "There had to be a better way," he thought to himself.

Determined to simplify the process, he called in his product team and hashed out ideas. Their brainstorming session resulted in VIP Smoothies, a new line of smoothie mixes which included four flavors: peach papaya twister, strawberry banana avalanche, cherry berry blizzard, and tropical isle hurricane. Inside each package are several varieties of individually, quick-frozen fruit and a packet of smoothie mix. Customers just add water or juice and in one minute, they've got a delicious thirty-two-ounce smoothie. For Lewis, who still drinks a smoothie every day, it's made his lunchtime meal even more convenient.

Since smoothie mixes are an entirely new category in the frozen food industry, the biggest job is making consumers aware that it's available. To promote the new product, VIP has been placing ads on radio, TV, national cable media, and billboards—in addition to doing in-store promotions.

Even with that success, Lewis isn't one to rest on his laurels. Ever the innovator, he is constantly trying to stay one step ahead of the competition. In 2004 VIP responded to the rising interest

Above: *Some of the products introduced in 1990.*

Above: *VIP introduced lo-carb meals in 2004.*

Below: *The industry's first non-caloric sliced strawberries were introduced in 1990.*

in low-carb diets by adding six low-carb entrées to its Tai Pei brand Asian cuisine.

In the near future, VIP will be rolling out a new line of frozen vegetables that Lewis thinks will be a big hit with consumers as well. Once again, the focus is on the packaging. What makes this product so special is new polyethylene packaging that comes with a "steam magic" valve. All customers have to do is take the bag out of the freezer and pop it in the microwave to get perfectly steamed vegetables.

This is yet another example of how Lewis and VIP have been making mealtime more convenient for Americans, while maintaining top quality for more than thirty years. With a success record like that, it's clear that Lewis learned more than enough from that initial business failure with Arctic Foods. By keeping his eyes open for new trends, there's no question that Lewis and VIP will continue to introduce groundbreaking new products and packaging for years to come.

VISITING NURSE ASSOCIATION OF TULSA

The Visiting Nurse Association of Tulsa puts an emphasis on care as a not-for-profit healthcare agency, serving the people of northeastern Oklahoma. Established to provide private care, the VNA has been an integral part of the community for nearly a quarter of a century.

The not-for-profit organization opened its doors on June 4, 1981 as NSI Health Care Inc. That agency was a division of Nursing Services Inc. (NSI), which had operational roots reaching back to the mid-1920s. Located on East Sixteenth Street and South Yale Avenue, the agency's purpose was to offer services to individuals and institutions which were offered by private care registered nurses, licensed practical nurses, and home health aides.

Medicare guidelines began to shift in the early 1980s, and the changes caused turbulence in the healthcare industry. During that time NSI was the second largest Medicare agency in Tulsa, and like many other large healthcare companies of its size, it folded. However, NSI Health Care Inc. remained opened, although it needed to better define itself if it was to continue.

The facility quickly introduced a visiting nurse program through the Tulsa United Way. This provided a much-needed local service and helped ensure the survival of the then four-year-old

A 1920s home health visit in Tulsa.

organization. The public program, which differed from the private care it originally offered, allowed for home health visits to members of the Tulsa community. The program filled an urgent need, as a large number of area residents either did not have Medicare, Medicaid, or any third-party coverage.

The traditional visiting nurse program became a fast success, and a year later the agency moved to a larger home at East Forty-First Street and South Sheridan Road. As word spread of NSI Health Care's services, the organization grew and joined the Visiting Nurse Association of America (VNNA), a national affiliation of not-for-profit agencies formed in 1888.

The agency's board of directors realized a name change was in order and in 1990 NSI Health Care Inc. became Visiting Nurse Association (VNA) of Tulsa. The change was made in an effort to better reflect its overall purpose, as well as maximize the name recognition of VNAA and its belief in home-care services.

The early '90s continued with more positive changes in store for VNA of Tulsa. While many other health-care

agencies were forced to close their doors, the agency continued to grow. Once again the organization was looking for a new home. It relocated to Skelly Drive, where it remains today.

In 1993 the agency introduced its wellness services with its first annual flu prevention program in Tulsa. This much-needed effort introduced VNA to the general community, giving the organization the opportunity to promote preventative healthcare measures. VNA began to focus on public outreach and established the wellness program in 1998—offering health screenings, corporate wellness services, and educational efforts.

The new program continued the flu immunizations and added vaccinations for pneumonia, hepatitis A and B, Lyme disease, and certain travel requirements. Screenings were also made available for blood pressure, cholesterol, and blood glucose.

The wellness program proved to be a service that not only made a difference in the lives of Tulsa residents, but in the viability of VNA. The program was pivotal to the agency's growth as it allowed for the expansion of services

Visiting Nurse Association of Tulsa management staff. Back row, left to right: Roberta Stapleton, clinical manager and George Beilke, CEO. Front row, left to right: Elizabeth Browne, clinical manager and Jan Guinn, director of wellness and business development.

into Oklahoma City in 2001, with a new office serving western Oklahoma.

Today's Visiting Nurses Association of Tulsa is Oklahoma's only freestanding, not-for-profit, home health agency. It has grown to employ more than 300 people and provide more than 180,000 annual home health visits through its visiting nurse program. The organization also administers hundreds of thousands of immunizations and offers health screenings and foot-care appointments through its wellness program.

VNA's wellness program, after just little more than a decade, has grown to be a major contribution to the community. During its "Fight the Flu" campaign every fall, tens of thousands of area residents are immunized against the potentially fatal ailment.

VNA provides vaccines at easily reachable public sites such as drug stores and supermarkets. They also offer corporate flu clinics and distribute shots to employees at local businesses. The program has grown to include pneumonia shots and the new FluMist vaccine—a needle-less immunization found favorable by many children and adults alike.

Other agency services include wound care, foot care, diabetes management, cardiovascular assessment, HIV/AIDS care and counseling, colostomy care, pain management, home safety assessment, paternity testing, Alzheimer's care, medication setup, physical and speech rehabilitation, social services, and respite care for caregivers.

In-home care begins with a consultation with the patient's physician. A registered nurse conducts an assessment and supervises all home health aides. VNA's staff works with the patient's doctors and family to ensure a complete, yet individualized, approach in addressing any specific healthcare needs.

The healthcare staff is licensed and accredited; however, VNA requires additional annual training. Each healthcare provider receives 12 hours of continuing education on topics such as universal precautions, fire and home safety, infection control, and the proper technique for lifting and transferring patients.

The growth and success of VNA has been guided by its CEO, George Beilke.

Beilke, who has extensive not-for-profit experience, joined the agency just months after it was formed and has shown unwavering dedication through its growth.

The board of directors, comprised of strong community leaders, has played an active role in shaping the VNA of today. These individuals are committed to the common good of community—and the agency. They are the backbone of the organization's mission which is "To be providers of the highest quality and ethical healthcare to the community through its private care, nursing program, wellness/

VNA program staff, from left to right: Pat Lemaster, LPN; Jean Willis, LPN; Roberta Stapleton, RN; Linda Barnhart, RN; Nelda Watson, LPN; Debbie Stoy, RN; Julie Evans, LPN; and Myrna Thompson, LPN.

A VNA drive-through flu clinic.

education program, and home healthcare services funded by the United Way."

VNA's stability is also a credit to its passionate and professional staff. The agency's licensed and certified nurses and home health aides provide the expert medical care and compassionate understanding that's required during difficult times. They bring with them the skills and knowledge to care for patients in any given situation.

The administrative personnel also support the values and beliefs of VNA and ensure its success as an important community partner. These staff members serve an average of more than eight years with the organization, which is outstanding in an industry that suffers from a high turnover rate and rapid burnout.

The Visiting Nurses Association of Tulsa has survived an ever-changing and unpredictable industry, while evolving into an agency that far exceeded its original goals. The organization provides expert in-home healthcare to the sick and dying, regardless of age or economic standing, as well as preventative and maintenance health services to all people of its community. VNA is truly living up to its vision statement as "the heart of home health."

WARD PETROLEUM CORPORATION

Like father like son. The saying resonates for Lew Ward, the founder and chairman of Ward Petroleum Corporation in Enid, Oklahoma. While growing up, Ward worked summers as a roughneck alongside his father who served as a field boss for an oil drilling company. Hoping Lew would follow in his footsteps with a career in oil, the elder Ward encouraged his son to go to college and become a petroleum engineer. The younger Ward took his father's advice and received his bachelor of science degree in petroleum engineering from the University of Oklahoma in 1953. By 1963 he'd started his own company in Enid, a town with a rich history as an oil and gas center.

The first oil well in Oklahoma was drilled in the Garber Field near Enid in September 1916. World War I was raging in Europe at the time, but the oil boom was on in Enid. Dozens of oil companies were popping up to capitalize on the discovery. By April 1917 at least 100 rigs were drilling in the Garber Field. And by 1931 approximately twenty major oil companies had offices in Enid.

Lew Ward first came to Enid in 1956 to work for his wife's father in the oil business. By 1963 he had drilled his first productive well located on the Petru Farm, south of Douglass. Production was at 5,800 feet and the well produced 220 barrels of oil a day. Based on that success, Ward started the company that would eventually become Ward Petroleum Corporation.

With all the drilling in Enid, Ward began to wonder if the area immediately surrounding the community would also produce oil. The enterprising petroleum engineer started trying to buy acreage,

Bill and Lew Ward meet to work on strategic planning.

Members of Ward Petroleum's advisory board.

but quickly discovered that other people had the same idea—the area was almost completely leased. There were some small acreages around town that were not leased, but it was considered too difficult to put together enough acreage to drill. Not knowing any better, Ward went ahead and bought some of the small acreages surrounding Enid that were still within the city limits.

One day Ward had a visitor from the National Cooperative Refining Association in McPherson, Kansas. They needed oil for their refinery and wanted to work out a deal to participate with Ward in drilling some of these small acreages. The first well, completed in 1964, was the number one Beasley just west of Thirtieth Street and Breckinridge Road. Proving that Ward had made a good move in buying the small acreages, the number one Beasley produced 175 barrels of oil per day at 6,800 feet.

The area south of Enid had indications that it might also produce oil and gas.

Ward approached the city council for an oil and gas lease on Meadowlake Park. He outbid all the other competitors and drilled the number one Meadowlake just south of the golf course driving range in 1965. Once again, Ward's instincts proved right and the well produced gas. There was some concern about drilling in the park, but the city council felt that encouraging drilling might benefit the economy.

Shortly after, Ward drilled another gas well east of Highway 81. There was only one problem with the gas wells: Ward didn't have a buyer for the gas. Ward decided that if nothing else he might be able to sell it to a local brick plant. Fortunately, he never had to go that route. The Oklahoma Natural Gas Company ended up coming to the rescue and hooking up the wells at no cost to Ward Petroleum.

From 1964 to 1975 the company drilled more than twenty-five wells within the city limits of Enid. The Oklahoma company and the oil industry were growing at a significant rate. That is, until something unforeseen happened.

The year 1973 proved to be a milestone in the industry. The first Arab oil

Number one Perry well in a city park in Enid, Oklahoma.

embargo took place in October of that year and due to the oil shortage, Ward Petroleum was focused on increasing oil production. When the second oil embargo occurred in 1979, oil prices increased to more than $40 a barrel and once again oil became the focus.

By 1980 the whole country was supporting a plan to become energy independent. At the time, President Jimmy Carter was urging conservation and increased oil and gas production. He also encouraged the banks to help. To do their part, financial institutions were calling oil companies like Ward Petroleum with offers to lend money. Ward

would be signing up for one of those loans sooner than he expected.

In 1981 Lew Ward was planning to drill several wells in Cheyenne Valley and as usual, he contacted his longtime drilling contractor about taking on the job. Rigs had become such a hot commodity by this time that the driller asked for several additional conditions that weren't acceptable to Ward. When they couldn't reach an agreement, Ward got upset and made a decision he would come to question many times. He decided he'd buy his own rigs. That's when he called one of the banks for a substantial loan.

Soon after Ward purchased the rigs, drilling intensity around Enid increased sharply. The area was a boomtown. People were living in their cars, and in tents in public parks, because there wasn't enough housing available. Enid and Abilene, Texas were listed in *U.S. News & World Report* as the two fastest-growing cities in the nation. By May 1982 there were 882 rigs running in Oklahoma.

Ward Petroleum continued to expand operations into Caddo, Grady, Custer, and Rogers Mills counties and drilled wells in the 12,000 to 14,000 feet range searching for natural gas. Around this time, the company developed an investment philosophy that is still in use today: take a smaller piece of several wells

The 16,000-foot Burton well in Grady County.

rather than a large piece of one well. To this day, Ward drills with partners within the industry.

Unfortunately, the drilling boom in Oklahoma was about to suffer a slow-down. Over the next decade the number of rigs declined steadily, reaching a low of about 100. Ward Petroleum survived these tough times by pioneering hybrid turnkey drilling contracts and developing what Ward called a "total performance package." This meant creating prospects, acquiring acreage, finding partners, and drilling. Companies who participated with Ward Petroleum in drilling prospects could be assured of quality geological prospects, fixed costs on drilling, and excellence in engineering. During slower times, Ward Petroleum would frantically compete for drilling contracts, often bidding below cost in order to keep the crews together.

It was during this downturn that the Penn Square Bank failure happened. This had devastating effects on local oil and gas companies. Many of the companies lost their funds in the bank failure and were forced to file for bankruptcy. That meant they couldn't pay their vendors. In turn, those vendors who couldn't collect

Ward Drilling Company operations in Grady County.

on their receivables subsequently couldn't pay their own bills. It was a vicious cycle.

After the Penn Square Bank failure, there was a general feeling of doom and gloom within the industry. Ward knew things were going to be tough. On top of that, the company had the daunting burden of bank debt for the drilling rigs. In spite of that, the company had a lot of things going for it, including an experienced staff, proven oil finders, capable engineers, and the respect of the people within the industry. Ward kept telling himself and his crew that failure was not

an option. During this time, he also constantly reminded himself not to get discouraged and to keep a positive mental attitude.

With a renewed sense of teamwork, the folks at Ward Petroleum stepped up their efforts to survive. The company sought out new partners for prospects it was ready to drill. Ward once said, "We often reminded ourselves that we had to sell our prospects just like they sell Fuller Brushes. Keep knocking on doors till you get the job done. One prospect we showed 121 times. Determination and persistence are traits we have found helpful."

Thanks to the increased efforts, Ward Petroleum managed to stay afloat during this trying time. One reason for their success was an emphasis on gas. The firm had been successful in drilling several gas wells, but was reluctant to continue until there was a market for the gas. To solve the problem, Ward entered into a joint venture with a party that had a market but no gas. Together, the companies built a pipeline to the marketplace.

A major milestone in the history of Ward Petroleum Corporation came on February 24, 1987. That's the day the company paid the last installment on the

Ward Drilling Company operations in Custer County.

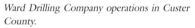

drilling rigs. The company threw a party in which Ward symbolically burned the mortgage and paid off the debt. Ward credits the company's team of explorationists for making it possible to make all those payments on time and pay off the note in full.

In the late 1980s the firm continued to build on its exploration expertise. Only now the explorationists were using more advanced 3-D seismic prospecting instead of the two-dimension seismic of years past. The three-dimensional seismic offers explorationists a look at everything within a large area—in three dimensions. With the more advanced equipment the firm began prospecting in the deep part of the Anadarko Basin.

Another important area for the company has been the Arkoma Basin. Since 1989 Ward has operated or participated in nearly 100 wells in the structurally complex Frontal Ouachita Thrust Belt in the Arkoma Basin of southern Oklahoma. The Arkoma possesses many of the same characteristics as the Anadarko. However, there are huge areas of undeveloped acreage, making the Arkoma a frontier area. To date, Ward Petroleum has drilled more than 800 wells in the Anadarko and

Ward's rig number one.

Lew Ward participating in a town festival and parade, circa 1979.

Arkoma Basins, some as deep as 22,000 feet. Those two basins are expected to provide Ward Petroleum with many more years of good opportunities to build and maintain a reserve base for oil and gas.

Ward's efforts to keep his business alive during the dark days of the 1980s paid off. By the early 1990s the firm was once again on the rise. In fact, Ward Petroleum grew so quickly that it was listed in *Inc. Magazine* as one of America's 500 fastest-growing private companies in 1991, 1992, and 1993.

With more than forty years of success in the oil and gas business, Ward has proven to be an industry leader and is often sought out for his expertise. Throughout the years he has served in various capacities on numerous national and local petroleum commissions and councils. In 1996 he was named "Energy Leader of the Year" by the National Association of Royalty Owners. He also received Lone Star Steel's "Chief Roughneck" award in 1999 for lifetime achievement in the oil and gas industry.

In addition to his noteworthy achievements in the oil and gas industry, Ward has become a role model in the community. Over the years he has served as the director of the Oklahoma State Chamber of Commerce and as president of the Enid Chamber of Commerce. He also held the title of president of the Enid Rotary Club and the American Business Club. To applaud Ward for his many efforts, the Enid Chamber of Commerce once named

him "Businessman of the Year." From 1996 to 1998 he served the oil industry as the national chairman of the Independent Petroleum Association of America.

In the future, the company plans to grow by continuing drilling and acquiring existing producing properties. Although the firm began by drilling for oil more than forty years ago, gas has become its main focus. Today, gas represents approximately 80 percent of its efforts while oil accounts for about 20 percent.

With the long-term success of Ward Petroleum, it's safe to say that Lew Ward is proud that he followed in his father's footsteps. And in keeping with that family tradition, he encouraged his own son, Bill, to join him in the business. In the late 1970s when Bill was a teenager, he started working summers at Ward Petroleum. After he graduated college in 1984 with a degree in petroleum engineering, he joined the firm on a full-time basis. Beginning as a staff engineer, he eventually took over as president in 1996.

Lew Ward handed over the reins as CEO to his son in 2001, but remains involved in the day-to-day activities of the company as chairman. Now it's up to the highly qualified third-generation Ward to carry the torch and lead the independent energy company into the future. Like father, like son.

DONALD G. WEINKAUF AND WEINKAUF PETROLEUM, INC.

The oil and gas industry has given and taken much in Oklahoma, yet behind it all has been one man who has been as steady as a pump jack on a solid producer—Donald G. Weinkauf. Weinkauf Petroleum, Inc. is a family-owned and operated oil and gas exploration and production company that generates drilling prospects for oil and gas wells in Oklahoma, Texas, Kansas, and Colorado. Donald G. (Don) Weinkauf and his wife, Julia (Judy), founded Weinkauf Petroleum, Inc. in 1980 and remain one of the few small oil and gas companies that survived the industry down turn of the '80s. Don Weinkauf's "nose for oil" and smart financial practices provided the foundation that has made Weinkauf Petroleum the strong and diverse company it is today.

Don Weinkauf was born November 18, 1928 in Banner, Oklahoma. His family moved to Orlando, a rural area in central Oklahoma, where he graduated from Hayward High School in 1946. Weinkauf then worked for two years with his dad,

farming and raising Angus cattle. Although his father never encouraged higher education, Weinkauf had a yearning to learn and experience more. The late 1940s brought a new commodity to Oklahoma's rural areas—electricity. Weinkauf studied and became a licensed electrician. From 1948 to 1950 he wired over 150 houses in the Orlando rural community.

Pictured here in their Tulsa office, Don and Judy Weinkauf founded Weinkauf Petroleum, Inc. in 1980.

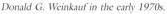

Donald G. Weinkauf in the early 1970s.

The Weinkauf Family in the mid-1990s. Front row: Don and Judy Weinkauf. Back row: Donnita Weinkauf Wynn and Douglas Kirk Weinkauf.

The Apache Corporation staff in 1962, with Don Weinkauf in the center of the front row.

in Oklahoma City. He was promoted to chief geologist prior to leaving Eason in 1961 to work for Honcho Oil & Gas. After a short stint with Honcho and with $50 in his pocket, Weinkauf moved his young family to Tulsa in January 1962 and went to work for Apache Corporation as a staff and well-site geologist.

After seven productive years with Apache, Doyle C. Cotton, Jr. of Cotton Petroleum Corporation offered Weinkauf the position of vice president of exploration, which he accepted in February of 1969. It was during his tenure with Cotton Petroleum that his success as a geologist was recognized. He was elected chairman of the board in 1973.

Under his leadership at Cotton Petroleum the net wells drilled per year went from five to thirty. In fact,

Weinkauf got his first taste of the oil and gas business when he went to work as a roughneck with his only sibling, R. H. Weinkauf. Together they worked for several different companies in central Oklahoma from 1950 to 1952. As he watched the well-site geologists study cuttings from the hole, he was fascinated that they could determine the quality of the rock formations below the surface and predict what might be produced from the well. As a result, he entered Oklahoma A&M (Oklahoma State University) in the fall of 1952 to study geology.

After completing his first year, Weinkauf had to go back to work to earn enough money to continue his education. He was a roughneck for Falcon-Seaboard Drilling Company and worked his way up to driller. In 1953 he joined the U.S. Army serving in the 82nd Airborne in Fort Bragg, North Carolina. After serving his country for two years, he returned to Oklahoma A&M using the GI Bill to help finance his education. He graduated at the top of his class in 1958 with a degree

in geology and a minor in chemistry. Weinkauf was one of only three students from the College of Geology that were recruited and hired after graduation.

Don Weinkauf was first employed as a staff geologist for Eason Oil Company

The corporate office of Weinkauf Petroleum, Inc.

at this point in Weinkauf's career he had been responsible for the drilling of over 200 producing wells with estimated reserve calculations of over 200 billion cubic feet of gas and 7.7 million barrels of oil. Weinkauf had earned the respect of his peers throughout the oil and gas industry as an expert explorer, having discovered or significantly developed the Perry Misener, May Basal Tonkawa and Morrow, Sparks Morrow, Arnett SE, and Randal fields in Oklahoma and Texas.

During the 1970s Weinkauf returned to his roots. He began buying land in the Orlando, Oklahoma area where he and his wife grew up with their parents, Herman and Ester Weinkauf and Jack and Alma Betchan, who were very active in their communities, helping to establish schools and churches. These land purchases resulted in he and his wife Judy co-owning and operating a 3,500-acre cattle ranch in Garfield and Logan Counties. Weinkauf enjoyed operating the ranch from his Tulsa office and going to work there when he had the opportunity. The original Weinkauf homestead claimed in the Oklahoma Land Run remains an inherited treasure in the Weinkauf family.

With confidence in his abilities as a geologist and businessman, and with his

Don Weinkauf, chairman of the board for Weinkauf Petroleum, Inc.

Kirk Weinkauf, president of Weinkauf Petroleum, Inc.

wife's support, Weinkauf made the decision to become an independent geologist. He went on retainer for Cotton Petroleum in 1974 and in 1976 similarly went on retainer for May Petroleum, Inc. of Dallas, Texas. Weinkauf maintained his office in Tulsa, Oklahoma and on September 2, 1980 he and his wife formed Weinkauf Petroleum, Inc. (WPI).

WPI started in 1980 with eight employees including Don Weinkauf as president and Judy Weinkauf as executive vice president. The staff also included two part-time employees who were geology students—one of which was his son, Kirk Weinkauf, who became president of WPI in January 2001 and his best friend, Erik VandenBorn, who is currently WPI's vice president of exploration. In keeping with the family-owned and operated business tradition, daughter Donnita Weinkauf Wynn joined WPI as an attorney for the land department in 1981 where she worked until 1992.

The mid to late 1980s brought dramatic changes in the oil and gas industry. Deregulation came into effect with the formation of the Federal Energy Regulatory Commission (FERC), which resulted in a chaotic period in the industry. Within a very short time the price of gas went from approximately $4.00 per MCF to $1.60 per MCF, decimating the industry. Over the next few years about half the oil and gas producers in the industry folded. WPI suffered as well but kept its doors open.

From 1984 to 1989 WPI was on retainer with Rosewood Resources, owned by Carolyn Rose Hunt, daughter of Texas oilman H. L. Hunt. In 1989 as the downturn in the oil and gas industry took its toll and contracts were renegotiated, Weinkauf's son, Kirk, was vocal about the numerous frustrations of working on retainer—WPI was doing a lot of the work, but not really having any control. He felt WPI could operate more efficiently, bringing in higher revenues to the company. At the urging of his son, Weinkauf made the agonizing decision to go it alone. Ties were severed amicably with Rosewood, and WPI entered into a new phase of turning prospects to select industry groups. It was a challenging task that met with great results.

With continued success, Kirk Weinkauf approached his father with the idea of purchasing existing wells where operating expenses were excessive and where production could be enhanced. He noted that through the 1980s WPI had been responsible for solving problems related to well operations. Weinkauf usually held a small working interest in these properties resulting in great rewards for the operator. He felt WPI would be better off economically, even though there would be risk involved, to take over operations of wells that met their criteria.

In November of 1991 WPI purchased two wells, the Rowan Trust #1-6 in Texas County, Oklahoma and the Urben #1-971 in Lipscomb County, Texas. Both of these properties are still producing today and have paid out many times their initial investment. This created a successful operations division for WPI, complementing the existing exploration component. By the end of 1998 WPI had acquired ten wells from which 10 percent of WPI's revenue was being derived.

Weinkauf and his son, Kirk, worked side-by-side both utilizing their unique styles successfully in the highly competitive oil and gas business. In 2001 Donald

The Rowan Trust #1-6. One of the first Weinkauf Petroleum, Inc. operated wells.

G. "Don" Weinkauf became chairman of the board and his son, Douglas "Kirk" Weinkauf became president of Weinkauf Petroleum, Inc. By the end of 2003 over 50 percent of WPI's revenue was derived from operated wells.

The main difference in the WPI philosophy of today, versus yesterday, is now it strives to control a larger interest of deals in which it participates. While some of the philosophies have changed through the years, some have remained the same. WPI would not exist today if Don Weinkauf had not run the company with the motto, "No debt!" This is one of the primary reasons they are currently a viable company and still adhere to that philosophy today. In addition, both Don and Kirk Weinkauf think of their employees as family. Any major decisions are based, in part, on how it will impact the families of their employees, as well as their own. That is evident, as six of their original eight employees remain employed by WPI today. Loyalty runs deep among WPI employees. Current full-time employee tenures range from thirteen to twenty-four years of service.

Although Don Weinkauf no longer plays an active role in the day-to-day activities of the company, his business philosophies will continue. He developed a great foundation that has given his son the financial tools, business ethics, and characteristics of a successful explorer, to take WPI to the next level while the integrity and philosophies of the company he created are preserved.

Following in the footsteps of a father who has been as successful as Don Weinkauf can be very difficult. Under his father's guidance, Kirk Weinkauf was prospecting at sixteen years of age and had worked up at least five prospects through his high school years. Cotton Petroleum drilled three of these prospects. At the age of eighteen he worked on a rig for Unit Drilling Company before entering Oklahoma State University (OSU) in September of 1978 as a geology student. One of the favorite stories he likes to tell occurred while taking a physical geology course in his first year at OSU. "The professor teaching the course, Dr. Naff, walked into the room and proceeded to call roll," Weinkauf says. "When he got to my name, he looked up and asked me, 'Is your father Don Weinkauf?' After replying 'yes,' he followed with, 'We'll be expecting great things from you. Your father was the best student this college has ever seen.' Dr. Naff had been one of my father's professors when he was in school. Let's just say I did not attain the same academic success that my father had achieved."

WPI has seen the work of three generations of Weinkauf men. From Donald G. Weinkauf as founder to Douglas "Kirk" Weinkauf as president, and now Kirk's two sons, Derek Kirk and Kent Jacob, have begun their journey working in the field and in the office. They, too, will find their area of talent.

Behind the Weinkauf men have been strong women who have supported the oil and gas industry as well. Both Don's wife, Judy, and Kirk's wife, Donna, have served as president of the Tulsa Geological Geophysical Auxiliary.

The Oklahoma oil and gas industry has been good to the Weinkauf family and they have in turn given back to the community. As a family they have created a successful company that has provided energy for the country, revenue for the state of Oklahoma, and jobs for individuals, all while remaining involved in community service. The Weinkauf family, young and old, has donated many hours and dollars to their respective areas of interest. Some of the major benefactors of their tireless contributions are Oklahoma State University, National Safety Council, National Association for Family & Community Education, Boy Scouts of America, 4-H Organization, Pilot Club International, Tulsa Boys Home, numerous schools and churches, and other local, state, and national charities. In addition, Don and Judy Weinkauf created a perpetual scholarship fund at Oklahoma State University for students studying in the field of geology or home economics.

For as long as the pump jack is a fixture on the Oklahoma horizon, the Weinkauf family will continue to be a part of the fuel that has driven Oklahoma's rich history.

UNITED WAY OF CENTRAL OKLAHOMA

In a state with a rich history, any business or agency that is eighty years old is unique—especially if it is a nonprofit organization. The United Way of Central Oklahoma, headquartered in Oklahoma City, is part of that rare and unique breed.

Most nonprofits are started to meet a specific need, and once that has been accomplished, they usually disappear. Many have come and gone since Oklahoma became a state in 1907. The United Way of Central Oklahoma has remained a strong and necessary part of the fabric of the state's life for two reasons: concern for the needs of its people, and the leadership to see that those needs are met, year after year.

Founded in 1924 by some of Oklahoma City's most revered forefathers, this organization, although known by several names over the years, has mirrored its counterparts throughout America. It began as a way to help people who could not otherwise help themselves and is funded through the generosity of local donors. It has always been locally governed by the strong, committed leadership of the city's top business, civic, and religious leaders who see it as the most efficient way to help the greatest number of people.

Beyond that, what has made this particular United Way special is its ability to

Left to right: Mike Packnett, president of Mercy Health Center; Jerry Maier, president of Oklahoma University Medical Center; Bob Spinks, president of United Way of Central Oklahoma; and Bill Swisher, retired CEO of CMI Corporation, gather to celebrate United Way's 2003 campaign.

Burns Hargis, vice chairman of the Bank of Oklahoma, presents Ray Ackerman with the first annual "Ray Ackerman Leadership Award" at United Way's annual meeting.

move and change with the community's ebb and flow. And that takes consistent, far-sighted leadership. Leaders such as Ray Ackerman, a successful Oklahoma City advertising executive and fifty-seven-year volunteer with United Way, have helped pave the way.

There are few positive initiatives in Oklahoma City's history that haven't benefited from Ackerman's vision and creative gifts. His United Way service began as a campaign worker in the late 1940s, asking small businesses to help fund the organization's efforts to help people in postwar Oklahoma City. He chaired the annual campaign in the 1960s and later headed United Way's board of directors. Today, he works the toughest calls in the annual fundraising drive. He is so respected for his work to help others, that in 2004 a new award for grassroots United Way leaders was named in his honor.

And there's also Lee Allan Smith. In the past forty years, no major effort or cause in Oklahoma City has succeeded without his strong leadership and direction. The Stars and Stripes Shows, the 1989 Olympic Festival, the Capitol Dome Dedication, and the State Centennial Celebration—he's led them all, and many, many more. He chaired the United Way campaign in the 1980s and remains a loyal, active volunteer today, recognizing how critically important it is to help people from all walks of life.

United Way's community leadership rolls are endless. Bill and Wanda Swisher

at CMI, Richard Clements of Clements Foods, Luke Corbett of Kerr McGee, Burns Hargis at Bank of Oklahoma, and many others have worked in support of the organization's crucial work. These people, and thousands of others from every part of the community, have led the organization in the past—and are guiding the United Way of Central Oklahoma through the twenty-first century.

However, any nonprofit also depends on the commitment and drive of its staff leadership. The person chosen to lead the organization through the new millennium is a native Oklahoman who was selected because of his history in the local community and his connection with the needs of the city and region.

Bob Spinks grew up in McAlester, seeing human need up-close. His father taught at rural schools, and his mother was a social worker who case managed welfare recipients. Bob learned early that some people just need extra help to get through life.

After receiving his education at Oklahoma State University, including a doctorate in educational administration, Spinks decided to follow his passion for helping others. He started his career in nonprofit leadership in Oklahoma City, first working for the Boy Scouts of America, then managing a regional research support organization, and now leading the United Way. He uses his thirty years of volunteer and professional nonprofit leadership training and experience every day.

Like most Oklahomans, Bob Spinks stubbornly refuses to accept the idea that social problems cannot be solved. It just takes leadership—twenty-four hours a day, seven days a week, 365 days a year.

Under his direction, the United Way of Central Oklahoma has continued to perform its traditional responsibilities of raising and distributing donated dollars to agencies that help the young and old, the sick and infirm, the homeless and hopeless. It still provides strong, accountable leadership in times of disaster, whether natural or man-made. However, that's not enough in today's Oklahoma.

The United Way is also attacking the new problems that face twenty-first century Oklahomans by creating and incubating programs that seek long-term, permanent solutions. Its successful leadership in recent efforts such as "Success by 6," which prepares children to start school healthy and prepared; "Turning Point," which addresses Oklahoma's serious health problems; and many other initiatives are creating a new United Way—one that is built on the traditions and successes of the past, but ready to tackle the new problems of the future.

As always, these challenges are met face-on because of strong leadership. Today, the United Way of Central Okla-

Above: Bob Spinks, president of United Way of Central Oklahoma; Luke Corbett, chairman and CEO of Kerr-McGee; Larry Nichols, president of Devon Energy Corporation; and Tom Price, senior vice president of Chesapeake Energy Corporation, honor United Way with yearly support as competitors in business, but partners in community from leaders of Oklahoma City's largest energy firms.

Right: Larry Nichols, president of Devon Energy; Lt. Governor Mary Fallin; and Jim Couch, city manager of Oklahoma City, stand in front of the new Centennial Fountain on United Way Plaza in Bricktown.

United Way of Central Oklahoma staff dressed up for the 2004 Snowflake Gala.

homa is staffed by talented, creative, empowered professionals, with an unsurpassed energy and passion for helping people. Most are native Oklahomans with a powerful respect and love for their state and all have a complete commitment to making Oklahoma the best place for everyone to live and work.

And, as it has been for eighty years, the United Way is led by volunteers who are completely committed to extending its history of public service far into the future. After all, that's what leadership is all about.

A TIMELINE OF OKLAHOMA HISTORY

1803
The Louisiana Purchase doubled the size of the U.S. and included what are now eight states.

1817
A.P. Chouteau established a trading post with Joseph Revoir at the present site of Salina.

1821
The Santa Fe Trail began.

1824
Forts Gibson and Towson were established in Indian Territory.

1830
Congress passed the Indian Removal Act.

1831-1850
The "Trail of Tears" forced the removal of the Five Civilized Tribes from the homelands in southeastern United States: Choctaw (1831-1834); Creeks (1832-1835); Chickasaws (1837); Cherokees (1838-1839); and the Seminoles (1835-1850).

1842
Fort Washita was established. The Slave Revolt in the Cherokee Nation took place.

1850
Goodland Mission was established for the Choctaws by Reverend O.P. Stark.

1855
The Chickasaws purchased land from the Choctaws to create their own nation in Indian Territory.

1861-1865
The Civil War engulfed Indian Territory.

1866
Treaties concluded with the Five Civilized Tribes after the war. One provision allowed

Water from the North Canadian River flooded the streets of Capitol Hill, circa 1923. Courtesy, OHS

A flood at the intersection of Reno and South Byers streets in Oklahoma City on July 29, 1963. Courtesy, Johnny Melton Collection, OHS

for territorial status to be created and another permitted railroads to cross Indian lands.

1869
Fort Sill was established in southwest Indian Territory.

1872
Missouri, Kansas, and Texas (MK&T) Railroad began construction near Vinita, Cherokee Nation. It followed the old Texas Road or what is now U.S. Highway 69.

1878
The International Councils of Indian Tribes met in Okmulgee, Creek. Nation stemmed efforts to create territorial status of Indian Territory by Congress.

1880
The Boomer Movement began under the leadership of Captain David L. Payne.

1884
Captain Payne died in Wellington, Kansas and William Couch assumed command of the Boomer Movement.

1886
The last Indian tribe removed to Indian Territory and the Apaches, including Geronimo, were relocated to Fort Sill. Cimarron Territory was created at Beaver City.

1889
Unassigned Lands in central Indian Territory were opened to settlement by non-Indians and 25,000 settlers made a dash for land.

1890
The Organic Act created Oklahoma Territory that included all of the panhandle in western Oklahoma.

1891
The Sac and Fox-Shawnee Indian Reservation was opened to land run by non-Indians.

1892
The Cheyenne and Arapaho Reservation was opened to land run by non-Indians.

1893
The Dawes Commission was established by an act of Congress to form a treaty for lands with the Five Civilized Tribes. The largest land opening took place just south of the Kansas border with over 100,000 people seeking lands to homestead.

1895
The Mexican Kickapoo Reservation was opened to non-Indians by land rush.

1898
The Curtis Act was passed by Congress and forced members of the Five Civilized Tribes to treaty with the Dawes Commission Rough Riders that had formed in Oklahoma Territory to fight in the Spanish American War.

1901
Kiowa, Comanche, and Wichita and Affiliated Bands lands opened to non-Indian settlement by lottery.

1905
The Sequoyah Convention convened in Muskogee, Indian Territory.

1906
Final rolls for the Five Civilized Tribes were closed by the Dawes Commission. The Constitutional Convention convened

The Oklahoma State Supreme Court with Justice Alma Wilson (far left) and Justice Yvonne Kauger (third from left), © 1984. Courtesy, OHS

in Guthrie, the territorial capitol of Oklahoma Territory.

1907

On November 16th Oklahoma became the 46th state to enter the union. Charles N. Haskell took the oath of office as Oklahoma's first governor.

1910

An election was held to determine the final location for the state capitol and Oklahoma City was chosen. Governor Haskell ordered official papers to be moved to Oklahoma City immediately after the election results were known.

1912

James Thorpe, a Sac and Fox Indian, won a gold medal at the Olympic Games in Sweden.

1914

Construction began on the state capitol in Oklahoma City, with Solomon Layton acting as the principal architect.

1915

The Rohrerbaugh-Brown Department Store was established in Oklahoma City,

with other locations opening later in Tulsa and Norman.

1917

The Capitol was essentially completed minus the domes, as monies to finish the structure were used for other purposes.

1920

Alice Robertson from Muskogee was elected to Congress.

1921

The Tulsa Race Riot resulted in thousands being left homeless.

1922

WKY Radio became the first radio station in Oklahoma. C.R. Anthony opened the first store in Cushing.

1923

John C. "Jack" Walton was impeached as governor. WNAD radio was established at the University of Oklahoma.

1926

Construction began on Route 66 in Oklahoma.

1928

WBBZ in Ponca City was founded.

1929

Governor Henry S. Johnston became the second governor to be impeached.

1931

The Great Depression hit Oklahoma hard. Oklahoma's own Wiley Post, a noted aviator, circled the globe in eight days. Post also invented what later became pressurized space suits, used in today's manned space flight.

1933

Drought hit western Oklahoma including the panhandle region. President Franklin Roosevelt created the Civilian Conservation Corps, Works Progress Administration, and other programs to assist in relief during the Depression years.

1934

KTUL radio was established in Tulsa. KADA radio was founded in Ada.

1935

Dust storms hit western Kansas, Oklahoma,

and the Texas panhandle. Wiley Post and Will Rogers, a Cherokee Indian and humorist, died in a plane crash in Alaska.
1941
KSWO radio in Lawton was established.
1942
Air Depot, later renamed Tinker Field for Osage Indian and General Clarence Tinker, was established near Oklahoma City. Robert S. Kerr was elected governor.
1944
WKY in Oklahoma City conducted a war bond drive in several state communities using television equipment for demonstration purposes.
1945
World War II ended.
1948
KGYN radio in Guymon went on the air and KIHN radio in Hugo was founded.
1949
Ada Lois Sipuel, a Black student from Langston University, was finally allowed to enroll at the University of Oklahoma School of Law. WKY-TV in Oklahoma City became the third television to go on the air in the United States with 15 hours of weekly programming.
1950-1959
Growing efforts by the NAACP and local Black leaders in Tulsa, Oklahoma City, and other communities began to tear down the walls of segregation. KSWO-TV in Lawton was founded.

Founded in 1915, retailer John A. Brown Company's men's department at Penn Square in 1972. Courtesy, OHS

In 2003 Otoe Indian family members presented important Lewis and Clark documents to the Oklahoma Historical Society. Courtesy, Terry Zinn

1954
KOED-TV was established as Tulsa's educational channel.
1955
The Rodgers and Hammerstein musical "Oklahoma!" opened on Broadway in New York City.
1956
The Turner Turnpike, named for former governor, Roy Turner, opened between Oklahoma City and Tulsa. The Kerr-McGee Oil Company entered the international financial market when its stock appeared on the New York Stock Exchange.
1957
Oklahoma celebrated its semi-centennial. Peaceful sit-ins began in Oklahoma City to help end segregation.

1958
The NAACP Youth Council, after consulting with local chapter president James Stewart, Sr., received approval for a sit-in demonstration at Katz Drug Store in Oklahoma City.
1959
Oklahoma became the last state to end Prohibition.
1961
Public sit-ins to end segregation continued.
1962
Henry L. Bellmon became the first Republican elected as governor since Oklahoma's statehood.
1963
Senator Robert S. Kerr died. Federal District Judge Luther Bohanon ruled that Oklahoma City schools were not truly integrated.
1965
Judge Bohanon ruled that the Oklahoma City school system had to take positive action to integrate schools. Astronaut Gordon Cooper of Shawnee commanded the last Mercury spacecraft into orbit. Thomas Stafford, a Weatherford native, piloted Gemini 6 into orbit. KTUL in Tulsa completed a 1,909-foot broadcast tower.
1966
Dewey F. Bartlett was elected as the second Republican governor succeeding

Henry Bellmon. KOTV in Tulsa began colorcasts.

1967
Jane Jayroe of Laverne was crowned Miss America.

1968
Hannah D. Atkins became the first Black woman elected to the Oklahoma legislature.

1969
Fort Sill celebrated a century as a military installation in Oklahoma.

1971
The Cherokee Nation reorganized with a new constitution.

1973
The McAlester prison riot occurred. Three inmates were killed by other prisoners before the riot was contained.

1974
Governor David Hall lost in his primary bid for reelection.

1975
David Boren became the second youngest governor in the U.S. Dr. Fred D. Moon of Wewoka, became the first Black person to serve as school board president in Oklahoma City.

1978
George Nigh was elected as governor.

1979
The centennial celebration of the birth of native son Will Rogers took place at Oolagah, Cherokee Nation.

1981
The county commissioners scandal oc-

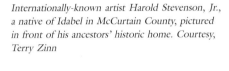

Internationally-known artist Harold Stevenson, Jr., a native of Idabel in McCurtain County, pictured in front of his ancestors' historic home. Courtesy, Terry Zinn

curred. Susan Powell, an Elk City native, was crowned Miss America.

1982
The diamond jubilee celebrating 75 years of statehood took place. Penn Square Bank failed, the first of many bank failures during the 1980s. Governor George Nigh appointed Judge Alma Wilson of Pauls Valley to the Oklahoma Supreme Court making her the first woman to serve on the high court.

1983
Tar Creek in northeast Oklahoma, near Miami, was listed as an Environmental Protection Agency Super Fund site.

1984
T. Boone Pickens tried a hostile takeover of Phillips Petroleum Company located at Bartlesville.

1986
Henry Bellmon was elected governor for the second time (his first administration was in 1963).

1987
Pari-mutuel betting began as Remington Park opened in Oklahoma City.

1989
The centennial celebration of the 1889 land run took place.

1990
J.C. Watts, of Eufaula, became the first Black person elected to statewide office since statehood.

1993
Alva, Cherokee, Perry, Blackwell, Ponca City, and Woodward took part in activities that celebrated the centennial of the land run that opened Cherokee Outlet.

1994
J.C. Watts became the first Black person elected from Oklahoma as a Republican to serve in Congress.

1995
The Murrah Federal Building was destroyed by a domestic terrorist, killing 168 people in Oklahoma City.

1997
James Stewart, Sr., civil rights activist and national member of the NAACP, died.

1999
An F-5 tornado destroyed communities from Chickasha to Stroud, killing 44 people and causing damage into the millions of dollars.

2002
A statehood celebration commemorated the new dome on the state capitol.

This photo titled Five Thoughts *was taken at the Cheyenne and Arapaho Pow Wow in Colony, Oklahoma in 1980. Courtesy, Terry Zinn*

BIBLIOGRAPHY

STATE HISTORIES

Barrett, Charles F. *Oklahoma After Fifty Years: A History.* 4 vols. Oklahoma City: Historical Record Association, 1940.

Dale, Edward E., and Morris L. Wardell. *History of Oklahoma.* Englewood Cliffs, NJ: Prentice Hall, 1948.

Foreman, Grant. *History of Oklahoma.* Norman: University of Oklahoma Press, 1942.

Gibson, Arrell M. Oklahoma: *A History of Five Centuries.* Second Edition. Norman: University of Oklahoma Press, 1981.

Harlow, Victor E. *Oklahoma History.* Oklahoma City: Harlow Publishing Company, 1961.

Litton, Gaston. *History of Oklahoma.* 4 vols. New York: Lewis History Publishing Company, 1957.

McReynolds, Edwin C. *Oklahoma: A History of the Sooner State.* Norman: University of Oklahoma Press, 1954.

Ruth, Kent, ed. *Oklahoma: A Guide to the Sooner State.* Norman: University of Oklahoma Press, 1957.

Thoburn, Joseph B. *History of Oklahoma.* 5 vols. Chicago: Warden Company, 1916.

___. and Muriel Wright. *Oklahoma: A History of the State and its People.* 4 vols. New York: Web Publishing Company, 1929.

GENERAL READINGS

Abel, Annie H. *The American Indian as Slave Holder and Secessionist.* Cleveland: A.H. Clark Company, 1915.

Allen, Clinton M. *The Sequoyah Movement.* Oklahoma City: Harlow Publishing Company, 1925.

Alley, John. *City Beginnings in Oklahoma Territory.* Norman: University Oklahoma Press, 1939.

Bailey, M. Thomas. *Reconstruction in the Indian Territory.* Port Washington: Kennikat, 1972.

Baldwin, Kathlyn. *The 89ers: Oklahoma Land Rush of 1889.* Oklahoma City: Western Heritage Books, 1981.

Barnard, Evan G. *A Rider in the Cherokee Strip.* Boston: Houghton Mifflin, 1935.

Bass, Althea. *The Story of Tullahassee.* Oklahoma City: Semco Color Press, 1960.

___. *The Arapaho Way.* New York: C.N. Potter, 1966.

Bell, Robert E. *Oklahoma Archaeology: An Annotated Bibliography.* Norman: University of Oklahoma Press, 1978.

Bellmon, Henry, with Pat Bellmon. *The Life and Times of Henry Bellmon.* Tulsa, Oklahoma, Council Oak Books, 1992.

Berthrong, Donald J. *The Southern Cheyennes.* Norman: University of Oklahoma Press, 1963.

___. *The Cheyenne and Arapaho Ordeal.* Norman, 1976.

Bischoff, John P. *Mr. Iba: Basketball's Aggie Iron Duke.* Oklahoma City: Oklahoma Heritage Association, 1980.

Blackburn, Bob L. *Heart of the Promised Land: An Illustrated History of Oklahoma County.* Woodland Hills: Windsor Publications, 1982.

___. *Images of Oklahoma: A Pictorial History.* Oklahoma City: The Oklahoma Historical Society, 1984.

Blair, Margaret B. *Scalpel in a Saddlebag: The Story of a Physician in Indian Territory.* Oklahoma City: Western Heritage Books, 1979.

Bolton, Herbert E. *Coronado: Knight of Pueblos and Plains.* New York: Whittsley House, 1949.

Bonnifield, Matthew P. *Oklahoma Innovator: The Life of Virgil Browne.* Norman: University of Oklahoma Press, 1976.

___. *The Dust Bowl: Men, Dirt, and Depression.* Albuquerque: University of New Mexico Press, 1979.

Boydstun, Q.B. *Growing Up in Oklahoma.* Oklahoma City: The Oklahoma Historical Society, 1982.

Burke, Bob. *Good Guys Wear White Hats: The Life of George Nigh.* Oklahoma City, Oklahoma, Oklahoma Heritage Association, 2000.

Bryant, Keith L. *Alfalfa Bill Murray.* Norman: University of Oklahoma Press, 1968.

Cantrell, M.L., and Mac Harris. *Kepis and Turkey Calls: An Anthology of the War Between the States in Indian Territory.* Oklahoma City: Western Heritage Books, 1982.

Carriker, Robert C. *Fort Supply, Indian Territory: Frontier Outpost on the Plains.* Norman: University of Oklahoma Press, 1970.

Carter, L. Edward. *The Story of Oklahoma Newspapers.* Oklahoma City: Oklahoma Heritage Association, 1984.

Chapman, Berlin B. *The Claim of Texas to Greer County.* Oklahoma City: Privately printed, 1950.

___. *The Otoes and Missouris: A Story of Indian Removal and the Legal Aftermath.* Oklahoma City: Journal-Record Publishing Company, 1965.

Colcord, Charles F. *The Autobiography of Charles Francis Colcord, 1859-1934.* Tulsa: Privately printed, 1970.

Collins, Ellsworth. *The 101 Ranch.* Norman: University of Oklahoma Press, 1971.

Conn, Jack T. *One Man in His Time: The Autobiography of Jack T. Conn.* Edited by O.B. Faulk. Oklahoma City: Oklahoma Heritage Association, 1979.

Constant, Alberta. *Oklahoma Run.* New York: Crowell, 1983.

Dale, Edward E. *The Range Cattle Industry.* Norman: University of Oklahoma Press, 1930.

___. *Cow Country.* Norman: University of Oklahoma Press, 1942.

Debo, Angie. *And Still the Waters Run.* Princeton, NJ: Princeton University Press, 1931.

___. *The Rise and Fall of the Choctaw Republic.* Norman: University of Oklahoma Press, 1934.

___. *The Road to Disappearance.* Norman: University of Oklahoma Press, 1941.

Edmunds, R. David. *The Potawatomis: Keepers of the Fire.* Norman: University of Oklahoma Press, 1978.

Ellis, Albert H. *A History of the Constitutional Convention of the State of Oklahoma.* Muskogee: Economy Printing Company, 1923.

Ezell, John S. *Innovations in Energy:*

The Story of Kerr-McGee. Norman: University of Oklahoma Press, 1979.

Faulk, Odie B. *A Man of Vision: The Life and Career of O.W. Coburn.* Oklahoma City: Western Heritage, 1979.

___. *The Making of a Merchant: R.A. Young and T.G.& Y. Stores.* Oklahoma City: Oklahoma Heritage Association, 1980.

___. *A Full Service Banker: The Life of Louis W. Duncan.* Oklahoma City: Oklahoma Heritage Association, 1981.

___. *A Specialist in Everything: The Life of Fred S. Watson, M.D.* Oklahoma City: Oklahoma Heritage Association, 1981.

___. *Dear Everybody: The Life of Henry B. Bass.* Oklahoma City Oklahoma Heritage Association, 1982.

___. *Muskogee, City and County.* Muskogee: Five Civilized Tribes Museum, 1982.

___. *Jennys to Jets: The Life of Clarence E. Page.* Oklahoma City: Oklahoma Heritage Association, 1983.

___. and B.M. Jones. *Fort Smith: An Illustrated History.* Fort Smith: Old Fort Museum, 1983.

___. and B.M. Jones. *Tahlequah, NSU, and the Cherokees.* Tahlequah: Northeastern State University Development Foundation, 1984.

___. J.H. Thomas, and C.N. Tyson. *The Gentleman: The Life of Joseph A. LaFortune.* Oklahoma City: Oklahoma Heritage Association, 1979.

___. K.A. Franks, and P.F. Lambert, eds. *Early Military Forts and Posts in Oklahoma.* Oklahoma City: The Oklahoma Historical Society, 1978.

Ferber, Edna. *Cimarron.* New York: Bantam, 1929.

Fischer, LeRoy H., ed. *The Civil War Era in the Indian Territory.* Los Angeles: L.L. Morrison, 1974.

___. ed. *Oklahoma's Governors, 1890-1907: The Territorial Years.* Oklahoma City: The Oklahoma Historical Society, 1975.

___. ed. *Oklahoma's Governors, 1907-1929: Turbulent Politics.* Oklahoma City: The Oklahoma Historical Society, 1981.

___. ed. *Oklahoma's Governors, 1955-1979: Growth and Reform.* Oklahoma City: The Oklahoma Historical Society, 1985.

Foreman, Carolyn. *Oklahoma Imprints.* Norman: University of Oklahoma Press, 1936.

Foreman, Grant. *The Five Civilized Tribes.* Norman: University of Oklahoma Press, 1934.

___. *Sequoyah.* Norman: University of Oklahoma Press, 1938.

___. *Marcy and the Gold Seekers.* Norman: University of Oklahoma Press, 1939.

Franklin, Jimmie L. *Born Sober: Prohibition in Oklahoma, 1907-1959.* Norman: University of Oklahoma Press, 1971.

Franks, Kenny A. *Stand Watie and the Agony of the Cherokee Nation.* Memphis: Memphis State University Press, 1979.

___. *The Oklahoma Petroleum Industry.* Norman: University of Oklahoma Press, 1980.

___. *You're Doin' Fine, Oklahoma: A History of the Diamond Jubilee.* Oklahoma City: The Oklahoma Historical Society, 1983.

___. *The Rush Begins: A History of the Red Fork, Cleveland and Glenn Pool Oil Fields.* Oklahoma City: Oklahoma Heritage Association, 1984.

___. P.F. Lambert, and C.N. Tyson. *Early Oklahoma Oil: A Photographic History, 1859-1936.* College Station, TX: Texas A & M University Press, 1981.

Gard, Wayne. *The Chisholm Trail.* Norman: University of Oklahoma Press, 1954.

___. *The Great Buffalo Hunt.* New York: Alfred A. Knopf, Inc., 1959.

Gibson, Arrell M. *The Kickapoos: Lords of the Middle Border.* Norman: University of Oklahoma Press, 1963.

___. *The Chickasaws.* Norman: University of Oklahoma Press, 1971.

___. *Wilderness Bonanza: The Tri-State District of Missouri, Kansas, and Oklahoma.* Norman: University of Oklahoma Press, 1972.

___. and E.C. Bearrs. *Fort Smith: Little Gibralter on the Arkansas.* Norman: University of Oklahoma Press, 1969.

___. ed. *America's Exiles: Indian Colonization in Oklahoma.* Oklahoma City: The Oklahoma Historical Society, 1976.

___. ed. *Will Rogers: A Centennial Tribute.* Oklahoma City: The Oklahoma Historical Society, 1979.

___. ed. *The West Wind Blows: The Autobiography of Edward Everett Dale.* Oklahoma City: The Oklahoma Historical Society, 1984.

Gittinger, Roy. *Formation of the State of Oklahoma.* Norman: University of Oklahoma Press, 1939.

Goble, Danney. *Progressive Oklahoma: The Making of a New Kind of State.* Norman: University of Oklahoma Press, 1980.

___. *Tulsa! Biography of the American City.* Tulsa, Oklahoma, Council Oak Books, 1997.

Gould, Charles N. *Travels Through Oklahoma.* Oklahoma City: Harlow Publishing Company, 1928.

Grady, Charles. Edited by Tim Zwink and Gordon Moore. *County Courthouses of Oklahoma.* Oklahoma City: The Oklahoma Historical Society, 1985.

Green, Donald E. *The Creek People.* Phoenix: Indian Tribal Series, 1973.

___. *Panhandle Pioneer: Henry C. Hitch, Ranch, and His Family.* Norman: University of Oklahoma Press, 1979.

___. ed. *Rural Oklahoma.* Oklahoma City: The Oklahoma Historical Society, 1977.

Guthrie, Woody. *Bound for Glory.* New York: E.P. Dutton, 1943.

Hammons, Terry. *Ranching from the Front Seat of a Buick: The Life of Oklahoma's A.A. "Jack" Drummond.* Oklahoma City: The Oklahoma Historical Society, 1980.

Hargrett, Lester. *Oklahoma Imprints, 1835-1890.* New York: Bowker, 1951.

Harlow, Rex F. *Oklahoma Leaders: Biographical Sketches of the Foremost Living Men of Oklahoma.* Oklahoma City: Harlow Publishing Company, 1951.

Harrison, Walter M. *Me and My Big Mouth.* Oklahoma City: Britton 1954.

Hauan, Martin. *How To Win Elections Without Hardly Cheatin' At All.* Oklahoma City, Oklahoma, Midwest Political Publications, 1983.

Hendrickson, Kenneth E., Jr. ed. *Hard Times in Oklahoma: The Depression Years.* Oklahoma City: The Oklahoma Historical Society, 1983.

Hofsommer, Donovan L. *Katy Northwest: The Story of a Branch Line Railroad.* Boulder, CO: Pruitt Publishing Company, 1976.

___. ed. *Railroads in Oklahoma.* Oklahoma City: The Oklahoma Historical Society, 1977.

Hoig, Stan. *The Peace Chiefs of the Cheyennes.* Norman, 1979.

___. David L. Payne: *The Oklahoma Boomer.* Oklahoma City: Western Heritage Books, 1980.

___. *The Oklahoma Land Rush of 1889.* Oklahoma City: The Oklahoma Historical Society, 1984.

Hurst, Irvin. *The Forty-Sixth Star: A History of Oklahoma's Constitutional Convention and Early Statehood.* Oklahoma City: Western Heritage Books, 1980.

Irving, Washington. *A Tour on the Prairies.* Oklahoma City: University of Oklahoma Press, 1955.

Isern, Thomas. *Custom Combining on the Great Plains: A History.* Norman: University of Oklahoma Press, 1981.

Jones, Billy M. *L.E. Phillips: Banker, Oil Man, Civic Leader.* Oklahoma City: Oklahoma Heritage Association, 1981.

___. and O.B. Faulk. *The Cherokees: An Illustrated History.* Muskogee: Five Civilized Tribes Museum, 1984.

Jones, Dick. *From Okemah to the State Court of Criminal Appeals: The Autobiography of Dick Jones.* Oklahoma City: The Oklahoma Historical Society, 1983.

Jones, Stephen. *Oklahoma Politics in State and Nation.* Enid: Haymaker Press, 1974.

Kappler, Charles J., comp. and ed. *Indian Affairs: Laws and Treaties.* 3 vols. Washington, DC: Government Printing Office, 1904.

Kirkpatrick, Samuel A. *The Legislative Process in Oklahoma.* Norman:

University of Oklahoma Press, 1978.

Lambert, Paul F. *Pioneer Historian and Archaeologist: The Life of Joseph B. Thoburn.* Oklahoma City: Oklahoma Heritage Association, 1980.

___. and K.A. Franks, eds. *Voices from the Oil Fields.* Norman: University of Oklahoma Press, 1984.

Latrobe, Charles J. *The Rambler in Oklahoma.* Edited by M.H. Wright and George Shirk. Oklahoma City: Harlow Publishing Company, 1955.

Leckie, William H. *The Military Conquest of the Southern Plains.* Norman: University of Oklahoma Press, 1977.

Logsdon, Guy W. *The University of Tulsa: A History, 1882-1972.* Norman: University of Oklahoma Press, 1977.

McReynolds, Edwin C. *The Seminoles.* Norman: University of Oklahoma Press, 1957.

Malone, James H. *The Chickasaw Nation.* Louisville, KY: J.P. Morton 1972.

Masterson, V.V. *The Katy Railroad and the Last Frontier.* Norman: University of Oklahoma Press, 1953.

Matthews, John Joseph. *Life and Death of an Oil Man: The Career of E.W. Marland.* Norman: University of Oklahoma Press, 1951.

___. *The Osages: Children of the Middle Waters.* Norman: University of Oklahoma Press, 1961.

Maxwell, Amos D. *The Sequoyah Constitutional Convention.* Boston: Meador Publishing Company, 1953.

Mayhall, Mildred. *The Kiowas.* Norman: University of Oklahoma Press, 1962.

Meredith, Howard L. and Mary Ellen Meredith. *Mr. Oklahoma History: The Life of George Shirk.* Oklahoma City: Oklahoma Heritage Association, 1982.

___. *Superior: The Life of B.D. Eddie.* Oklahoma City: Oklahoma Heritage Association, 1982.

___. eds. *Of the Earth: Oklahoma's Architectural History.* Oklahoma City: The Oklahoma Historical Society, 1980.

Morgan, Anne. *Robert S. Kerr: The Senate Years.* Norman: University of Oklahoma Press, 1977.

___. and Rennard Strickland, eds. *Oklahoma Memories.* Norman: University of Oklahoma Press, 1981.

Morris, Cheryl H. *The Cutting Edge: The Life of John Rogers.* Norman: University of Oklahoma Press, 1976.

Morris, John W. *Ghost Towns of Oklahoma.* Norman: University of Oklahoma Press, 1977.

___. ed. *Geography of Oklahoma.* Oklahoma City: The Oklahoma Historical Society, 1977.

___. ed. *Boundaries of Oklahoma.* Oklahoma City: The Oklahoma Historical Society, 1980.

___. ed. *Drill Bits, Picks, and Shovels: History of Mineral Resources in Oklahoma.* Oklahoma City: The Oklahoma Historical Society, 1982.

___. C.R. Goins, and E.C. McReynolds. *Historical Atlas of Oklahoma.* Norman: University of Oklahoma Press, 1976.

Moulton, Gary. *John Ross: Cherokee Chief.* Athens, GA: University of Georgia Press, 1978.

Murray, William H. *Memoirs of Governor Murray.* 3 vols. Boston: Meador Publishing Company, 1945.

Nichols, Max J. *John & Eleanor: A Sense of Community.* Tulsa, Oklahoma, Council Oaks Books, 1995.

Nye, Wilbur S. *Carbine and Lance.* Norman: University of Oklahoma Press, 1937.

Opie, John. *Ogallala: Water for a Dry Land.* Lincoln, Nebraska: University of Nebraska Press, 1993.

Patterson, Zella J. *Langston University: A History.* Norman: University of Oklahoma Press, 1979.

Pickens, T. Boone, Jr. *Boone.* Boston, Houghton Mifflin Company, 1987.

Rainey, George. *The Cherokee Strip.* Guthrie: Co-operative Publishing Company, 1933.

Rister, Carl C. *No Man's Land.* Norman: University of Oklahoma Press, 1948.

Rosser, Linda K. *Christmas in Oklahoma.* Oklahoma City: Western Heritage Books, 1983.

Ruth, Kent, and Jim Argo. *Window on the Past.* Oklahoma City: Western Heritage Books, 1984.

Savage, William. *The Cherokee Strip*

Live Stock Association: Federal Regulation and the Cattleman's Last Frontier. Norman: University of Oklahoma Press, 1973.

____. *Singing Cowboys and All That Jazz.* Norman: University of Oklahoma Press, 1982.

Scales, James R., and Danney Goble. *Oklahoma Politics: A History.* Norman: University of Oklahoma Press, 1982.

Shirk, George. *Oklahoma Place Names.* Norman: University of Oklahoma Press, 1974.

Shirley, Glenn. *Law West of Fort Smith.* Lincoln: University of Nebraska Press, 1968.

____. *Heck Thomas: Frontier Marshal.* Philadelphia: Chilton Company, 1962.

____. *Henry Starr: Last of the Real Badmen.* New York: Mckay, 1965.

____. *West of Hell's Fringe: Crime, Criminals, and the Federal Peace Officer in Oklahoma Territory.* Norman: University of Oklahoma Press, 1978.

____. ed. *Ranch and Range in Oklahoma.* Oklahoma City: The Oklahoma Historical Society, 1978.

Skaggs, Jimmy. *The Cattle-Trailing Industry: Between Supply and Demand, 1866-1890.* Lawrence, KS: University of Kansas Press, 1973.

Smallgood, James. *Urban Builder: The Life and Times of Stanley Draper.* Norman: University of Oklahoma Press, 1977.

____. ed. *And Gladly Teach: Reminiscence Teachers from Frontier Dugout to Modern Module.* Norman: University of Oklahoma Press, 1976.

Smith, Robert, ed. *Oklahoma's Forgotten Indians.* Oklahoma City: The Oklahoma Historical Society, 1979.

Stewart, Roy P. *Born Grown: An Oklahoma City History.* Oklahoma City: Fidelity Bank, 1974.

____. *Programs for People: Oklahoma Vocational Education.* Oklahoma City: Western Heritage Books, 1982.

____. and Pendleton Woods. *One of a Kind: The Life of C.R. Anthony.* Oklahoma City: Oklahoma Heritage Association, 1981.

Strickland, Rennad. *Fire and Spirits: Cherokee Law from Clan to Court.* Norman: University of Oklahoma Press, 1975.

Teall, Kay M. *Black History in Oklahoma.* Oklahoma City: Oklahoma City Public Schools, 1971.

Thomas, James H. *The Bunion Derby: Andy Payne and the Great Transcontinental Footrace.* Oklahoma City: Western Heritage Books, 1980.

Thurman, Melvina, ed. *Women in Oklahoma.* Oklahoma City: The Oklahoma Historical Society, 1982.

Tilghman, Zoe A. *Outlaw Days: A True History of Early-Day Oklahoma Characters.* Oklahoma City: Harlow Publishing Company, 1926.

Tolson, A.L. *The Black Oklahomans: A History, 1541-1972.* New Orleans Edwards Publishing Company, 1972.

Trafzer, Clifford E. *The Judge: The Life of Robert A. Hefner.* Norman: University of Oklahoma Press, 1975.

Tucker, Howard A. *History of Governor Walton's War on the Ku Klux Klan, the Invisible Empire.* Oklahoma City: Southwestern Publishing Company, 1923.

Tyson, Carl N. *The History of Vocational and Technical Education in Oklahoma.* Stillwater: State Department of Vocational-Technical Education, 1976.

____. *The Pawnee People.* Phoenix: Indian Tribal Series, 1976.

____. *The Red River in Southwestern History.* Norman: University of Oklahoma Press, 1981.

____. O.B. Faulk, and J.H. Thomas. *The McMan: The Lives of Robert M. McFarlin and James A. Chapman.* Norman: University of Oklahoma Press, 1977.

Unknown Author. *Presbyterian Health Foundation: A Celebration of 10 Years / 1985-1995.* Oklahoma City, Oklahoma, Presbyterian Health Foundation, 1995.

Waldby, H.O. *The Patronage System in Oklahoma.* Norman: University of Oklahoma Press, 1950.

Wallace, Allie B. *Frontier Life in Oklahoma.* Washington, DC: Public Affairs Press, 1964.

Wallace, Ernest, and E.A. Hoebel. *The Comanches: Lords of the South Plains.* Norman: University of Oklahoma Press, 1952.

Wardell, Morris L. *A Political History of the Cherokee Nation.* Norman: University of Oklahoma Press, 1938.

Webb, Walter P. *The Great Plains.* Boston: Ginn and Company, 1931.

Welsh, Louise, W.M. Townes, and John W. Morris. *A History of the Greater Seminole Oil Field.* Oklahoma City: Oklahoma Heritage Association, 1981.

West, C.W. *Tahlequah and the Cherokee Nation.* Muskogee: Muskogee Publishing Company, 1978.

Wheeler, Robert W. *Jim Thorpe: The World's Greatest Athlete.* Norman: University of Oklahoma Press, 1979.

Wilson, Steve. *Oklahoma Treasures and Treasure Tales.* Norman: University of Oklahoma Press, 1976.

Wilson, Terry. *The Cart That Changed the World: The Career of Sylvan N. Goldman.* Norman: University of Oklahoma Press, 1978.

Woodward, Grace S. *The Cherokees.* Norman: University of Oklahoma Press, 1963.

Wright, Muriel H. *A Guide to the Indian Tribes of Oklahoma.* Norman: University of Oklahoma Press, 1951.

Wright, Peggy Q., and O.B. Faulk. *Coletta: A Sister of Mercy.* Oklahoma City: Oklahoma Heritage Association, 1981.

Zwink, Timothy A. and B.D. Evans. *The Flying Farmer Organization: First in Oklahoma.* Oklahoma City: Western Heritage Books, 1983.

JOURNALS

Chronicles of Oklahoma
The Oklahoma Historical Society Historical Building, Oklahoma City, OK 73105

Oklahoma Today
Will Rogers Memorial Building State Capitol, Oklahoma City, OK 73105

Great Plains Journal
Museum of the Great Plains P.O. Box 68, Lawton, OK 73502

ARTICLES

Carson, Brad. "Renewing Oklahoma's Frontier: Congressman Brad Carson's Commitment to Western Oklahoma." 6-10.

Gumprecht, Blake. "Giants on the Plains: Grain Elevators and the Making of Enid, Oklahoma." *Great Plains Quarterly* 18:4 (Fall 1998): 305-325.

NEWSPAPERS

Boise City News
Capitol Hill Beacon
Daily Oklahoman
Journal Record
Stillwater News Press
Tulsa World
USA Today
Watonga Republican

GOVERNMENT DOCUMENTS

Oklahoma Bank Commissioner, *Report of the Bank Commissioner of the State of Oklahoma* (Oklahoma City, OK, 1984).

Oklahoma Corporation Commission, Biography Bob Anthony.<http://www.occ.state.ok.us/Divisions/COMM/Bio-Anthony.HTM> 14 April 2004.

Oklahoma Department of Environmental Quality, *Oklahoma Plan for Tar Creek 2003* (Oklahoma City, OK, 2003).

Oklahoma Department of Libraries, *Directory of Oklahoma 1979* (Oklahoma City, OK, 1980).
Directory of Oklahoma 1981
Directory of Oklahoma 1983
Directory of Oklahoma 1985-1986
Directory of Oklahoma 1987-1988
Directory of Oklahoma 1989-1990
Directory of Oklahoma 1991-1992

Oklahoma Department of Libraries, *Oklahoma Almanac 1993-1994,* Oklahoma City, OK 1995.
Oklahoma Almanac 2001-2002
Oklahoma Almanac 2003-2004

Oklahoma Space Industry Development Authority, (Oklahoma City, OK, 2002).

INTERVIEWS

John Marshall, interview by William D. Welge, Oklahoma Historical Society, April 7, 2004.

Rick Moore, interview by William D. Welge, Oklahoma Historical Society, April 8, 2004.

Susan Savage, interview by William D. Welge, Oklahoma Historical Society, April 20, 2004.

Gary Thurman, interview by William D. Welge, Oklahoma Historical Society, May 23, 2004.

INDEX